A HANDBOOK AND GUIDE FOR THE COLLEGE AND UNIVERSITY COUNSELING CENTER

A HANDBOOK AND GUIDE FOR THE COLLEGE AND UNIVERSITY COUNSELING CENTER

EDITED BY
B. MARK SCHOENBERG

GREENWOOD PRESS
WESTPORT, CONNECTICUT • LONDON, ENGLAND

Library of Congress Cataloging in Publication Data

Main entry under title:

A Handbook and guide for the college and university
    counseling center.

    Includes index.
    1. Personnel service in higher education--Addresses,
essays, lectures.   I. Schoenberg, B. Mark, 1928-
LB2343.H272   378.1'94   77-87975
ISBN 0-313-20050-5

Library of Congress Catalog Card Number: 77-87975
ISBN: 0-313-20050-5

First published in 1978

Greenwood Press, Inc.
51 Riverside Avenue, Westport, Connecticut 06880

Printed in the United States of America

10 9 8 7 6 5 4 3 2 1

To Mr. Frank G. Lawson,
*in grateful appreciation
of his continued support
to counseling.*

CONTENTS

CONTRIBUTORS

R. D. Archiband is director of the Counseling and Consultation Service at the Ohio State University and adjunct assistant professor of Psychology, Management Science and Education. His primary interests are in the area of intra- and interpersonal effects of the person in the work environment. He has also worked extensively with the influence process in decision-making groups.

Carolyn T. Aguren is a counselor at the Richland College Campus of the Dallas County Community College District. Her experiences as a counselor at both the university level at Southern Methodist University and the community college level at Richland College give her a broad perspective. She has also directed a community college counseling program. One of her special interests concerns mature women students, and she has published an article entitled *How Mature Women Students Cope with Current Life Situations*.

Charles R. Brasfield is assistant to the director of Simon Fraser University Counselling Services and has held appointments in university counseling centers in both Canada and the United States. He has been involved in clinical application of biofeedback techniques for several years and has been a frequent contributor to local and national professional organizations on the topics of biofeedback and stress management.

Donald A. Brown is director of the counseling center at the University of Michigan-Dearborn and formerly held appointments at several other universities. His interests are broad but recently have focused on two major areas, the relationship between sexuality and vocational choice and the treatment of sexual dysfunction. He is active as an educational and industrial consultant and as a therapist with the Amity Mental Health Clinic. His publications include "Counseling the Youthful Homosexual" and "Career Counseling for the Homosexual." In conjunction with his wife, Roberta Brown, he currently is editing and coauthoring a book dealing with sexual dysfunction.

Roberta S. Brown served as dean of student affairs and assistant professor of music at two midwestern colleges. At the University of Michigan she worked as a counselor and financial aid advisor and as director of admissions in the School of Nursing. She did pastoral counseling at the University of Iowa Hospital and conducted sexuality workshops in conjunction with the Menninger Clinic. Recently she has joined her husband, Donald A. Brown, as cotherapist in a series of Human Sexuality and Career Development Workshops and as coauthor of several articles.

William A. Cass is director of the Student Counseling Center and is a full professor in the Department of Psychology at Washington State University. He has served for over twenty-five years as a counseling center director and has held leadership positions within the Association of University and College Counseling Center Directors and the International Association of Counseling Services. His current professional and research interests focus upon the possible effects of National Health Insurance upon university counseling centers.

Larry R. Cochran is the assistant director of the Counselling Centre at Memorial University and coordinator of the centre's program in learning to learn. His research has focused upon the way cognitive structures are consolidated and disrupted, with applications to personality change, career decision-making, and learning from reading. His recent interests have been concerned with what goes on between the pretest and the posttest in psychological experiments.

John T. Deines established the counseling center at Texas Woman's University and continues as its director. He has also served as a consultant for counseling center development. He has published locally and nationally, primarily through symposia.

William M. Gilbert is a professor of psychology and director emeritus of the Psychological and Counseling Center at the University of Illinois, Urbana-Champaign. He has been an active therapist and counselor for thirty-seven years, has published widely, and with collaborators has been the recipient of two national awards for innovative research. He initiated and contributed to the development of the internationally recognized and used *Self-Counseling Manual* for university students.

Gary E. Green is a counselor at the counseling center of Memorial University. He has had a keen interest in architecture and interior design for several years. Together with his wife, Ruth, he is involved in several organizations concerned with the preservation and restoration of historical and unique buildings.

John E. Hechlik is director of University Counseling Services at Wayne State University. In addition to a traditional background in individual, personal, and vocational counseling, he brings to his present administrative work past professional experience in special education, student personnel work, and group work. As a result of his involvement with ERIC-CAPS at the University of Michigan, his professional and administrative orientation emphasizes responding to the developmental needs of students in as wide range as possible of growth-potential contexts.

Beulah M. Hedahl is director of the counseling center and professor in the Department of Psychology at the University of North Dakota. She has been active in professional organizations, particularly in the Division of Counseling Psychology of the American Psychological Association and in the American College Personnel Association.

Robert I. Hudson is professor and counselor at the University of Manitoba, where for thirteen years he was director of the counseling service. His more than twenty-five years of counseling and counseling administration experience contributed to his authorship of the *Guidelines for Canadian University Counselling Services,* adopted by the Canadian University and College Counselling Association in 1971. This was the first publication of its kind in North America.

David L. Jordan is associate professor and director of counseling at Brock University. He is a clinical psychologist and has worked in university counseling services for the past ten years. His primary interest is in group and community approaches to individual develop-ment. His recent research has focused on institutional goals and the role of academic advising in student development.

Robert D. King is assistant director of University Counseling Services at Wayne State University. His orientation to counseling was initially influenced at the University of Chicago by Rogers' "Client-Centered Psychotherapy" and Havighurst's "Research in Human Development," later by Ellis's "Rational-Emotive Approach" and by work as Veterans Administration Counseling Psychologist in Vocational Rehabilitation. During his past twenty years of counseling and administrative experience at Wayne State Univer-sity, these diverse backgrounds have become integrated in his approach to the counseling of university students.

Janet C. Lindeman is a family therapist at the Alaska Clinic, Section of Psychiatry and Family Therapy, Anchorage, Alaska. Her research interests have focused on the impact of public policies on the delivery of counseling services. While working at Washington State University's student counseling center, she completed a dissertation on the implications of national health insurance for student counseling centers.

Beatrice G. Lipinski is director of the University Counselling Service at Simon Fraser University in British Columbia, Canada. She has held positions in a wide variety of clinical and research settings. With a considerable background in developmental psychol-ogy, she has initiated a number of preventive counseling programs, especially for mature students, couples, single parents, and women on campus.

Sheridan P. Mc Cabe is the director of the Center for Student Development and associate professor in the psychology department at the University of Notre Dame. Prior to coming to Notre Dame to establish their first counseling center in 1967, he served as chairman of the psychology department at the University of Portland. He is the author of numerous articles relating to counseling. His present research interests include the role of psycholog-ical and organizational climates in student development.

David H. Mills is assistant director of the University Counseling Center and a full profes-sor in the Department of Psychology at the University of Maryland. Currently president-elect of the International Association of Counseling Services, he is a member of the review panel for and a research consultant to the National Register of Health Service Providers in Psychology. The author of many published research articles, his current research interests are in the general area of the availability of psychological manpower.

Ted Packard is currently chairman and associate professor in the Department of Educa-tional Psychology at the University of Utah. He was formerly the director of the counsel-ing center at the University of Utah for a number of years. He is currently president of the Utah Psychological Association and also serves on the State Psychology Licensing Board.

Charles F. Preston is professor of psychology and coordinator of Applied Clinical Train-ing at Memorial University. He holds degrees in theology from Wycliffe College and psy-chology from the University of Toronto. He has pursued a diverse career as a clergyman in the Anglican Church, a psychologist, and the founder of the counseling centers at the University of Waterloo and Memorial University. He has served in an advisory and con-sulting capacity to the Government of Newfoundland and Labrador and the Government of Uganda, and his institutional experience includes university, hospital, and correctional settings. He is presently president and board chairman of the St. John's Community Counselling Centre, a member of the Minister's Advisory Committee on Mental Health, Newfoundland Provincial Department of Health, and a member of the Advisory Committee of the General Hospital School of Nursing.

Harriett A. Rose is director of the University Counseling and Testing Center and an associate professor in psychology at the University of Kentucky. She has published extensively in the area of college student personality, vocational choice, and attrition, and currently serves on the Editorial Board of the Journal of Vocational Behavior and the Board of Directors of the International Association of Counseling Services.

John H. Russel is a counseling psychologist at the Memorial University Counselling Centre as well as a consultant with the St. John's Community Counselling Centre. He has instructed both graduate and undergraduate level courses and has had extensive involvement with career-related issues in both a research and applied setting. He is the author or coauthor of several articles and projects related to career development theory and the application of systems methodology to career planning.

Philip Ron Spinelli is a staff psychologist at the University Counseling Center, University of Utah. He also holds an adjunct appointment on the Educational Psychology Faculty there. As coordinator for Outreach Services he has been responsible for the design and implementation of a variety of paraprofessional training programs, workshops, and classes that have allowed university students the opportunity to engage in meaningful work experiences in conjunction with their formal academic learning. His published research is in the area of stress management, particularly as it relates to academic performance anxiety, and has utilized undergraduate paraprofessionals extensively in the offerings of specific anxiety treatment programs to large university populations.

John C. Wolf is a counseling psychologist for the United States Veterans Administration in Lubbock, Texas, and an adjunct faculty member in psychology and human services at South Plains College of Lubbock. He has worked in the rehabilitation field in private, state, and federal settings, and he has held college faculty and counselor appointments. A frequent contributor to professional publications, he has published in such journals as the *Journal of College Student Personnel, The Vocational Guidance Quarterly,* and *The School Counselor.*

FOREWORD

College and university counseling centers have established themselves over the past forty years in such a way that there is widespread conviction that they are here to stay. From the half-dozen or so existing in the late 1930s, they have proliferated so that any university or college of whatever size is uneasy about its obligations to students, and indeed its very purpose, should it lack such a program.

Why should there be such institutions? There are many ways to respond to this question. Education itself is costly, especially at the higher levels utilized by our most valuable national product: the people who are being educated to be our leaders in all walks of life—sciences, professions, government, education, military—the people who will set far-reaching policies and ultimately cause and implement the circumstances through which high quality of life is assured.

The quality of life of these very students is at issue. They enter higher education at a formative period, a time when they are in flux. In developmental terms, their tasks are separation from home and family, attainment of individual identity and adulthood, establishing the base for future vocation and career, establishing adult forms of socialization as well as relations with the opposite sex, and emotional life in general.

They come frequently ill-prepared, surely from the standpoint of counseling and/or guidance by secondary counselors. These counselors are usually in no position to give much attention to individuals, nor are they commonly skilled in any of the special areas in which students need developmental facilitation. And there are, as we know, a great range of skills among parents in dealing with the great number of adolescents and their problems.

The American Council of Education's surveys of incoming freshmen informs us year after year that these freshmen declare their intention of seeking counseling, especially vocational counseling. Research has made all too clear the degree of instability of interests in the adolescent and early adult years. In 1976 nearly 10 percent knew in advance that they would seek counseling services; more became aware of such a need as they got underway; and estimates run around 41 percent that seek counseling at some point in their entire college program.

Some are more in need than others, and my own research indicates that such need has a good deal to do with the individual student's make-up, ascertainable at matriculation. Many surveys report that students recognize their own needs. With the complexity of the changing work world and labor market, with problems in surmounting the many difficult developmental tasks of this period, a segment of all students find that professional help is required for them to maximize their college experience and to obtain full benefits from their educational opportunities. Counseling centers are established to serve, on the average, 10 to 15 percent (usually 12 percent) of all students per year.

Whatever the funding fortunes of the higher educational institution, can it afford *not* to provide counseling service? There are many ways of funding in practice, including socialized student fees.

Students profess need, and their performance in seeking it validates their words. How do counseling centers meet these requests beyond counting numbers of students served? This book addresses this topic. The authors are among the best known, best informed, and best performing members of the profession, and all are directly associated with counseling centers.

The "hows" of insuring quality service involve the status and interaction of the counseling center with its campus—its place in the organizational structure, its relationships with academic and administrative campus personnel, its budget, but above all, the caliber of its personnel and its commitment to meeting the student and campus needs through well-designed programs and careful apportionment of its resources.

If the needs of the staff are at variance with those of the consumers, as sometimes happens, services may not be appropriate as well as of less then high quality.

Because of the nature of their work, counseling psychologists often have administrative interests and abilities, and thus to satisfy them they reach out or "out-reach" to effect changes administratively, to offer prevention, or to implement broad programs. These administrative interests and abilities represent positive growth, but they constitute a contribution only if they are well performed, fruitful, and do not detract from expressed needs for other services, particularly individual or group counseling. Innovation must always be encouraged, but not for its own sake alone, and must endure only as it provides substantive solutions to problems and needs.

Another trend has been the move away from vocational/career counseling to the therapy model for counseling services. Both are needed, neither at the expense of the other. Educational/vocational counseling is more sought in terms of numbers but less attractive to staff and interns to provide. Vocational/educational counseling is critically needed by university and college students. No less critical is the need to revive and expand sophisticated training in clinical vocational counseling.

It is hoped that the comprehensive treatment in this book will reinforce the

already strong case for a comprehensive counseling program on every university
and college campus.

Barbara A. Kirk
Director, Counseling Center
Dean of Counseling (Emeritus)
University of California, Berkeley

Berkeley, California
November, 1977

PREFACE

Those who collect data and report on it, especially in the behavioral sciences, have frequently noted that the United States specifically and North America generally tend to provide the laboratory as well as the testing ground for trends and developments that are later accorded near universality. It strikes me that the counseling center on the college and university campus is a prime example of the creativity that North Americans have repeatedly demonstrated: not only has the concept of the center received universal acceptance, but it would be difficult to cite an area of academia that has had more of a direct and lasting effect on a generation of students.

Educational innovations have a way of diminishing from the initial unique concept to levels of mediocrity that would not long be tolerated in either business or industry. I do not propose to give examples of this, for the informed reader will undoubtedly recognize the truth inherent in the statement. But the counseling center on campus does provide a refreshing countertrend to academia's general movement toward mediocrity through standardization and regimentation. I think that the one facet contributing to the strength of the counseling center is the fact that it is a unique entity on campus, made that way not only because it does not ''fit'' into the organization as do other departments and faculties, but also because the director and his/her staff can usually respond quickly to student needs provided that they have been given complete freedom of operation by an enlightened administration.

Yet if uniqueness from campus to campus is one of the strengths of the center, this same uniqueness must be labeled a weakness as well. The reason for this is simple and straightforward. Since there are few rules guiding the operation of the center and since the director does not fit neatly into an organizational hierarchy, the impact that the center makes on campus is too frequently a result of the prestige (or clout) that the director enjoys with the higher levels of administration and/or the sensitivity and awareness of this same administration. Several of the contributors make this point, so it is unnecessary to give any detail at this juncture. Certainly every college or university should seek to engage the most prominent and prestigious director (and staff) that the budget allows, but it is complete folly that the impact of the center should be determined solely by such considerations. If this text serves no other purpose than to encourage the top administration of colleges and universities to take an active role in the development and maintenance of high-quality, comprehensive counseling centers on their campuses, then bringing it together will have been very worthwhile.

It occurs to me that one of the most important things that directors can do for their centers is to ensure that they are accredited by the International Association of Counseling Services, Inc. Guidelines for accreditation of a center can be an important point for reference in discussions of objectives with the college or university administration. Most directors will agree that the occasions are too frequent when we need all the support we can muster as we are buffeted (seemingly) from all sides.

Serving as editor has been a wonderful experience. The fact that each contributor did an excellent job made possible the application of that old rule of thumb, the least editing means the best editing. It was gratifying to me that some of the most respected names in the field of counseling psychology felt the project to be of such merit that they were willing to invest large amounts of their time and energy.

And I gratefully acknowledge the cooperation of Barbara Cadigan, Michael Doyle, Elise Hurd, Jane Rogers, and Debbie Noseworthy in the final preparation of the manuscript.

B. Mark Schoenberg

St. John's, Newfoundland
July, 1977

PART I History and Philosophy

1

CONCEPTIONS OF MAN AS GUIDES TO LIVING

Larry R. Cochran
MEMORIAL UNIVERSITY

Counseling centers are in the business of promoting change in people. Notions of how people change and toward what they should change stem largely from theories of personality or, more generally, from views on the nature of man. Under the banners of different theories, psychologists might use "working through" to build ego strength, or conditioning to selectively strengthen and weaken stimulus-response connections, or modeling and role playing to add new repertoires of performance, or rational argument to challenge irrational beliefs and to support more rational ones, or reflection to facilitate more openness to experience. The means and ends of counseling are bounded by conceptions of man.

Indeed, the very possibility of guiding change depends upon a conception of what man is—what is fixed and what is variable. Psychoanalysts, for instance, do not ordinarily treat symptoms, since substitute symptoms would inevitably arise to take their places. Rather, they would go beyond symptoms to their cause, issuing from early childhood experience. In contrast, behaviorists would not even see a symptom as such. They would see the problematic behavior or reaction as part of a functional relationship, and it would be the relationship that would command attention. Theories define what to look for, what to expect, and what to hope for.

To paraphrase W. I. Thomas,[1] whatever vision of persons is defined as real *is* real in its consequences. Whether true or false, theories define different versions of reality. The practical consequences of holding different theories of persons are different ways of seeing, planning, and acting.

To facilitate change, psychologists do not ordinarily communicate their orientations directly and systematically. A Rogerian, for instance, does not explain Rogerian theory to get on with the business of facilitating change. Rather, clients usually receive the psychologists's vision of man (and of themselves) indirectly through expressions or projections of that vision. Counselors tend to present sustained foci of attention that can be taken as rhetorical appeals to different resources thought to be important for change. Stereotypically, Rogerians appeal to the elaboration of feelings, radical behaviorists to the control of environmental stimuli, psychoanalysts to the uncovering of repressed experiences, and rational-emotive therapists to the refinement of reason. Counselors call attention to some things rather than others, introduce new terminologies and rationales, model stances toward people and situations, provide commentary, and communicate what they are trying to do. They explain, interpret, illustrate, describe, and evaluate. In short, they offer a way of seeing people and their situations, however attenuated and piecemeal that offering might be.

Just as psychologists require a personality theory to order their views and actions toward clients in promoting change, so do people in general require a more or less coherent vision of persons, an "implicit personality theory" to establish an orientation toward themselves and others (Kelly, 1955). It is only natural that people would be receptive to definitions of man communicated by people whose business is to understand personality more fully than others. In one way or another, psychologists communicate their orientations that people can use to extend and refine their own orientations. Yet it is precisely this—the influence of the psychologist's orientation upon the orientations of other people (in particular, clients)—which is so often an inadvertent by-product of service. Counselors tend to focus upon the production of some type of change, not upon the image of persons they are projecting in the way that they stimulate and guide change. The broader influence of practice can easily be left unrecognized and undefined.

For the sake of distance, consider the following example, which is remote from the services of a counseling center, but has considerable impact upon the way in which people take those services. Personality theories are relentlessly popularized. Television dramas repeatedly call in the authoritative psychiatrist who, on the basis of the sketchiest of evidence, outlines a personality profile that would befog even the keenest of observers. With such predictability does the pathological killer turn out to be asserting his manhood against an overprotective mother that one wonders why detectives continue to bother with consultations. With a few notable exceptions (for example, *Psychology Today*), popular magazines continually feature articles on psychological problems (that are usually written in a very fatherly and very Freudian tone), by presumed authorities with names I seldom recognize. They always seem to end up advising people to see their family physician, should they run up against that particular problem. With articles ranging from the perils of not taking your antidepressants to the vigilance a mother must have to spot minimal brain damage (the signs of which can be spotted in almost anyone), the only thing that seems clear is that spooky-sounding notions of personality can render even the most innocent of actions suspect, make even the most natural of situations problematic. Like Jonathan Edwards's eighteenth-century parishioners, we hang by a slender thread over the hell-pit of problems.

It is quite unfortunate that personality theory should be so tied to problems. Is life best conceived as a problem to be solved? With this obsessive focus upon problems, there are apt to be a number of probable, inadvertent effects. First, the manifestations of problems are usually treated as pseudo-problems, behind which the real problems lurk, whether they be repressed experiences, closedness to experience, lack of sensory awareness, or whatever. Moral dilemmas might become manifestations of reaction formation, conditioning, and so on. In short, psychological terms can cast doubt upon a person's normal way of giving definition to life and, by casting doubt, dislodge people from the banners under which they act. To act under the name of justice could become a reinforced response, which redefines the very nature of the act. It would be extremely difficult, if not impossible, to act in the name of justice if one's acts were interpreted merely as self-serving, greedy, and self-congratulatory. As Campbell (1975) has recently pointed out, psychological descriptions of man tend to assert not only that people are selfishly motivated, but also that they ought to be so. Second, once problems are defined in professional terms, they can be solved only in those terms. This requires dependence upon professionals. If one agrees that the only effective daily care is self-care, then this usurpation of individual autonomy is very serious indeed. For instance, Carlson (1975) and Illich (1974) have argued convincingly that the cultivated dependence of people upon the medical profession for health care has divested them of the confidence and competence to take care of themselves.

A third effect of this focus is that recognition of professionally defined problems and solutions requires a conception of man that defines what will count as a problem and a solution. To accept problem definitions requires the adoption of a theoretical stance. By adopting a theoretical stance, people can also embrace the limitations and possibilities of that stance in their daily living and in their efforts to live well. Fourth, popularizations have little to say about living well, other than that it might be the temporary absence of problems. The standards erected do not stimulate positive living as much as tell people how far short they fall. People can feel guilty or drastically impaired if they do not have sexual intercourse often enough, if they are not experiencing joy and pleasure all of the time, if they get walked over once in a while, or if they have failed to be open and honest all day long. These effects exist, however, and they are largely inadvertent. No one seriously wants to plunge people into Hamlet-like doubt about their views of self and others, to create professional dependence, to convert people to a theory of personality that will probably be discarded or unrecognizable in fifty years, or to give them a terminology for having bigger and better problems.

The conceptions of persons projected by counseling services can be as important, if not more important, than the effectiveness of those services in producing change. With the dramatic rise of cognitive psychology, old theories have gained new respectability, while established theories have been radically altered to maintain respectability. There has been a general convergence upon the notion that cognitions matter and, in particular, conceptions of oneself and others matter. Raimy (1976) has recently argued that counseling is largely a matter of correcting misconceptions, particularly mistaken conceptions of oneself. Adler's ingenious elaboration of such concepts as compensation, life-style, fictional finalism, and mistaken goals (Ansbacher & Ansbacher, 1956) provides a framework for identifying sources of misconceptions and determining their modes of correction. Ellis (1962) provides one way of viewing misconceptions and their correction through his emphasis upon irrationality. Kelly's theory of personal constructs (1955) places stress not simply upon misconceptions, but upon types of constructions. For example, constructions can be tight or loose, consistent or inconsistent, fragmented or integrated, and the like. Even Freudians and behaviorists (at least social learning theorists), who have traditionally given cognition a trivial role to play in human affairs, have come increasingly to stress the importance of what people think and how they think (for example, Bandura, 1974; Mischel, 1973; Peterfreund, 1971).

If projections of man do influence the orientations of clients, it becomes imperative to assess not only what is being communicated, but how. For to the extent that these influences are inadvertent, they are beyond professional awareness and control. Consequently, the benefits and detriments of these influences would be largely a matter of chance. Bergin (1971), in an extensive and painstaking reanalysis of outcome studies of counseling and therapy, has shown that a substantial percentage of clients get worse. Rather than assume, as Bergin appears to, that this detrimental effect is due to "psychonoxious" counselors, might it not be equally well assumed that it is partially due to highly skilled counselors? Some clients might get worse not because counseling has failed, but because it has succeeded only too well. In light of this prospect, models of man are not merely theoretical. Their study is eminently practical and deserving of close consideration in the establishment of any psychological service.

Orientation and Position

In the present age, an adequate orientation is a major achievement. Cultural lag has its analogue in personal lag, as one adapts or attempts to adapt to situations that disappear one after the other. Society now contains a plurality of life-worlds (that is, divergent orderings of reality that give meaning to the conduct of life; Berger, Berger, & Kellner, 1973), whose requirements for choice in major areas of life (career, life-style, identifications) can be as bewildering as liberating. Like gravity in the physical world, new modes of communication (for example, Innis, 1951; McLuhan, 1964) contract the social world. From decisions about family size to underarm deodorant (spray or roll-on), we witness our individual actions being collectively magnified into issues of global importance. Organizations multiply with incredible speed, and their impact on people can be staggering as they increasingly and sometimes conflictingly seek to structure our lives according to maxims that are personally alien (Seidenberg, 1950). The impact of technology requires major changes in beliefs and values (Baier & Rescher, 1969). The sheer rate of information flow holds out the possibility (if not the actuality) of chronic states of anxiety, of informational overload. The rates of change in jobs, friendships, neighborhoods, and homes create a transient, shifting reality in which it is becoming increasingly more difficult to establish an anchor (Toffler, 1970). Work roles are rife with ambiguity and conflict (Kahn et al., 1964). Personal identity, which was perhaps once as natural as growing up, is now problematic (Klapp, 1969); it must be earned and re-earned over and over again (McCall & Simmons, 1966).

The current requirements for orienting and reorienting to life situations are unprecedented, heightening the possibility of misorientation and disorientation. Discontinuous leaps from one life-world to another require major changes to avoid massive invalidation. And certainly one of the most demanding periods of change occurs during a student's career at the university. During this period many of the more discontinuous leaps occur, from individual to husband or wife, from dependence to independence, from adolescence to adulthood, from belief in unlimited possibilities to recognition of definite limits, and from student to professional. Rapid personal changes take place within the context of a highly demanding environment in which even small difficulties can easily ramify into pervasive maladjustment.

Too much order might be stultifying, but too little is crippling. An orientation builds on pattern, regularity, order, or, more simply, meaning. Friedman (1975) has recently argued that an orientation is the fundamental requirement for human adaptation, because a predictable relationship with one's environment is necessary to take any effective action. It is more basic than self-actualization, for instance, since, without order, there would be no coherent possibilities to actualize. Similarly, it is more basic than pleasure, since predictability is necessary to take the actions required to satisfy wants and needs.

Organizing concepts such as identity, role, status, and even personality are most appropriately understood, I believe, as relational concepts, not as entities. For example, identity rests on identifications, in the sense of being able both to identify something and to identify with something. Although varying in many ways, these organizing concepts find common meaning in the idea of position. People take positions in argument, assume positions in business, have a position in families, develop positions on events, establish positions on the future, and so on. Position is ubiquitous in human affairs, so much so that it is strange to find it so little used in psychology. As position is central to the theme of this paper, let me point out some of its more obvious features.

To be oriented is to have position in some scheme of things or to have a definable place in an intelligible situation. Position can be defined physically or more personally as identity, or more socially as role and status. But the way position is defined must be relational. There is no position without an intelligible scheme of things that allows placement to occur. Consider the age-old, but serviceable analogy of a ship at sea. Without placement upon the longitudinal and latitudinal coordinates of a map, the ship has no position. If a map—an intelligible frame of reference—exists, then various locating strategies can be performed. But without a map, there is no possibility for ever discovering position because there is nothing in which to establish it. Position, then, whether physical, personal, social, or all combined, must be defined in relation to something.

Positioning is a way of imposing structure on oneself within the context of a larger framework. In the context of other people, positioning establishes the type of person one is. To assert one's fairness, for instance, requires a dimension or construct of, say, fair to unfair that makes comparison and contrast with other people possible. One is distinctive by contrast, and to contrast anything requires a dimension in common. If a person were wholly novel at time 1, time 2, time 3, and so on, then no regularity, no predictable relationship, could exist upon which to form self-expectancies. Without self-expectancies (which define capacities, interests, desires, and the like), there can be no intelligible guide to action. To maintain a predictable relationship, there must be two knowns, oneself in relation to something. What a person cannot be (and still remain functional) is a novelty to his or her own self.

A construct such as self-esteem might explain at least part of a person's strivings to maintain a given self-conception. But structuring itself requires acting, thinking, and feeling that are in accordance with it, since not to do so puts one outside order, where it is difficult or impossible to be oriented at all. This does not imply a stagnant rigidity, for people do thrust themselves into novel situations, do enjoy exploration and variety, and do strive for extensions and developments of themselves. Rather, it stresses the point that some degree of structure is necessary to do anything at all.[2] In a laborious series of studies, Fransella (1972) has shown that personal transformations (from stutterer to fluent speaker, from obese person to trim person, and so forth) are not apt to be maintained or even achieved until the person has structured—that is, endowed meaning and predictability on—the position sought. For example, an obese person might lose weight under treatment, but fail to maintain the weight loss until he has given definition to the position of a trim person. Obese persons do not live in the same world as trim persons, or stutterers in the same world as fluent speakers. Both the new world (the different reactions of people, for instance) and one's position in it must be reconstructed to maintain a predictable relationship with one's environment. Without preparation then, what a person who has made a radical transformation might experience is a radical restriction in the ability to anticipate. In a quote that might do justice to Kelly (1955) and numerous others (Bruner, Goodnow & Austin, 1956; Kagan, 1971, for example), Bandura (1974) asserts that "people learn to predict them [events] and to summon up appropriate anticipatory reactions." It is this capability for anticipating events that positioning supports.

Without position in some scheme of things, there is little possibility for purposeful action, because effective action is dependent upon anticipating what the effects of action might be. To extend this one step, consider a backpacker who blunders into unfamiliar territory. Without a map or a compass, perhaps, she would be thoroughly disoriented. In deference to the here-and-now, she could position herself with reference to the trees and undergrowth in her immediate surroundings. Actions could certainly be performed, but only actions with a radically limited scope—she would still be lost. Orientation, then, can be seen as relative to the level of action contemplated.[3]

Conceptions of man underlie personal orientations to living. They have impact upon the way people define position, establish and elaborate position, interpret schemes of things, and plan levels of action. For example, conceptions of man offer different personality dimensions for imposing structure upon oneself and others. Classical Greece offered the four cardinal virtues of courage, temperance, justness, and wisdom. Rogerian thought offers openness to experience, trust, and what might be termed existential awareness and involvement. These dimensions are both descriptive and prescriptive. To call certain people friendly, for instance, is to see them in a particular way and to take a definite stance toward them. To highlight the construct of friendly/unfriendly in one's orientation limits the way people will be construed and the stances that can be taken. The adoption of different constructs has different implications for living.

Conceptions of man offer different perspectives, angles of vision, or frames against which man is placed. Gilbert Murray has suggested that the Greeks erected the golden mean—of nothing in excess—to restrain their tendencies toward uncontrolled extremes of passion, indulgence, and action (Brinton, 1959). Campbell (1975) has recently sketched a similar role for social ideals of conduct. Perhaps also, the development of the city-state required a different frame to give sense to the business of living. For in the heroic age of Homer, conflict was the essence of living and honor the guiding purpose. There was little room here for moderation. Similarly, the Dionysian pursuit of excess to break the boundaries of ordinary experience scorns the middle of the road (for example, Benedict, 1934). And romantic visions of humanity have little but contempt for sniveling appeals to moderation (for example, Brinton, 1959). Different frames give significance to different codes. The angle of vision also matters. Framed upward as a child of God, against the heavens and atop the Great Chain of Being (Tillyard, 1959), as in the Elizabethan age, man appears spiritually inviolate and superior to all living things. But framed downward against the molecules that compose his being, man does not appear spiritually inclined at all, nor for that matter does he appear to be particularly different from any other animal. The adoption of different perspectives has different implications for the appropriateness of situations and the significance of personality constructs.

Last, conceptions offer different ordering assumptions involving rationales that serve to bind constructs into wholes and to guide their elaboration.

Rationales prescribe forms of representation (chains, hierarchies, agons, intertwining circles), connectors (causal, analogical, conceptual, contiguous, valuative), and modes of elaboration (dialectical, logical, empirical, intuitive). The adoption of different ordering assumptions has different implications for elaborating and consolidating orientations to living.

Through the nature of their jobs, psychologists communicate these conceptions. As this brief characterization of orientation suggests, these communications can affect the orientations of others in a variety of ways that are not immediately obvious. What requires consideration now is the extent to which these communications are inadvertent.

Inadvertent Projections of Man

Inadvertent projection is a problem of construing. Any way of seeing is also a way of not seeing. Wittgenstein's famous duck-rabbit (1968) can be seen as a duck or as a rabbit, but not as both at the same time. To use Veblen's magnificent juxtaposition of "trained incapacity," training capacitates as well as incapacitates (see Burke, 1965). Studies of Duncker's functional fixedness (see Johnson, 1972, for a summary of evidence) demonstrate convincingly that defining objects and circumstances in one set of terms can blind one to definitions using other terms. Perhaps the most notorious example of a blinding definition is the psychiatric interpretation of personal difficulties in living as mental illness (Szasz, 1961). This assumption allowed and still allows mental hospitals and wards to impose the most devastating role definitions upon patients (for example, Goffman, 1961; Rosenhan, 1973; Scheff, 1966). The strange and demoralized behavior of patients could be attributed to the disease working its way out rather than to the role definition working its way in. Here is inadvertency with a vengance.

To be trained in the dominant forms of therapy (psychoanalysis, behaviorism, and humanistic psychology) is to be trained into a particular way of seeing or not seeing the role of projected definitions and cognition in counseling practice. For classical analysts, man is the center of forces beyond his (but not the analysts') understanding. Obviously, what patients think is irrevelant except insofar as it points indirectly toward hidden causal forces in the unconscious. If patients try to explain their positions, they are rationalizing. If they become disgusted with minute introspections and retrospections, they are resisting. If they go along with the rules of the game, they are improving. But this odd transaction is also a negotiation of identities. What projected definitions of themselves must persons accept to cooperate with a psychoanalyst?

Behaviorists have long asserted that "goodies" matter, while definitions do not. Cognitive definitions of self and others, being either epiphenomenal or minimally influential, could be disregarded. Behavioral reports of therapeutic practices came to look very scientific and remarkably uncluttered in comparison with the sloppy, ill-defined reports from other standpoints. Yet, is this not a case of bad reporting, of very selective attention? Like other therapies, behavioral therapists must give some rationale to encourage a person to carry out the procedures and to anticipate benefit from them. Client's must accept a re-definition of their problems and, by accepting, adopt a theoretical stance that gives them a different meaning. Indeed, it must be a very powerful rationale if clients are to perform many of the time-consuming tasks required in behavioral programs. But of this inducement into a new orientation, a new way of seeing, we are told little. Behavioral therapy can be legitimately viewed as a way of initially changing a client's orientation coupled with elaborate procedures for testing the validity of that new orientation in the person's life.

Under the constructive impact of social learning theory, behaviorism has changed radically in the past decade. Behavioral techniques of recent years would be more appropriately termed cognitive techniques. The mind-boggling assertion that cognitions are behaviors has more to do with legitimizing a transfer of attention than with making a defensible claim about the nature of thought. However, the same argument applies to these newer, more powerful techniques as to the more traditional ones. For example, Kanfer's self-regulation model (1975) ends with reinforcement or self-praise. The three stages of this model are self-monitoring, self-evaluation, and self-reinforcement. It seems clear, however, that if self-praise is to be anything more than hollow verbiage, people must have some basis for praising themselves—some orientation, some stance, or some vision of things that makes self-praise appropriate and deserved. They deserve it because they've earned it in some way. With the introduction of merit (oneself being defined as a person who merits praise once in a while), a vision of man with pervasive implications is already being offered. Yet this envisioning experience is not a stage in Kanfer's model, although the projected vision of man implicit in this technique would seem to be the key aspect of it: self-praise will not work without an orientation that makes certain self-statements ones of praise. Again, about the orientation that is cultivated to make reality different for the person, we are told little. Might it not be the case that this shift in vision, along with experiential testing of it, will lead to desired changes even without the carefully executed program of reinforcement? Or might not reinforcement be more appropriately construed as validation, the confirmation of a new position?

Some third-force psychologists do not seem to ignore cognitions so much as scorn them. Affect appears to be something separate from and opposed to intellect, as if feelings popped out of nowhere. Far from being an impediment, structuring capacities are the very means by which persons are able to see things coherently enough to have feelings about them (for example, Neisser, 1976). As Hanson has phrased it in demonstrating that scientific observation is necessarily theory-laden, "to see what the aeronaut sees, we would have to know what he knows" (1969, p. 101). Kuhn (1962) offers a similar view in his example of a student learning to comprehend a bubble-chamber photograph. This is not to say that all feelings result from a way of construing. People can feel overloaded due to the rate of information flow, which is not so much a matter of what is construed as how adequately and in what amount it is construed. Similarly, Kelly's definition of anxiety (1955) suggests that feeling can result from a failure to construe coherently, which is about all humanists are apt to feel if they are successful in banishing the "cold intellect." Instead of separating thinking and feeling (which is scarcely defensible anymore), it would seem more reasonable to acknowledge the stance toward life that they offer and the stances that they argue against. Part of the position might run as follows:

People, or the same person at different times, take different stances toward life. In particular, one stance is analogous to a slightly bored computer technologist debugging a routine program. The task requires little experiential involvement (little interest, joy, and so on) and a lot of monotonous, methodical thinking. Now this stance might be okay for some things, but it is no way to live your life. There may be times when such deliberation and detachment are necessary to be able to function at all, but if used continually, they will stultify your capacity for experiencing in variety and depth. Also, there are some problems that cannot be solved by detachment. A detached stance toward yourself and others takes away richness and is apt to be the very reason for your problems.

It is perfectly reasonable for a humanist to discourage a detached stance toward living and to encourage a more involving one. But what a source arises for inadvertent projection and sheer bewilderment when people are made to feel guilty or suspicious about thinking, about having it all "in their heads."

In a stimulating investigation of orientations and their transformations, literary critic Kenneth Burke (1965) argued that therapeutic practices "cured" by providing a secular conversion. People are converted from an orientation that offers no solution to their problems to an orientation that does offer a solution. For instance, guilt might be transformed into a conditioned reaction or a remnant of parental discipline, neither of which seem to be so very awful or intractable.

Certainly Burke is on solid ground in stressing belief and expectancy. For instance, systematic desensitization has perhaps been the subject of more studies than any other therapeutic technique in psychology. Yet scores of studies have failed to demonstrate that it does anything more than alter client beliefs and expectancies. And when expectancy is controlled, the "evidence does not strongly support the efficacy of desensitization as a specific treatment strategy" (Kazdin & Wilcoxon, 1976).

Many therapeutic techniques might better be viewed as rituals that cure more by rhetorical excellence than by their assumed, specific effects. Or at a minimum, some techniques might be fruitfully approached as rhetorical devices. Without doubt, the incantatory force of desensitization rites is very powerful indeed. Implosive techniques, to take one more instance, are therapy with a will. Clients are driven into a corner with the very stuff of which nightmares are made. In movies, this is what the bad guy does to drive the victim crazy. But in counseling, this is what the counselor does to cure a client. Why the striking difference in effect? Suppose the client assumes that the counselor knows what she is doing and that she is solely concerned with the client's welfare. How could the client then interpret the counselor putting him through the very experience he fears? It is plausible that the client might assume that the therapist knows more than he does, knows he is stronger than he thought he was, knows he can handle the experience, all of which would be very reassuring. Like the proverbial mouse in a corner, she may learn to fight back or to view the situation more realistically. Or implosive therapy might work in a fashion analogous to the strategy a father might use to help overcome his son's fear of water; let the child swim first with someone to rely upon until he is confident enough to rely upon himself. Or it might work for the same reason any procedure will work if people have faith in it. Whether these possibilities are suggestive or not, it is surprising that the rhetorical dimensions of such a highly dramatic procedure as implosive therapy should be so neglected.

Therapies, too, offer ingenious strategies of rhetoric. For example, Rogerian therapy might gain its effects by the peculiarly forceful way in which the counselor's communications are stylistically emphasized. The client states his position, anticipating some form of threat. Rogerians assume that although the client is prepared to be defensive, he meets absolutely no resistance, nothing whatever to be threatened or defensive about. Instead, he finds someone who appears to be totally absorbed in experiencing, understanding, and appreciating his side of things. On the principle of reciprocity in human relations, it can be supposed that just as the counselor is wholly open to the client's side of things, so will the client be disposed to be more open to the counselor's side of things (Young, Becker, & Pike, 1970). There is every reason to believe that such a strategy, if carried out skillfully, could not fail to encourage the client to attempt to understand the counselor's position, if he would ever state it.

But a complication ensues. The counselor never explicitly proposes a counter-position. If the client is to reciprocate, he must make a more active effort to uncover exactly what the counselor's stance really is (what a truly remarkable switch this would be from a defensive person!). The counselor's orientation can be read indirectly through the way he vividly enacts an alternative way of thinking, feeling, and acting. If the client adopted even part of this openness, honesty, and warmth that is so clearly modeled for him, surely it would alter his own orientation. Rogerians believe that their method of therapy releases a natural growth process. But from the slightly different angle presented here, it appears more likely that what they witness are clients adopting in varying degrees their own stance toward themselves and others. If the client learned to view himself in the way the counselor appears to, there would be much more involved than a releasing of potential. There would also be a forceful directing of potential.

When growth potential is released, can the person grow in any direction? The answer is no. The direction of growth is defined by the attributes of a fully functioning person. And the fully functioning person is but a variant of the model a Rogerian counselor portrays. Growth is recognized to the extent that a client emulates the stance of the counselor. From a rhetorical viewpoint, this is what Burke has termed secular conversion, pure and simple. It is not necessarily a release of growth potential. If this mystification of position is removed, then the basis for considering some attributes as important and others as unimportant is also removed. We are left with a stance toward living, an orientation that is but one of many and that might be better than some and worse than others.

The danger of inadvertency, of course, is that detrimental effects can occur without knowledge or control. Studies of pragmatic communication (Bateson, 1972; Watzlawick, Beavin, & Jackson, 1967) have been particularly revealing of the profound upset that can occur through inadvertent and contradictory communications. A wife, let us say, might domineeringly demand that her husband be more assertive and assume a more dominant role in the family. The content of the message is contradicted by the manner of its delivery. While the content requests more dominance, the style requests more submissiveness. The command aspect of the communication projects a definition of the husband (submissive weakling?) that could be wholly inadvertent.

Encounter groups seem to offer a rich source of bewilderment. Consider the demand to be known. A person might shout, "I want to get to know you," with all the force of a barroom tough on Saturday night. In ordinary life, it would be obvious that if this person wanted to get to know you better, he is certainly not acting like it. But in groups, all manner of requests to know can be sanctioned as legitimate. That is, the report aspect of the message (I want to get to know you) can be, and often is, at odds with the command aspect of the message. The onus is upon the person to reveal or not reveal; he cannot for long combat the stylistics of the communication without appearing defensive, evasive, and closed. Ordinary terms such as *sharing* and *honesty* are operationalized quite differently in groups, a circumstance which could be bewildering to the novitiate. For example, sharing can be swapping tales of woe; honesty can be a willingness to dwell excessively upon weaknesses. At least initially, common positions or bonds appear to be forged on the basis of weakness, hidden secrets, and guilts.

In response to Koch's penetrating essay (1971) on the image of man implicit in encounter groups, Haigh (1971) replied that he did not force groups to do anything. Rather, groups take on predictable directions, and he lets them go as they will. What a curiously myopic stance that is! Can a group leader seriously believe that members of a group do not learn rather quickly what is expected of them, that when their turn comes, they are supposed to reveal their weaknesses and to convince the group that their appearances belie a starker reality? The demand characteristics of a group speak loud and clear; there is no need for explicit statement.

The obsession with techniques can also have detrimental consequences. Consider the following hypothetical example. X, a client, has developed a sense of helplessness, a loss of agency in a variety of situations. X is not a person who makes things happen, but a person to whom things happen. He enters counseling upon the prodding of a friend to see if somebody can do something about one particular situation, his severe anxiety during tests. The counselor elects to use systematic desensitization (SD). While SD is certainly one of the most effective techniques available, it also usually requires in practice a considerable amount of passivity in the client's role. Under the directions of the counselor, the client constructs a hierarchy (or hierarchies) of related situations, undergoes relaxation training, and proceeds through the hierarchy of imagined situations by learning to relax in their presence. During the entire procedure, the client must only follow instructions. He does not have to take an active role at all. That is, X could follow the procedure with little sense of agency or competence, since it is undergone, more than done. Let us assume that the procedure was effective, X's anxiety decreased during tests. In this sense, the technique was effective in promoting desirable change. But what X learned from such a service could well have been that he was very helpless indeed without the intervention of others. To get things done, X might be further disposed to rely upon others and further convinced that he could not depend upon himself. In this sense, the by-product of service would have been an image that consolidated a detrimental and incapacitating orientation to living. The very effectiveness of a technique can be harmful if it fosters a deficient orientation toward onself and others.

It is not enough to use a technique in an effective manner. The influence of the entire experience on a person's orientation requires consideration. The above situation could not necessarily be corrected by a more extensive use of SD. A series of hierarchies could be constructed for each area of difficulty. But still, if X regards the treatments as something he undergoes with little sense of contribution to his own welfare and as evidence of his own inability, then it would merely underline his perceived incapability further. But SD can be used differently. For example, people can learn to self-administer SD with no loss in effectiveness (for example, Clark, 1973). Equipped with both rationale and method, X could become more of an agent. Techniques are blind. The way they are used to elaborate one role or another, agent or patient, has radically different implications for one's orientation, potentially different implications for one's future well-being (Chein, 1972).

Projections also arise from professional stances rather than theoretical ones. One familiar stance, which might be called the code of the headache pill, prescribes that anything that is bothersome should be removed or alleviated as efficiently as possible. Guilt, for example, is variously regarded as a hang-up, an irrationality, or an unrewarding association, among other things (consult Mowrer, 1967). Since it plays no constructive role (it is not pleasurable), the only rational thing to do with guilt is to get rid of it as soon as possible. Gilligan's recent proclamation (1976) that morality is dead—and deserves to be dead since it is antagonistic to life—is certainly not uncharacteristic of the mental health movement.[4] Yet, as Rawls (1971) has demonstrated, one cannot do away with moral feelings without doing away with the natural sentiments to which they are necessarily attached. To love others, for instance, is to care about their welfare, to take joy from their benefit and sadness from their detriment, and to assume guilt for having hurt or wrongly treated them. To clarify by a comparative example, striving for success necessarily involves the risk of failure. Each term is defined by its opposite. If a person remained unaffected following failure (no sadness, deflation, or depression), it could be safely assumed that he had not really cared about success. Similarly, to do right necessarily involves the possibility of doing wrong. If guilt were removed from the human condition, it would imply the lack of any sense of right and wrong and of the natural sentiments underlying moral conduct.

Suppose that psychologists could get rid of bothers just as a headache pill gets rid of headaches. Would people be any better for such a service? First, like headaches, guilt and other emotions are consequences of living; they are apt to signal something about the life a person is leading. Might not the very availability of effective analogues to headache pills encourage a person to ignore the consequences of the perhaps stupid and harmful way he is conducting his life? How guilt and other states of mental suffering are resolved is apt to make a great deal of difference to the way in which people approach the next turn in the road. Second, the very effectiveness of such a service could disarm people, undermining the age-old strategies for standing up to and even benefiting from mental suffering. If mental suffering is merely something to be rid of, something unnatural and unnecessary, then people are more likely to feel cheated when suffering comes their way.

The complement to the code of the headache pill is the code of the pig. Discussing the principle that behavior is influenced by anticipated consequences, Bandura (1974) observed that images of man depend upon the consequences acknowledged. Modern epicureanism, as Campbell (1975) has recently criticized, projects an image of man that is self-serving, self-congratulatory, and pleasure-loving. According to the code of the pig, the only consequences worth discussing are feeling good, experiencing pleasure and enjoyment, and the like. Consider the impact of this image upon a program such as self-assertion. In considering the examples set forth by Alberti and Emmons (1970), assertiveness training appears to be concerned primarily with justice in human affairs. There was perhaps an overconcern with rights rather than obligations and duties, but the stress upon justice is unmistakable. To recognize situations requiring assertion, a person must have a well-developed sense of justice. In its advocacy of justice for oneself and others, assertiveness training is perhaps the most significant innovation in some years. However, shift its appeal, and it becomes just another program to help individuals "do their thing" (whatever that means). For example, it can become a way to be more self-serving, more self-congratulatory, and more successful in obtaining pleasures. To recognize a situation requiring assertion in this case, the person need have only a sense of self-interest. To capture the flavor of the radically different implications for living that assertiveness training projects, it is necessary only to compare a selection of recent, popular books on the subject.

Professions arise in response to demand, but are maintained by generating a continued demand for service. Demand need not be generated by malicious intent or by deliberate invention (however, see Schrang & Divoky, 1975, on the myth of the hyperactive child), but can arise by professionals' defining their domains of influence. Certain phenomena are defined in professional terms to be solved in professional terms. This advocacy is made public and legitimate: professional prerogatives are asserted, and to the extent that people accept those claims or are required to do so by law, they will yield to higher authority presumably for their own benefit. Dependence is thus created by convention or legislation. For example, the recent legislative proposal that would make biofeedback available only upon the prescription of a physician illustrates one form of legislated dependency. Professions also expand by staking out more territory to be defined in professional terms and by creating a more pervasive dependence. In this development, professions refine and assert a role definition that requires a complementary role to fulfill it.

That is, professions take a stance toward people that demands a complementary stance from them in return. It is here that psychologists (particularly in counseling centers) have recently broken tradition in refusing to cultivate the role of consumers, patients, and even clients. Counseling centers have been one of the few professional institutions to insist in recent years upon defining people as agents. Although there is no space to elaborate this distinction, a few issues might be mentioned. In cultivating patiency rather than agency, professions typically guard or obscure knowledge, insist upon consummatory dependency, and focus almost exclusively upon problems, weaknesses, and deficits. In guarding knowledge, which of course preserves professional stances of authority, simple ideas are obscured behind technical-sounding terminologies that serve to keep people in the dark. For example, the term *anorexia nervosa* scarcely adds to the fact that a person has stopped eating, but it can certainly alter one's stance toward that fact. In contrast to this tradition, psychologists have taken seriously Miller's call (1969) to give information away to promote human welfare. Most programs in counseling centers are now oriented to the development of agency. Most are devoted to skill building (not unblocking and other ''depth'' pursuits), to self-regulation (not to dependence), and to self-administration (not treatment). There is more respect for agency and less respect for blind compliance. After all, the idea of man implicit in self-administration rather than treatment is truly radical! In contrast to North American psychiatry, which seems to have opted almost exclusively for consumptive patient roles (taking drugs, undergoing shock treatment, undergoing psychotherapy, and so forth), psychology has developed the reverse stand in fostering productive agent roles.

Last, with a reorientation toward people as agents, there has been much more attention directed to living well rather than to coping adequately. Circumscribed problem solving has been expanded to a concern for the conduct of life, a rediscovery that "curing illness" is one thing while promoting health and well-being is quite another. In lieu of an elaboration of this significant professional reorientation, I might simply ask the question whose implications I have been hastily spelling out: What if Freud had been an anthropologist?[5]

In summary, the point of these examples is not to show that the methods and techniques of counseling are damaging. On the contrary, most have been of demonstrated value. For instance, systematic desensitization for test anxiety has been shown to have a positive effect upon self-concept (Ryan, Krall, & Hodges, 1976), perhaps, as the authors suggest, because it requires people to imagine themselves as more successful "copers." But this effect, which in itself could very well account for the effectiveness of systematic desensitization, is wholly inadvertent as this treatment is presently conceived. The point, then, is simply that the effects of counseling upon the way people define themselves and others, either beneficial or detrimental, can be largely inadvertent. Consequently, a broader perspective on the way interventions are conducted is required if these effects are to be made predictable and manageable.

Frames and Cages

Orientations differ in a variety of ways.[6] According to different theorists, they can be more or less veridical, coherent, consistent, precise, differentiated, fruitful, fulfilling, complex, demanding, ambiguous, ambivalent, broad, and manageable, to name a few. These criteria, with their huge overlap in meaning, can best be understood as different ways in which an orientation's predictive capabilities are expandable or limited. A veridical orientation, for instance, generates anticipations that are apt to be validated, while a broad orientation generates anticipations allowing higher levels of action to be envisioned and performed. Orientations generate anticipations, and anticipations allow actions to be constructed and events to be seen (for example, Neisser, 1976).

A number of scholars have converged on the fundamental assumption that people are directed toward the development of their ability to anticipate events. Kelly's choice corollary (1955) states that persons are directed toward the extension and refinement of their personal construct systems. Hinkle (1965), in revising the corollary slightly, states that people are directed toward an increase in the meaning and significance of their lives, toward an avoidance of "the anxiety of chaos and the despair of absolute certainty." Friedman (1975) asserts that man is inherently impelled to increase his ability to predict. Kagan (1971) frames it as a motive to resolve uncertainty, to seek uncertainty when it can be managed, and to avoid it when it cannot be managed. Such a principle is implicit in many works on the experimental psychology of cognition. For instance, it was all but formulated explicitly in Neisser's recent book (1976) on the conception of human nature implicit in the idea of cognition (see particularly his explanation of the perceptual cycle and the origins of schemata). It is also implicit in principles that stress self-competence and self-mastery and, less obviously, in models of self-fulfillment. For example, Rawls developed an Aristotelian principle of motivation stating roughly that people will engage in those activities in which they are proficient and which offer the greatest range for making "more intricate and subtle distinctions" (1971, p. 426). Applied to plans of life, people will be directed toward those activities which will exercise their proficiencies and allow for the greatest range of meaningful elaboration.

To maintain a meaningful contact with reality, individuals' orientations must be capable of extension and refinement or, in light of invalidation, of revision. To thrive or perhaps even to survive, orientations must be capable of meaningful elaboration, adaptation to changing circumstances. Frames for endowing life with meaning can be subtly transformed into cages in which people endure what they cannot escape. Where once there were only possibilities, there are now only limitations. Kuhn (1962) has emphasized the framing and caging aspects of scientific orientations in his study of paradigm change, of revolution in science. which strikingly parallels the activity of counseling. Kuhn's chapter on paradigm changes can be compared, for instance, with Kelly's view of counseling (1955) as a way to facilitate a psychological reconstruction of life.

Frames can become cages in many ways. Like the dinosaur, the concept of honor has died due to dependence upon highly specific circumstances (Berger, Berger, & Kellner, 1973). The very inflexibility and lack of scope that gave it incredible power and significance render honor incapable of extension to changing circumstances. Or, for another example, the Elizabethan passion for order (Tillyard, 1959) was countered by an inability to establish a unifying order amidst constant threats of chaos. Their vast epistemology of correspondences and similitudes defied unification of knowledge (Foucault, 1970). To discover the meaning of something required a search for resemblances, which, being infinite, became a search without end and resulted in a staggering accumulation of similitudes. What should have emerged as order became in practice an unmanageable list of similarities.

Orientations can be limited in their capability for meaningful elaboration by a lack of veridicality, scope, consistency, or precision, or by fragmented constructions lacking in overall unity, and so on. It is through criteria such as these that the orientations that counselors project, either intentionally or inadvertently, can be assessed. For example, is self-identity best construed as a treasure chest that one discovers through introspection or as an accomplishment that is earned and re-earned over and over again? To diminish aggressiveness, should it be released or expressed, or should it be controlled by appropriate strategies and models? Which will conflict with evidence? How far can people go, doing their own thing, as though any activity were just as good as any other? What limits are attached to the maxim, Be yourself? Does it mean that one should act the same way at all times and to all people? What kind of guide to living is the Gestalt prayer? How would people really feel if no one expected anything of them? While these criteria and their applications to psychological orientations cannot be elaborated further here, it is hoped that they provide a useful way to view the practical consequences of counseling. Namely, how do counseling practices help to frame or to encage a person's orientation to living?

Counselors have been obsessed with the means of personal change, and perhaps rightly so. If psychology has contributed anything novel to traditional images of humanity, it is this broadened conception of what it is possible to change. What was once fixed is now variable. People can change and, to a large extent, control the direction of change. They need not wait upon miracles, spells, the wheel of fortune, or the fickle affections of the gods. Yet this very fascination with change can be blinding in its neglect of the ends toward which human nature can change. Noble-sounding statements of purpose are no substitute for careful consideration and study of the way in which ends are communicated in practice. The ends that are now implicit within means of change must be made explicit, be made subject to the same rigors of debate and evidence to which means are now subject.

Notes

This chapter owes much to the writings of George Kelly and Kenneth Burke. Discussions with Michael Stones were also of great value.

1. Perhaps the best introduction to Thomas's work can be found in Janowitz (1966).

2. Attribution theorists (e.g., Valins & Nisbett, 1971) have shown how damaging can be self-attributions that put one outside normal ways of imposing structure on oneself. The common practice of labeling people as neurotic or whatever can be seen as one way people are put outside normal orders and normal explanations. Raimy (1976) has argued that the fear of going mad is a major contributor to personal difficulties, even for people who are supposed to be mad. Madness, of course, is conceived as the ultimate plunge into unpredictability by popularizations of personality theory and by significant portions of the mental health movement. But if people are disposed to read their own thoughts, feelings, and actions as signs of impending chaos, then they are reading them in just the opposite way to that which would establish order. People need assistance in extending and refining stagnant orientations, in tightening overextended ones, and in revising ones that collide with reality, but it is unlikely that they need help in anticipating total chaos. For a person experiencing difficulties in structuring the world, the assurance of a total plunge could hardly be of much comfort.

3. The whole force of such new fields as systems theory (e.g., Buckley, 1968; Weiss, 1971) is that higher levels of understanding allow higher levels of action to be contemplated and performed. Or consider the role of objective knowledge in expanding the possibility of effective action. For example, a person does not take antibiotics because they feel good, because intuitive experience recommends them, or because they just seem right. Instead he does so because of objective knowledge that they will help fight infection.

4. It is striking that current images of moral persons as downtrodden and guilt-ridden are so at odds with traditional images of moral persons as upright and healthy. There is no doubt a moral lag taking place at least in North America—a lag in which old morals become imprisoning—but this scarcely justifies the ill-conceived notion that morals are somehow bad for you. On the contrary, it should demand more careful and penetrating consideration of the right and the good. Feinberg (1970) has noted that the role of the ancient moral philosophers was to recommend life goals and standards of personal excellence; they advised people how to live well. I believe this role of assisting people to build plans of life now rather accurately defines the guidance services of a counseling center. Yet guidance workers are apt to operate in ignorance of over two thousand years of accumulated knowledge in this area, since moral traditions are certainly not a part of professional preparation. Personally, I think it most unfortunate that guidance has become so tied to personality theories rather than to relevant aspects of moral philosophy. After all, it was Freud who defined the multiple ways in which people can live miserably and the Greek philosophers who first defined the multiple ways in which people can live well.

5. For an excellent book on the way anthropologists facilitate change, see Goodenough (1966).

6. The title, "Frames and Cages," was taken from Ryle's excellent book (1975) on personal construct systems. Therapies, to a greater or lesser extent, do stress or offer new personality constructs, perspectives, and ordering assumptions that people can use to define and to elaborate their positions. Openness, for instance, not only establishes a direction of change, but also can define the way in which a person is deficient. It is striking to observe how clients of different types of therapists go about expanding or revising their positions. How, for example, do Rogerian clients differ from clients of behavioral therapists in elaborating their visions of things? These considerations, however, must await another time.

References

Alberti, R., and Emmons, M. 1970. *Your perfect right: a guide to assertive behavior*. San Luis Obispo, Calif.: Impact.

Ansbacher, H., and Ansbacher, R. 1956. *The individual psychology of Alfred Adler*. New York: Basic Books.

Baier, K., and Rescher, N. 1969. *Values and the future*. New York: Macmillan.

Bandura, A. 1974. Behavior theory and models of man. *American Psychologist* 29: 859–69.

Bateson, G. 1972. *Steps to an ecology of mind*. New York: Ballantine Books.

Benedict, R. 1934. *Patterns of culture*. Boston: Houghton Mifflin.

Berger, P.; Berger, B.; and Kellner, H. 1973. *The homeless mind*. New York: Random House.

Bergin, A. 1971. The evaluation of therapeutic outcomes. In A. Bergin and S. Garfield, eds., *Handbook of psychotherapy and behavior change*. New York: John Wiley.

Brinton, C. 1959. *A history of Western morals*. New York: Harcourt, Brace and Company.

Bruner, O.; Goodnow, J.; and Austin, G. 1956. *A study in thinking*. New York: John Wiley.

Buckley, W., ed. 1968. *Modern systems research for the behavioral scientist: a source book*. Chicago: Aldine.

Burke, K. 1965. *Permanence and change: an anatomy of purpose*. Indianapolis: Bobbs-Merrill.

Campbell, P. 1975. On conflicts between biological and social evolution and between psychology and moral tradition. *American Psychologist* 30: 1103–26.

Carlson, R. 1975. *The end of medicine*. New York: John Wiley.

Chein, I. 1972. *The science of behavior and the image of man*. New York: Basic Books.

Clark, F. 1973. Self-administered desensitization. *Behavior Research and Therapy*. 11: 335–38.

Ellis, A. 1962. *Reason and emotion in psychotherapy*. New York: Lyle Stuart.

Feinberg, J. 1970. *Moral concepts*. London and New York: Oxford University Press.

Foucault, M. 1970. *The order of things*. London: Tavistock.

Fransella, F. 1972. *Personal change and reconstruction*. New York: Academic Press.

Friedman, M. 1975. *Rational behavior*. Columbia, S.C.: University of South Carolina Press.

Gilligan, J. 1976. Beyond morality: psychoanalytic reflections on shame, guilt, and love. In T. Lickon, ed., *Moral development and behavior*. New York: Holt, Rinehart and Winston.

Goffman, E. 1961. *Asylums*. New York: Doubleday & Co.

Goodenough, W. 1966. *Cooperation in change*. New York: John Wiley.

Haigh, G. 1971. Response to Koch's assumption about group process. *Journal of Humanistic Psychology*. 11: 129–32.

Hanson, N. 1969. *Perception and discovery*. San Francisco: Freeman, Cooper & Company.

Hinkle, D. 1965. The change in personal constructs from the viewpoint of a theory of construct implications. Unpublished doctoral dissertation, Ohio State University.

Illich, I. 1974. *Medical nemesis*. London: Calder and Boyars.

Innis, H. 1951. *The bias of communication*. Toronto: University of Toronto Press.

Janowitz, M. 1966. *W. I. Thomas on social organization and social personality*. Chicago: University of Chicago Press.

Johnson, D. 1972. *The psychology of thinking*. New York: Harper & Row.

Kagan, J. 1971. *Understanding children: behavior, motives, and thoughts*. New York: Harcourt Brace Jovanovich.

Kahn, R., et al. 1964. *Organizational stress: studies in role conflict and ambiguity*. New York: John Wiley.

Kanfer, F. 1975. Self-management methods. In F. Kanfer and A. Goldstein, eds., *Helping people change*. New York: Pergamon Press.

Kazdin, A., and Wilcoxon, L. 1976. Systematic desensitization and nonspecific treatment effects: a methodological evaluation. *Psychological Bulletin* 83: 729–58.

Kelly, G. 1955. *The psychology of personal constructs*. New York: W. W. Norton.

Klapp, O. 1969. *Collective search for identity*. New York: Holt, Rinehart and Winston.

Koch, S. 1971. The image of man implicit in encounter group theory. *Journal of Humanistic Psychology* 11: 109–28.

Kuhn, T. 1962. *The structure of scientific revolutions*. Chicago: University of Chicago Press.

McCall, G., and Simmons, J. 1966. *Identities and interactions*. New York: Macmillan.

McLuhan, M. 1964. *Understanding media: the extension of man*. New York: McGraw-Hill.

Miller, G. 1969. Psychology as a means of promoting human welfare. *American Psychologist* 24: 1063–75.

Mischel, W. 1973. Toward a cognitive social learning reconceptualization of personality. *Psychological Review* 80: 252–83.

Mowrer, O., ed. 1967. *Morality and mental health*. Chicago: Rand McNally.

Neisser, U. 1976. *Cognition and reality*. San Francisco: W. H. Freeman.

Peterfreund, E. 1971. *Information, systems, and psychoanalysis*. New York: International Universities Press.

Raimy, V. 1976. *Misunderstandings of the self*. San Francisco: Jossey-Bass.

Rawls, J. 1971. *A theory of justice*. Cambridge: Harvard University Press.

Rosenhan, D. 1973. On being insane in insane places. *Science* 179: 250–58.

Ryan, V.; Krall, C.; and Hodges, W. 1976. Self-concept change in behavior modification. *Journal of Consulting and Clinical Psychology* 44: 638–45.

Ryle, A. 1975. *Frames and cages*. London: Sussex University Press.

Scheff, T. 1966. *Being mentally ill*. Chicago: Aldine.

Schrang, R., and Divoky, D. 1975. *The myth of the hyperactive child*. New York: Pantheon Books.

Seidenberg, R. 1950. *Post-historic man*. New York: Viking Press.

Szasz, T. 1961. *The myth of mental illness* New York: Hoeber-Harper.

Tillyard, E. 1959. *The Elizabethan world picture*. New York: Random House.

Toffler, A. 1970. *Future shock*. New York: Random House.

Valins, S., and Nisbett, R. 1971. Attribution processes in the development and treatment of emotional disorder. In E. Jones et al., eds., *Attribution: receiving the causes of behavior*. Morristown, N.J.: General Learning Press.

Watzlawick, R.; Beavin, J.; and Jackson, D. 1967. *Pragmatics of human communication*. New York: W. W. Norton.

Weiss, P., ed. 1971. *Hierarchically organized systems in theory and practice*. New York: Hafner.

Wittgenstein, L. 1968. *Philosophical investigations*. New York: Macmillan.

Young, R.; Becker, A.; and Pike, K. 1970. *Rhetoric: discovery and change*. New York: Harcourt, Brace and World.

2

THE PROFESSIONALIZATION OF CHANGE AGENTS: GROWTH AND DEVELOPMENT OF COUNSELING CENTERS AS INSTITUTIONS

Beulah M. Hedahl

UNIVERSITY OF NORTH DAKOTA

The counseling center as an office or agency with its own identity is a relative newcomer on the university or college campus. It is still less than fifty years since the University Testing Bureau was established at the University of Minnesota in 1932 (Williamson & Sarbin, 1940; Paterson, Schneidler, & Williamson, 1938; Paterson, 1976; Kirk, 1966). This appears to have been the earliest separate unit organized to offer professionalized educational and vocational guidance, although the need for such counseling had been recognized since the early 1900s, and responsibility for it had been assigned to faculty and to deans of men and women. Indeed, as Paterson (1976) has pointed out, the University Testing Bureau was an outgrowth of a decade of activity at Minnesota attempting to individualize mass education through the Committee of Faculty Counselors (which he headed), the development of general education courses, the use of subject-matter achievement examinations for sectioning, various how-to-study and orientation courses, and a mental hygiene program staffed by psychiatrists.

This activity was paralleled at other institutions. In 1927, Cowley (1964) became director of the Board of Vocational Guidance and Placement at the University of Chicago and was assigned the task of coordinating counseling activities of various special service officers; and at the University of Illinois the Student Personnel Bureau was founded in 1938 with a staff of seven part-time faculty counselors, a technical director who was a psychologist, and an administrative director who was a mathematics professor (Bailey, Gilbert, & Berg, 1946; Ewing, 1973). At Ohio State University the Occupational Opportunities Service was established first as an off-campus service to the state as a whole and was moved onto the campus in the early 1940s, gradually taking on functions of counseling for students (Thrush, 1957). About 1938 a College Adjustment Clinic developed at the University of Missouri as an outgrowth of the student health service, but its testing and counseling service developed separately at a later time (Embree, 1950).

A check of the annual membership list of the American College Personnel Association revealed that during the early 1930s relatively few people bore titles indicating relationship to a separate counseling center, but by the late 1930s and early 1940s there was a definite increase in the number of departments, offices, or bureaus with titles indicative of functions in testing, vocational guidance, and counseling (Hedahl, 1958).

By 1950 the movement toward establishment of counseling bureaus or clinics had reached the point at which Embree could describe it as "one of the most striking and productive phases of the personnel-guidance mental hygiene movement during the past two decades" (1950, p. 465).

What were the trends and developments during the first half of the century that led to the emergence of counseling centers as separate administrative units on an increasing number of campuses? Three major sources of influence were the developments in student personnel work, vocational guidance, and psychology. These developments were closely interrelated—in fact, many of the leaders in one field were leaders in one or both of the others—yet each area made its own contribution to the growth of counseling services within higher education.

The Student Personnel Movement

An emphasis on counseling was a significant aspect of the development of student personnel services in colleges and universities. The need for counseling (or advising) was frequently mentioned as one of the justifications for appointing advisors, counselors, or deans and thus was part of student personnel work since Gilman appointed the first Chief of the Advisors at Johns Hopkins in 1889 (Cowley, 1949).

Many of the factors favoring the development of student personnel work also favored counseling as one of the central concerns of student personnel: the individualization movement in elementary and secondary education; the contributions of psychological, sociological, and educational research to the knowledge of the problems and capabilities of adolescents; the development of psychometric techniques; and the increasing emphasis upon the worth of the individual (Williamson & Sarbin, 1950).

So closely was counseling connected with student personnel that it was often used to mean the whole of student personnel work rather than one function of the student personnel program (Wrenn, 1941). Counseling was considered to be one of the responsibilities of faculty members in general or of particular faculty members appointed to serve as counselors. For example, the discussion of counseling in *A Student Personnel Program for Higher Education* by Lloyd-Jones and Smith (1938) centered on counseling performed by faculty counselors, preferably with some professional training in counseling, and coordinated by a professional student personnel worker. In *Educational Counseling of College Students,* a brochure published by the American Council on Education, it was recommended that all faculty do some counseling; that some faculty be selected for further training; that trained persons be responsible for remedial reading, remedial speech, and psychological measurement; and that a central agency be set up to coordinate counseling data and personnel (Bragdon et al., 1939).

During the 1930s and 1940s student personnel work was characterized by an increased emphasis on counseling and on professional training for counseling. A 1933 report of personnel activities in colleges belonging to the North Central Association of Colleges and Secondary Schools showed that almost three-fourths of the people classified as personnel workers in colleges or professional schools listed counseling as one of their functions. These personnel staff members were mostly college teachers, with two-thirds of them devoting less than one-fourth of their time to personnel work (Brumbaugh, 1937).

In 1936, Lloyd-Jones studied the catalogs of 521 universities and colleges for the listings of faculty and administrative staff connected with student personnel work and found 216 different job titles. Although titles that suggested professional counseling were relatively few (about 20) and appeared in very few of the catalogs, some titles that implied special training in counseling—personnel counselor, vocational counselor, student counselor, advisor of vocational guidance, director of personnel guidance, and mental hygiene counselor—were beginning to appear (Lloyd-Jones & Smith, 1938).

As a part of their plan for a total counseling program, Paterson, Schneidler, and Williamson (1938) pointed out the need for professionally trained general counselors whose primary function would be diagnosis, but whose concerns would also include treatment, analysis of student needs, and coordination of personnel services in the interest of the student.

In 1949, Cowley stressed the need for professionalization in student personnel work through the setting of professional standards, the establishment of curricula in personnel work in several universities, and the requirement that professional standards be met by people subsequently to be employed in personnel (Cowley, 1949).

Appraising the extent to which college personnel work was moving toward professionalization, Wrenn reached the conclusion "that of the several vocations in college student personnel work, that of a qualified psychological counselor comes closest to meeting the criteria of a profession" (1951b, p. 191). Darley (1949) also noted the trend toward professionalization. The general recognition of the need for specific skills and training for professional counseling paved the way for the establishment of separate administrative units in an increasing number of universities and colleges.

The Vocational Guidance Movement

The vocational guidance movement in the United States, which is generally dated from 1908 with the work of Parsons in Boston, grew rapidly as a civic service within the communities and as a service for young people within the high schools. Although higher education did not generally acknowledge the need for vocational guidance for students, it provided training for vocational guidance workers for positions in the community, served as a center for research in occupations, or provided service to the state in a consultative capacity (Brewer, 1942).

TRAINING OF VOCATIONAL GUIDANCE WORKERS

As centers for training, the universities were part of the vocational guidance movement from the very start. The first course in vocational guidance was given in Boston in 1908 and was sponsored by the YMCA as a School for Vocational Counselors. The first university-sponsored course came soon after, at Harvard in 1911; the University of Chicago scheduled a course in 1912; and Columbia University and the University of Missouri gave classes in 1913. By 1925, between thirty and fifty colleges offered summer courses in vocational guidance (Brewer, 1942). That year Kitson was invited to organize a sequence for graduate-level training of vocational counselors at Teachers College, Columbia University, where the first doctoral degree in vocational guidance was granted in 1927 (Kitson, 1946). By 1938, twenty or more colleges had set up a curriculum of courses leading to professional work in personnel or guidance (Brewer, 1942).

The 1940s brought two attempts to set up general standards for the training of professional personnel in vocational guidance. In 1944 the War Manpower Commission issued a bulletin, *The Training of Vocational Counselors,* prepared by the Advisory Committee on Vocational Counseling; and in 1949 a brochure entitled *Counselor Preparation* was prepared by the Joint National Committee on Counselor Preparation of eight national personnel organizations and agencies, including the American College Personnel Association, the National Vocational Guidance Association, and the Division of Counseling and Guidance of the American Psychological Association (Wrenn, 1951b).

The addition of the category of professional membership in the National Voca-

tional Guidance Association in 1948 was another indication of growing professionalization (Blum & Balinsky, 1951).

VOCATIONAL GUIDANCE FOR COLLEGE STUDENTS

A summary of the early vocational guidance in the colleges has been made by
Brewer. In some instances vocational guidance was carried on in connection with
the placement services that had developed somewhat earlier. In other cases the
deans of women or men assumed some responsibility for vocational guidance.
Commenting on the sparsity of vocational guidance for students in colleges,
Brewer wrote, "On the whole the colleges have shown reluctance toward vocational guidance; some professors do not distinguish it from vocational education" (1942, p. 249).

The impact of the vocational guidance movement on higher education was
relatively small in terms of stimulating vocational guidance for college students
except as this was performed by individual people, by particular institutions, or
in connection with placement departments; however, in terms of stimulating the
growth of education and training facilities for counselors and guidance workers,
the impact was truly great.

In both the student personnel and the vocational guidance movements many of
the leaders were psychologists by training, and many of the tools with which they
worked were developed by psychologists.

Professional Psychology

One of the earliest influences of psychology on counseling in higher education
came in the field of psychometrics. The work of individuals like Scott, Bingham,
and Otis just prior to World War I made possible the extensive development of
psychometrics during the war years. Subsequently, many psychologists who had
gained much experience and training during this period returned to colleges and
universities with an interest in the measurement of intelligence, aptitudes, and
interests. This led to the development of a wide range of tests that could be used
in both secondary and higher education (Paterson, 1950). Later, in an attempt to
meet some of the needs brought on by the economic depression of the late 1930s,
the Minnesota Employment Stabilization Research Institute experimented with
psychological tests, occupational information, and retraining as methods of getting adult workers back into the active labor force (Super, 1955). Throughout the
1920s and 1930s psychologists led the way in the expansion of research and
faculty counseling programs on college campuses and added their knowledge of
psychometrics and diagnostics to provide professional assistance for the faculty
counselors (Viteles, 1961).

An interest in psychotherapy began to influence developments in the 1930s,
largely stemming from work that was being done in clinical psychology. The
work of Carl Rogers (1942, 1951) was one product of this interest. Following its

publication the interest in psychotherapeutic procedures became even greater than the interest in psychometrics (Super, 1955). According to Kirk, Rogers's greatest impact on counseling within higher education was the emphasis "upon 'personal' counseling, self-knowledge from the internal frame of reference, and self-actualization" (Kirk, 1966, p. 22).

In 1957, Wrenn described counseling as a product of the convergence of vocational guidance and occupational information, individual differences and psychometrics, personality dynamics, and the psychology of learning. His statement reflected the increasing awareness by counseling educators of the importance of training in such areas of psychology as individual differences, learning, and personality dynamics.

Psychology also influenced counseling in higher education through the growing sense of professional identity among applied psychologists. Formed in 1937, the American Association for Applied Psychology included sections for clinical, consulting, educational, and industrial psychology. During World War II this group merged with the American Psychological Association, and a Division of Counseling and Guidance was set up. This became the Division of Counseling Psychology in 1951. Another instance of the increased awareness of professional status within psychology was the establishment of the American Board of Examiners in Professional Psychology; since 1947 the ABEPP (now ABPP) has issued the Diploma in Counseling Psychology to those meeting the necessary qualifications (Super, 1955). In 1951 the Division of Counseling Psychology recommended a doctoral program for counseling psychologists, and in 1953 the Committee on Ethical Standards published the APA's Code of Ethics, which includes principles related to the practice of counseling (Bordin & Wrenn, 1954).

The developments within psychology were interwoven with those within vocational guidance and student personnel work because of the considerable overlap of personnel. Although many of the leaders were college professors in departments of psychology, they were active in various vocational guidance organizations. From the area of psychology came most of the skills, tools, and techniques: psychometrics; psychotherapy; the knowledge of human behavior from the areas of individual differences, learning theory, and personality dynamics; and the growing sense of professional status within the field of psychology as a whole.

Developments Since World War II

THE VETERANS ADMINISTRATION AND THE GROWTH OF COUNSELING CENTERS

The end of World War II brought an unprecedented flood of students to the campuses, and student personnel counseling services expanded to match this growth. However, in order to meet the needs of veterans more effectively the

Veterans Administration undertook a college and university guidance program that led to the establishment of many new counseling facilities on college campuses and to the expansion of many already existing facilities. This VA guidance program was called the "major contributing factor to the expansion of college counseling services" by Embree (1950, p. 471). Having studied 154 of the 415 guidance centers activated on college and university campuses, Dreese (1949) found that prior to having a VA center more than half of the institutions had not had a central testing and vocational counseling service with a director. Brayfield (1961) reported that 75 percent of the work load of VA guidance centers was carried by the 429 guidance centers at colleges and universities; most of these centers continued to operate after the VA contract was discontinued.

Other developments came from within the Veterans Administration's counseling facilities themselves. In 1951 the position of counseling psychologist (vocational counselor) was established in VA hospitals with a Ph.D. in Counseling Psychology as one requirement. The same year the title of VA vocational advisor in veterans' guidance centers was changed to counseling psychologist (vocational counselor), a position calling for a doctorate in psychology or two years of graduate work in specified fields (Bordin & Wrenn, 1954).

Counseling in higher education has thus been part of the developments in the student personnel movement, the vocational guidance movement, and professional psychology and has been influenced by the interactions among them. It responded to the growing trend toward professional status in these areas and to the influence of the Veterans Administration as the latter attempted to meet the needs of student veterans particularly in the decade after World War II. These developments in the importance of counseling in colleges and universities often necessitated a change in the administrative structure and the establishment of new agencies or bureaus for the administration of the counseling services.

COUNSELING CENTERS SINCE 1950

The period from 1950 until the present has been one of change and stress throughout the world: The Korean War, the cold war, the Vietnam War, Cambodia, Kent State, the space age, the population explosion, nuclear energy, automation, electronics, computers, the Lost Generation, the Beat Generation, hippies, missiles, protest marches, sit-ins, the drug culture, the sexual revolution, racism, sexism, equal opportunity employment, affirmative action, encounter groups, the Third World, Watergate, assassination, riots, crime, urban renewal and urban blight—these are but a few of the forces that have affected the college and university campuses in the past quarter of a century. The stimulus for the development of counseling centers that came from the increased enrollments and the VA guidance center contracts after World War II continued with the tremendous growth in college enrollments and the increasingly impersonal nature of university student-faculty relationships.

Two examples of university counseling centers furnish typical patterns of development. The center at Michigan State University began with a VA contract, but grew dramatically during the 1950s along with the university to become one of the largest centers in the country. In a retrospective look at its twenty-five year history, Grummon (1970), its director from 1953 to 1966, affirmed that the greatest strength of the center had been the delivery of high-quality counseling services to a large number of students. The center recruited a highly competent professional staff, added graduate student training in the mid-1950s as a stimulus to counseling excellence, and kept responsible to its environment through the establishment of subcenters in residence hall complexes in the mid-1960s and through a variety of programs designed to serve the campus as a whole as well as special groups of students.

More typical of smaller universities, the counseling center at the University of North Dakota was established in 1959 as the result of recommendations made by a committee that had been directed to review the counseling and guidance services on the campus. Opening with one full-time director (who also taught in the psychology department) and half-time commitments from two faculty members from psychology, the center was immediately involved in graduate training and offered internships to students in the small counseling psychology program. As part of the Division of Student Affairs, the center has provided individual and group counseling, crisis intervention, and other special programs. Its staff have participated actively in university governance and self-study.

In a 1965 survey Oetting, Ivey, and Weigel (1970) sent questionnaires to the presidents of the 1,155 colleges and universities in the United States conferring the bachelor's degree and asked for the name of the individual responsible for counseling on each campus. Seventy-five percent of the institutions responded, with 603 providing the name of the counseling director. The authors concluded that the "acceptance of the counseling facility as an integral unit of the campus has spread to over two-thirds of the institutions of higher education" (p. 9). Also in 1965, Nugent and Pareis (1968) sent questionnaires to 1,166 institutions. Of the 785 institutions that responded, 320 had no counseling center. Still another survey (Albert, 1968) sent questionnaires to 1,136 accredited senior colleges; 415 completed questionnaires were returned, and 169 additional returns indicated no counseling services. The different terminology used in the three surveys might account for the discrepancies in results.

On the whole, counseling centers seem to have become well established in their roles on the campuses. Even though the growth in enrollments has been tapering off, Magoon (1973) interprets data from surveys of counseling centers in 1967 and in 1971 as showing a modest increase in the ratio of professional staff to students. He did not, however, predict a continued growth period.

In an overview of counseling center development, Gilbert (1973) commented that the 1950s represented a kind of consolidation phase, while the 1960s brought the behavioristic movement. He looked to the 1970s as a time of hard decisions, budget cuts, staff cuts, increased interest in vocational counseling, and emphasis on accountability.

GRADUATE TRAINING

Another evidence of professionalization is counseling center involvement in graduate training. Professional counselors in the centers early responded to departments of psychology and of counselor education in need of part-time staff and of training facilities. Although most counseling centers stressed services to students, many of them offered practicum or internship opportunities to graduate students as well. Offering training programs provided an additional source of staffing, but also necessitated the hiring of professional staff qualified to supervise the work of the graduate trainees. As in the Michigan State model, the goal was to use the interaction between the services and the training programs to enhance the quality of services provided. A 1970 survey of 203 university and college counseling centers (Kirk & Chin, 1971) revealed that 51 percent reported internship programs.

COUNSELING CENTER DIRECTORS' CONFERENCES

In 1951 about fifty counseling center directors (Warnath, 1971), primarily from midwestern schools, met to discuss mutual problems and concerns in the first of what has become an annual series of conferences. Although avoiding formal organizational structure, this group has expanded to include participants from universities and colleges throughout the United States and Canada. Participation has been limited to directors from four-year schools with at least two professional counselors on the center staff. Serving as a forum in which the practical concerns of counseling center operation are shared, annual conferences over the years have considered topics reflecting an awareness of student and institutional problems: new programs, relationship to other units of the university, staff recruitment, responses to ethnic and minority students, accountability, confidentiality, and ethical standards, to name but a few.

The directors have also established task forces, sometimes continuing work over a period of years, to consider some problems in greater depth. One such task force developed guidelines for university and college counseling services (Kirk et al., 1971).

Most directors affiliate with the APA and its Division of Counseling Psychology, but almost as many identify with the American Personnel and Guidance Association (APGA) and two of its divisions, the American College Personnel Association (ACPA) and the Association for Counselor Education and Supervision (ACES) (Warman, 1965). In recent years an increasing number have not been members of any of these organizations.

The directors who have been regular participants in the annual conferences have also tended to be leaders in the Division of Counseling Psychology of the

APA and in the ACPA. This has prompted a sharing of programs and ideas with professional counselors in the other organizations. One example is the program on counseling innovations presented each year at the ACPA convention, in which selected directors share innovative programs and developments from their institutions (Magoon, 1964).

Another evidence of the growing professionalization within the field of counseling with implications for counseling centers have been two special conferences.

In 1966 the APA's Division of Counseling Psychology conducted a conference on the professional preparation of counseling psychologists at the Greyston Conference Center of Teachers College, Columbia. The report of this conference (Thompson & Super, 1964) provided a summary of the status of counseling psychology at that time and outlined recommendations or guidelines for counseling psychology training programs.

The APA conference on patterns and levels of professional training, held at Vail in 1973, also considered issues relevant to counseling practice (Vail conference, 1973). The full impact of this report has yet to be assessed (Ivey & Leppaluoto, 1975), but it has implications for both counseling training and practice.

INTERASSOCIATIONAL COOPERATION

The joint committee of the American College Health Association and the American College Personnel Association and the recent founding of the International Association of Counseling Services both represent professional activities with an impact on counseling center operation.

In 1964 a joint committee of the American College Health Association and the American College Personnel Association was appointed to study the relationships between counseling services and psychiatric services in college health services. This committee, whose members included several college counselors and directors, published its recommendations in 1969 (Recommended practices and relations).

A step in the direction of standards has been the establishment of the International Association of Counseling Services (IACS) in 1973. It is an affiliate of APGA and was founded by and replaced the American Board on Counseling Services.

The Counseling Center Data Bank, supported by the center directors, the Counseling Commission of the ACPA, and the University of Maryland, makes annual surveys of counseling centers. The data have proved useful for a variety of administrative and research purposes.

THE NATIONAL DEFENSE EDUCATION ACTS

The 1958 National Defense Education Act provided for counseling or guidance institutes aimed at increasing the supply of school counselors as a response to increased enrollments and the challenge of Sputnik (Wrenn, 1962). These summer and year-long institutes, which were continued until the mid-1960s, provided "new insights for thousands of counselors now in service as well as the beginning of professional education for others" (p. 180).

Although not directed toward providing training for college counselors, the institutes served to interest many students in continuing their graduate education in the area of counseling. This led to an increase in counselor education programs and to a demand for doctorate-level faculty to staff them. To meet federal guidelines, counselor education programs developed on a model somewhat different from that proposed for counseling psychology.

As counseling centers expanded, however, the need for trained counselors exceeded the supply, and graduates of counselor education programs who preferred counseling to teaching were a ready source of personnel. The demand for graduates of the counselor education programs was great enough that they felt little need to seek APA accreditation, and many counselor-educators questioned the usefulness of affiliation with APA.

STUDIES OF COUNSELING CENTER PROGRAMS AND FUNCTIONS

A number of studies of the roles and functions of counseling centers have been reported. The Warman study of counseling role (1960, 1961) was readministered by Kohlan (1975) fifteen years later. Surveys of services offered by counseling centers have also been conducted by Anderson (1970); Graff, Raque, and Danish (1974); Lombardi (1974); and Crane, Anderson, and Kirchner (1975).

An example of counseling center self-study is the monograph describing both the programs of and the action research conducted by the Counseling Center at Georgia State University (Worthy & Bell, 1975). It provides a model of ways in which counseling centers can assess campus needs and develop programs to respond to those needs. Programs such as facilitation skills training, divorce adjustment counseling, responses to ethnic groups, and development of a learning resources center were reviewed.

In his book *New Myths and Old Realities,* Warnath (1971) presented an analysis of college counseling in the late 1960s based on his experience as a counselor and a director, his long-time acquaintance with directors at other institutions, and the descriptive and comparative data collected on visits to centers on fourteen campuses in 1967. He reviewed the variety of activities in addition to counseling in which counselors and centers are engaged, and he asked hard questions about the future of counseling on the campus.

EXPANSION OF THE COUNSELING CENTER ROLE IN THE INSTITUTION

For several reasons, counseling centers and personnel have been moving toward a number of functions besides counseling. During most of the years since 1950, college enrollments have been increasing. No matter how willing the administrative support of the center, demand for services has tended to exceed the availability of counseling hours. This situation has led to innovations in counseling practice to make more efficient use of the center resources—for example, orientation programs, learning resources centers, use of paraprofessionals, computer-assisted counseling, and personal adjustment courses.

Nygreen (1962), Bond (1972), Volsky (1972), and Sharp (1974) are administrators who have looked at the resources on the counseling center staff and asked for greater involvement in the consultative role within the university. The general tenor of their writings is that knowledge of students, professional skills, and psychological understandings should be directed toward improving the institution as well as changing the individual students. Many centers have been serving such functions all along. Certainly the Michigan State Center has been actively involved in many aspects of university life and operation. Further evidence of center influence in various institutions is apparent in the series of *Proceedings* from the annual counseling center directors' conferences.

However, a group from Colorado has developed the most complete model of expanded center function. In 1968, Morrill, Ivey, and Oetting reported on the attempt by the Colorado State University Counseling Center to create a new model for mental health intervention. Emphasis is on movement out into the community, creation of programs based on primary prevention, mobilization of community resources, and definition of the role of counselor and service as developmental rather than therapeutic. The model also placed the center as an internal feedback mechanism for the university and identified the counselor as a human development consultant. An ACPA monograph, *The College and University Counseling Center* (Oetting, Ivey, & Weigel, 1970), and Morrill and Hurst (1971) also discuss this model.

The reports of the four task forces for the Western Interstate Commission for Higher Educations program on improving mental health services on western campuses are all aimed at expanding the role of the counseling center professionals into one of direct intervention in the campus environment (WICHE, 1972a, 1972b, 1972c, 1973). Packard (1975) served as facilitator for a directors' task force on the ecosystem model at a recent directors' conference.

Counseling Centers as Change Agents

Counseling centers and counselors perceive themselves to be agents or facilitators of change. The profession has its roots in the psychological theories of behavior, learning, and personality—all of which emphasize how change occurs. Research on counseling process studies how change occurs, and the goal of training programs is to enable counselors to help clients achieve change.

Counselors in centers are generally in a position to have an institution-wide perspective about students and the campus community and often have become aware of changes in the student culture before many other units on the campus. Even when they have seen their role as primarily that of remediation, they have been concerned about prevention, about ways in which their knowledge and awareness of student problems could be used to reduce or eliminate stress and to prevent problems before they occur.

This chapter has attempted to trace some of the developments that have changed the counseling role from that of friendly advisor to that of competent professional functioning in an administratively distinct unit on the campus. Many of the recent forces that have changed counselors and counseling centers have only been implied. For example, the developments in career development theory and the critical look at testing by ethnic minorities and feminists have changed the practice of vocational counseling. Developments in counseling theory also change the counselor and the counseling center.

It is, indeed, the extent to which centers and counselors can use their professional knowledge to respond to change themselves that will enable them to assist their individual and institutional clientele to plan for and to make the changes that lie ahead.

References

Albert, G. 1968. A survey of college counseling facilities. *Personnel and Guidance Journal* 46: 540–43.

Anderson, W. 1970. Services offered by college counseling centers. *Journal of Counseling Psychology.* 17: 380–82.

Bailey, H. W.; Gilbert, W. M.; and Berg, I. A. 1946. Counseling and the use of tests in the student personnel bureau at the University of Illinois. *Educational and Psychological Measurement* 6: 37–60.

Blum, M. L., and Balinsky, B. 1951. *Counseling and psychology.* Englewood Cliffs, N.J.: Prentice-Hall.

Bond, J. 1972. Address. In *Proceedings: Twenty-First Annual Conference of University and College Counseling Center Directors,* eds. J. C. Hurst and R. G. Taylor. Ft. Collins, Co.: Colorado State University, pp. 2–10.

Bordin, E. S., and Wrenn, C. G. 1954. The counseling function. *Review of Educational Research* 24: 134–46.

Bragdon, H. D., et al. 1939. Educational counseling of college students. *American Council on Education Studies*, vol. 3, ser. 6, no. 1.

Brayfield, A. H. 1961. Vocational counseling today. In M. S. Viteles, A. H. Brayfield, and L. E. Tyler, *Vocational counseling: a reappraisal in honor of Donald G. Paterson,* Minnesota Studies in Student Personnel Work, no. 11. Minneapolis: University of Minnesota Press.

Brewer, J. M. 1942. *History of vocational guidance.* New York: Harper & Bros.

Brumbaugh, A. J. 1937. Preliminary report on the activities, training and experience of college personnel workers. *Report of Fourteenth Annual Meeting of the American College Personnel Association,* pp. 3–9.

Cowley, W. H. 1964. Reflections of a troublesome but hopeful Rip Van Winkle. *Journal of College Student Personnel* 6: 66–73.

———. 1949. Some history and a venture in prophecy. In E. G. Williamson, ed. *Trends in student personnel work.* Minneapolis: University of Minnesota Press.

Crane, J.; Anderson, W.; and Kirchner, K. 1975. Counseling center directors' attitudes toward paraprofessionals. *Journal of College Student Personnel* 16: 119-22.

Darley, J. G. 1949. An appraisal of the professional status of personnel work, part II. In E. G. Williamson, ed., *Trends in student personnel work*. Minneapolis: University of Minnesota Press.

Dreese, M. 1949. Present policies and future plans of college guidance centers operating under V.A. contracts: a survey of the American Council on Education. *Educational and Psychological Measurement* 9: 558-78.

Embree, R. B. 1950. Developments in counseling bureaus and clinics. *Educational and Psychological Measurement* 10: 465-75.

Ewing, T. N. 1973. Perspectives on counseling, 1938-1973. In *Proceedings: Twenty-Second Annual Conference of University and College Counseling Center Directors,* eds. P. E. Comer and J. F. Carruth. Morgantown, W. Va.: West Virginia University, pp. 3-13.

Gilbert, W. M. 1973. Perspectives in counseling and psychotherapy, 1940-1975. In *Proceedings: Twenty-Second Annual Conference of University and College Counseling Center Directors,* eds. P. E. Comer and J. F. Carruth. Morgantown, W. Va., pp. 17-27.

Graff, R. W.; Raque, D.: and Danish, S. 1974. Vocational-educational counseling practices: a survey of university counseling centers. *Journal of Counseling Psychology* 21: 579-80.

Grummon, D. L. 1970. An overview: prospect in retrospect. In *Procedings: 25th Anniversary Share-In,* Counseling Center, Michigan State University, pp. 83-90.

Hedahl, B. M. 1958. A study of the role expectations of counselors in three university student counseling centers. Doctoral dissertation, University of Minnesota. *Dissertation Abstracts International,* University Microfilms no. 58-07007.

Ivey, A. E., and Leppaluoto, J. R. 1975. Changes ahead! Implications of the Vail conference. *The Personnel and Guidance Journal* 53: 747-52.

Kirk, B. A. 1966. The challenges ahead in counseling and testing. In G. J. Klopf, ed., *College student personnel work in the years ahead.* Student Personnel Series, no. 7. Washington, D.C.: American Personnel and Guidance Association.

Kirk, B. A., and Chin, A. H. 1971. Internship in counseling psychology. *Journal of Counseling Psychology.* 18: 524-30.

Kirk, B. A., et al., 1971. Guidelines for university and college counseling services. *American Psychologist* 26: 585-89.

Kitson, H. D. 1946. Autobiographical sketch. *Occupations* 25: 27-29.

Kohlan, R. G. 1975. Problems appropriate for discussion in counseling centers: 15 years later. *Journal of Counseling Psychology* 22: 560-62.

Lloyd-Jones, E. McD., and Smith, M. R. 1938. *A student personnel program for higher education.* New York: McGraw-Hill.

Lombardi, J. S. 1974. The college counseling center and preventive mental health activities. *Journal of College Student Personnel.* 15, 6: 435-38.

Magoon, T. 1964. Innovations in counseling. *Journal of Counseling Psychology* 11: 342-47.

———. 1973. Outlook in higher education: changing functions. *Personnel and Guidance Journal.* 52: 175-79.

Morrill, W. H., and Hurst, J. C. 1971. A preventative and developmental role for the college counselor. *The Counseling Psychologist* 2: 90-95.

Morrill, W. H.; Ivey, A. E.; and Oetting, E. R. 1968. The college counseling center: a center for student development. In J. C. Heston and W. B. Frick, eds., *Counseling for the liberal arts campus*. Yellow Springs, Ohio: Antioch Press.

Nugent, F. K., and Pareis, E. N. 1968. Survey of present policies and practices in college counseling centers in the United States of America. *Journal of Counseling Psychology* 15: 94–97.

Nygreen, G. T. 1962. The college counseling center of the future. *Journal of College Student Personnel*. 4: 32–34, 46.

Oetting, E. R.; Ivey, A. E.; and Weigel, R. G. 1970. *The college and university counseling center*. Student Personnel Series, no. 11. Washington, D.C.: American Personnel and Guidance Association.

Packard, T. 1975. Ecosystem model: assessing and designing campus environments. In *Proceedings: Twenty-Fourth Annual Conference of University and College Counseling Center Directors*, ed. C. O. Grant. Orono, Me.: University of Maine, pp. 45–72.

Paterson, D. G. 1950. The genesis of modern guidance. In A. H. Brayfield, ed., *Readings in modern methods in counseling*. New York: Appleton-Century-Crofts.

————. 1976. Reminiscences concerning the development of student personnel work at the University of Minnesota. *Journal of College Student Personnel* 17: 380–85.

Paterson, D. G.; Schneidler, G. G.; and Williamson, E. G. 1938. *Student guidance techniques*. New York: McGraw-Hill.

Pierson, R. R. 1970. Foreword. In *Proceedings: 25th Anniversary Share-In*, Counseling Center, Michigan State University.

Recommended practices and relations for counseling and psychiatric services in the university and college community: report of the Joint ACHA-ACPA Committee. 1969. *Journal of College Student Personnel* 10: 210–14.

Rogers, C. R. 1951. *Client-centered therapy*. Boston: Houghton Mifflin.

————. 1942. *Counseling and psychotherapy: newer concepts in practice*. Boston: Houghton Mifflin.

Sharp, W. H. 1974. The counselor from a different desk. In *Proceedings: Twenty-Third Annual Conference of University and College Counseling Center Directors*, ed. J. P. Schnitzen, pp. 3–16. Houston: University of Houston.

Super, D. E. 1955. Transition from vocational guidance to counseling psychology. *Journal of Counseling Psychology* 2: 3–9.

Thompson, A. S., and Super, D. E., eds. 1964. *The professional preparation of counseling psychologists: report of the 1964 Greyston conference*. New York: Bureau of Publications, Teachers College, Columbia University.

Thrush, R. S. 1957. An agency in transition: the case study of a counseling center. *Journal of Counseling Psychology* 4: 183–89.

Vail conference endorses professional model of training. 1973. *APA Monitor* 4: 1, 4.

Viteles, M. S. 1961. Psychological perspectives in vocational guidance. In M. S. Viteles, A. H. Brayfield, and L. E. Tyler, *Vocational counseling: a reappraisal in honor of Donald G. Paterson*. Minnesota Studies in Student Personnel Work, no. 11. Minneapolis: University of Minnesota Press.

Volsky, T. 1972. Counseling in higher education? The views from here. In *Proceedings: Twenty-First Annual Conference of University and College Counseling Center Directors* eds. J. C. Hurst and R. G. Taylor. Ft. Collins, Co.: Colorado State University. pp. 15–18.

Warman, R. E. 1965. A call to action. *Counseling News and Views* 17: 13–15.

————. 1961. The counseling role of college and university counseling centers. *Journal of Counseling Psychology* 8: 231–37.

————. 1960. Differential perceptions of counseling role. *Journal of Counseling Psychology* 7: 269–74.

Warnath, C. F. 1971. *New myths and old realities: college counseling in transition.* San Francisco: Jossey-Bass.

WICHE. 1972a. *Consultation: a process for continuous institutional renewal.* "Improving Mental Health Services on Western Campuses" project, report of the Mental Health Consultation on the Campus Task Force.

————. 1972b. *New designs: prevent educational casualties, promote educational growth.* "Improving Mental Health Services on Western Campuses" project, report of the Preventive Intervention Task Force.

————. 1972c. *Quality of educational life: priorities for today.* "Improving Mental Health Services on Western Campuses" project, report of the Mental Health Services and the Changing University Community Task Force.

————. 1973. *The ecosystem model: designing campus environments.* "Improving Mental Health Services on Western Campuses" project, report of the Epidemiology, Campus Ecology, and Program Evaluation Task Force.

Williamson, E. G. 1961. Introduction. In M. S. Viteles, A. H. Brayfield, and L. E. Tyler, *Vocational counseling: a reappraisal in honor of Donald G. Paterson.* Minnesota Studies in Student Personnel Work, no. 11. Minneapolis: University of Minnesota Press.

Williamson, E. G., and Sarbin, T. R. 1950. The nature and scope of student personnel work. In W. S. Monroe, ed., *Encyclopedia of educational research,* rev. ed. New York: Macmillan.

————. 1940. *Student personnel work in the university.* Minneapolis: Burgess.

Worthy, M., and Bell, G. L., eds. 1975. *Counseling center functions in an urban university: a research monograph.* Atlanta: Counseling Center, Georgia State University.

Wrenn, C. G. 1949. An appraisal of the professional status of personnel work, part I. In E. G. Williamson, ed., *Trends in student personnel work.* Minneapolis: University of Minnesota Press.

————. 1962. *The counselor in a changing world.* Washington, D.C.: American Personnel and Guidance Association.

————. 1941. General counseling procedures. In W. S. Monroe, ed., *Encyclopedia of educational research.* New York: Macmillan.

————. 1957. Status and roles of the school counselor. *Personnel and Guidance Journal.* 36: 175–83.

————. 1951a. *Student personnel work in college.* New York: Ronald Press.

————. 1951b. Training of vocational guidance workers. *Occupations* 29: 414–19.

3

PROFESSIONAL AND ETHICAL CONSIDERATIONS IN THE OPERATION OF COUNSELING CENTERS

Harriett A. Rose

UNIVERSITY OF KENTUCKY

In so-called normal times, the directors of counseling services are probably the people most concerned about the ethical relationships between counselor and client or agency and clientele. Now that we Americans are living not in merely abnormal times, but in the most litigious times of our national history, such concern is dictated for the protection of both the client and the practitioner and agency; and our concern is shared by the administrators within our institutions.

Until recently most ethical expectations about operating a counseling service were unspoken. In fact, most knowledge about the operation and management of such a service has been learned by trial and error, or as younger practitioners sat at the feet of more experienced ones and profited from their direction. Lately, some additions to the literature have made the acquisition of administrative know-how easier. I refer specifically to Gallagher and Demos (1970), the monograph by Oetting, Ivey and Weigel (1970), the two books contributed by Charles Warnath (1971, 1973) and now this handbook. The indexes of the former four volumes, however, list a total of one specific reference to ethics.

Even the counseling journals provide little in the way of practical advice about the ethics of operating a counseling service. Perhaps the only way to deal with this issue has been by trial and error; perhaps the problems that pose the most perplexing dilemmas are those which arise so rarely that there would be no expectation of them and no precedent established for their solution.

One informal source of real help to directors new to the position has been the Annual Conference of University and College Counseling Center Directors. At every meeting for several years there was at least one program on administrative problems and a significant one entitled "Legal and Moral Responsibilities of Counseling Centers" was presented at Tantara, Missouri, in 1971. On that program Dr. Robert Callis and Dr. Charles Krauskopf, psychologists, and Ms. Jo Krauskopf, attorney, dealt with privileged communication, with personal confidentiality and agency confidentiality as separate but related issues, and with truth in advertising. Dr. Krauskopf warned that "California is suit-happy, and the California Medical Association reports that 25 percent of its members have been sued at least once." The account was an early notification and reminder that we could expect the same problems to arise in the rest of the country within five years, and so they have. The directors present who took notice were able to examine their policies, the law of their states, and the malpractice arrangements available to them before the fever for litigation spread eastward.

The more formal professional organizations, the American Psychological Association (APA) and the American Personnel and Guidance Association (APGA), have supplied us with various codes of ethics; all of us were introduced to these codes during graduate school, but they deal with practice as individual psychologists and counselors. The newest code is the APA's "Standards for Providers of Psychological Services" (1974). To my mind, this is a most useful guide for the administrator, provided the standards are viewed as minimal standards and used as they were intended. Similar standards that are directly pertinent to counseling services in higher education are those developed by the University and College Counseling Director's Task Force (Kirk et al., 1971), subsequently adopted by the International Association of Counseling Services as criteria for evaluation and accreditation. But all centers do not seek evaluation and accreditation, and only about half of those in attendance at a recent Annual Conference of College and University Counseling Center Directors were members of the APA, the ACPA, or the APGA. For such agencies and directors, my recommendations are immediate professional affiliation and adherence to the codes produced by professional colleagues, or at least the purchase, study, and conscientious implementation of the published standards and codes of ethics.

Why should this advice about ethical codes and administration be warranted in a book like this? All too often, the Peter Principle—that everyone rises to the level of his or her incompetence—is seen in the appointment of the director of a counseling center. Administration is an art all its own; seldom are we trained to be good administrators. Directors are often gentle souls who chose to study psychology in order to be able to relieve pain. They accepted the dictum of their training—to be nonjudgmental and nondirective—but now they are expected to make judgments, to lead, and, in short, to direct. Observation tells us that too frequently superior psychotherapists may be the bumbling administrators, that they loathe the role and play it protesting all the way. Vocational theory based on personality (Holland, 1973) dictates the impracticality of such duty assignment; follow-up empirical research (Kelly & Goldberg, 1959) validates the theory, finding that among those celebrated trainees of the Kelly & Fiske (1951) study the therapists were later more satisfied with their career choice than those who became administrators. But we continue to accept the appointments—we, too, have status and money needs, and frequently we burn out as counselors, as Warnath (1976) reminds us. And, in truth, who should direct a psychological service? Only a qualified psychologist, enjoins principle 2.3 of the "Standards for Providers of Psychological Services."

Psychologists alone among student personnel workers have an academic discipline as the theoretical basis for their applied skills. That discipline conveys a framework that helps us establish priorities. The typical administrator in higher education is a person with increasingly divided loyalties and responsibilities, "on the margin of many groups, many ideas, many endeavors," as Clark Kerr (1963) describes his "marginal man." Becoming administrator of a psychological service combines concepts. Can we still identify with psychology or must we then be marginal men and women? We must set and maintain our priorities, often in a setting where the discipline on which we depend is not understood by our sources of financial support, who are busy mediating between conflicting pressures for space, staff, and money. Our ethical responsibility as psychologists is to define the kind of service we provide and the manner of delivery of that service—in other words, to be an "independent, autonomous profession." (APA, 1972). This practice will in many instances put us in conflict with those administrators who operate without a prescribed set of standards. Even so, we must proceed cautiously. Can we afford to be marginal men? If we are not, then are we at the mercy of marginal men? What protects us from them—perhaps nothing—and is the source of whatever strength we possess? First, our academic discipline; second, professional identification and affiliation; third, thoughtful, conscientious adherence to published standards and codes; fourth, voluntary evaluations and accreditation efforts.

At the 1973 Conference of University and College Counseling Center Directors, James Carruth reflected, "Over the years, I've subjectively felt I was being exhorted to be brave enough to do intensive psychotherapy; to stop doing psychotherapy unless it was on the curbstone; to do nothing but group counseling; to give up group counseling and do T-groups instead; to stop hiding in my office and go seek the masses who need me whether they realize it or not; to stop licking the hand that feeds me and overthrow the "system"; to stop being a practitioner and begin training technicians and concentrate on research; to become a minority group advocate, a crisis intervener, a power behind the throne; a student life determiner; to solve the national manpower problem; and recently, to become an accountant." That quotation conveys the frustration I have felt at attempts, usually outside the center, to define the role of the center.

The decision that a university will have a counseling center is not ours to make. But what role a counseling center will play *is* our responsibility to decide, and that decision can be based most securely on the standards and guidelines available to us through our professional identification. A profession defines what it is, establishes rules for its members, polices itself, and trains its neophytes. Are we a profession? Can we—directors of centers—claim and maintain this categorization?

Recently, I heard a former center director, now a vice-president of student affairs, say that a mark of a unified division of student affairs is the self-professed identification of the counselors in it as "student personnel workers." For him, the division of student affairs was primary. To me, that designation might indicate health for student affairs, but not well-being for the counseling center or the psychologists who make up its staff. In fact, I might like to make the same statement about the staff of the counseling center. Whether their assignment is in counseling, testing, or learning skills, I would hope their identification would be with the center, and not with one of its component parts. During counselor training, it was made clear to me that my client's welfare was my primary concern—not the client's parents, the university, or the people on whom the client impinged. After I accepted the responsibility for directing the counseling center, it gradually became apparent to me that the center is my client—not the university, not the individual staff member, not even the individual client, if that means the sacrifice of the center. I am primarily concerned with the preservation, protection, and welfare of the center. Therefore, my ethical choices should be those which keep the center performing at its best level and earning credibility not only with its clients, but also with the faculty and administration of the university.

This broader perspective of the good of the center as primary has grown so imperceptibly that I had not even contemplated its enunciation until the sort of reflection that precedes the writing of such an article as this. The reactions of the graduate student counselors on the staff to some of my administrative and professional decisions have seemed inexplicable to me at times. They are steeped, I now realize, in the ethic of "the client's welfare is always primary"—still in the always-or-never stage of professional development that precedes the necessity for making fine discriminations—while I have evolved into a different frame of reference. In the vernacular of today, we are "coming from" different places.

My present perspective takes into account more than individual clients, while not forgetting them and their needs. These issues of difference between the staff and me include such items as how long treatment should last, what experimental methods should be used, whether or not to hop on new bandwagons, and whether or not to permit the consumers to define our service. We all know that effective therapy may take a long time, but our staff is limited. How much is justifiable? Which comes first, the counselor work load or the waiting list? The client's right to privacy or the center's need to evaluate its service and the quality of its offerings? Absolute, total confidentiality or other agencies' need and right to information? My broader perspective takes me, I think, to a more professional level: computers and clerks can follow directives; minds must decide when and how much to bend directives, and the right and the obligation to do this accompany the responsibility of professional administration.

The center's policy on confidentiality, for instance, is clearly stated: no information about any individual client is to be communicated to anyone outside the center at any time by any staff member, without express written consent of the client and, beyond that, express permission of the associate director or me. And yet, in my judgment, there are occasions when other members of the university community are properly concerned and involved in the welfare of that client. There are professional colleagues outside the center whom I would not trust with information; there are nonprofessionals I would trust to the end of time. Judgment is involved; continuity and longevity of relationship play a role; an appropriate decision is suggested, but certainly not dictated, by the ethical code. It is the administrator—the director—who must make the decision of when to abrogate the policy. Beyond the administrator's responsibility for making fine distinctions, there is also the responsibility for teaching that concept to the trainees, some of whom will inevitably wind up as directors of counseling centers. In discussions at the annual conference of directors, one frequently hears the Young Turks expounding, "Total confidentiality," while the long-time directors who fought for and won that right years ago in their institutions add, ". . . but sometimes . . ."

Directors must be aware that the graduate student trainees learn not only from what is said, but also from what is done. What we reward is what the students do. In other words, if directors value and reward only psychotherapy, that is the role the students will aspire to; if directors value and reward outreach or groups or biofeedback, the student will learn those things. If directors value and require good records, the staff will keep them. The tone and orientation of any center are a function of the preferences of the director, no matter how subtly those pressures are exerted. Therefore, it is the obligation of directors to urge students to accept *broad* training, the job market being what it is, has been, and promises to be. Also, directors need to share administrative problems and their resolutions with the student trainees; they should be aware of the general expectations of the office. Directors then, provide a role model; their deviations from standard operating procedure should be explained as well as their reasons for whatever policies they have established. Especially when the deviations involve ethical principles, it is important that they be clearly communicated.

A frequent complaint from center directors is that new doctoral-level staff have been trained to be private practioners working for an agency. Somewhere those new staff members worked as trainees in a center; the director of that center should have trained them to comply with the policies of the agency in which they worked. Just as supervisees are given training in test interpretation and effective psychotherapy, they also need training in agency requirements and problems of

administration. Examples of such sharing with the staff might be the establishment of developmental studies units that appear to duplicate the services offered
by the center, the increasing encroachment of placement offices in the area of
vocational counseling, and the newly established services offering counseling to
specialized groups such as veterans, mature women, and minorities, in response
to the ever increasing demands of ever enlarging consumer groups.

Questions requiring professional and ethical decisions by the director frequently reflect pressures that come from outside the counseling center. Such
pressures include such varied areas as hiring practices, use of paraprofessionals,
requests for cooperation with other campus agencies whose version of vocational
and personal counseling is less professionally based and whose staff consists of
people who would not qualify to be staff members in our centers, and suggestions
that we modify our practice in ways that might *appear* to provide counseling, but
would in fact offer only the shadow, not the substance. Current pressure is for
"career counseling if students will invest no more than one hour of their time,"
but there have been other suggestions in other years.

One of the practical problems that can be dealt with by reliance on ethical
standards is the push by university administrators (who are themselves pushed
by budgets) for the use of paraprofessionals in the counseling center. The director
can rely on the codes to decline such suggestions, since the roles appropriate for
parapros are defined, as in the amount of supervision necessary to see that those
limitations are maintained. These may be penny-wise, pound-foolish maneuvers
involving the use of untrained people. In the long run, training costs, supervision
costs, and turnover render any savings meaningless, and endangering the center's
reputation for competence is costly indeed.

Another external pressure is provided by qualified-on-paper, but unqualified-
by-nature professors who wish to use the counseling skills they *should* have and
who volunteer their services for free to see clients of the center. Is it possible to
turn down free, technically qualified service when everyone needs more staff? Of
course, and tactfully as possible! Volunteers are frequently available, but they
are accountable to nobody in the real sense and, in my experience, harder to get
rid of than to get. A wise acquaintance once said, "Never hire anyone you cannot
fire." A few times I have wished I had listened more intently to that aphorism.

Remembering that choice of staff (and everyone can make mistakes) and
supervision of them are what determine the stature and reputation of the counseling center, we are well advised to shop carefully and supervise well. Pressures to
choose minorities or women are legitimate, while pressures to opt for less than
competence in order to "balance the staff" are not. High standards are not a
crime, and competent blacks and women do exist; fortunately, we are entering a
time when respect for competence also exists. It is no longer enough just to be a
minority group member or a female; it is also necessary to be competent and to
grow in the job. Many centers now have the staff members they accepted during
the years of yielding to indiscriminate pressure. If those staff members have

demonstrated their inability to grow when given every opportunity, the ethical duty of the director toward the center and its clients is to counsel the inept counselor into another, more appropriate line of endeavor.

An even more difficult situation than the staff member who has reached the disappointing level of her competence is that of the advanced graduate student who has worked devotedly in your center for three or four years and has always been a little paranoid—but, then, aren't we all? One day, a fellow professional calls to tell you what a frightened client has reported to him about this counselor. Investigation of the allegations reveals an alarming loss of control and a full-blown delusional system. The counselor submits to psychiatric examination, which verifies your findings. There is no question about the immediate need to suspend him as a counselor until he is better; no one needs a code to make this decision. The ethical problem is this: should you protect him, keeping knowledge of this situation from his academic department and from your vice-president, when the counselor refuses treatment? Who is the client here? Not the counselor, not the center, not the center's clients—is it the profession that is the client? Or is the public, for whom ethical codes are the only protection, the client? The situation is not common, fortunately.

Where does one find guidance for this kind of situation? Michael Scriven, in *Primary Philosophy* (1966), says that bad decisions and actions are the result of irrationality or of a failure to use the "known-to-be-best" alternatives arrived at through the process of reason. "In many instances, the most rational action does not result in the greatest happiness; it is the way, however, to do the best with what one has and to choose the alternative most likely to result in equal consideration of individuals." (Dalton, 1975).

The greater the number of elements within the university that are served by the center, the more important it is that we keep in mind the identity of the client. When an individual student seeks our services voluntarily, she is without question "the client." In the days when deans of students sought to refer their disciplinary cases, we declined those referrals, knowing we could not serve the student as client and the dean as client, too. We frequently do academic evaluations for readmissions; however, in these cases the referring academic dean is our client, and the student being evaluated is his problem, not ours. What the dean wants from us is our expert opinion as to the probability that the student will perform differently if he is given another chance. The student had no choice in coming to us; it is unlikely that his story to us will differ from his story to the dean. What we can offer the dean, our client, is a recommendation based on data from our test battery and our clinical experience. The last thing he needs is our bleeding heart; he has one of his own. It is always more pleasant to give everyone another chance regardless of the probability of success, but a succession of false positive recommendations does not build credibility for the counseling center, nor does it help the dean, our client, to make decisions that really benefit the student, his client.

Similarly, in the administration of our national testing program, the identity of the client is important. In the final analysis, the client is probably the national testing service that has entrusted us with ethical administration of its test so that the graduate or professional school using the test data for admission purposes can rely on its findings. The ethical operation of a testing center requires on occasion that we refuse certain members of the university community some conveniences that they ask, either in their ignorance of their deleterious effect on the security of test materials or because they are concerned only with their own priorities. In those instances, principle 13 of "Ethical Standards of Psychologists" (1972) is the basis for our position; here the client has to be the profession and the preservation of the utility of testing. If the violations concern students and consist of "ringers" attempting to sit for tests or of attempted appropriations of test booklets, the appropriate academic department chairpersons are informed. These students are not clients and are not therefore entitled to our protection by confidentiality.

Another obligation of the center director is to stay aware of the programs being offered at other institutions and the evaluations of such programs. Higher education, like psychology, is fraught with "fads, fashions, and folderol" (Dunnette, 1966); the news of innovative programs travels quickly, west to east, like the prevailing winds; reports of their success or failure take slow freight trains and frequently suffer derailments. By our familiarity with all aspects of new programs we may be able to keep from having to reinvent the wheel at every institution. Sometimes we and our instituions are able to profit from our knowledge of the unsuccessful ideas of others as well as their good ones.

In the same way, we are urged to stay abreast of current research and to make it possible for our staff members to attend workshops for their professional development. In-service training is helpful for staff members as well as trainees, and travel money is frequently more productively spent by bringing in consultants to interact with the whole staff than by sending one person to a meeting.

In the research done with center clients, the director must protect at all times the identity of the sources of data and must see that the subjects in control groups in research projects are not the victims of research design. Many times, would-be researchers seek to use the center to attract subjects to their own treatment—biofeedback, or assertiveness training, or systematic desensitization, or whatever. Some respondents are then put off, offered delayed treatment, or told that groups are full, in order to fulfill the requirements of a control group for the study. It is the responsibility of the director to protect both the would-be client and the center by ensuring that control groups get treatment, even if delayed. No-treatment groups are not in the best interests of the center—only of the researcher.

The job description of the counseling center director is growing more and more complex. Good therapist, good manager, consultant to other parts of the university, teacher, supervisor, researcher, public relations expert—can any one person play all those roles effectively? Many of us try, at least, keeping in mind the many entities served. Directors must continually be aware of who the client being served is, and they must accede to or withstand both internal and external pressures, depending on their effect on the preeminent client—the counseling center, for whose welfare directors are responsible. As they attempt to fill as many of the roles of the directorship as possible, it is unlikely that they will find better sources of assistance and support than the various ethical codes supplied by professional associations.

There were several different types of counseling centers when Oetting, Ivey, and Weigel (1970) analyzed them, and there are probably even more varieties now. Obviously, the point of view expressed in this paper is representative of a rather traditional model, with minor modifications. Similarly, the director described is a traditional one, with minor modifications. The center and the director described are, I think, the ones most likely to last for the long haul. While the population of today's university differs in many ways from that of the 1960s, counseling is still needed and valued by the present college student and will continue to be needed by the college population of the 1980s and beyond. Counseling centers based on ethical and professional standards earned the respect in which they are held; perhaps that respect is the reason so many other student personnel workers seek to imitate our service, only they profess to do it more quickly and more cheaply for larger numbers of clients. But then, as John Ruskin is supposed to have said, "There is hardly anything in the world that some man cannot make a little worse and sell a little cheaper, and the people who consider price only are this man's lawful prey". (Stevenson, 1967).

References

American Psychological Association. 1972. *Ethical standards of psychologists.* Washington D.C.: American Psychological Association.

———. 1975. *Standards for providers of psychological services.* Washington, D.C.: American Psychological Association.

Dalton, J. C. 1975. *A theory of moral accountability for administrators in higher education.* Unpublished doctoral dissertation, University of Kentucky.

Dunnette, M. D. 1966. Fads, fashions and folderol in psychology. *American Psychologist* 21: 343–52.

Gallagher, P. J., and Demos, G. D. 1970. *The counseling center in higher education.* Springfield, Ill.: Charles C. Thomas.

Holland, J. L. 1973. *Making vocational choices: a theory of careers.* Englewood Cliffs, N.J.: Prentice-Hall.

Kelly, E. R., and Fiske, D. W. 1951. *The prediction of performance in clinical psychology.* Ann Arbor: University of Michigan Press.

Kelly, E. R., and Goldberg, L. R. 1959. Correlates of later performance and specialization in psychology. *Psychol. Monographs* 73: no. 12.

Kerr, C. 1963. *The uses of the university.* Cambridge: Harvard University Press.

Kirk, B. A., et al., 1971. Guidelines for university and college counseling services. *American Psychologist* 26: 585–89.

Oetting, E. R.; Ivey, A. E.; and Weigel, R. G. 1970. *The college and university counseling center.* Student Personnel Series, no. 11. Washington, D.C.: American Personnel and Guidance Association.

Scriven, M. 1966. *Primary philosophy.* New York: McGraw-Hill.

Stevenson, B. 1967. *The home book of quotations.* New York: Dodd, Mead and Company, p. 1605.

Warnath, C. F. 1971. *New myths and old realities: college counseling in transition.* San Francisco: Jossey-Bass.

Warnath, C. F., ed. and Associates. *New directions for college counselors: a handbook for redesigning professional roles,* ed. San Francisco: Jossey-Bass, 1973.

———. 1976. The ultimate disappointment: the burned-out counselor. *Personnel and Guidance Journal* 55: 4, 172–75.

PART II Structure and Organization

4

PHYSICAL FACILITIES

Gary E. Green
MEMORIAL UNIVERSITY

The space requirements of the center will vary with considerations ranging from the number of the professional staff to the size and scope of programs, services, and activities. Those who plan, develop, and maintain centers must direct their attention to two separate requirements at the same time. Of course, sufficient physical space in terms of square footage is a necessity. But the effect of setting upon behavior and person perception has been reported in a number of studies (Maslow & Mintz, 1956; Mintz, 1956; Rosenthal, 1966; Canter & Wools, 1970; Canter, West, & Wools, 1974). Each of these investigations noted that a significant relationship existed between the aesthetic (or pleasing) quality of the room and subjective perception. Thus, this chapter will examine the aspects of creating an aesthetically pleasing environment in addition to providing adequate physical space for the comprehensive counseling center.

Aesthetic Considerations in Interior Design

The subject of aesthetics, or what constitutes "good taste," has for a long time been the source of arguments among countless philosophers and lay persons. Unfortunately the results of these deliberations have been disappointing, for no clear definition of what constitutes good taste has emerged. In its place has developed a virtual myriad of opinions or standards, which gain and lose popularity with the ages of man. Dorfles (1968) suggests that the reason for this is that over a period of time the requirements of our civilization and our society change and with them our values. In short, there can be no absolute "good taste" since the basis of such judgment is in a state of almost constant flux. This may account for the acceptability of the definition offered by Hume. He reasoned that beauty per se is not inherent in an object but is reflected in the emotional response of the observer. In other words, "good taste" is a mental quality that is capable of being interpreted many ways by many different people. Whiton (1963) agrees with this interpretation, suggesting that the art of interior design is invariably linked to a personal value judgment. On the surface, the words of Hume and Whiton seem to suggest that whatever appeals to any one individual is in good taste.

However, this is not the case. An individual's values are not inherent, they are developed within a society that may greatly influence an individual's value system. Hence, a personal value judgment is, in part, a reflection of the values of the society of which the individual is a member. The issue of aesthetics must transcend individual preferences for the broader issue of the society's values. Furthermore, the society's values must not be regarded as fixed but as continuously evolving.

In interior design, taste is not simply reflected in the choice of individual elements of decoration. Our contemporary society requires that elements must achieve an orderly arrangement that both serves the function of a room and makes it pleasing to the eye. Efficiency, comfort, and convenience should guide the placement of objects within any room. In order to place the objects to maximize these three requirements, the habits and needs of the individuals who utilize the room should be studied carefully. A private office requires special consideration because it should reflect the personality of the person who uses it. The room should appear natural and not strictly rigid; it should look as though it is used by a person who enjoys both being and working in it. Obviously, the individual who will use the room must be encouraged to make a "personal statement."

All of the space occupied by the center should be made appealing to the eye, but special attention should be given to the reception areas and to the private offices. In coordinating the total effect, five elements require a harmonious treatment.

Walls

Most rooms are rectangular in shape, with four walls that must be considered, for the purpose of design, both separately and in relation to one another. Each wall has its own unique characteristics requiring that it be treated separately. Though most rooms have walls of uniform height, there is likely to be some degree of variation in width and architectural features, such as windows, doors, built-in storage, heating controls, and light switches. These features, in addition to moveable elements such as pictures and furniture, must be considered in developing a wall composition. In turn, the four compositions must be unified to present an overall pleasing effect.

The term *composition* in relation to a wall implies an arrangement of related lines, areas, or masses that appears orderly and produces a unified effect. Unity is obtained through each part's contributing its share to the grouping as a whole. Elements of the composition may be related through position, size, shape, color, texture, material, or any combination of these. The essential design of both walls and their fixtures form both horizontal and vertical lines with which the room must harmonize or balance.

Horizontal balance requires that a wall be divided horizontally by either real or imaginary lines. Real lines may be supplied by architectural features—windows, doors, built-in units such as bookcases, and room decorations such as moldings. Imaginary lines are provided by the designer to break down the wall into pleasing proportions and may be marked by such items as mirrors or pictures. These lines form the boundaries or guidelines for the placement of elements upon or against a wall.

In addition to horizontal balance, a wall must have vertical balance, which refers to the placement of elements along the length of a wall. Elements should be spaced along a wall so that it gives the impression of being evenly balanced. Vertical balance may be achieved either optically or symmetrically. Symmetrical balance refers to the placing of identical or near identical elements so that one half of a wall is a mirror image of the other. For example, two similar chairs might be placed on either side of a table. Optical balance is attained by placing an element or elements along a wall to give the impression of equal mass. For example, a bookcase may be placed along a wall containing a door. The door and bookcase are not identical, but they do balance optically.

For the purpose of explanation, horizontal and vertical balance have been separated, but in reality this cannot be done.

Furniture Arrangement

As pointed out by Whiton (1963), furniture arrangement is essentially a consideration of floor composition, and unlike wall composition, it must be approached from the point of utility and convenience, rather than from the perspective of line, form, and mass. Although practicality must take precedence over appearance in the placing of furniture, appearance should not be totally ignored. Principal elements should be placed so that they serve their function best, and then balancing may be achieved by the placement of secondary furnishings. For example, in a counselor's office, the desk, filing cabinet, and interviewing chairs may be the most important furniture for allowing the counselor to work efficiently. Their placement is critical; notions of balance may be ignored in order to assure their correct positioning. Secondary furniture such as bookcases, lamps, and tables may then be used to create balance. This may mean that balance is not completely achieved, but there is little value to a balanced room if it does not lend itself to efficient and functional utilization.

The prime consideration in furniture arranging must always be the purpose of the room and the work patterns of the people who make use of it. For example, a much-used filing cabinet should not be placed across the room from the user's desk. Also, the furniture must be in proportion to the room in which it is placed. Except in situations where it is desirable to tone down the straight lines of a room or to create a special area within a room, furniture should be placed parallel to the walls. In general, the center area of the room should be kept free for traffic flow. This is not a hard-and-fast rule, since efficiency may require desks and other elements to be placed away from walls. In this case, care should be given to traffic patterns and aisles created to allow as free a flow as possible. Finally, where possible, furniture should be placed to take advantage of any natural light.

Floor Coverings

Modern buildings have floors of wood or masonry that may be covered with a variety of materials, but high-quality carpeting is by far the most satisfactory for use in the center. Tile, vinyl, and linoleum can be installed at less initial cost, and these floor coverings are available in a wide variety of colors and patterns. As they are quite easy to maintain, they should be considered especially for high traffic areas. Hard floors are extremely difficult to maintain, especially in high traffic areas, and therefore cannot be recommended. Still, the major drawback to all hard floor coverings is that they do not deaden sound and, in some cases, actually serve to amplify it. Thus, wall-to-wall carpeting throughout the center is the most desirable floor covering.

Carpeting is available in a variety of colors and patterns that makes it suitable for every kind of office. Good-quality industrial carpeting will hold up well in heavy traffic areas and will require only routine maintenance, while area rugs may be used quite effectively for special effect. The texture of carpeting can do much to soften the appearance of a room.

Finally, it is important to avoid floor coverings with intricate patterns or curving lines. These lines are "busy" and may tend to disturb, rather than relax, the room's occupants. Plain coverings or those incorporating straight lines in a simple pattern are more useful and pleasing to the eye in an office setting.

Color

Color plays a major part in both the aesthetic and psychological features of a room. While the intricacies of color coordination are beyond the scope of this chapter, it may be of interest to examine some of the properties of color.

According to Whiton (1963), colors seem to have certain accepted qualities, although the source of these qualities is uncertain. Orange and its adjacent colors are considered "warm," and their use in decoration is to add warmth and gaiety to a room. Blue and its adjacent colors, considered to be "cool," may be used to tone down rooms that receive large amounts of direct sunlight. In general, colors with light tonal values and the variations of greens, blues, and violets are referred to as "distant" or "receding." These may be used in small rooms to give the effect of space. Colors with dark tonal values, particularly the variations of red and orange, are considered to be "near" or "approaching" colors and may be used most effectively to give warmth to an exceedingly large room. Green, the middle color of the spectrum, is considered to be the most relaxing color. Both warm and cool colors are used as accents without upsetting the desired effect of the room; that is, in a blue color scheme, red may be used as an accent to offset the coolness created by the blue.

Whiton (1963) reports that the color of a room has a psychological effect upon its occupants. Light, cool colors such as lavender, light blues and foilage greens suggest quiet, freshness, and repose. Light, warm colors, such as tan and ivory, suggest cheer. Bright, warm colors, especially red and orange, are suggestive of excitement and exhilaration, while darker colors give a dignified, somber impression. Thus, a room may become cheerful or gloomy, friendly or cold, depending upon its color treatment.

Lighting

Lighting is of great importance to a room. Depending upon the type and method of illumination, the whole appearance of a room can be changed.

Light fixtures, both stationary and movable, come in a variety of shapes and sizes. These fixtures illuminate a room in one of three methods; direct, indirect, or semidirect. Direct lighting, as the name implies, occurs as a result of a light source directly illuminating an area. Some ceiling lights, spotlights, and table lamps belong in the category, having a direct line between the source of light and the area being illuminated. Indirect lighting is the illumination of an area by the reflection of light, usually using the ceiling as a reflector. Some wall fixtures are of this type. Usually the source of light is hidden from view behind a solid covering, and, unlike direct lighting, indirect lighting creates almost no shadows. Semidirect lighting is a combination of the other two types. Part of the light is allowed to shine directly on the area, while the remainder is either reflected or diffused. Desk lamps with a diffusing lens of either glass or plastic belong to this category. The efficient lighting of any room may require any one or combination of these methods. Offices especially require good diffused ceiling lighting for overall illumination and the reduction of shadows. Lower-level fixtures such as table and floor lamps may be used to accentuate certain areas or to give direct lighting to work areas.

The type of lighting source used will also affect the colors in a room. Incandescent bulbs, unless specially tinted, give warm, yellow rays that will alter colors toward the red end of the spectrum. Fluorescent tubes, except those known as warm tubes, give cool, blue rays that will alter colors toward the violet end of the spectrum. Color schemes that appear quite pleasing with one type of light may not look quite as pleasing when illuminated with a different type.

Another factor influencing the overall illumination of a room is the color and texture of the walls and ceiling. Light colors, such as white or ivory, will reflect almost 80 percent of the light, while dark colors, like dark blue or green, may reflect only 5 to 10 percent of the light. A room with dark walls and furnishings may require substantially more light in terms of wattage to produce a desired level of illumination than a room of comparable size and lighter color. Likewise, walls and ceilings with a gloss or semigloss finish will reflect more light than those with a dull or mat finish.

Work Space

As previously noted, the actual size and type of physical facilities required by a counseling center will be largely determined by its programs and activities. A center that has a small staff offering mainly individual counseling will require little more than a reception area and the necessary number of private offices. On the other hand, a center that has a large staff offering a wide range of services to individuals and groups will require more extensive facilities. The variance will be in size or quantity, however, because the quality of the space, as well as its accessibility, should be the primary consideration.

RECEPTION AREA

Regardless of size, a counseling center will require an attractive and spacious reception area. It is important to recognize that this is one of the most important rooms in the center. Every client utilizing the center will spend some time in it, so in a sense it is the clients' room. It is here that new clients start to form their impressions of the center, impressions that may ultimately affect the tone of the overall counseling situation. As such, the room should project feelings of warmth and acceptance to the clients, and it should be a pleasant room in which clients are able to feel comfortable and relaxed.

Several factors influence the size and/or design of the room. First is the size or client load of the center. The room must provide sufficient seating to accommodate the volume of clients, for a room that is too small and lacks adequate seating will give the impression of clutter and confusion. Conversely, a very large area requires special attention to ensure that it is neither cold nor foreboding. A good rule of thumb is to have three seating spaces for each professional staff member. Such a ratio allows adequate seating for peak periods to accommodate people waiting for groups to begin and should suffice at other times when each counselor may have someone waiting.

If a receptionist is to be placed in the reception area, certain points need to be considered in the design of the room. Of prime consideration is the role of the receptionist. A receptionist may perform several functions, such as greeting the clients, making appointments, and answering the phone, in addition to a variety of clerical and secretarial work. The contact with students requires that the receptionist's desk be easily accessible, but a clerical work load means that semiprivacy and adequate work space must be provided. These conflicting objectives can be attained through the discrete use of distance, partition, or, best of all, careful arrangement of furniture. The use of distance would require a large room in which the receptionist's work space could be physically distant from the actual waiting area. The use of partitions, such as counters or room dividers, may achieve the desired result of providing a private work space, but the physical barriers may not be conducive to an open, accepting atmosphere. A selective furniture arrangement would allow the receptionist to be placed closer to the clients, while maintaining the physical distance that promotes efficiency. Entrances and exits to the reception area must be placed in such a way as to allow a free flow of traffic. Further, the arrangement of furniture in the area must not be allowed to impede this flow, nor should the furniture be grouped in such a way as to leave any part of the area either empty or cluttered.

Standard office furniture will be provided for the receptionist, but furnishings for the clients should include comfortable chairs, sofas, table lamps, and end tables. The chairs and sofas should be arranged in a manner affording clients varying amounts of privacy. For example, a corner arrangement of chairs around a coffee table provides a small group of clients an informal place to talk among themselves without feeling hemmed in by other people. Privacy may be added by placing coffee tables or large potted plants between chairs. The addition of free-standing ash trays and floor lamps may also create privacy areas.

The atmosphere may be enhanced through a judicious use of wall coverings. Wallpapers with subtle designs and warm colors will do much to create a relaxed atmosphere, Paintings and prints can add an attractive dimension, but the most important consideration is that the total effect of the area must be warm and inviting to the client. Attempts should be made to keep conversational and other noises muffled, but soundproofing is not the absolute requirement that it is in all other rooms of the center.

ADMINISTRATOR'S OFFICE

The administrator's office is essentially the hub of the physical and financial operation of the counseling center. Its prime function is to provide the administrator with a pleasant and efficient work space to carry out his or her duties. If there is only one room, it would probably be best to create two distinct work areas. Part of the room would be a conventional office work area in which the director can perform all those tasks requiring desk space, while the second area would be a consultation work area allowing comfortable visits with either counselors or clients. Depending upon the director's preference, the arrangement of furniture could create two distinct areas or could permit one area to flow into the other. If separation of space is desirable, it could be effected through use of area rugs that define the boundaries of each area.

The room should have overhead lighting with one or two low-level units to allow additional illumination for the work area and to create atmosphere in the conversation area. Where possible, heavy-use areas should be situated to avail of the natural light. Wall coverings should be of a light color to allow for a good reflection of light.

SECRETARY'S OFFICE

In addition to a secretary or receptionist in the waiting area, larger counseling centers may have one or two additional secretaries or stenographers in a separate office. Intended primarily to provide a pleasant and efficient work space, this room should be large enough to accommodate the secretary's desk and chair, an occasional chair or two for other staff, filing cabinets, and other storage units.

Lighting is an important element in this room. Good overhead lighting is essential and, where possible, the desk should be positioned to take advantage of the natural light. Wall coverings should be of a light color to reflect as much light as possible, and bright colors should be avoided, as they tend to create a glare that may strain the eyes.

STAFF OFFICES

Like the director's office, each private office should provide two different spaces, one for desk work and one for consultation with clients. Whether or not these areas are kept separate or integrated is a matter of personal choice by the counselors. Integration of the two areas usually places the counselor's desk close to the center of the room. Filing cabinets, bookshelves, tables and other storage furnishings can then be located behind the desk so that they are easily accessible to the counselor. The majority of counselors do not sit behind their desks when seeing clients, so a small consultation area with two or more comfortable chairs is reserved in front of the desk. Again, separation of the two areas may be achieved through careful furniture arrangement.

The room should have good overhead lighting supplemented by low-level lighting to allow direct illumination of work areas and to help create atmosphere in the conversation area.

GROUP ROOMS

Most counseling centers are now offering a variety of group programs. Unless the center has sufficient facilities to allow a room to be permanently set up for a particular group, a group room will have to be flexible enough to serve the needs of several groups. Though people seem to prefer rooms that are rectangular in shape as opposed to square, the group room is an exception to this. A square room forces the participants to be positioned in a circle, whereas a rectangular room might encourage the group to move into an oval arrangement. A room measuring twenty feet square should be adequate for most groups up to fifteen in number.

Furnishings should consist of a number of comfortable armchairs arranged in a circle and several small coffee tables conveniently placed to accommodate ash trays and coffee cups. Other than a table for a coffee urn, little or no additional furnishings are needed. If space allows for a second or third group room, less conventional furnishings might be considered. One of our small group rooms at Memorial contains a dozen large bean bags—and nothing else.

Wall coverings play an important part in making the group room flexible. For some groups the presence of blackboards and flip charts are important factors, but for others they are a hindrance. These permanent wall fixtures need not be the problem they first seem, for they may be tastefully hidden by draperies. One or more walls of the room may be fitted with traveling curtains that can be opened or closed to expose or conceal fixed wall features.

Lighting is critical in the group room. If at all possible, the overhead lighting should be on a dimmer mechanism that allows the overall lighting to be varied from zero to full. This is especially useful in groups wishing to create a more relaxed atmosphere. Additional lighting from floor and table lamps can also be used effectively to create such an effect.

The floor should be covered with a good quality carpet to absorb sound and to allow comfort in relaxation.

RELAXATION ROOM

The relaxation room may come under the heading of a special group room; however, it will be treated separately here. A relaxation room calls for a bare minimum of decoration and, like the group room, should be square to allow people to be evenly spaced. Furnishings are relatively simple: a number of large, comfortable armchairs or recliners arranged in a circle, facing either in or out. The direction of the chairs is a matter of counselor preference: some feel that facing the chairs away from the circle is more conducive to relaxation; others do not. If the group is to focus on a variety of relaxation positions or if clients are required to sit or lay on the floor, the addition of large pillows may be helpful.

The walls should be painted a light, relaxing color and be free from any unnecessary decoration such as paintings or posters. Soundproofing is a must, including carpeting on the floor. Lighting control may be a critical factor. Heavy, lined curtains may be used to eliminate any unwanted natural light, while variable light switches would be an asset for both overhead and lower lighting.

The room may require special electronic wiring if the training exercises involve pretaped instructions or music. Speakers strategically placed around the room will ensure that everyone is able to hear the material clearly.

BIOFEEDBACK LAB

A biofeedback lab should consist of two rooms, one for the client and the other for the counselor and the equipment.

The client's room must provide a quiet space, free from any visual distractions. Ideally, the room should be windowless with artificial lighting being regulated by a dimmer switch. Heating and air conditioning must be controlled by a thermostat within the room. Sensors for auditory and visual feedback can be mounted on a wall or set on small tables. In most cases the client will sit in a recliner, but other arrangements can be made depending upon the counselor's preferences.

The equipment room should provide ample space for operating and housing all equipment as well as space for the storage of supplies. Independent regulation of lighting and room temperature are also required.

Since the electrical equipment will occasionally place heavy demand upon the power source, it is preferable to have the circuit breaker within the room. Much of the present equipment is highly sensitive to even small electrical impulses. Operating several pieces of equipment in close proximity may have adverse effects upon each machine. There are various ways of minimizing this interference for each machine, which are best explained by operators' manuals and electrical engineers.

In order that the counselor may observe the client, a one-way mirror should be set into the wall between the two rooms. An intercom system must also be installed.

CLASSROOMS

Some programs offered by counseling centers require the use of classrooms. The size and number of classrooms will vary with the demand for the courses and/or the class limits.

The instructor will require a desk or table, a chair, a blackboard, and perhaps a screen. Students will require some kind of seating-writing arrangement, either desk-chair combinations or separate tables and chairs. These furnishings may be arranged in any number of ways; the important point is to ensure that the arrangement allows both instructor and students free access to their work areas.

The room should be equipped with sufficient electrical outlets and storage units to allow for proper utilization of learning materials. Good ventilation, heating, and overhead lighting are essential.

READING LAB

The reading lab is a specialized classroom that must be utilized for teaching as well as individual practice. To separate these functions, the teaching area may be concentrated in the center of the room, with individual practice areas spaced along the walls. Separation is particularly important if the students use electronic devices in their practice, for such an arrangement makes more efficient use of electrical outlets. The practice area may be furnished either with individual tables and chairs or with carrels.

VIDEOTAPE ROOM

More and more counseling centers are making use of videotaping, or VTR, in training and therapy. The VTR equipment should be located in a windowless room where maximum control can be exerted over the environment.

The VTR room needs to provide three work spaces: the set, the camera area, and the recording area. The set, which refers to that part of the room used by the people being recorded, may vary from one taping session to another, so the furniture must lend itself to ease in arrangement. The camera area, that space in which the camera moves, should be kept clear of any objects such as furniture or electrical cables that may interfere with the movement of the camera. The recording area refers to the area in which the actual recording equipment and monitors are placed. This equipment should be isolated behind a screen or a room divider.

The room should be kept free from dust, and smoking should not be permitted near the recording equipment, for dust and smoke can damage both the recording heads and the magnetic tape. A large number of electrical outlets will minimize the use of extension cords. Soundproofing is required to ensure a good quality sound tape, and lighting is critical, especially if color equipment is being used.

By positioning a VTR room between a practicum room and a group room, activities in these rooms could be recorded through one-way mirror systems.

CAREER LIBRARY

The nature of career libraries vary greatly from center to center. Some centers contain libraries that are essentially information rooms in which literature on various careers is displayed, while other libraries are really vocational guidance centers.

A career library requires that storage units such as bookcases, filing cabinets, and display racks be placed along the walls. The center of the room will contain tables and chairs so that clients may examine the materials without having to take them from the room.

A vocational guidance center requires more extensive space. In addition to an information area, the vocational guidance center requires both teaching and counseling areas. The teaching area, which is used with groups involved in career planning programs, requires additional tables and chairs for clients and appropriate teaching aids such as blackboard and a screen. This setting would possibly be more informal than that of a classroom. The counseling area should be set apart from the other two areas—ideally, a separate room within the larger room. This would enable career counselors to talk privately with clients without being disturbed by other users of the facility.

PRACTICUM ROOMS

Practicum rooms are those offices which are used by counselors-in-training. Offices like those of professional staff members are quite satisfactory, except that each room should be adjacent to a viewing room used by the supervising psychologist. A one-way mirror set into the wall between the two rooms is an important requirement of many supervisors. Many supervisors prefer that counselors-in-training tape-record counseling sessions, but others favor a direct communication link-up. Whether the supervisor elects the one-way mirror or the direct communication link-up, it is recommended that centers constructing practicum facilities include the plans in their blueprints. Clients are usually no more reluctant to give permission that this specialized equipment be used than they are to agree to see a counselor-in-training.

TESTING ROOM

The administration of testing instruments to large groups may require more spacious facilities than those usually found in a college or university counseling center. However, most routine testing of small groups or individuals—

personality, interest, aptitude, and intelligence testing—can be done within the center. A testing room may be arranged with individual tables or carrels arranged along the walls, leaving the center of the room open. This area may then contain one or two additional tables capable of being used by both client and counselor for individual testing.

The walls should be a light, but not bright, color and should be as free of distractions as possible. Cabinets or shelves should be provided for the storage of tests and other related materials. The room should have good overhead lighting, especially in the writing areas.

PROFESSIONAL LIBRARY

The main purpose of a counseling center library is to provide storage for center-owned journals and books and to provide counselors with easy access to them. Books and journals may be conveniently stored in bookshelves and display racks placed around the walls. In addition, the room should contain several comfortable chairs and at least one writing table with a chair. Good overhead lighting should be supplemented with lower lighting for reading and writing areas.

STAFF FACILITIES

A pleasantly decorated and comfortably furnished room should be maintained to encourage informal interchanges between staff members, support personnel, and visitors to the center. The staff room at Memorial is furnished with a sofa and five comfortable chairs and has facilities for making coffee and tea. There is an informal agreement that neither office nor professional concerns are discussed in the staff room. Clients are not invited into this room, but coffee or tea may be served to them in any of the offices or group rooms.

Design

Each center must be laid out in accordance with the overall floor plan of the building in which it is located. Designing a center to be housed in a building yet to be constructed may be a relatively simple task, since there can be great flexibility in the placement of walls and corridors. Designing centers to be housed in existing buildings proves to be more difficult. To obtain a suitable arrangement of rooms, extensive renovations may have to be undertaken.

The elimination of noise should be of major concern in center design. Traffic is another primary consideration: while it is important that the center be in an easily accessible part of the campus, particular attention must be given to the entrance to the reception area and other facilities to ensure a free flow of traffic. The center should have its own corridor for access to rooms, and it is important that those facilities having the heaviest traffic flow be placed closest to the reception area.

In most instances, the size of rooms has not been suggested because it is impossible to give concrete figures without knowing the planned use for a room. However, the approximate floor space required by various rooms and offices can be determined by considering the furniture to be placed in each room.

Office furniture may vary in size depending upon style and manufacture, but in general, the following dimensions are reasonable estimates.

Item	Square Feet
Bookcase (3 feet long)	3
Desk	13
Secretary's desk	18
Filing cabinet (closed)	3.5
Chair	4
Table (small)	6
Recliner (open)	15
Desk-Chair (classroom)	6
Coffee table	6
Sofa (two-seat)	8

To obtain the square footage needed for offices, add up the total square footage of furniture and multiply by 3. For classrooms, add the furniture area, aisles (about 2 feet wide), and the instructor's lecturing area (approximately ⅓ of aisle plus furniture area). Multiply the area of furniture by 4 to obtain the size for group rooms. Space for a career library (information area only) may be approximated by multiplying the furniture area by 3. The VTR room is perhaps the most complex room to estimate. The size of the camera and set will vary, as will furnishings and sound equipment. However, the lens in the camera will dictate the area needed to obtain full and close shots of the set. When designing this room, a competent technician should be consulted.

Conclusion

This chapter has attempted to demonstrate that aesthetics and practical considerations should be of equal concern in the design of a counseling center. No attempt was made to discuss all types of rooms, for some facilities (research rooms, office for student assistants, and so on) involve special consideration. My main objective was to raise some points that could be helpful to anyone planning to build or renovate and might stimulate additional literature on the subject of center design.

Information and ideas for the chapter were a result of both a review of existing facilities at Memorial University and the plans for our new center. Six different areas have been suggested for the relocation of the center, and this has resulted in six different sets of plans. A confusing procedure, perhaps, but it has forced us to give considerable thought to center planning.

References

Canter, D.; West, S.; and Wools, R. 1974. Judgements of people and their rooms. *British Journal of Social and Clinical Psychology* 13: 113–18.

Canter, D., and Wools, R. 1970. A technique for the subjective appraisal of buildings. *Building Science* 5: 187–98.

Dorfles, G. 1968. *Kitsch: The World of Bad Taste*. New York: Bell Publishing Company.

Maslow, A. H., and Mintz, N. L. 1956. Effects of aesthetic surroundings: I. Initial effects of three esthetic conditions upon perceiving "energy" and "well-being" in faces. *Journal of Psychology* 41: 247–54.

Mintz, N. L. 1956. Effects of esthetic surroundings: II. Prolonged and repeated experience in a "beautiful" and "ugly" room. *Journal of Psychology* 41: 459–66.

Rosenthal, R. 1966. *Experimentor effects in behavioural research*. New York: Appleton-Century-Crofts.

Whiton, S. 1963. *Elements of interior design and decoration*. New York: J. B. Lippincott Company.

5

THE PLACE OF COUNSELING IN THE UNIVERSITY ORGANIZATION

Charles F. Preston

MEMORIAL UNIVERSITY

General Principles

Universities claim to be institutions dedicated to education and the advancement of knowledge. A good indication of the validity of this claim is found by asking whether any given university uses its counseling center as a piece of window dressing, a palliative, or an effective force for student development. A secondary question considers whether the university provides the counseling center with resources for service only, or whether it also attempts at an adequate level to permit innovative programs and research. The university's budgetary allocation to counseling is, therefore, the best measure of the sincerity of its concern for student development.

A favorite ploy in budget competition is to imply that one's own department is essential to the university by suggesting that some other department (for example, classics) should be abolished as nonessential or irrelevent. In fact, any discipline that attracts fine scholars producing fine scholarship and enhances knowledge and culture has a right to a secure place in the university. Of course, process and structure are not always the same. The *functions* of the counseling center are the quintessence of the university and have always been of tremendous importance. But as a *structure*, the counseling center should not have a monopoly on them, any more than the philosophy department on the use of logic, or the mathematics department on the use of mathematics.

The importance of a counseling center as an independent entity is not to be minimized, however. It is unlikely that the essential educational functions to which I refer below will be effectively carried out in any university without a department whose primary responsibility is their implementation and investigation. The center may serve as a conscience, reminding some faculty in other departments of their counseling responsibility, or as a source of support and consultation to other faculty in their contacts with students. It may enable yet other faculty to engage in more significant contact with students, secure in the knowledge that if they get in over their heads, they have a group of professionals to fall back on. And it can provide a safety valve for students who have mismanaged an encounter with an instructor or another authority figure. The existence of the counseling center is very important as a catalyst in producing the type of academic climate that will facilitate education as full personal, intellectual, and cultural development.

It would be unduly naive to suggest a detailed plan for all counseling centers everywhere and always. Universities have a wide range of individual differences in "personality." It may be possible, however, to describe an abstract model suggesting the principles in terms of which a counseling center could be expected to achieve real influence and effective working relationships. The embodiment of such a model in any given university would obviously be modified by the particular structure and the specific context.

Any adequate model or plan for a university counseling center will provide for the tripartite thrust of counselors as educators, integrators, and change agents in the lives of both the institution and the community.

COUNSELORS AS EDUCATORS

The belief that education means student development in the fullest sense has become universally accepted. However, not every department in the university can or should give the single-minded attention to student development in the fullest sense that student service development can and should. Probably Mark Twain's definition of the University—a log with a professor on one end and a student on the other—is an ideal more closely approximated by student counselors than by any other group of academics. To state this fact, however, is not to magnify this group's importance relative to their colleagues in the various academic disciplines; rather, it is to indicate that the effective presence of a counseling center in the university community can be the catalyst enabling faculty in all departments to be not only scholars and researchers, but also educators. In this way counseling centers can help to counter, at least in part, the divisive and competitive nature of the modern university.

Five implications involved in a conception of counselors as educators are relevant here.

First, as a university department, a university counseling center should be more than a community clinic or psychologist's office. As a center for innovative techniques and their evaluation, a university counseling center should be a model for its psychological counterparts in elementary schools and high schools, in hospitals and community clinics. Ideally, the counseling center should help to make the university a model community or perhaps, in our larger institutions, a model set of communities.

Second, the personnel of a university counseling center must be the right kind of people to be members of a university faculty. Thoroughly grounded in their own discipline and profession, they must be competent to deal with the specific problems that students bring, but in such a way that the solutions of these problems become part of each student's fuller personal development and education for life. Nor can we overlook the counselor's own character and value system.

Third, as competent members of a university faculty, counselors will be able to keep a balance between service functions, on the one hand, and feedback and research functions, on the other.

Fourth, the organizational structure of the university must provide for policy input from counselors. All programs in the university, academic or otherwise, should be open to examination and, if they prove to be nonfacilitative or destructive of student development, ready to change. Of course one is almost sure to encounter an obstacle here, perhaps in the form of a department chairman who claims that his discipline is so esoteric that only the initiated—that is, he and his own department members—can possibly understand the needs of his students or can do anything for them. I suppose he would include in this claim the decision as to whether they wish to continue to be his students or not. Just as the walls, towers, and moat of a feudal castle entrapped the serfs and preserved their lord in isolated splendor, so can specialization be used to defend an insecure academic ego against creative interaction with others. We know how counselors themselves are sometimes tempted to take refuge in professionalism or confidentiality.

Finally, as educators, counselors need to remember that education is not always giving students what they want, but enabling them to discover what they need.

COUNSELORS AS INTEGRATORS

One of the axioms that reasonable human beings accept as self-evident is that education requires something more than the accumulation of knowledge. That something more is often called wisdom. Serving as central agencies whose constituency is the whole university, counseling centers have an integrative role, at the heart of the educational process, similar in this respect to that of the president's office, and perhaps to the board or senate.

The modern university has a tendency to separate into an aggregation of self-sufficient and self-centered departments that often utilize faculty councils and other interdepartmental committees in order to safeguard or advance their own peculiar interests in competition with other departments. (Perhaps academics have something in common with politicians!) Fortunately, counseling centers and other student service departments could not play this game even if they wanted to. By their very existence as departments committed to the well-being of the whole university community, they have an effect on the thinking of faculty and students far beyond their direct efforts.

If this impact is to be maximized (and who can gainsay its importance), then student service departments need to be highly visible and continuously involved in strategic decision-making bodies; I refer to certain faculty and senate committees. It is important that decisions concerning the human consequences of building designs, academic programs, timetables, and so on receive the benefit of feedback from student counselors while they are still at a formative stage and can still be readily modified. The apparent waste of time involved in attending such meetings is, in fact, time well spent in assisting the university to achieve a unified orientation toward its educational responsibilities. If so, then human wisdom may be prevented from degenerating into a meaningless conglomerate of isolated bits of knowledge.

The story is told of a delightful young bride who always wore her hat to bed. Her young husband, not wanting to get their marriage off on the wrong foot, at first said nothing about this. Finally, however, he gathered his courage and, approaching the topic indirectly, asked his bride whether any of her family had ever been treated for mental illness. "No," she said. "You don't have an aunt or uncle, or a grandparent perhaps, who has been in the mental hospital?" "No," she said, "but why do you ask?" "Well," he said, "it seems a bit unusual that you always wear your hat to bed!" "Oh," she said, "That's easily enough explained. You see the night before we were married, my mother drew me aside and told me that there had been a number of things that she had always meant to explain to me, but now there would not be time. But she told me that one thing I should remember is that a nice girl always wears something to bed!"

O tempora, O mores! The ludicrous results of disjointed bits of knowledge! Can we save the university from such a reductio ad absurdum?

COUNSELORS AS CHANGE AGENTS

One of the ways to a positive conception of the counselors' role as educators and integrators is to think of them as personal and institutional change agents. This model includes remedial action, but goes beyond it to action directed at modifying and maintaining a campus climate facilitating student development in the fullest sense.

Remedial action is, of course, a major method of change for the individual. Consider the impact in a trimester system—when examinations are never more than three months away—of even a relatively short disruption in a student's life. Even in the more traditional two-term academic year with finals in the spring, a student may experience a severe setback as a result of a few days of sickness, or the selection of the wrong course or program, or a spiritual crisis, or dating trouble, or a love affair. To these we might add many others, such as disruption in a student's housing situation, homesickness, or loneliness. Every counselor who has been in a helping or advisory relationship with students would be able to add to this list. On the other hand, every experienced counselor could also describe instances in which what seemed to be very little help, easily given, has had tremendously beneficial effects, spreading far beyond the counselor's expectation and out to every area of a student's life, as the ripples from a stone dropped into a pool go out in ever widening circles.

In seeking to provide the opportunity of a personal interview with a well-equipped counselor for every student who needs it, professional counselors could perhaps do a great deal more to upgrade the skills and mobilize the resources of their colleagues in academic departments, residences, admissions, athletics, and so on than has already been done. Interesting attempts have been made to use fellow students as counselors for certain types of concerns. Perhaps this sharing of competence, while obviously an illustration of the counseling center's educational and integrative roles, is also the most readily available channel for influence as change agents on the campus.

The counseling center, in conjunction with other student service departments, can fulfill its role adequately only by going beyond the remedial function to act as a change agent, not only for the individual but also for the institution.

As Jean Piaget (1952) has pointed out, adaptation is a two-way process of accommodation and assimilation. The individual does not always have to change in order to cope with the environment. Sometimes the environment can be changed to suit the individual. And moreover, these two processes are continually interacting in an ascending spiral to enable ever more highly differentiated and complex patterns of behavior and environmental control.

In the old days the wife in a marriage was expected to conform to her husband's desires; today, some people claim, the husband shapes up, or the wife ships him out! Where were student affairs departments in times past? If students didn't like the university, they left it; if they didn't fit in, they dropped out. More often than not, if more recent research can be applied retroactively, they left for personal, social, or financial reasons rather than for academic ones, more narrowly conceived. In recent research at Haverford College, Heath has shown that even students with outstanding academic records may suffer in later life from the fact that liberal arts faculties do not "pay as much attention to developing their students' moral and social character as to developing their intellect" (Jacobson, 1977).

We are not surprised to read in a study of *Youth Guidance in the Soviet Bloc* (Drapela, 1970) that individuals are expected to adapt themselves to rigid and relatively unchanging institutions; but we are less likely to realize that in our free democratic countries there are also many instances in which it would be appropriate for the institution to change, instead of, or together with, the students and faculty who constitute it.

On many campuses the climate for social and spiritual development is not particularly propitious. Housing and finances often constitute serious problems or the individual may feel overwhelmed and bewildered in a megalithic temple to learning, where human sacrifice is still practiced.

In all of these areas and many others, a positive program to provide for the all-around personal, physical, and intellectual development of university students is obviously preferable to a mere troubleshooting function, valuable as that is to those who need it. The ever increasing number of students who seem to need professional help is one indicator of the deterioration in the cultural and personal climate of the modern multiversity.

It would not do, of course, to minimize the importance of all that counseling centers have been doing and attempting over the last generation or two. Counselors have learned to deal at some level of effectiveness with these and many other concerns, often with very limited resources. Those students who have taken the initiative and made maximum use of the opportunities provided have sometimes managed to graduate not only with a degree, but also with a meaningful philosophy of life, a committment to service, a set of cultural and recreational skills, a career, and a spouse.

But not all students do avail themselves of the often scanty resources available. And so over and beyond its service to the individual students whose names appear on its appointment schedule, a student service department must be concerned to make such an impact on university policy and programming that all students will find themselves in a situation that challenges and fosters their full development as thinking, feeling, caring, and active human beings. Based on first-hand knowledge of student needs, student services can function as change agents in the institutions of which they are a part by continuous feedback and input; this will be effective not as a once-for-all-time intervention, but rather as a continual interaction. Then, perhaps, some of our universities may become centers of excellence in producing the citizens of tomorrow, as well as in developing some of our more esoteric research specialties.

Specific Organizational Concerns

The position of the counseling center and its director in the organizational nexus of the university is decisive in determining its effectiveness as a resource for students and as a change agent for the institution. Its effectiveness will depend on how the administration sees it, how the faculty see it, and how the students see it. These perceptions of the center will determine its resources, its referrals (both their number and their nature), the use made of the counseling center, and its impact in the university community.

A structure is required that fosters relationships not only with academics, faculty councils, and boards, but also with personnel in placement, health, the registrar's office, student affairs, and residences as well as those providing athletic and cultural resources. Such a structure may be achieved in several ways:

first, by having the director of the center report directly to the chief executive officer of the university; second, by setting up a widely representative advisory board for the center; and third, by achieving effective working relationships with the major divisions of the university, whether by some decentralization of the center's personnel or by other stratagems.

Historically, a center often begins with the appointment of a director. Obviously, if the director is a junior assistant professor, the concern for student development is not very realistic. If the director reports to the director of medical services, for example, the center is probably intended to be little more than a band-aid operation for scraped knees. If—as a slight improvement—the director is a senior academic, but is given inadequate resources or excluded from the decision-making group in the university, this will amount to a mere gesture, an acknowledgment of the importance of student development, but no real commitment to it.

The director of the counseling service should report directly to the president or chief executive officer of the university. Many counseling centers were initiated in order to improve and extend the existing advisory services offered by deans of men and women or by health centers, chaplains, and individual professors in various departments such as psychology. It was anomalous to have the director of the new center reporting to one of the groups or individuals that the center was in fact set up to supplement or replace. In some instances, the work of the counseling service was frustrated from the beginning; in others, because of the dedication of people on both sides to student development, the organizational confusion was prevented from seriously impeding the job to be done.

There are a number of reasons why it is likely to be more effective, as well as most logical, to have the counseling director report directly to the president. This arrangement removes the center from the ordinary hierarchy of executive authority. (Parallel developments are found in the personnel departments in some industrial settings or in certain general staff and support services in military ones.) It makes it clear that the center serves the entire university community and not only certain favored subsections of it. Possibilities of rivalry and jealousy are thus removed, and counseling services are made equally accessible to all departments. This position helps to offset any idea that the center can serve as a disciplinary agent and makes it clear that its work is to facilitate the effectiveness of others. In addition, this arrangement can help to preserve the confidential nature of the center's work, while ensuring continuous feedback to policy-making bodies concerning the impact of every aspect of the university on individual students' personal and intellectual development.

A committee or board, representing the whole university, chaired by the director of the center, and advising the president on all matters connected with it, is a necessary adjunct to any center with the structure outlined above. Such a board will protect the center from being, or seeming to be, a body beyond the reach of the rest of the university or a foreign element unaware of and unresponsive to the very community it was set up to serve. This board will also help the center to maintain some long-term stability and independence, in the sense that the style and approach of successive presidents would not determine the center's activities too directly.

Corwin and Clarke (1969) have shown how important it is for a center to be able to counter distortion resulting from bureaucratic pressures. The existence of an advisory board and the direct line of responsibility to the university president should make this possible.

The professional staff of the center need to have regular working contacts with their colleagues in the rest of the academic community. This can be achieved in a number of ways, including joint appointments with academic departments; location of counselors in auxiliary offices in various schools, colleges, or faculties; designation of specific counselors to serve particular divisions of the university and appropriate membership in faculty councils or departmental committees for such designates. Each of these arrangements has its peculiar advantages and disadvantages. Because they are not mutually exclusive, however, various combinations may be desirable in particular settings.

The center at York University stresses the value of viable cross-appointments for its professional staff in these words: "This policy has prevented the development of cultural and academic isolation which sometimes occurs in departments of this kind. As part of this liaison, the center provides facilities and staff for the training of graduate students" (York, 1975). It would appear that joint appointments with suitable departments may provide the best method of keeping counselors in touch with their psychological colleagues. In addition, such appointments can be arranged in such a way as to make it clear that counselors are members of faculty. This can help to foster their acceptance by the academic community and can ensure the usual rights and opportunities for research and professional development that are likely to be important, at least to the kind of counselor needed in a university setting. The chief disadvantage of joint appointments is that they are administratively cumbersome, requiring consultation between both departments in decisions about increments, promotion, and tenure. There is also a danger that a joint appointee may be tempted to emphasize one or the other aspect of the joint responsibility, as pressures or individual preference may dictate. The counterbalancing asset, however, is the greater flexibility for joint appointees in career plan or work pattern. It is, of course, important to ensure that the counseling center is compensated for the loss of time inherent in joint appointments.

Charging counselors with responsibility for particular sections of the university can be of great help on a large campus in personalizing the service. It becomes possible for such a counselor to know most of the faculty members in that division of the university and to develop working relationships with them. An office in the appropriate building in which the counselor maintains regular office hours, perhaps every morning or every afternoon, can significantly increase the counselor's visibility and availability. As Blocher (1974) points out, a student who can *find* the way to the counseling center in many of our universities probably has such problem-solving ability as to obviate much *need* of counseling. There is the risk, however, in such a designation of one or two counselors that only a limited range of services will be utilized in accordance with the special skills or biases of the particular counselor or counselors assigned to that section of the campus. Further, students may see such counselors as too closely identified with the dean, the professors, or the other authority figures who constitute that division of the university. Provided that a strong central service is maintained as a home base, both of these risks can be handled in such a way as to become assets, so that such designated counselors are seen as representatives of the central service with a special interest and concern for a particular group of students and faculty. Their offices in various regions of the campus will then be seen as outposts of the central counseling center.

The issue of centralized or decentralized service cannot be dealt with simply. The larger the campus, the more important some decentralization is likely to be, in order to facilitate accessibility and the kinds of working relationships already referred to. On the other hand, no matter how large a campus may be, a strong central service is necessary, both to ensure an adequately wide range of service and to enhance effective interaction among counselors. Other functions that require such a central service are qualified supervision of the various counselors, such as a director and group of professional colleagues can provide, and coordination of various advertising programs intended to make the nature and location of various counseling services better known to the student body.

Elsewhere in this handbook, the issues of consultation and referral procedures are discussed in detail. Obviously, the director must establish a procedure for guaranteeing that there is reasonable consistency in the way such matters are handled. It is all too easy for letters to committees and officials from an inexperienced counselor to create all sorts of problems and so to undermine the center's credibility with academics and administrators. The solution to this and many other problems is a carefully designed operations manual.

So-called academic advising is an important counseling function that requires interviewing and interpersonal skills of a high order, as well as familiarity with the programs and course options available to students. Not every faculty member is well suited to this task. Those who are should be selected, trained, and given suitable recognition or reward. In this way, counseling centers can go beyond the mere rescuing of a few victims of biased and insensitive academic advisors and can engage in their proper role by offering training programs to advisors. They can also use their specialized techniques to select and appropriately evaluate those faculty who shall be entrusted with the psychologically complex interpersonal task of academic advising. In the third edition of her book, *The Work of the Counselor,* Leona Tyler (1969) provides a framework and guidelines for such selection, training, and evaluation. Academic advising has a natural and inevitable interface with a student's articulation of a value system or philosophy of life and with a student's consequent career planning and pursuit of the prerequisite skills and knowledge.

In concluding this discussion of the place of counseling services in the organization of a university, there remains the delicate question of evaluation. In the past, attempts to evaluate the work and impact of a counseling services department have too often taken place in the hostile context of threatened budget cuts. Actually, periodic evaluation can be of great benefit to a center. At least every year, and preferably every semester, informative reports on the center's work should be submitted for discussion by the relevant committees, councils, and boards. The counseling center advisory board should have at least monthly meetings, which should routinely include an assessment of the past month's work and progress. This seemingly onerous task is actually a valuable opportunity for feedback to the institution, for enhanced understanding of the center's functions and working relations with faculty, and finally for healthy self-evaluation. As Tyler (1969) has shown, the question of whether counseling does any good has only an affirmative answer. The important evaluatory questions now concern what counseling is good for and how to improve counselor effectiveness in both the selection of the best techniques and their application in particular cases. This is a significant administrative and organizational problem.

References

Blocher, D. H. 1974. *Developmental counseling*. 2d ed. New York: Ronald Press.

Corwin, R. G., and Clarke, A. C. 1969. Social change and social values: further reflections on the counseling movement. In D.A. Hansen, ed., *Explorations in sociology and counseling*. Boston: Houghton Mifflin.

Drapela, V. J. 1970. *Youth guidance in the Soviet bloc*. Tampa: International Education Press.

Hansen, D. A., ed. 1969. *Explorations in sociology and counseling*. Boston: Houghton Mifflin.

Jacobson, R. L. 1977. Does high academic achievement create problems later on? *Chronicle of Higher Education* 14 (May 23, 1977).

Piaget, J. 1952. *The origins of intelligence in children*. New York: International Universities Press.

Tyler, L. E. 1969. *The work of the counselor*. 3d ed. New York: Appleton-Century-Crofts.

York University Counselling and Development Centre. 1975. *The counselling and development centre, 1975–1976*. Toronto: York University.

6

THE COUNSELING CENTER IN THE COMMUNITY/JUNIOR COLLEGE

John C. Wolf

SOUTH PLAINS COLLEGE

Carolyn T. Aguren

RICHLAND COLLEGE

Perspective: The Community/Junior College Counseling Center in the Context of the Handbook

The decade of the 1970s has produced a remarkable growth in both the number and size of community and junior colleges. Originally created to fill specific student and institutional needs (such as two-year academic preparation for subsequent transfer to a senior college) and later viewed as a vocational-technical preparation resource, the two-year college has greatly expanded its role in the last twenty years. Although the basic goal of any educational institution remains the same in both four-year and two-year colleges—service to the student population—the diversity in student population institutional objectives, and curricular, extracurricular, and cocurricular offerings found in the community/junior college dictates innovative counseling strategies and commensurate innovativeness in implementation of these strategies.

In a handbook devoted to the college counseling center, a chapter devoted exclusively to the two-year colleges counseling center is of particular importance in order to provide a complete overview of the role of the counseling center in higher education. Handbooks and other reference sources treating the college counseling center have often focused upon functions of the counseling center as traditionally defined for the senior college and university. For example, the comprehensive and concise discussion of the college counseling center in the ACPA monograph of Oetting, Ivey, and Weigel (1970) makes no specific mention of counseling services at the community/junior college level, thereby implying that their presentation may be generalized to all college counseling centers at all levels of preparation. The treatment that follows demonstrates not only the similarities in objectives and processes, but also the dissimilarities that exist between the counseling center functions at the two levels of educational preparation. The primary intent of this chapter is not to present the community/junior college counseling center as a separate model functioning within its own conceptual framework, but to illustrate how each concept described in this handbook is developed and incorporated in the counseling process at the community/junior college.

Warnath (1972) has provided the college counseling profession with a well-defined challenge to document counseling objectives and processes with an emphasis upon student development and facilitation of student growth in the face of administration- and institution-defined goals and objectives for counseling. Nowhere has this challenge been faced more directly than in the community/junior college counseling center, as indicated clearly by reviews of such centers' services by Hinko (1971), Goodman (1975), and Wolf and Dameron (1975). In fact, the impact of many factors directly associated with the community/junior college setting, such as open enrollment, has in some cases dictated revision of counseling practices at senior colleges (Martorana, 1972).

THE COMMUNITY COLLEGE: LEARNING RESOURCE FOR THE ENTIRE COMMUNITY

The community college concept represents an attempt by higher education to fulfill a commitment to extend universal educational opportunity to all members of the community. This commitment and orientation is reflected in the development of the instructional format from the original junior college institution, which was designed mainly as a transfer or feeder facility for the senior college, to the very broad, multidimensioned educational facility of today. This development has mandated certain responsibilities to the counseling processes that must be implemented in the framework of the counseling center at the community college. Originally, the term "junior college" referred to a residentially oriented, transfer and technical-vocational training facility functioning as a downward extension of the senior college; in contrast, "community college" designated a nonresidential, noncentralized training facility blending transfer curricula, technical-vocational curricula, and continuing community education programs. Although both terms are still in use, much of this distinction is now only semantical. In certain areas, geographical and community circumstances dictate the preservation of this distinction, and for that reason both the connotative and denotative implications of such a distinction retain relevance for the reader. The current trend is for the two-year college to draw closer and closer to the community college concept and to assume the posture of an extension of the community.

The commitment of the community college to its philosophy of comprehensive community service is manifested in the type of student whom it serves. Students at the two-year college are more likely to come from a lower socioeconomic level, have more limited financial resources, receive less parental encouragement, possess less confidence in their ability to do college work, and have a poorer understanding of college programs and their objectives than do their counterparts at the four-year college (Cross, 1972). This "new student in higher education," reflecting the nature of the community college and its objectives, demands not only different counseling strategies and student personnel services but a differing emphasis in curricular offerings.

Transfer courses that provide instruction for the student having limited income or residing in an area distant from a four-year college remain a significant part of the community college curriculum, but other offerings in the areas of continuing education, cocurricular and extracurricular activities, and resource programs based upon community needs represent a significant trend toward the fulfillment of the commitment of the community college. Wolf and Marshall (1976) have noted that the largest source of postsecondary technical and vocational training is presently found at the community college, where constant expansion in number and type of technical-vocational programs and in instructional divisions specifically designed to provide such training further documents the willingness of the community college to fulfill its obligation to all members of the community.

THE COUNSELING CENTER: COMMUNITY COLLEGE AND UNIVERSITY

Previous reviews of college counseling center functioning have concentrated primarily upon counseling services, at times addressing staff qualifications as well. Detailed investigations of the counseling center on the four-year college campus by Albert (1968), Clark (1966), and Nugent and Pareis (1968) have described these counseling center facets adequately, while Hinko (1971) and Goodman (1975) have followed much the same format for the community college counseling center. In the present chapter, attention will be focused upon all facets of counseling center functioning at the community college. Wherever possible, illustrations of similarities and dissimilarities in counseling services and staffing, as well as institutional goals and objectives, student characteristics, curricular offerings, and resultant effects of these factors upon counseling goals, objectives, and delivery systems at the two levels of instruction are provided. Particular emphasis is placed upon the various differences in structure and organization of counseling centers on community college and university campuses. To illustrate, the comparison of counseling center function in two-year and four-year colleges provided by Wolf and Dameron (1975) has demonstrated that community college counseling services concentrate much more upon academic advisement than upon personal-social-emotional counseling, while at senior colleges and universities the opposite is the case. From such a comparison of counseling services, consideration of the implications of all facets of counseling center function is a logical progression.

A CONCEPTUAL AND PRACTICAL AMALGAMATION

The present trend in student services literature is to emphasize the basic similarity in overall goals existing in both two-year and four-year college counseling centers. Specifically, considerable emphasis is now being placed upon a student development model (Grant, 1972) that suggests a priority be given to counseling as a change agent centered on total student growth, acquisition of self-help skills, and preparation for life as a fully functioning member of society. Collins (1972) has discussed in particular the characteristics of the student at the two-year college as well as the implications of these characteristics for the student personnel worker. The opportunity now afforded almost all who desire to attend college through the widespread application of the policy of open-door admission in the community college has led Collins to suggest that perhaps an institutional reordering of priorities is in order—deemphasizing at least to some degree academic and cognitive learning and stressing a new direction that places greater value on affective learning and concern for human morality, relationships, and ethics.

Diversity in student characteristics, admission criteria, curricular offerings and objectives, as well as in the ever changing economic and employment scene, has created a challenge leading O'Banion (1972) to call for the development of "exceptional practices in community junior college student personnel programs." New delivery systems utilizing not only professional, but also paraprofessional personnel have added new dimension and flexibility to the counseling process, both of which have become increasingly evident in the community college counseling center. Although the principles and concepts described in all chapters of this handbook apply equally to both community college and university counseling centers, the manner in which the various components of the counseling center and the counseling process are combined in delivery of services contributes most to the uniqueness of the community college counseling center. Delineation and discussion of the two-year college counseling center will demonstrate that these combinations are simultaneously currently operational as well as in a constant state of change and revision. This dynamic evolutionary process in the community college deserves recognition, but also requires continual evaluation to ensure that the change is constructive and purposeful.

Goals and Objectives of the Community College

Since the foundation of America as a democratic nation, there has been a recognition of the need for a well-educated citizenry to support a constituional government. In addition, education has traditionally been viewed as a vehicle for upward social mobility. The educational opportunities for citizens of the United

States have historically been continually expanded in adherence to the ideals of social and political democracy. In addition, education is based upon a concept of individual worth: citizens are encouraged to make the most of their abilities in the quest for personally satisfying lives.

These general goals of education are found in a variety of forms in a review of the history of education. For example, in many ways the educational philosophy of today remains a reflection of the propositions of the Commission on the Reorganization of Secondary Education of 1918. This commission proposed the "seven cardinal principles" of education that were addressed to the education of the "total person" (Blount & Klausmeier, 1968). The development of skills in the areas of vocational preparation, family life, citizenship, and productive use of leisure time remain viable goals of education.

With the growth of the economy and technology of the nation, demographic characteristics have changed, life expectancy of the population has increased, and education for increasing numbers of people has assumed even greater importance. Education is being viewed as a lifelong process for all, and communities are moving toward providing all citizens with opportunities for developing skills and knowledge useful in society and in their personal lives.

STATEMENT OF PHILOSOPHY, GOALS, AND OBJECTIVES

The community college is a logical vehicle for meeting the educational needs of the diverse segments of the population now entering higher education and for implementing the general goals of education. The objectives of the community college were aptly stated by the Dallas County Community College District (DCCCD, 1976):

1. Providing leadership in the community in cultural and educational matters;
2. Being sensitive to changing needs of the community and adapting to them;
3. Serving a great variety of citizens of all ability levels and interests;
4. Offering a broad curriculum designed to assist each community member attain his desired level of cultural, intellectual, physical, and social development as well as technical competence;
5. Providing counseling and guidance to individuals to assist them in making responsible, mature decisions in all areas from career planning to personal problems;
6. Promoting and maintaining high standards of scholarship and academic performance.

To attain such goals and objectives, the following programs and services are offered:

1. Transfer degree programs leading to subsequent study at a four-year educational institution;
2. Occupational-technical programs, degree and certificate, preparing students for immediate employment;
3. Adult continuing education and community services providing opportunities for part-time instruction in both credit and non-credit courses;

4. General education courses as a requirement for graduation or as a special interest area for personal growth;
5. Educational, occupational, and personal counseling services.

These statements of community college philosophy, goals, and objectives are broadly representative of those of two-year educational institutions and reflect the pronounced emphasis upon the community- and student-centered atmosphere of the community college.

OBJECTIVES OF COMMUNITY COLLEGE AND UNIVERSITY: A COMPARISON

Thornton (1972) has defined the basic differences in the objectives of the university and the community college. The community college does duplicate the goals of the university in the sense that the community college provides lower-division academic course work leading to the bachelor's degree for students of similar abilities, backgrounds, and interest. However, the community college goes considerably further to avoid limiting the student clientele it serves. The community college extends its services to the entire population of the community through open-door admissions policies and a diversified curriculum of credit, technical-occupational, and noncredit courses.

A second difference may be defined by the pronounced emphasis upon counseling and guidance services in the community college. While in the university setting these services are viewed as ancillary to instructional services, in the community college they are integrated into the instructional format to augment instruction. Academic advisement and career counseling supplement the more traditional psychological testing and personal counseling services offered in the university, and the community college counselor is also beginning to implement the applied behavioral scientist concept of Berdie (1972) in serving as a consultant to the faculty.

A third major point of divergence is found in the emphasis in the community college on the role of teaching excellence in implementing the mission of the community college. In a university setting, research and publication are goals frequently stressed as a major portion of the academic mission and, either implicitly or explicitly, as requirements for promotion. The community college is far more inclined to reward competence in student-centered teaching. In fact, a fourth difference between the objectives of the community college and of the university is that the entire community college program format is couched in student-centered terms. This point assumes major importance when the potential student population is the entire community and when the college is attempting to identify and respond to all needs of the community and its residents.

Community colleges and universities are both needed if the general goals of education are to be met, since each meets certain goals better than the other. The university has the programs and facilities to educate that segment of the population itself, thus indicating many characteristics that make the community college training at the bachelor's, master's and doctoral degree levels. The community college serves a different function in providing ready access to a wide variety of educational programs that may enhance the total functioning of any and all members of the community.

The Community College Student

The student population of the community college is a reflection of the institution itself, thus indicating many characteristics that make the community college far more than a mere downward extension of the senior college and university. Comprehensive discussions by Collins (1972) and Cross (1972) allow a profile of the community college student to be drawn and, in so doing, raise both interesting and demanding questions and challenges for counseling at the two-year-college level. The factors describing community college students of today and to a considerable degree differentiating them from university students are complex and diverse and reflect the cultural and social flux in which the country as a whole now finds itself.

Typically, community college students come from families of lower socioeconomic status than that of their senior college counterparts; their financial resources are commensurately more limited; and this leads to demands on their time that are often unrelated to academic work—the necessity for working on either a part-time or even a full-time basis while attending classes at the community college. Harris (1973) has reported that frequently community college students are part-time students and full-time employees, with financial commitments extending not only to support of educational endeavors but also to family obligations. Thain (1976) has pointed to the needs of part-time students at the community college, particularly those who attend at night, as justifying increased emphasis on career and vocational counseling service provision. Collins (1972) has stressed the importance of the community college as the major educational vehicle for the minority student, and the concomitant cultural and ethnic factors have raised questions about the role and value of much of the standardized testing presently in use for selection, placement, and advisement.

POPULATION OF THE COMMUNITY COLLEGE: A SURVEY

Who then does the community college serve, from where do they come, and why? What portions of the community might be conceptualized as primary targets for the community college? Surveyed very broadly, the population of the community college does follow some general patterns.

1. On the basis of traditional criteria for conceptualization of academic achievement, the community college serves those with lower levels of measured and perceived academic achievement.
2. The community college student is from a lower socioeconomic level, with parental educational level and encouragement below that of the senior college student.

3. The community college student is often part-time, working and/or attending at night.
4. As Wolf (1977) and Krings (1976) have described, the community college student is older than the typical college student.
5. The educational and aspiration levels of the community college student differ from those of the senior college student: not only are transfer degree, terminal degree, and technical-vocational certificate programs pursued, but the latter two are often preferred over the transfer degree program.
6. The community college provides minority and disadvantaged students the opportunity for access to higher education.
7. All members of the community are potential students of the community college.

NEEDS AND PROBLEMS OF THE COMMUNITY COLLEGE STUDENT

In the identification of specific needs, problems, and resultant goals of community college students, all characteristics of these students must be considered. The resulting description, combined with definition of the populations served by the community college, leads to identification of several critical areas for counseling priority assignment.

1. Academic advisement is a central service in the counseling of the community college student. Actual practice (Wolf & Dameron, 1975) has documented this hypothesis.
2. Financial aid and related services assume a high priority in counseling the community college student.
3. A need for recognition of nonacademic goals is noted for many community college students, and the desire for education to deal with human values and social-cultural concerns, rather than just academic objectives, is central to serving the community college student.
4. Relevance in use of standardized measurement techniques is a basic concern for the community college counselor. Wolf (1977) has demonstrated, for example, the relevance of the GED as a valid predictor of community college performance for non-high-school graduates.
5. Demand exists for a general student services program including a redefined counseling process that will broaden the scope of services, recognize and embrace diversity of all types, and, above all, maximize flexibility.

IMPLICATIONS OF CHARACTERISTICS OF THE COMMUNITY COLLEGE STUDENT FOR COUNSELING

One factor becomes obvious in the discussion of the individual characteristics of the community college student: the student described will not be adequately served through reapplication of counseling procedures and structure found in the senior college and university. Moughamian (1969) has suggested that intensification of counseling program services, defined primarily as an increase in number of counseling contacts, might be one viable alternative to better serving the community college student. Yet, the reconsideration by Collins (1972) of the purposes of the educational process in the community college examines the point that academic aptitude may be only *one* dimension of human beings that has relevance for the educational process. This view has a decided implication for counseling in the community college, since affective learning and relationship concerns enter the list of priorities along with cognitive learning in the educational process. Models for student services emphasizing the "whole man," such as that described by O'Banion, Thurston, and Gulden (1972), suggest that more than a shift in counseling intensity is needed if Collins's viewpoint has relevance. The counselor becomes a "human development facilitator," and the direction of the counseling process is altered in accordance with the revised view of the nature of the educated person.

Perhaps the most perceptive statement on redirection of counseling for community college student service is that of Cross (1972), wherein the student personnel field is challenged to investigate the ways in which the community college student differs in *kind*, rather than *degree,* from the traditional senior college student. Cross believes that the development of counseling programs for the community college student on the same dimensions as services for the senior college student will lead to two inevitable and equally undesirable results: first, the community college student will be seen as an intellectually less capable student, as a less striving and motivated individual, and a poorer risk for higher education than the senior college student; and second, the purpose of the community college concept of education is inalterably subverted since it is to meet the different types of needs of the community college student that the community college was created.

The basic premise with which we are then left is this: To be different is neither better nor worse, but merely distinctive in many ways. Community college students are in many ways unique in their needs and goals for the educational process, and the challenge of counseling at the community college level is to meet not only those requirements which community college students have in common with senior college and university students but also those requirements which differentiate them from that more traditional concept of a student.

The Counseling Process at the Community College

A statement of goals and objectives of counseling in higher education should inevitably be tied to the goals and objectives of the educational process itself. This philosophy is applied most appropriately in the community college, where perhaps the highest degree of integration of counseling and general education goals has been attained in the "student development point of view in education" described by Grant (1972). If, as Grant states, the overall goal of education is to facilitate behavioral development from a multidisciplinary base, then the objectives of the counseling process are logical extensions of this general educational objective. In the holistic view of humanity dominant in education today, behavior is conceptualized as the embodiment of all facets of an individual's being, cognitive and conative.

COUNSELING GOALS AND OBJECTIVES IN THE COMMUNITY COLLEGE

Following the student development approach of both Grant (1972) and O'Banion (1971), the goals of the counseling process at the community college may be succinctly stated:

1. To assess and solidify behaviors already present in the repertoire of the student;
2. To discover with the student appropriate behaviors that will lead to educational objectives and develop general behaviors appropriate for all aspects of living: that is, formulation of specific behavioral objectives leading to facilitation of overall student self-direction;
3. To outline student development programs that will result in attainment of objectives formulated, building upon those behaviors already in the repertoire of the student as the foundation for subsequent development;
4. To modify existing behaviors that are identified as barriers to the attainment of the behavioral objectives formulated;
5. To facilitate development of a value structure that will allow the student to evaluate the functionality of his or her behaviors toward meeting the needs of society and attaining behavioral objectives while providing movement toward self-direction;
6. To clarify interaction patterns of cause-effect relationships in behavioral terms for diverse cultural environments including those which might be encountered subsequent to the educational experience.

A central point in all of the counseling objectives stated above is the implicit goal to facilitate development of *coping behaviors and attitudes* applicable in both academic and nonacademic environments.

THE STUDENT AS THE FOCUS OF THE COUNSELING PROCESS

As the counseling process may be considered the hub of student services in the community college, so might the student be considered the center of the entire educational process and therefore the focal point of the counseling process. O'Banion (1971) has described a basis for what he terms the "humanistic ethic" in education, in which an individual is conceptualized as a dynamic and vibrant organism, constantly growing and possessing the capacity for actualization of the potential for personal and social worth. In his opinion, this capacity has been inadequately expressed in other approaches, which failed to base their system about and upon students themselves. O'Banion defined the approach to helping that considers the student to be a developing person and centers on a behavioral orientation for learning as constituting the "student development point of view" (1972). A central value of the student development model that Grant (1972) suggests is the translation of the humanistic, developmentally oriented statement into specific behaviors and behavioral objectives around which a student-development-based counseling system might be designed and implemented.

DELIVERY SYSTEM FOR COUNSELING AT THE COMMUNITY COLLEGE

The trend in counseling at the community-college level today is to describe the delivery strategies as models; and models designed to integrate such varied tools as counseling psychology, sociology, vocational development theory, developmental principles, learning theory and behavior modification, and even management techniques from business have been developed. A review by O'Banion, Thurston, and Gulden (1970) of existing models for student services delivery found all to be inadequate, prompting O'Banion to introduce his student development-student personnel model (1971). This model is one in which students (1) are provided the freedom to choose their own direction for learning, (2) assume responsibility for these choices, and (3) experience interpersonal interactions that embrace all aspects of development with student development facilitators. Some models have concentrated upon a specific counseling service, such as the model for implementation of academic advisement described by Dameron and Wolf (1974). It incorporates the O'Banion concept of student development into a career ladder format, using faculty, professional counseling, and paraprofessional to facilitate the advisement process.

More broadly, Young and Harris (1977) have provided a description of alternatives for delivery of counseling services at the community college, resolving the issue in favor of an interdependent model. Including the student, the counseling services, and the institution as equal partners, it represents an interacting process designed to facilitate that portion of student development which is the province of counseling. In contrast to Warnath (1972), who has cautioned against subversion of counseling objectives by adherence to institution-defined goals, Young and Harris feel that an interdependence of the community college objectives and structure and the community college counseling programs and structure is essential if the student-centered philosophy of the community college is to be reflected in the counseling services. Both O'Banion and Young and Harris conceive of the counselor as an active interventionist, "encountering" in order to implement the counseling process.

Sophistication extending beyond the delivery of counseling services is found in the systematic training model of Stilwell and Santoro (1976). The professional working counselor is transformed into a learning development consultant with competence-based modular components training the consultant in an extended graduate curricula. Inasmuch as it is behaviorally oriented, the model may be a positive step toward their goal of a training model for the 1980s. The concept of interdisciplinary counseling orientation is found in all of the models mentioned, and perhaps the applied behavioral scientist envisioned by Berdie (1972) may become a reality in the community college through implementation of the counseling process. Added flexibility is given to counseling, especially at the community college level, by the increasing use of paraprofessionals in counseling, a practice given generally positive marks in a comprehensive review by Hoffman and Warner (1976) of research investigating the effectiveness of paraprofessional usage.

Some conclusions can be drawn about the delivery of counseling services at the community college. All models stress the nature of counseling as developmental and process-oriented. Individual strategies for delivery will no doubt continue to vary with institution size, staffing, needs, and orientation, with no single model being universally applicable. However, the philosophical bases for the counseling services and the resultant services should reflect a concern for the student as a total person, acquiring not only knowledge, but also the everyday skills necessary to make productive use of that knowledge in today's social and employment worlds.

Structure and Organization of the Community College Counseling Center

In many ways, the student personnel programs on community college campuses are organized much like those on senior college and university campuses. As a rule, the counseling center staff in a community college report directly or indirectly to the chief administrator of student services. This administrator frequently holds the title of dean of student affairs, dean of student development, or dean of student services. However, recently there has been a move on some community college campuses to elevate the chief student personnel administrator to the rank of vice-president. O'Banion (1971) has noted that this may be a recognition of the importance of student personnel programs in the community college education process, but that time will tell whether such vice-presidents in student personnel are afforded the same status as instructional and administrative vice-presidents.

The size of community college counseling center staffs vary considerably, with an ideal staffing formula of 300 to 350 students per counselor frequently utilized. The formula may be based upon student head count or FTE (full-time equivalents), the former being the most desirable in the community college in which part-time students are prevalent. The 1965 AAJC-Carnegie Corporation study of student personnel services in colleges of various sizes recommended the following staffing patterns:

STAFF LEVELS	ENROLLMENT			
	500	*1,000*	*2,500*	*5,000*
Dean (or Director) of Counseling	1	1	1	1
Head Counselor or Supervisor	0	0	1	2
Professional Counselors	1	2	8	16
Support Personnel (clerical)	1	1½	2½	5

Obviously, *ideal* programs of this magnitude cost in proportion to their size. Few counseling centers in the larger community colleges reach these ideal levels, largely due to space and budgetary considerations. For this reason, alternatives allowing an approximation of these levels have been explored. One innovative practice in organization has been utilized at Fulton-Montgomery Community College in New York, where the student personnel program has been organized as an academic division (O'Banion, 1971). The staff members offer credit courses in addition to performing counseling duties, are represented on campus committees responsible for making curriculum decisions, and are, therefore, afforded the opportunity to offer expertise and to influence the college curricula. The practice of using counselors as academic instructors is also followed in the Dallas County Community College District and numerous others. Giddan, Healy, and Price (1976) found in a nationwide survey of 72 counseling centers that many university and college counseling centers utilize joint appointments to provide adequate staffing for student services. Although such solutions have not proved to be without their problems, nonetheless ingenuity has been nurtured and has flourished in the community college.

DECENTRALIZATION: AN EXPERIMENT IN ORGANIZATION

O'Banion has stated, "The major question is no longer 'should the counselor work more closely with faculty?' The question now is 'should the counselor be literally moved out of the counseling office and housed with faculty members?'" (1971, p. 15). Some campuses are experimenting with a completely decentralized system, in which counselors are assigned and housed in academic divisions and are administratively responsible to the division chairperson. Other campuses have modified the total decentralization schema somewhat by placing counselors in the academic divisions while also having the division-based counselors serve in the centralized counseling center to maintain both the continuity of the services and the professional identities of the counselors. Another version of a decentralized system is actually more of a liaison system, in which the counselors are housed in a central counseling center, report to the dean or the vice-president of student services, and are subsequently assigned as liaison personnel to academic divisions. Such approaches reflect the concept that the counselor must go out into the student community to meet both student and faculty rather than waiting for them to come to the counseling center.

Still another approach to decentralization is the placement of satellite centers around the campus. One center may provide career exploration services; another, curriculum and academic advisement; another, intervention for personal problems; and others, those services identified as need areas by a specific campus. Faculty advisors are also part of some approaches to counseling, both in centralized and decentralized settings. Siewert (1975) has described an academic counseling center utilizing faculty members on a part-time-basis (with released time) to supplement counselors in facilitating the academic advisement process. There is increasing recognition that faculty members have valuable knowledge about their specific disciplines and can often provide a valuable source of support to the student after counseling assistance has led to career choice and selection of a major field. Such concepts further employ a team composed of faculty and counselors to facilitate the overall student development process.

DIFFERENTIATED STAFFING IN THE COMMUNITY COLLEGE COUNSELING CENTER

As Hinko (1971) has described, counseling centers in senior colleges and universities are usually staffed with doctoral-level counselors and offer a more limited range of services to students than in the community college, where the broad range of services offered lends itself well to the concept of differentiated staffing. An ideal staffing arrangement in the community college would include a base of doctoral- and master's-degree-level professional counselors augmented by bachelor's-degree- and associate-degree-level preprofessional guidance workers and supported by student and nonstudent paraprofessionals and student peer counselors. As noted before, Hoffman and Warner (1976) have documented the general effectiveness of paraprofessionals in delivery of helping services in the college setting.

The increasing utilization of preprofessional and paraprofessional guidance workers is in some measure indicative of the attempts of community college counseling centers to provide the diversity in services already described, while staying within reasonable staffing levels and budgets. Tasks such as group test administration, career information presentation, freshman orientation, academic advisement, and general intake processing are areas in which such support personnel have been effectively used, while activities appropriately facilitated in a group setting have also proved a worthwhile use of support personnel for the professional counselors. Crane, Anderson, and Kirchner (1975) surveyed the attitudes of counseling center directors toward paraprofessionals and found that the directors viewed them as desirable and most useful in supporting counseling in the areas of freshman orientation, study skills, personal problems relating to general college life adjustment, and drug abuse problems.

A TEAM APPROACH FOR SUPPORT AND LIAISON

A student-centered climate in the community college educational process demands that all components of the institution work in concert to deliver programs and services meeting student needs and supporting the overall student development concept. Formal and informal channels of communication must be established and maintained for both student personnel administrators and instructional administrators to endorse and support actively the integration of counseling-oriented services into the instructional programs.

To illustrate, at Richland College in Dallas, a team composed of counselors, faculty, student activities personnel, media specialists, and students plan and implement a Human Potential Week during which speakers, activities, and multimedia presentations focus on the development of human potential. This same team designs a Career Awareness Week. Another example of the sharing of expertise is the interaction of counselors and faculty at Richland College, using the technique of cognitive mapping. Cognitive mapping identifies the teaching type of the instructor and the learning styles of the students. Instructors can then be made aware of ways to modify their teaching methods to reach more students, while students can learn different study skills to adapt their learning styles to a variety of teaching methods.

To extend further the need for integration of all the resources of the community college, as counseling services become more "systematic," support from such areas as the library, for gathering of books and materials for career counseling, and the media services for preparing videotapes and slide-tape programs to be used in activities such as orientation. In short, counseling services must have at their disposal the same support and resources as do the academic divisions if the integrated, interdependent model of student development education is to function efficiently.

Counseling Services in the Community College

To attempt a categorization of community college services would undoubtedly lead to an arbitrary, controversial system that might confuse more than clarify. Therefore, a quite general, gross distinction between the more traditional, established counseling services of the community and junior colleges and the newer, innovative developments in the community college is used to present a summary of the actual helping intervention techniques offered to community college students.

TRADITIONAL SERVICES

In 1965, a nationwide study helped define essential counseling and counseling-related services at the community college level within the overall framework of student services. Interestingly, of the twenty-one functions identified as basic to community college student personnel work, such services as career information, orientation, academic advisement, program articulation, and testing were listed separately from the function of student counseling (National Committee for Appraisal and Development of Junior College Student Personnel Programs, 1965). Hinko (1971) has provided perhaps the largest survey of community college counseling services to date, identifying the most frequently offered, traditional counseling services. At that time, vocational counseling, educational counseling, testing, academic advising, and social-personal counseling were found to be those services most frequently offered in the community college, although others were mentioned.

Some of the more traditional services have been reconceptualized in an attempt to keep them in the mainstream of community college counseling. Parker (1975) has developed a recent model for organization and coordination of career placement services in the community college, while the concept of open admission at the community/junior college has had articulation implications both downward to the high school level (Simmons, 1970) and upward to the senior college and university (Martorana, 1972). Vocational counseling has been expanded into career and decision planning, and Babcock and Kaufman (1976) have described the utility of a career course offering in facilitating vocational development in college students.

RECENT DEVELOPMENTS

The articulate statement of Cochran (1974) has pointed to the obligatory nature of the implications of career education for counseling in general. Traditionally, vocational curricula, either at the high school or the community college level, have been considered as occupying second place to academic programs. As Cochran states, "Students in vocational curricula, along with other noncollege-bound students, have long been stepchildren of the American system" (1974, p. 585). This statement is quite logically extended to the community college technical-vocational curricula and makes the counseling function of program articulation a most important one. Not only must the academic curricula be articulated, but now, just as importantly, so must the technical programs. We now realize that the community and junior colleges are in fact training many of the so-called noncollege-bound students.

The past few years have been a period of great activity and innovation both in counseling and in the entire two-year college educational process. Community college counseling programs targeted at specific student subgroups—mature students, female students, adult education participants, non-high-school-graduate students, attrition-prone students, married students, part-time students—and, beyond the student clientele, at nonstudent clients have been developed and discussed in the professional literature. Computer-assisted counseling centers for adults wishing to investigate possible career change have been piloted to tie into the community college (Farmer, 1975), and counseling capability utilizing such computer systems as SIGI (System of Interactive Guidance and Information) to aid students in making career decisions is no longer a novelty in the community college counseling center. O'Banion (1971) has discussed in detail the movement of community college counseling services from behind the center walls out into the campus itself through the many options of the decentralization approach to organization.

The center approach has been extended through development of such techniques as a "Center for 'Undecided' College Students" (Bonar & Mahler, 1976), a "Learning Skills Center in a College without a Campus" (Bopp, 1974) whereby the counseling service is offered at several places in the community college district, and a community college counseling center extending so completely into the community that marriage and family counseling is viewed as a major function (Fischer & Rankin, 1973). Perhaps the epitome of community service by the community college counseling center is found in the outreach service of the Human Resources Development Center at Richland College in Dallas. Here, all members of the community, student and nonstudent, may receive such services as individual personal counseling, group counseling, family counseling, and special topic and interest counseling and training programs. The center utilizes mainly members of the professional community outside the community college to provide the services, operating on a break-even financial basis (Ott, 1976).

COMPARISON OF COUNSELING SERVICES: COMMUNITY COLLEGE AND UNIVERSITY

The function of college counseling centers and their services has been investigated in some detail, but the majority of the studies, such as those of Clark (1966), Albert (1968), and Nugent and Pareis (1968), have centered on senior colleges and universities. The survey of Hinko (1971) remains perhaps the only adequate survey of community college counseling services, although Goodman (1975) conducted a small-scale, regional survey of community college counseling services and the survey of Wolf and Dameron (1975) outlines them to some extent. The latter report is also the only available comparative study of counseling services at the community college and senior college/university levels. The two most frequently offered counseling services in both settings were those already noted as traditional—academic advisement and personal-social-emotional counseling. However, the percentage of counselor time in the community college counseling center spent in academic advisement was significantly greater than time spent in personal-social-adjustment counseling, while in the senior college/university counseling center the opposite was true. Counseling related to educational concerns such as course choice and load was considerably more prevalent at the community college, while short- and long-term counseling for emotional disorder was more prevalent in the senior college/university setting. Such a finding is consistent with the basic commitment of the community college, in terms of both educational philosophy and staffing interest and qualifications. Research was also noted to be less prevalent in the community college than in the senior college/university. Although other differences were noted, the reported differences in research activities is of significant importance at this time for the status of counseling as a profession. In reviewing the literature of community college counseling, perhaps the most glaring shortcoming is the absence of re-search adequately evaluating the effectiveness of counseling techniques and programs.

ASSESSMENT OF COMMUNITY COLLEGE COUNSELING OUTCOME

The finding that research is apparently given a relatively low priority does not mean that efforts to measure the effectiveness of community college counseling outcome have not been made. However, the adequacy of many studies that have been conducted has been widely debated on a variety of grounds. To illustrate, the value of a detailed review of paraprofessional effectiveness conducted by Hoffman and Warner (1976) is at least partially diluted by the fact that the literature regarding paraprofessional use in counseling includes almost as many definitions of effectiveness and criteria for measuring positive counseling out-come as there are studies reviewed. Hedlund and Jones (1970) investigated the effect of student personnel services upon completion rate in the community college using self-report questionnaires to gather data, leading even the authors to qualify all subsequent positive findings due to potential bias in methodology. An extreme example of looseness in counseling effectiveness research is found in a report from Leeward Community College, Hawaii: a questionnaire sampling technique was used to obtain counseling outcome information measured through respondent ratings of "excellent," "good," "fair," or "poor" (University of Hawaii, 1975).

Studies such as that of Krivatsy and Magoon (1976) have approached the investigation of counseling effectiveness from an economic standpoint, while a systems-analysis-based method for evaluation of counselor training programs was proposed by Bergland and Quatrano (1973). An interesting approach has been employed by Thompson and Wise (1976) to identify useful outcome criteria for assessing effects of counseling. In a series of studies, information was statisti-cally extracted from questionnaires administered to university counseling center clients to derive specific outcome criteria. Unfortunately, this approach suffers from many of the methodological problems inherent in questionnaire-based data. Further, there has not been a noticeable trend to adopt these criteria in other, better-controlled studies, although this potential exists.

The "era of accountability" has led, therefore, to evaluation of both counseling outcomes and counselor training programs. Have the pressures of account-ability resulted in wholesale research of counseling effectiveness without really attending to the primary concern of *evaluating* intervention strategies? Burck and Peterson (1975) have distinguished between evaluation and research: evalua-tion, an explanation of relationships between events and goals and objectives, is a much more task-oriented, pragmatic exercise than is scientific research, which is viewed by the authors as subject to greater controls, but more theoretically oriented and concerned with prediction of future events. Oetting (1976, 1976b) has offered an excellent discussion of "evaluative research" that emphasizes behavior goals to implement such evaluative research and thus to deal more efficiently with the issue of counselor accountability. Ivey (1977) has provided a start toward defining externally based outcome criteria for counseling, so op-timism for future assessment of counseling outcomes seems justified at this point.

COMMUNITY COLLEGE COUNSELING SERVICES: AN EVOLUTIONARY VIEW

A review of the 1965 AAJC report, more than ten years later, illustrates how responsive community college counseling has been to the rapid changes in stu-dent population, curricula, and general educational philosophy. The surveys of Hinko (1971) and of Wolf and Dameron (1975) have demonstrated that the traditional services are being subdivided; and as specific need areas are iden-tified, special counseling programs and techniques are being developed to meet these needs, often in highly innovative ways. Concern for accountability has drawn the community college counselor into research assessing counseling out-comes and effectiveness. What the future holds for counseling in the community college will no doubt be heavily influenced by trends in educational process and philosophy at that level, but Jonassen and Stripling (1977) suggest that student development and career planning appear major areas of emphasis for the future, with articulation, advisement, and community service programs to assume a larger role as well.

Counselor and Administrator: Cooperation, Not Confrontation

SOURCES OF CONFLICT

If we accept the basic premises that the educational institution exists to serve the student and that counseling services exist for the same reason, then situations in which student needs conflict with institutional policies, needs, and priorities should not arise. Yet they do arise; and when individual student needs conflict with those of the institution, counselors may indeed find themselves in confronta-tion with the administration of the community college.

As previously discussed, the diversified student population and the diversified curricula of the community college demand commensurate diversity in counseling services and delivery systems. Community college counselors are developing new models and filling new roles to better meet student needs, and community college counseling is having an impact upon academic programs and the entire educational milieu of the community college. Such influence has not come without its own set of problems, however. Herrick (1971) found that college administrators generally lacked insight into the functions that counselors should perform. Warnath has pointed out another difficulty:

As long as the counselor seems to be helping the misfits, the confused, or the rebellious find their way back into productive roles in the mainstream of the institution, he may be a useful tool for the institution. But when he begins calling attention to facets of the institution that may be contributing to the disruption of human lives or the alienation of people from the system, he becomes an annoyance. When he moves to effect changes in the system, he becomes a clear and present danger. (1972, p. 231).

Implicit in the philosophy of the community college is a responsiveness to the needs of the community as well as the students'. Counselors are in a strategic position to assess both student needs and community needs and to provide input toward the definition of institutional priorities and goals. However, such a stance may involve abandoning some counseling services viewed as traditionally necessary by the administration, thus risking direct confrontation with administrators.

METHODS OF IMPLEMENTING COUNSELOR-ADMINISTRATOR INTERFACE

In order to fulfill their responsibilities as counselors, it is imperative that community college counselors assume responsibility for educating other members of the institutional setting (such as faculty and administrators) about student needs and appropriate roles and services of counselors. In addition, community college counselors must recognize the absolute necessity of developing evaluation programs that will allow for the determination of effectiveness of intervention outcomes. Documentation of effectiveness and relevance of counseling services through program evaluation will provide an avenue to gain the attention, respect, and cooperation of the community college administration.

Counselors must be able to define their role in relation to the administration and students: not only must counselors know who they are and what they are about in the counseling business, but they must also be able to communicate this to both constituencies. A desirable approach to developing a functional relationship with the administration is to establish counseling programs based upon both assessment of student needs and institutional statements of goals and objectives and then to conduct ongoing program evaluation. An interesting approach to program evaluation combining community college counseling accountability with administrative participation has been used by Hecht and Henry (1976); a sematic differential instrument for student evaluation of counseling effectiveness was developed jointly by a committee of counselors, counselor educators, and administrators. Using approaches that accept input from both the administration and the student, community college counselors may maximize their potential to deliver relevant services to the students while ensuring the ability to document the positive effects of the counseling efforts made to meet both student and institutional goals.

Community College Counseling: Present and Future

The counseling profession as a whole has been dutifully concerned about the future of counseling and student personnel services in the college setting. Certainly the emphasis is upon the future in the article by Berdie (1972) entitled "The 1980 Counselor: Applied Behavioral Scientist," as it is in the more recent article by Stilwell and Santoro (1976), "A Training Model for the 1980's." Counseling is obviously preparing conceptually for the next decade, but upon what is this preparation based? Has the counseling profession become so concerned with the future that it has neglected the present? The relative lack of studies comparing actual counseling services in the community college and the senior college and university is in itself evidence that more attention might be profitably devoted to examination of the current state of affairs. *Adequate* studies measuring the outcome of counseling strategies now in use in the community college remain in short supply, despite an emphasis that suggests this decade be described as the era of accountability for counseling at all levels.

THE PRESENT

A combination of factors—including the emphasis upon counselor accountability, orientation of counseling and institution toward a posture of student development, and the movement toward a pragmatic eclecticism in helping intervention that stresses O'Banion's "humanistic ethic"—has provided a most positive base for the future of community college counseling. Despite methodological difficulties in implementing research evaluation of counseling process and outcome, the importance of demonstrating that counseling services do make a difference has now been recognized by all levels of the profession. The interdisciplinary nature of helping has also become an accepted orientation in community college counseling, as the recent model described by Young and Harris (1977) aptly documents. The growing use of paraprofessionals has provided a diversity and flexibility of services demanded by the nature of the community college objectives and student needs. However, the present has demonstrated enough for counselors to realize that the task that lies ahead in providing counseling services to the community college student far outweighs that which has already been accomplished.

THE FUTURE

If the task that lies ahead for community college counseling is one requiring assessment of the present and resultant appropriate redirection in the future, what areas should be examined and how should the examination be conducted?

The role of counseling in the overall student services program at the community college must be distinctly defined in order for priorities in service delivery to be outlined. The recent survey of Jonassen and Stripling (1977) of all public community colleges in Florida noted that student personnel workers ranked such services as student counseling, student development, career and decision-making facilitation, student advisement, and faculty consultation among the top eight student personnel service priorities for the next ten years. Recognition of the counselor as an integral part of the overall student development education model has led to extension of the counselor's role beyond directly delivering counseling service to functioning as an educator (for example, human development courses) and as a consultant to both faculty and administration. Models describing organization and function of counseling and student services in the community college have adopted an interdisciplinary approach that will promote emphasis upon integration of services, personnel, and physical facilities toward the general goal of student development. A systems approach to service delivery may prove the most efficient method to provide counseling to the community college student of the future.

SUMMARY

Counseling in the community college does seem to be adequately meeting student needs at present, but this conclusion is based primarily upon the observed correlation between intervention strategies currently in use and postulated student and institutional needs and goals, rather than upon sound educational research, evaluative or other. The "emerging model" of O'Banion (1971) has emerged; the "learning development consultant" system for training and helping has been nicely presented by Stilwell and Santoro (1976); and the direction of counseling in the community college appears to be headed toward the "student development view" of Grant (1972), in which the counselor does function as the "applied behavioral scientist" that Berdie (1972) envisioned. How productive the proposed models, strategies, and redefinitions of the counselor role prove to be in the community college environment remains to be demonstrated. Although this should not necessarily be construed as criticism—since by definition the future cannot be tested in the present—much of the planning for the future rests upon what is being done today in the community college. And as Oetting (1976a, 1976b) and Burck and Peterson (1975) have stressed, the methodologies used to demonstrate current accountability in counseling might profitably be subjected to their own tests of accountability.

The final standard for evaluation of counseling practices at the community college may be the Krumboltz (1968) "test of relevancy"—what will counselors do differently if the results of the research come out one way or another? Extending the test further to include intervention techniques, what will clients do differently after participation in community college counseling? Counselors would be well advised to be prepared in the years to come to respond to such inquiries and to have relevant, sound research evidence to support their responses. Therein lies both the challenge and the promise of community college counseling for the future, as well as the present.

References

Albert, G. 1968. A survey of college counseling facilities. *The Personnel and Guidance Journal* 46: 540–43.

Babcock, R. J., and Kaufman, M. A. 1976. Effectiveness of a career course. *Vocational Guidance Quarterly* 24: 261–65.

Berdie, R. F. 1972. The 1980 counselor: applied behavioral scientist. *The Personnel and Guidance Journal* 50: 451–56.

Bergland, B. W., and Quatrano, L. 1973. Systems evaluation in counselor education. *Counselor Education and Supervision* 12: 190–98.

Blount, N. D., and Klausmeier, H. J. 1968. *Teaching in the secondary school*. New York: Harper & Row.

Bonar, J. R., and Mahler, L. R. 1976. A center for "undecided" college students. *The Personnel and Guidance Journal* 54: 481–84.

Bopp, B. J. 1974. The realities of learning skills center in a college without a campus. Paper presented at the Western College Reading Association, Oakland, Calif., April 1974.

Burck, H. D., and Peterson, G. W. 1975. Needed: more evaluation, not research. *The Personnel and Guidance Journal* 53: 563–69.

Clark, D. D. 1966. Characteristics of counseling centers in large universities. *The Personnel and Guidance Journal* 44: 817–23.

Cochran, L. H. 1974. Counselors and the noncollege-bound student. *The Personnel and Guidance Journal* 52: 582–85.

Collins, C. 1972. Student characteristics and their implications for student personnel work. In T. O'Banion and A. Thurston, eds., *Student development programs in the community junior college*. Englewood Cliffs, N.J.: Prentice-Hall.

Crane, J.; Anderson, W.; and Kirchner, K. 1975. Counseling center directors' attitudes toward paraprofessionals. *Journal of College Student Personnel* 16: 119–22.

Cross, K. P. 1972. Higher education's newest student: a research description. In T. O'Banion and A. Thurston, eds., *Student development programs in the community junior college*. Englewood Cliffs, N.J.: Prentice-Hall.

Dallas County Community College District. 1976. *DCCCD manual: Policies and procedures, section 1*. Dallas: Dallas County Community College District.

Dameron, J. D., and Wolf, J. C. 1974. Academic advisement in higher education: a new model. *Journal of College Student Personnel* 15: 470–73.

Farmer, H. 1975. Inquiry project: computer-assisted counseling centers for adults. Paper presented at the American Association of Higher Education, Drake University, Des Moines, Iowa, May 1975.

Fischer, G. A., and Rankin, G. 1973. A community counseling center for total community service. *Community and Junior College Journal* 43: 48–50.

Giddan, N. S.; Healy, J. M.; and Price, M. K. 1976. The status and future of joint appointments in counseling centers. *Journal of College Student Personnel* 17: 2–6.

Goodman, L. H. 1975. Counseling services in the two-year college: a southeastern survey. *NASPA Journal* 12: 241–48.

Grant, W. H. 1972. Student development in the community college. In T. O'Banion and A. Thurston, eds., *Student development programs in the community junior college* Englewood Cliffs, N.J.: Prentice-Hall.

Harris, M. L. 1973. Urban influence on student personnel services. *Community and Junior College Journal* 43: 42–44.

Hecht, A. R., and Henry, B. 1976. Development of a semantic differential instrument for student evaluation of community college counseling conferences. Paper presented at the North Central Region AERA Special Interest Group on Community/Junior College Research, Madison, Wis., July 1976.

Hedlund, D. E., and Jones, J. T. 1970. Effect of student personnel services on completion rate in two-year colleges. *Journal of College Student Personnel* 11: 196–99.

Herrick, G. D. 1971. The administrator and the counselor: perception of counselor role in two-year colleges. *Journal of College Student Personnel* 365–69.

Hinko, P. M. 1971. A national survey of counseling services. *Junior College Journal* 42: 20–24.

Hoffman, A. M., and Warner, R. W. 1976. Paraprofessional effectiveness. *The Personnel and Guidance Journal* 54: 494–97.

Ivey, A. E. 1977. Cultural expertise: toward systematic outcome criteria in counseling and psychological education. *The Personnel and Guidance Journal* 55: 296–302.

Jonassen, E. O., and Stripling, R. O. 1977. Priorities for community college student personnel services during the next decade. *Journal of College Student Personnel* 18: 83–86.

Krings, D. 1976. Meeting the counseling needs. *Adult Leadership* 24: 311–13.

Krivatsy, S. E., and Magoon, T. M. 1976. Differential effects of three vocational counseling treatments. *Journal of Counseling Psychology* 23: 112–17.

Krumboltz, J. 1968. Future directions for counseling research. In J. Whiteley, ed., *Research in counseling*. Columbus, Ohio: Charles E. Merrill.

Martorana, S. V. 1972. Open enrollments in senior institutions. *Community Services Catalyst* 2: 17–26.

Moughamian, H. 1969. *The effects of an intensified counseling program on sophomore junior college students: final report*. Washington D.C.: Office of Education (DHEW), Bureau of Research.

National Committee for Appraisal and Development of Junior College Student Personnel Programs. 1965. *Junior college student personnel programs appraisal and development—a report to the Carnegie Corporation*. Washington, D.C.: American Association of Junior Colleges.

Nugent, F. A., and Pareis, E. N. 1968. Survey of present policies and practices in college counseling centers in the U.S. *Journal of Counseling Psychology* 15: 94–97.

O'Banion, T. 1972. Exceptional practices in community junior college student personnel programs. In T. O'Banion and A. Thurston, eds., *Student development programs in the community junior college*. Englewood Cliffs, N.J.: Prentice-Hall.

———. 1971. *New directions in community college student personnel programs*. Student Personnel Series, no. 15. Washington, D.C.: American College Personnel Association.

————; Thurston, A.; and Gulden, J. 1972. Junior college student personnel work: an emerging model. In T. O'Banion and A. Thurston, eds., *Student development programs in the community junior college*. Englewood Cliffs, N.J.: Prentice-Hall.

————. 1970. Student personnel work: an emerging model. *Junior College Journal* 41: 6–14.

Oetting, E. R. 1976a. Evaluative research and orthodox science: part I. *The Personnel and Guidance Journal* 55: 11–15.

————. 1976b. Planning and reporting evaluative research: part II. *The Personnel and Guidance Journal* 55: 60–64.

Oetting, E. R.; Ivey, A. E.; and Weigel, R. G. *The college and university counseling center*. Student Personnel Series, no. 11. Washington, D.C.: American College Personnel Association.

Ott, E. 1976. Community outreach—a definition. 1976. Unpublished report (ERIC), Richland College, Dallas, Tex.

Parker, V. 1975. Placement programs: a new philosophy. *Community and Junior College Journal* 45: 30–31, 34.

Siewert, J. A. 1975. The academic counseling center: a centralized advising and counseling concept. *Journal of College Student Personnel* 16: 163–64.

Simmons, W. D. 1970. *Survey and analysis of higher education programs for the disadvantaged student: final report*. Washington, D.C.: Office of Education (DHEW), Bureau of Research.

Stilwell, W. E., and Santoro, D. A. 1976. A training model for the 1980's. *The Personnel and Guidance Journal* 54: 323–26.

Thain, R. J. 1976. The night-school graduate dilemma. *Journal of College Placement* 36: 45–48.

Thompson, A., and Wise, W. 1976. Steps toward outcome criteria. *Journal of Counseling Psychology* 23: 202–8.

Thornton, J. W. 1972. *The community/junior college*. New York: John Wiley.

University of Hawaii. 1975. A report of the satisfaction of recent vocational-technical graduates with the academic counseling and registration assistance received. Unpublished manuscript (ERIC), Leeward Community College, Honolulu, Hawaii.

Warnath, C. 1972. College counseling: between the rock and the hard place. *The Personnel and Guidance Journal* 51: 229–35.

Wolf, J. C. 1977. An investigation of the predictive validity of the Tests of General Educational Development for two-year college study. *Dissertation Abstracts International* 37: 11, 128.

Wolf, J. C., and Dameron, J. D. 1975. Counseling center function in two-year and four-year colleges. *Journal of College Student Personnel* 16: 482–85.

Wolf, J. C., and Marshall, E. W. 1976. Alternatives to post-secondary academic training in Texas. *Guidelines* 24: 5.

Young, J. W., and Harris, K. A. 1977. A community college model of counseling. *Journal of College Student Personnel* 18: 133–37.

7

PROFESSIONAL PERSONNEL

William M. Gilbert

UNIVERSITY OF ILLINOIS, URBANA-CHAMPAIGN

When asked to write this chapter, I agreed to do so on the condition that I be permitted to write frankly and with the provision that what I wrote would be based mainly on my own experiences with the development of the large-scale Psychological and Counseling Center at the University of Illinois at Urbana-Champaign. Consequently, the general problems relating to professional staff will be discussed in three segments: the selection of professional staff, the retention (or nonretention) of staff, and the administrative structure within the staff and its relationship to other parts of the University. For other details readers should refresh their acquaintance with "Guidelines for University and College Counseling Services" in the June 1971 issue of the *American Psychologist*.

The fundamental conditions favorably affecting all of these areas can be stated in a very few words. In order to secure and retain a high-quality professional staff, it is necessary that salaries be equivalent to those of persons engaged in straight teaching in related areas and that some form of job security, such as the possibility of tenure, be available. No amount of morale boosting will effectively substitute for these basic conditions. Without them, professional staff members themselves will not have the self-respect they deserve, nor will they be adequately respected throughout the rest of the university. However, it may be of use to present some details and to discuss some of the other issues relating to a professional staff.

Selection of a Professional Staff

Before becoming involved in the selection of a professional staff, someone or some group must, obviously, have a reasonably clear idea of the purposes that the staff members should serve. These purposes will necessarily vary with the historical setting, the immediate conditions, the already existing services, and the general philosophy upon which the counseling center is based. Back in 1937 the intention to supply professional-level counseling to university students was quite new and innovative. Most counseling that did not directly relate to academic courses was supplied by the offices of deans of men or deans of women. Often these were persons who had broad interests in student welfare, but little or no professional psychological training. To my knowledge the only large-scale functioning counseling center in a university at that time was at the University of Minnesota. Fortunately, it was possible to secure the consulting services of Dr. E. G. Williamson from Minnesota, who made some very farseeing and astute recommendations regarding the establishment of a center at the University of Illinois. Clearly, the conditions existing then presented quite different staff needs from those which would be present in an ongoing counseling center today. In those early days the director of the Counseling Center at the University of Illinois was not a psychologist, nor did he have any psychological training. He was Dr. H. W. Bailey, a mathematician who had served on many university committees and was widely respected by the faculty. A very compassionate but firm man who was genuinely interested in student welfare, he never harbored any delusions of being a psychotherapist or even a psychologist. He was, however, an excellent general counselor and knew when and how to make referrals to the small number of psychologists on the staff. More than any other person on campus this man was accurately knowledgeable concerning the rules, regulations, and possibilities of exceptions that existed in all the various colleges of the university. Not only was he careful not to interfere with the functioning of the psychologists on the staff, but he was highly supportive of them. As I look back, it is clear to me that Bailey was a great and wise man who through his policies and philosophy greatly influenced the whole further development of the Psychological and Counseling Center.

In addition to the director, the early staff of the center consisted of three psychologists: one who acted as associate director, another who was primarily engaged in a group reading and study skills program, and a third who was to be concerned mainly with the emotional problems of the students and with the training of a relatively large group of so-called faculty counselors. There was also a graduate assistant who was in charge of testing. Almost without exception, the faculty counselors, who were carefully selected by the deans of their colleges and by members of the counseling center's staff, were very superior teachers. They were carefully trained and supervised by the staff of the center, they learned how and when to make referrals to the central staff, and they in fact made them. These counselors probably represented the first carefully selected and highly trained group of paraprofessionals in any counseling center. Over the years they contributed importantly to the general faculty acceptance of professional psychological counseling as distinguished from the general counseling that had existed previously.

Because of this increase in acceptance, it was possible over time to replace these faculty counselors with psychologists who were or who soon became fully competent clinical counselors in the Williamson sense. In some cases it was also less expensive to employ psychologists, because some of the faculty counselors had advanced to associate or full professorships in their own areas. Since we carried a proportionate share of their salaries in our budget, they actually cost the center more than new Ph.D's in psychology. This brief description of our own birth and adolescent strivings should make it clear that the selection of a staff should be consonant with the general conditions that exist at any particular time.

That some specialization was involved in our early development is evident from the description above. In addition, I was employed to replace a psychiatrist who spent a half-day each week at the center and who wrote voluminous reports on the clients he interviewed, primarily from an analytical viewpoint. It soon became evident, however, that clients rarely had nicely segregated problems. Emotionally disturbed students could also be having difficulties with their study procedures and grades as well as with the selections of curriculum and career. The analytic approach did not seem to be very appropriate for such an admixture of interacting problems, and the Rogerian approach was also largely ineffective. The problem-solving approach of Williamson seemed to be, in general, most appropriate, with two very critical differences. I personally could not accept (and in our circumstances it was not necessary to accept) Williamson's notion that all seriously emotionally disturbed clients should be referred to a psychiatrist. In my prior experience with psychiatrists, I had not been overly impressed with their astuteness, their conceptual competence or their adherence to sound scientific principles. I was also negatively impressed with their dogmatism. Consequently, a decision evolved that the professional staff of the counseling service would deal with all the students' problems in an integrated way and that referrals would be made only when there was reason for believing that clients had a strictly medical condition. The other policy that evolved gradually and without fanfare was that all counseling would be strictly confidential unless students gave their clear-cut permission for any of the contents of counseling to be disclosed or unless it was necessary to hospitalize forcibly clients because they were functioning in a way that was imminently dangerous to their own lives or to the lives of others. It is not quite true to say that this policy evolved, because, in fact, it was there from the start. But it was clearly enunciated only at a later time when it became necessary to do so. This general way of viewing counseling, along with a primary emphasis on individual counseling and therapy (except for the group reading and study skills program), led to the selection of staff members who were willing and able to function in a variety of ways with a variety of clients.

Closely related to this was the viewpoint that no one had yet developed a sufficiently supported overall theory of counseling or therapy. Unfortunately, it appears that this is still the case today. This opinion almost mandated selection of staff members who were not too enamored of any one narrow viewpoint and who appeared to be sufficiently open-minded that they would at least learn from the mistakes they made with their clients. Since the already existing staff of the counseling center also possessed some degree of open-mindedness, there were a few occasions on which persons were employed who had had a particular type of training. For example, two persons who had worked with Rogers were employed. One of these counselors was not personally as strongly wedded to Rogers's philosophical viewpoint and technique as the other. Thus, that counselor was more flexible and was able to modify both the viewpoint and the technique as more experience with clients was gained. The other counselor had a stronger personal commitment, was not as readily able to do this, and consequently had many clients who did not return after a first interview. There resulted a direct conflict in the counselor between clinical experience and viewpoint, and after a few years this counselor resigned.

What all this means is that the counseling center itself must be very clear in terms of its own viewpoints, policies, functions that the prospective staff member will be expected to perform. A center must decide whether it wishes to emphasize individual counseling and therapy, group counseling, outreach programs, workshops, research, graduate teaching, or whatever. In this connection there is another guiding principle that we have quite closely adhered to: anything we do must prove its worth in terms of contributing toward helping clients make effective use of their academic opportunities. It is not enough that what is done appears to satisfy some so-called student need or even makes a student happier. As someone said at the most recent national meeting of directors of counseling centers, "The only real student needs are those which are related to academic performance." Most of the other supposed needs are popular ones that are related only to entertainment value or to an uninformed search for "magic keys." Particularly in days of tight budgets, as most of us are now experiencing, higher university administrators will not long support unproductive frills even if hundreds of students indicate their desire to partake of them. If one wishes to spend significant staff time on such things as sensitivity groups, encounter groups, Gestalt groups, weight reduction groups, and anxiety reduction groups, or on such individual endeavors as desensitization or biofeedback procedures for tension reduction and headache relief, one should be prepared to set these programs up in such a manner that the participants will not in fact be harmed and that the programs can be evaluated objectively in terms of their contributions to the students' success in their regular academic courses.

Since most counseling center staff members will usually be involved in other activities in addition to counseling and therapy, it is also important to consider the particular kinds of training and experience that prospective staff members have had and their present and probable future special interests. In addition to setting minimum qualifications, the center needs to answer for itself some very important questions. Should Ph.D.'s in Clinical or in Counseling Psychology be employed? Is it possible to find individuals who have had both kinds of training? Does it make any difference whether this training has been in a Department of

Psychology or a College of Education? Should any social workers or psychiatrists be employed as a part of the center's staff? What should be the mix of Ph.D.-level staff with master's-level staff, with interns or advanced practicum students? How many of the staff members should engage in teaching and/or research? Should the director or assistant director of an agency as well as those engaged in teaching also be expected to continue to function as counselors and therapists?

There are no easy answers to such questions, and the best answers will probably vary somewhat from one agency to another and from one time to another in the development of an agency. From what has been written previously it is clear that the answers to all these questions ought to be related to the general goals and philosophy of the counseling center. Our broad goals at the University of Illinois have always been to provide the highest possible quality of integrated counseling and therapy services to clients; to provide excellent teaching and solid practicum and internship supervision for graduate students in the Department of Psychology; and to produce a reasonable amount of sound research related to counseling and therapy or to supervise relevant master's theses and doctoral dissertations. From the time the center was first formed, the director and associate director continued to see clients on at least a half-time basis. An instructor, a researcher, or a director needs continued first-hand experience with clients instead of just using secondary sources, highly fragmented and often incoherent research, or almost pure speculation, if good counseling, good teaching, good research, and good administration are to occur.

The University of Illinois Counseling Center has not always employed only people at the Ph.D. level. There have been and there still are some staff members who have their master's plus. However, all of these persons are the kind of individuals who could readily learn from further experience and in-service training. Three of our present seventeen staff members are in this category: two spend part of their time in our group reading and study skills program. The third, Miriam Sperber, had to retire officially some three years ago, but has been on a year-to-year appointment since then; she has been and continues to be one of the most effective therapists on our staff. We have also regularly utilized second- or third-year practicum students in psychology and from two to four full-time interns. It is extremely important for the practicum students and the interns that a sufficient amount of time is provided for genuinely adequate instruction and case supervision by experienced staff members.

At present we are actually providing some four different practicum experiences for graduate students in psychology. All of the persons who are in charge of these practica have rank either in the Department of Psychology or in the counseling center itself. This is also true for Associate Director, Thomas N. Ewing, who for many years has headed the research efforts of the center and has coordinated the research of individual staff members. Normally he has also directly supervised the work of from two to four half-time research assistants. It is his extremely calm and competent way of handling this part of his work that has made it possible for us to produce some really significant research. In a similar fashion Dr. Robert P. Larsen, in addition to his counseling work on our staff, has been in charge of our career information materials and has seen to it, with the help of either graduate assistants or clerical workers, that this material is kept both up-to-date and in order. I mention these particular names at this point because Dr. Ewing, Dr. Larsen, and I will have retired shortly before this handbook's publication and because I wish to express my hope that at least the most important elements of their work will be carried on. It seems clear, then, that some staff members should be employed who will be expected to perform other, more specialized functions in addition to their counseling loads.

Some of the other questions posed above have possible answers that are more controversial. If a counseling center provides integrated services, so that a given counselor helps with all the problems—educational-vocational and emotional-personal—that a student may have, and if clients are assigned randomly to practicum students, interns, and staff members, then there is no need for formal intake interviews. This eliminates one of the possible reasons for employing social workers. There is even some question as to whether a social worker would be the most appropriate person to perform intake interviews in centers where clients are referred to special counselors or programs. Under such circumstances a highly accurate assessment of the client's difficulties must be made during the intake interview so that the client can be referred to the most appropriate counselor or group. Accurate assessment is one of the most complex and difficult aspects of counseling and therapy, and it often needs to be an ongoing process, at least during the first four or five interviews. It would seem that the most highly educated and experienced counselor-therapist ought to perform this function. But this function is not particularly prized by experienced counselors, the usual result being that intake interviewing is done on a rotational basis or by the least well trained and the least experienced persons on the staff. In turn, the counselor to whom the client is assigned must reassess the client's difficulties, all of which leads to an inefficient use of staff and funds. To state it very generally, the nature of the tasks performed by a psychological and counseling center are not such as to utilize the special talents and training of social workers. Of course, there may always be special circumstances in which an unusual background of experience could justify the employment of such persons.

Whether a prospective employee should have a Ph.D. in Psychology or Education or a Doctor of Psychology degree or Doctor of Education degree may be a somewhat more complex question. However, if one simply considers averages, the preference probably should go to individuals who have a Ph.D. from a Department of Psychology that provides training in both so-called clinical and so-called counseling functions. The qualifier *so-called* is used because, in my judgment, good therapy cannot take place in the absence of good counseling and vice versa. A somewhat similar situation exists with respect to the employment of persons with master's degrees. If acceptance by the academic staff within the university is deemed desirable (and I think it is, if for no other reason than that the teaching faculty is the most powerful group in a university), and if tenure possibilities or other forms of job security are considered desirable, then it is certainly preferable to hire counselors at the doctoral level.

The question remains as to whether the degree should be in psychology or in education. Generally speaking, Colleges of Education quite properly require that their graduate students know more about the history and philosophy of education and related subjects; the result is that their students have not had as much strictly psychological training as those in Departments of Psychology. Admission procedures for students in guidance and counseling programs within Departments of Education also tend not to be as highly selective as those for Departments of Psychology.

The strictly psychological training in Colleges of Education tends to be somewhat less broad and somewhat less intensive than in Departments of Psychology. Thus, *other things being equal,* preference should be given to persons trained in a Department of Psychology if they are to be expected to function in the integrated fashion that has been described earlier.

There are, of course, always exceptions. For example, if a counseling center wishes to conduct a reading and study skills program, it may be necessary and desirable to seek a person who has had the requisite type of training that more often than not is provided in Colleges of Education. It would be ideal if such prospective staff members could also have had additional training in behavior disorders and related areas so that they could quickly learn to provide integrated counseling services. Whether the most desirable prospective staff members should have received their training in a counseling psychology program, in a clinical psychology program, or in a program that provides training in both clinical and counseling functions again is dependent upon the kinds of services they will be expected to render. My own view is that in actual practice it is necessary to be able to function in both ways if one is to render the best services to clients. The human being, after all, is probably the most integratively functioning ecological system in the world. Consequently, altering any one part of this system may have profound desirable or undesirable effects on some other part of this system. In addition, it is all too abundantly clear that not so much is really known in a scientific sense about either counseling or psychotherapy except that any student who is accepted into any of the major graduate colleges and is reasonably well motivated will be able to learn to function well in both areas. In my judgment the APA has made an important historical error in separating clinical and counseling into two divisions. I expect the separation exists because of political pressures rather than any logical educational or scientific reasons. Fortunately, there are a number of universities that do produce persons who are able to provide counseling and psychotherapy to a whole individual.

At the beginning of this chapter I indicated that I would try to speak to the point, forthrightly, with regard to any of my opinions. Interestingly, I have some hesitancy in doing this when considering the relationship of psychiatrists to a psychological and counseling center. On our campus this relationship for a number of years has been a very good one. And on occasion the psychiatrists have provided very badly needed services. Nevertheless, if the choice on a given campus came down to deciding whether to employ the average psychiatrist or the average psychologist trained in a clinical-counseling program, my strong recommendation would be in favor of the psychologist. Because of the somewhat unjustified professional respect accorded all physicians, including psychiatrists, and because of the more effective way they have publicly promoted a belief in their professional expertise, there is a tendency on the part of the public to believe that psychiatrists are better trained and more competent as psychotherapists. The real facts are that psychiatrists are medical doctors first of all and that an extremely large part of their medical school training is designed to prepare them to treat physical ailments. The question as to whether acute emotional and behavioral disturbances are physical in nature is controversial. There is some concern that medication for such conditions is far too widely used. However, there are occasions when it is highly desirable to be able to refer the rare students who are so acutely anxious or so psychotic that they cannot profit from psychotherapy alone. Clinical-counseling psychologists, in contrast, have had much training in learning, in perception, in aptitude, interest, and personality measurement as well as in the nature of attitudes and beliefs and the ways in which these can be altered by counseling or psychotherapy. In addition, they have had considerably more training in research, which makes them less inclined to become committed to a single viewpoint or technique. Instead, in their didactic practicum and internship training they are usually trained in the utilization of a number of different psychotherapeutic viewpoints and in a considerable variety of counseling or therapeutic techniques. Because of the research nature of their training they are also more inclined to examine and evaluate the practical outcomes of their procedures.

What this implies for the university as a whole is twofold: a trained psychologist can supply services to a much larger range of students and can deal effectively with the large number of interacting problems that individuals have, but it is desirable to have some psychiatric help available for the minority of individuals who may profit from medication. Thus, in general it would make sense to have a relatively large clinical-counseling staff and a relatively small psychiatric staff.

If we assume that the university's higher administration and the counseling center are both very clear about philosophy and functions, there is still the problem of determining whether a given person will best be able to fulfill the needs of a given counseling center. First of all, this requires both forthrightness and honesty on the part of the staff and the director. Applicants need to be clearly informed of the nature of the duties they will be expected to perform, the provisions for advancement in both salary and rank, and the conditions of job security, as well as the nature of fringe benefits.

Conversely, the staff of the counseling center also needs an opportunity to make their own judgments about the qualifications of applicants. In addition to careful examination of the standard credentials, including letters or recommendations and possibly phone calls to the recommenders, it is often useful to have applicants make a relatively informal presentation of some research they have done, possibly their dissertations, and of their work with some typical client. To the greatest possible extent, this should be conducted in a friendly atmosphere in which the staff members and the applicants can freely ask questions.

Since even psychologists are fallible on occasion and make mistakes in selection, and since new staff members could and should develop questions about the manner in which the center operates, it may be useful to discuss the problems related to the retention or nonretention of staff members.

Retention of Staff Members

If the selection of a staff member is accomplished in some conformity with the preceding suggestions, a very large part of the task of retaining a staff member will already have been accomplished. The initial question that needs to be addressed is whether it is desirable to attempt to retain staff members. My own answer to this question is an unequivocal yes. Probably the soundest research finding on counseling and therapy is that experience does make a difference in relationship to counseling outcomes. In addition, if one is not forced to attempt to publicize services in a marketing manner by capitalizing either on student fads or psychological fads (such as Gestalt groups, meditation groups, self-hypnosis groups, sexuality groups, assertiveness training groups and the like), the center must depend ultimately on word-of-mouth recommendations from satisfied clients and on the reputation the center is able to build over time with the academic deans' offices, the campus affairs offices, and, perhaps most importantly, the faculty. To put it simply, it just takes time for individual staff members to earn a good reputation. If turnover is too high, staff members themselves will have no time to improve with experience, and it will be impossible to establish any very solid reputations either within the student population or in the other parts of the university.

Because new staff members are ordinarily employed at much lower salaries than older staff members, there is a temptation on occasion to react to tightened budgets by employing less well trained persons or by anticipating or even promoting a rapid turnover of staff. Industry has long since discovered that rapid turnover is highly expensive in the long run. If it became necessary for a center to function on a reduced budget, the reputation and respect of the center would be promoted in the long run if it refused to lower the overall quality of its services and instead provided them to fewer clients. Under these circumstances a center could readily recover when budgets became more favorable. Under contrary circumstances, the center could have developed a reputation as a kind of extracurricular frill that did not contribute significantly to the educational mission of the university.

If one wishes to retain a professional-level counseling staff, it is essential that salary level and salary advancement be at least directly equivalent to that earned by psychologists who are engaged only in teaching and research. For example, if there is a general provision for increasing salaries by 5 percent, then the counseling center itself should be able to increase the salaries of its staff members by the same 5 percent. Even under these conditions the counseling staff members will probably be at some slight disadvantage. Because of the nature of their primary duties, they will be neither able nor expected to produce the same amount of research as persons employed for these purposes. Through their publications the latter group will become more widely known and may receive more outside offers. On most occasions this means some increase in salary for those faculty members if the university wishes to retain them. There seems to be no genuinely adequate way to compensate for this factor. Fortunately, most staff members most of the time come to accept this as a natural fact of life.

The manner in which advances in salary and/or rank are accomplished is of considerable importance. One might think that the best way to assign salary increases would be on the basis of recommendations from an elected advisory committee. This procedure has certain fairly obvious advantages. Whatever dissatisfactions are produced would be shared not only by the director or associate director, but also by the elected members of the advisory committee. However, this very spreading of possible onus to other staff members can create divisions and possible hostilities within the staff. There is probably always some amount of politicking that goes on within a staff, but it can become more acute and can lead to the formation of small cliques or parties when an election is to be held. At the University of Illinois Counseling Center there have been at least three occasions during the past fifteen years when the staff was given an opportunity to recommend how salaries should be distributed. On one occasion in the late 1960s there was agitation by a few staff members for the election of such an advisory committee. It was clear to me during the few weeks preceding open discussion with the staff that concerned small groups were forming. A general staff meeting was arranged as soon as possible, and the whole problem was openly discussed. A very large majority of the staff voted to continue the usual practice of having the director and associate director make such decisions. The same thing happened on another occasion when the university administration encouraged the utilization of advisory committees for such purposes. Without a committee, considerable responsibility is placed on the associate director and the director. But properly exercised, this responsibility may eliminate to a considerable extent the development of intrastaff disharmony. This is not to say that all staff members are always satisfied with the amounts of their salary increases. A relatively low degree of acute dissatisfaction is probably all that one can reasonably hope for. In terms of our own staff retention rate, which will be mentioned briefly at the end of this general discussion, our procedure seems to have functioned quite well.

The determination of salary increases would be much easier if there were a way of measuring, even crudely, the efficiency and effectiveness of counseling and therapy. Presumably, when clear-cut errors have been made in the selection of staff members, one fairly quickly becomes aware that a mistake was made. In other cases, at least two or three years are often required before enough information is gleaned about staff members' performance to make adequate judgments.

With this problem in mind, a client survey form was constructed at our center early in the second semester of 1976 and was mailed to some 1,900 clients in the early spring. Among other things it requested a rating of the expertness of the counselor in general and in particular areas and asked the client to compare the usefulness of the counseling received with the usefulness of an average academic course not in the client's major field. The somewhat surprising finding was that clients on the average rated counseling as more useful than the course. It is also clear from the mean scores of various counselors that there were considerable individual differences between counselors. On the whole, the results of the survey (which was returned by some 65 percent of the clients) were quite favorable. There were also answers to open-ended questions that were very frankly and specifically critical. All of these results were fed back to the individual counselors, and the director received his own ratings as well as the mean scores of the other ratings with the counselors unidentified. Because of some of the critical comments, the staff voted later to make the names of individual counselors available to the director. For the present year a similar survey is planned, and in this case the results for the first semester will be made available to the director and will be utilized as one factor in determining individual salary increases. In general, the survey results corresponded very closely to the judgments of counselor effectiveness and efficiency made by the associate director and director earlier.

Increases in rank present an even more difficult problem. As indicated at the beginning of this chapter, adequate salaries and adequate job security are the basic elements in retaining staff. Real job security in most university settings can be provided in only one of two ways, either by making it possible for a staff member to attain tenure in a teaching department or in a counseling center itself or by having staff members become nonacademic civil service employees. A kind of in-between situation, in which the counselors are designated as academic professionals, is probably somewhat more prestigious than being a nonacademic employee, but it provides less security than a civil service position. As an academic professional, the counselor really serves at the pleasure of the higher administrators within the university. Obviously, the best arrangement would make it possible for the staff member to earn academic tenure. Usually this would mean the possibility of advancement to the associate professorship level.

Since most teaching departments, such as a Department of Psychology, recommend rank increase primarily or even exclusively on the basis of published research, the counselor who has a split appointment with a teaching department is at a disadvantage, unless the teaching department establishes different criteria for persons on such split appointments. Counselor-therapists are usually expected to devote a major proportion of their time to service activities and so have much less time to carry out and publish research than do department members who simply teach. If the teaching department is willing to establish criteria for advancement that take this time constraint into account, then there is no problem, and rank within the teaching department is a highly desirable status. However, since a department's national reputation depends largely upon the amount of published research, a department head may be loath to take such a step.

Under such conditions the fairest and most desirable solution consists in having academic rank with tenure possibilities available within the counseling center itself. In this circumstance it is obviously necessary for the counseling center to establish criteria for rank advancement that will be acceptable to higher administrators. This would ordinarily involve a stated number of publications in referred journals over a given period of years and/or substantiated excellence in teaching and counseling.

Unless counselors' salaries are equitable with those of their teaching peers, and unless some means for tenure possibility are provided, the counselors and eventually the whole counseling service will certainly be looked upon as second- or even third-class citizens, even though the counselors themselves may be first-class clinical-counseling psychologists who, if they wished, could secure equally well-paying and prestigious teaching positions.

Once the basic considerations of salary and job security are satisfied, other factors begin to affect staff retention. How well staff members like what they are expected to do, how well they feel they have accomplished these tasks, how much positive feedback they get from their clients, how well they personally get along with other staff members, and the extent to which they seem to be appreciated by coworkers—all are conditions affecting counselors' comfort and desire to remain on the staff. If counselors expect—or are expected—to have a lot of individual counseling, but then are saddled with a requirement to write up very long reports, to participate in many workshops, to run so-called developmental groups, or to spend considerable time on negotiating their activities, or to punch a cost-benefit clock, they will not be very happy. Satisfaction will be promoted if counselors have freedom to try out new approaches, new techniques, or new ideas of any kind (even if they are required to do some adequate screening of clients and an adequate evaluation of the effects of their procedures).

The importance of these factors was brought to my attention when I asked a number of our staff members, both younger and older ones, what it was about our setting that contributed to their having remained or wishing to remain in our center. All of them concurred in saying that it was the fact that they could devote their time to working with clients; they did not have to write long case reports, nor did they have to serve on a lot of unproductive committees or task forces. I was not surprised that they mentioned this, but I was a little surprised by the emphasis that they put on it. Earlier in our history, counselors were expected to write fairly lengthy reports of their interviews, the idea being that these could be used for research purposes or would be helpful if a client decided later on to see another counselor. Experience taught us that clients differed so much and counselors differed so much in what they reported that the data supplied by such reports was essentially useless for research purposes. Consequently, at present our counselors write down only enough notes on a half sheet of paper to remind them personally of what has been happening with the client. In some instances this may be just a few sentences. And yet in most cases it is enough to remind the counselor of the whole context of the student's problems or is even useful if the client should decide to see another counselor at a later time.

One of the most valuable offices in our center is not an office at all: it is the library and coffee room, which is private for our staff. Small groups of counselors meet there from time to time during the day for a quick cup of coffee between appointments or during their free time. A great amount of easy and informal consultation regarding difficult clients occurs at such times. Questions and complaints are openly transmitted. In time the different staff members also get to know each other well, both professionally and personally. Not all of the conversations are about business. Two staff members could be discussing a client, while two others might be talking about the lousy job some mechanic did with their car or how good the fishing was in Minnesota. This kind of ongoing communication is more conducive to staff members' really getting to know and appreciate each other other than are arranged social get-togethers.

Since counseling center staff members, applicants for positions, and even directors are not perfect predictors, mistakes will be made on occasion. Sometimes employment is given to persons who simply do not appreciate the philosophy of the center, who are not as competent as had been anticipated, or who for many other reasons simply do not fit in. Under such circumstances it is both kind and necessary to discuss with the staff member whatever difficulties exist and to make whatever changes are possible. If either the staff member or the director is unwilling or unable to make appropriate changes, an unhappy outcome could ensue. In my thirty-six years with the counseling center there was only one occasion when it became necessary for me to suggest to the staff member that he/she would probably be happier in some other position. This occurred because of repeated violations of confidence and questionable ethical procedures. In all other instances the poorly selected staff members decided on their own to seek other positions. One can only speculate about the real reasons for such moves. It is likely that the staff members themselves recognize that they were not as competent as the others, that they discovered there was quiet staff disapproval of some of their voiced procedures or attitudes, or that they simply felt they would be more successful and more appreciated in a different setting. Staff members were also lost through what could be considered normal attrition over such a long period of time. Two of our early staff members died, one retired three years ago, and three more are retiring this year.

It is reasonable to ask what the retention rate has been at the Psychological and Counseling Center at the University of Illinois on the Urbana-Champaign campus. Our staff retention rate over the years appears to have been reasonably good: six have served for more than twenty-five years, ten have been on staff for more than fifteen years, and eighteen have functioned for five years or more. During this time a total of twenty-eight staff members served for five years or less; and of this last number there were eleven persons who held postinternships or similar positions in which it was never anticipated that they would remain longer than a year or two.

Influence of Administrative Structure on Staff

Unless a psychological and counseling center is administratively responsible to the highest administrative officer on campus (who presumably will be equally concerned with all parts of the campus), there is a likelihood that a center will be gently or not so gently pushed in the direction of the experiences and biases of the vice chancellors to whom it reports. Thus, if a counseling center is responsible to a vice chancellor for campus affairs or to a dean of students, it is probable that the push will be in the direction that fits that vice chancellor's view of student problems. Unless that vice chancellor happens by chance to be a clinical-counseling psychologist or unless he/she is unusually open to information and factual evidence, he/she will not make a very sharp distinction between the kinds of counseling that used to go on in deans of students' offices or the kinds of programs that respond irresponsibly to students wants as influenced by popular fads. He/she will not make any very clear distinction between the kinds of "counseling" that can be supplied by student peers, residence hall assistants, or other campus affairs people who are relatively untrained as psychologists and those services which can effectively be supplied only by highly trained professionals. Under these circumstances the director of the counseling service will either be in conflict with the vice chancellor or will need to have the counseling staff conform, at least to some extent, with a resulting loss of time for the rendering of genuinely professional services. If this superior officer is in fact also in charge of disciplinary and regulatory functions, the problems or conflicts could readily be compounded.

If on a given campus some high official is charged with the general problem of administrative organization or reorganization, it is unfortunately too easy for such an individual to decide that all persons rendering service of any kind to students, other than teaching as such, ought to be responsible to the same head. Such a viewpoint simply fails to take into account the particularized functions of the different service agencies. The health service, for example, might be responsible to a vice chancellor for campus affairs without significant problems because the medical profession generally is perceived as a highly professional group, and no attempt is made to influence the manner in which they function. Unfortunately, such is not yet the case with clinical counselors, since many persons, from barkeepers and kindly janitors to lawyers and ministers, perform some kinds of "counseling" functions. What probably is needed is a new semantic term that could help make such a differentiation easier than it now is.

Ideally, then, a psychological and counseling center ought to be directly responsible to the chancellor or similar officer in the university. If this cannot be managed, for any one of a number of historical reasons, and if the center sees its main mission as that of aiding students to take full advantage of their academic opportunities, it would make most sense to have the center responsible to a vice chancellor for academic affairs. This would be especially true if the center in fact contributed significantly in the teaching program and in research. Of course, there are always exceptions to general rules. But, it is important to make certain that these are exceptions with respect to particular persons and not with respect to principle.

In general, then—but particularly in times of tight budgets—it is essential that counseling centers provide the kinds of services that, on the basis of research findings, can be shown to contribute significantly to the academic and career success of students. At our present stage of knowledge this can best be accomplished by a carefully selected and well-retained staff of high-quality clinical-counseling psychologists who provide integrated individual counseling and therapy to clients who have significant problems and to faculty members who teach them.

8

PARAPROFESSIONAL AND SUPPORT PERSONNEL

Philip Ron Spinelli and Ted Packard

UNIVERSITY OF UTAH

The Student Paraprofessional: A New Approach

A PERSPECTIVE

For over a decade college and university counseling centers have been undergoing a process of evolution as regard their *raison d'être*. Reflecting the demand for a reexamination of the entire higher educational enterprise during the "tumultuous sixties," counseling centers have found themselves increasingly confronted by new demands for varied services from an expanded clientele. No longer are counselors being asked to remedy the psychological ills of a few troubled students. Rather, they are being asked to potentiate the abilities of all students. No longer are counselors expected to wait within the peaceful confines of their consulting rooms for a troubled clientele to present themselves for help. Rather, they are encouraged to leave the office—indeed, the building—and reach out to a student population that includes many who have been traditionally unavailable for psychological intervention, for example, the minorities, the poor, and the returning homemakers. Through attempts to grapple with the increased complexity of demand, it has become clear that traditional models of service delivery are inadequate. Specifically, the older remedial model has had to be expanded to include a vigorous proactive commitment to the developmental needs of all students and to the prevention of obstacles to growth within the college environment.

Given this expanded mission, counseling centers have had to develop new methods for implementing services. Basic to the question of delivering services was the question "Who can and should deliver them?" Traditional thinking quickly answered that only trained professionals could and should. Unfortunately, such an answer seemed untenable and on closer analysis somewhat unreasonable. Services rendered solely by professionals were untenable on the grounds that service needs exceeded time available to meet them. Heavy case loads, waiting lists, and the like have been part of the human service provider's working situation for many years. On the other hand, it seemed unreasonable to continue to utilize professionals when there was a growing body of evidence that non-professional persons, given specific training and supervision, were effectively engaging in activities and services once carried out exclusively by professionals. The impetus for this strategy grew out of the antipoverty programs of the 1960s, the OEO model of "service to indigenous people by indigenous people," and the subsequent "new careers movement" (Pearl & Riessman, 1965). These programs offered employment and concurrent education as a way out of poverty. Evidence appeared that the poor, minorities, and others could be trained to provide effective service in community action programs (Gartner, 1969; Gordon, 1965), mental health settings (Carkhuff & Truax, 1965; Nicoletti & Flater-Benz, 1974), public school programs (Hamburg and Varenhorst, 1972), and a host of other human services once rendered only by credentialed personnel.

The paraprofessional movement, as it is generally referred to, is unquestionably a revolutionary approach to the delivery of a wide range of human services. Born out of the crises of the 1960s, the paraprofessional appears headed for an alive, robust adolescence, struggling to achieve a semblance of identity as a legitimate service agent. Such legitimacy seems to be gaining, particularly among college counseling centers. In addition to the obvious advantage of more service to more people, Delworth (1972) has provided additional rationale for using student service agents:

1. Student paraprofessionals make possible an extension of the work of the professionals by freeing them for more appropriate tasks.
2. A paraprofessional program offers services to students by their peers.
3. Paraprofessional programming provides the opportunity for regular representative input into the system by students.

Taken collectively, these arguments speak cogently to the concept that a student paraprofessional program will relate as much to the needs of the counseling center (and the professional) as to the clients that are served. Paraprofessionals are seen as potentially powerful *additive* components that might be expected not only to contribute to the professional's growth, but also to influence services in innovative ways.

The purpose of this section is to provide a framework within which the reader might begin to consider the utilization of paraprofessional resources within a college or university counseling center. While the goal is not to provide the reader with a step-by-step manual for the development and implementation of paraprofessional programs, it is hoped that significant parameters and related issues can be identified and discussed.

One of the difficulties in discussing paraprofessional programming lies in the definition of the term. Who is a paraprofessional? In casting about for an operational definition specific enough to be useful and inclusive enough to relate to the diverse roles and settings reported in the literature, we again turned to Delworth (1972):

A paraprofessional is defined as a person without extended professional training who is specifically selected, trained and given ongoing supervision to perform some part of a portion of the tasks usually performed by the human services professional. This does not include the offering of support services, i.e., clerical, as a major function.

Embodied in this definition are several specific ingredients that are essential in defining the role of the paraprofessional: *selection, training, supervision,* and *participation* in professional activity. These concepts will serve as topical headings within which student paraprofessionals will be considered as they relate to the role of provider of human services within a college or university counseling center. In addition, the evaluation of such programs as well as incentives needed to attract and retain students in such positions will be discussed. Finally, some of the larger issues that need to be recognized as potential hazards when professionals and paraprofessionals share the helping enterprise will be examined.

SELECTION AND TRAINING

A discussion of selection and training issues needs to start with a careful consideration of the task that the student paraprofessional is expected to carry out. Considerable time and energy should go into analyzing a potential paraprofessional activity in terms of specific skills needed. This requires operationally defining vague terms: for example, "establish rapport" becomes "communicate accurate empathy." In addition, it is important to make clear that specific knowledge and information will be essential in performing such duties (for example, referral sources or drug information). What are the salient client characteristics? How do these characteristics (for example, minority group membership) relate to the student paraprofessional, for example, a minority student? Do values and attitudes affect successful implementation of potentially controversial programs (for example, birth control information)? In short, a thorough analysis of the demands related to a specific program must be considered prior to any consideration of who should implement them.

Selection decisions and training issues must be discussed jointly since they are reciprocally related. Decisions affecting one will directly influence the other. In some instances considerable time and effort are expanded on selection procedures that identify persons already possessing necessary skills. Training needs would presumably then be minimal. This is analogous to the "professional model" of job placement, in which selection committees review credentials and resumés in hopes of identifying candidates with the best fit between skills already available and demand characteristics of the job. At the other extreme of job selection (what might be referred to as a "nonprofessional model") there is no assumption of prior skills, and selection procedures focus on attempting to identify those persons with the best potential for training. Since the paraprofessional usually fits this latter category, selection techniques have often reflected this approach.

Recently, selection procedures have become more and more behavioral in nature, demanding that applicants demonstrate some potential. Thus, simulation experiences asking persons to approximate the specific skills that will be called for on the job (a mock interview, for example) are being utilized. Group interviews have afforded a sample of applicants' interaction behavior that is useful in ascertaining leadership skills, cooperative qualities, and so on.

A recent approach to selection/training issues emphasizes sequence. The above discussion presents a straightforward model calling for definition of the task, followed by selection procedure and ending with training. An emerging model being increasingly used among student paraprofessional programs employs training as a preferred mode of selection. This "paraprofessional model" assumes that providing systematic training in basic dimensions of the helping process is the first step in selecting paraprofessionals. This thinking, of course, is the direct outgrowth of considerable research demonstrating that previously unskilled persons can be systematically trained to provide effective service to client populations (Carkhuff, 1969; Ivey, 1971; Kagan, 1972). Thus, many programs have initiated intensive, relatively short-term skills-training workshops as a first step in identifying potential student paraprofessionals. Such workshops have the distinct advantage of providing a significant sample of behavior from which to make selection decisions, as well as producing individuals with specific skills that will be directly applicable to human service activity.

An interesting variation of the above core training concept that lends itself well to a college setting has been the introduction of a formal helping-skills class for undergraduates. Students are invited to participate in such a class in order to (1) increase their interpersonal effectiveness, (2) gain additional insight for career decisions by experiencing the helping profession's process, or (3) receive specific training necessary to participate in a variety of student paraprofessional programs. The advantage of this educational format is that there is "something for everybody." Students gain valuable skills, academic credit, and some insights whether or not they end up working in a paraprofessional position. Agencies that use paraprofessionals have a pool of persons with basic training in helping skills and can focus on training for specific tasks.

While the approach to selection and training will vary in both sequence and investment of energy, it is clear that the trend is toward the more behavioral methodologies for both processes. The emphasis is on implementing programs that develop behavioral skills and demonstrated competencies.

SUPERVISION

The development and implementation of a student paraprofessional program must take place within the framework of a viable supervisory commitment by those professionals who will be involved with paraprofessionals. Supervision serves three broad functions: (1) ensuring that a quality service is rendered to the agency clientele, (2) developing a climate of respect and openness within which the paraprofessional can be expected to grow, (3) providing ongoing learning experiences that will increase the paraprofessional's effectiveness and experience.

Implied in each of these broad functions are a number of specific characteristics of an effective supervisor. First, the supervisor should be closely involved with the activity or program in which the paraprofessional is engaged. Ideally, the professional should have had direct experience carrying out the functions required of the paraprofessional. Second, the supervisor needs to be accessible routinely to the paraprofessional and to have developed training procedures detailing paraprofessional-client interactions via tapes, observations, and the like. In addition, the professional should be skilled in evaluation methodology and able to develop assessment techniques that will provide assurance that service goals are being met. It is important that the supervisory relationship promote mutual acceptance and trust, that the professional supervisor communicate his or her value for the paraprofessional effort, and that feedback be shared in a constructive, supportive manner.

Finally, the professional supervisor must not only possess a high skill level, but, more importantly, be willing to share such skills with paraprofessionals through in-service training efforts. The supervisor not only provides a powerful influence as a model, but actively seeks to impart new learning and to encourage increased competence as a natural extension of the relationship with the paraprofessional.

Formats for supervision vary, depending on time constraints and number of paraprofessionals involved. Ideally, each paraprofessional should meet individually with his or her supervisor on a weekly basis. Where several paraprofessionals are involved in the same or similar endeavors, small group supervision has proved satisfactory. The most important aspect of the supervisory experience is that it occur routinely. Since this represents a significant time commitment by the professional, it is essential that agency support is explicit and that supervisory activity is given priority equal to other agency efforts.

PARTICIPATION IN PROFESSIONAL ACTIVITY

Delworth's working definition of a paraprofessional (1972) makes it explicit that paraprofessionals share in the real enterprise of helping (that is, offering at least a portion of direct services to clientele) rather than to function merely in clerical, secretarial, or other support capacities to professional activity. To what extent is this happening? Research surveys of college and university counseling centers have revealed widespread use of paraprofessionals in a variety of activities (Geer, 1971; Crane, Anderson, & Kirchner, 1975; Steenland, 1973). Such studies have provided evidence of the effective use of student paraprofessionals in such activities as academic advising (Brown, 1965), minority counseling (Gravitz & Woods, 1976), peer counseling (Wolff, 1969; Hauer, 1973), and crisis intervention programs (Dana, Heynen & Burdette, 1974; Delworth, Rudow, & Taub, 1972). Thus, it would seem that student paraprofessionals are gaining widespread acceptance as human service providers to the college population. At the same time, however, many of the surveys mentioned above revealed a consistent attitude among counseling center directors reflecting specific limitations on paraprofessional activity. Strong disapproval, for instance, has been expressed for utilizing student paraprofessionals in such areas as marriage counseling, sex therapy, or testing and dealing with pathological symptons (Crane, Anderson, & Kirchner, 1975).

EVALUATION

Paraprofessional programming in no way implies a reduction in an agency's commitment to providing quality service, for paraprofessionals should be employed only in services and activities in which they have demonstrated competence. Fortunately, an evaluation component has been a significant part of many of the paraprofessional programs reported in the literature. The results have generally supported the notion of quality service being rendered by paraprofessionals. However, this should not be interpreted to mean that evaluation, indeed *ongoing* assessment, is no longer necessary. On the contrary, a significant portion of time and energy needs to be committed to such continuous, evaluation of paraprofessional programs. Evaluation should include not only the effect on the recipient of services—the client—but also the impact of the paraprofessional on the employing agency. Relevant questions to be answered include the following: (1) To what extent was the paraprofessional's training experience effective in the acquisition of specific helping skills? (2) Do clients feel that they have been satisfactorily served? (3) How do paraprofessionals compare to professionals in their effectiveness in delivering identical services? (4) What is the impact of the paraprofessional on the way professionals use their time? (5) What influences has paraprofessional programming had on the agency in terms of numbers of clients served? (6) What are the comparative costs of paraprofessionally and professionally implemented programs?

INCENTIVES

Basic to the question of developing and implementing the student paraprofessional program is the issue of incentives. What are the concrete, external rewards that will produce and maintain helping behavior on the part of student paraprofessionals? Three sources of reward that generally ensure a high level of performance are: money, the opportunity to engage in relevant learning experiences, and grades and academic credit. We are unaware of any empirical data showing the differential effects of these incentives. All have been successfully employed either individually or jointly in various combinations as part of an overall reward system for paraprofessional activity.

While it is hardly surprising to learn that student paraprofessionals will toil for money, the amount is rarely commensurate with the energy expended. Nevertheless, monetary remuneration, no matter the amount, communicates that the work is valued. It is generally recommended that efforts be made to provide financial support for student paraprofessionals. Potential sources that have been reported (Delworth, 1972) include funding from within the institution:

1. operating budget of the counseling center,
2. student services administration budget,
3. profits of specific student services,
4. financial aid programs,
5. student work-study funds;

and funding from outside:

1. government grants,
2. grants from private foundations,
3. funds from service clubs and/or mental health associations.

Student paraprofessionals are provided a unique and potentially rewarding learning experience. The skills that are acquired and, more importantly, the opportunity to implement them in human service can be a source of significant personal reward. In addition, student paraprofessionals gain valuable work experience that can serve them well in competing for future jobs and acquiring recommendations from associated professionals. For these reasons many paraprofessional programs are able to rely on the intrinsic value of the experience as a major incentive for involvement.

Traditional academic incentives such as credits and grades have also been applied to the nontraditional learning experiences that accompany student paraprofessional programs. This reflects the growing effort on the part of academic departments to individualize student programs and encourage educational experiences beyond the classroom.

ISSUES

Despite the documented success of such programs on college campuses, there are issues that remain. The extent to which these are addressed and resolved will in large measure determine the success or failure of a student paraprofessional program.

One crucial issue concerns the acceptance and active support of the professional community within which the paraprofessionals will reside. To what extent can the professional let go of some of the responsibilities that were earned through rigorous training and, in many cases, battle with rival professions for identity and status? To trust a nonprofessional with duties for which the professional must take ultimate responsibility is, indeed, a risk. While the pragmatic argument that use of paraprofessionals serves to free professionals to engage in creative new tasks has its appeal, it assumes that professionals are inherently creative and would launch into new and exciting directions if given a chance. Reality suggests that this is not always the case.

While it is true that no paraprofessional program will succeed when professionals are resistant, there is little hope of success unless professionals are actively involved. A stance of active commitment that fosters a climate of respect and encouragement is necessary to expand the paraprofessionals' experience in new ways. No paraprofessional program can be foisted on a negative or even an impassive professional community without a guaranteed experience of failure for both. Thus, professional commitment must be assessed before any paraprofessional program is started.

If acceptance and support by professional persons is an essential prerequisite to *initiating* any student paraprofessional program, the extent to which paraprofessionals can experience a sense of personal satisfaction in what they are doing is the key to *implementing* one. As already mentioned above, meaningful and relevant work is inherent in the definition of the paraprofessional, and many college students are, in fact, being given such an opportunity. Nevertheless, there is growing evidence that many paraprofessionals have been actively recruited, provided extensive training, and then made to languish in irrelevant or remote job situations (Delworth, 1974; Weber & Palmer 1969). The result is often frustration, low morale, and open conflict among agency personnel.

A fourth issue that must be dealt with in order to establish the viability of a paraprofessional program concerns maintenance functions. This issue relates to those ingredients which serve to ensure a sustained level of satisfactory performance: such things as encouragement, feedback, and opportunity to resolve conflicts as they arise. For paraprofessionals the main source of support is usually derived from an open, ongoing relationship with the professionals responsible for their supervision. As in any good working relationship, there must be developed an atmosphere of respect and trust that invites the paraprofessional to share concerns as well as results. While there is little doubt that paraprofessionals depend heavily on their supervisors for feedback, there remains another source of psychological support that should not be overlooked—that of peer support. Paraprofessionals find themselves in a unique place. In many ways they are like their clients in age, developmental stage, and so forth, and yet their activities and responsibilities give them identity with their professional colleagues. In short, they are neither student nor professional. In an effort to provide opportunity for resolving issues and feelings associated with this special identity crisis, paraprofessionals have profited greatly from developing among themselves support groups in which they come together to check out their own perceptions with others like themselves. Programs that have encouraged, even formalized, such peer support groups have found them to contribute greatly into effective functioning of student paraprofessionals.

Another issue that needs to be faced is the availability of paraprofessional input. Opportunity should be afforded student paraprofessionals to have input into the system within which they reside. The payoff, of course, potentially affects everyone. The paraprofessionals gain in self-respect and potency as individuals who can impact their environment and can share in decisions that affect their own lives. At the same time, bringing to the setting a perspective that in many ways reflects the clientele served, paraprofessionals can provide useful feedback regarding program needs and strategies. It makes sense, therefore, to include paraprofessionals in all phases of decision making with respect to program planning as well as implementation. Their views should be actively sought and considered.

A truly viable student paraprofessional program allows room for growth and development. Basic to the new careers model is the notion of "ladders and lattices," whereby a person gains entry to work settings through the acquisition of a specific set of helping skills. Once into the system, however, the paraprofessional can have the opportunity to work at different jobs at the same skill level or to gain additional skills and move upward. Allen (1974) proposed a "levels" model of paraprofessional intervention that allows for systematic introduction of paraprofessionals into increasingly complex and responsible activities if they are ready and able. Four distinct training levels proposed were level 1, observer; level 2, technician; level 3, advanced specialist; and level 4, psychological associate. Such an approach assures a diversity of training opportunities as well as advancement and upward mobility.

Support Personnel

Support personnel are the unsung heroines and heroes of most counseling centers. Without their necessary contributions, appointments would not be made, tests would never be given, organizational "nuts and bolts" would go unattended, and the counseling center, be it a thirty- or a two-person enterprise, would simply not function. Although most counseling center directors will readily acknowledge the significant functions performed by various support staff, little attention is paid to ways of integrating selection and effective utilization of these important people. For example, there is probably no one within the typical work environment who receives, processes, and transmits more information (Gordon, Miller, & Mindell, 1976) or who more frequently acts as the initial contact between the organization and its larger environment than does the secretary.

FUNCTIONS

Even the smallest of counseling centers generally has at least a part-time secretary who of necessity ends up wearing many hats. Larger staffs typically have several individuals among whom various support functions are assigned.

Possible job titles and descriptions include the following:

Secretaries - process information; operate office machines; maintain record systems; attend to operational details; and often perform many of the functions noted below.

Executive Secretaries - sometimes called office managers or administrative assistants; manage purchasing and payroll functions; monitor budget expenditures; coordinate and supervise other support staff; assist the director with innumerable projects and are indispensable in an agency of more than a few staff members.

Receptionists - serve as all-important initial contact point with clientele and public; coordinate scheduling of professional staff, programs, and facilities; gather and collate information for accountability reports.

Record Clerks - maintain testing, counseling, and/or management information systems by coding, entering, and retrieving data.

Testing Clerks - sometimes called test supervisors or proctors; administer, proctor, and score standardized paper-and-pencil tests; supervise testing room operations.

Support personnel are the maintenance specialists in any organization. Their value is attested by the frequently heard lament of the administrator—"a good secretary just cannot be found." Good secretaries (and other support personnel) can be found, trained, and maintained in an organizational setting if sufficient time and energy are invested in the process. Frequently the agency spends significant sums of money locating and hiring the "right" professional staff member, then invests months of effort in a program development activity, only to have the system founder because too little time and attention have been paid to the necessary contributions of support personnel. Selection, training, and supervision of support personnel is a vital and high-priority activity.

SELECTION

Affirmative action guidelines affect virtually all colleges and universities and dictate that searches for all levels of staff be conducted in an open and accessible fashion. Undoubtedly, the first requisite for a successful search is to commit sufficient time to the project. Applicants should be screened for basic job qualifications and then interviewed by the immediate supervisor involved, often an executive secretary. Those that pass this initial assessment can then be interviewed by the professional staff member responsible for the program area in which the new staff member will primarily function. Final decisions are best made by consensus, using input from all staff involved in the interview process. College personnel departments often supply information on applicants' specific job skills (typing speed and accuracy, for example) although such information may not be as critical as other qualities. A generalized list of selection criteria would likely include three items:

Interpersonal Competence

Receptionists, testing supervisors, secretaries, and virtually all other support personnel have frequent contact with clients, faculty, administrators, parents, and the myriad others who have reason to contact a college counseling center. Since these interactions are often the initial contact, they are influential in fixing attitudes and "sets" that color the consumers' subsequent involvements with the agency. An anxious college student seeking counseling may or may not follow through based on his/her initial interpersonal experience with the agency.

In addition, the tone and morale of a total staff are significantly affected by the interpersonal qualities of key support personnel. The human relations skills taught in the structured developmental group programs of many counseling centers are critically needed in the interactions between support and professional staff members. The receptionist in a large counseling center with primary responsibility for coordinating the schedules of twenty or thirty staff members (sometimes including an ever changing cadre of graduate students) must of necessity be a human relations specialist in order to survive long in the job. Training programs can help refine such skills, but locating potential support personnel who initially possess basic maturity and interpersonal sensitivity is of critical importance.

Although few, if any, standardized instruments that directly measure interpersonal competence are on the market, better-than-chance judgments should result from judicious use of structured interviews by more than one staff member, consideration of recommendations from prior employers, role-playing situations or similar behavior samples, and the clinical judgment of professionals trained in the assessment and development of human qualities and characteristics. Interpersonal competence is often the single most important selection criteria to be assessed.

Capacity to Learn

Since support personnel often have major responsibility for operating the maintenance side of the enterprise, they must of necessity exercise frequent independent judgment requiring understanding of the overall purposes of the organization as well as knowledge of specific operating procedures. Individuals willing and able to learn obviously make more effective staff members than those who lack the requisite ability or motivation. Evidence of effective performance in prior vocational and educational settings is therefore an important selection consideration and can be reviewed through written and verbal recommendations, work histories, and the like. If objective information concerning prior job performance is not available, then transcripts of educational attainment and scores on standardized tests may sometimes be helpful.

Specific Job Skills

Different jobs require different specific skills. In-service training programs can sometimes build such competencies, but cost-efficiency factors often dictate that necessary basic skills already be acquired. Secretaries must process information, a task that usually includes efficient typing (80 words per minute) and operating various business machines, including dictating equipment. Records clerks may need to operate card-punch machines, while executive secretaries or administrative assistants will probably need to understand account summaries and budget projections. The list could go on depending on the circumstances. Specific job skills are generally identified in an objective job analysis. Many college personnel offices routinely carry out such analyses and may be willing to help in specific situations. Counseling center personnel involved in the selection process should also analyze the position in order to identify specific job skills needed.

TRAINING

Counseling centers, like many other student personnel services, are often caught up in reactively responding to a long succession of crises and pressures. The training needs of secretaries and other support staff can be easily overlooked in such an atmosphere, often to the detriment of the agency. In-service training for support personnel is both desirable and necessary and needs to be routinely planned.

Specific job training during the first six months of employment will facilitate new staff members' learning agency procedures, clarify expectations of supervisors and other staff members, and make for a smoother initial transition. Biweekly or monthly review meetings with the immediate supervisor are in order, with possibly a three-month and six-month general follow-up with the responsible professional staff member. Some university personnel departments indicate the initial six months, or a similar period, as a probationary period and require specific feedback sessions between new employees and supervisory personnel. In the absence of such requirements, initial job training can occur informally, although regularly scheduled review meetings can have the added advantage of communicating the value and importance placed by the agency on both the new staff members and their jobs.

Some sort of ongoing in-service training programs for support staff is desirable following the period of initial training. Such training programs will at times be specific to changing job demands (for example, implementation of new record system). Beyond such ad hoc needs, however, there are possibilities for the development of more generalized job-related skills. For example, many counseling centers offer various programs designed to enhance the communication and interpersonal skills of participants. Little adaptation would be needed to relate such programs to in-service training needs of receptionists and secretaries.

At the University of Utah a comprehensive staff development program for all personnel in the Student Affairs Division of the university has been in operation since 1975. The majority of individuals participating have been support personnel. Counseling center staff have had a primary role in formulating and implementing the program. Two basic objectives have been to provide all staff members with opportunities for personal growth experiences (for example, stress management training) and to encourage the development of job-related skills (for example, communication skills). General workshops for all staff as well as specialized sessions for particular categories of employees (secretarial, administrative, professional, and so on) are scheduled. Self-contained workshops, ninety minutes in length, have proved to be the most popular and practical format. Examples of general workshop titles include "Communication Skills Training," "Assessing Your Interpersonal Work Style," and, "Your Job—A Means or An End?" Special workshops designed for support personnel have included "Interpersonal Effectiveness Training," "Helping Skills," and a "Front-Line" luncheon and seminar. During the first year of the program's operation (the 1975-1976 academic year), 166 staff members, or approximately 75 percent of the total Student Affairs staff, participated in at least one activity. Evaluation questionnaires distributed at the end of each workshop indicated an overwhelmingly positive response from participants, with many comments requesting the continuation of such programming. The program has strongly attested to the consistent interest of staff, including support personnel, in participation of such training.

A final and usually overlooked aspect of staff development has to do with special in-service training for "bosses." Agency directors and other professional staff with administrative responsibilities often have difficulty effectively utilizing the services of various support personnel. Executive secretaries, administrative assistants, and office managers in particular are capable of handling a variety of administrative and quasi-management functions that harried administrators sometimes tend to keep to themselves. Kozoll (1974) has outlined an approach to secretarial "training for bosses" that includes the following three components: (1) developing a functional profile of management tasks regularly performed by an administrator (regularly scheduled meetings and events, number of reports and memos that accumulate per week, and so on); (2) defining the variety of tasks performed by support staff that directly contribute to effective performance of the manager or supervisor; and (3) analyzing the two profiles to pinpoint areas of inefficiency and to identify tasks done by the administrator that could be performed by supporting staff.

SUPERVISION AND JOB SATISFACTION

In a narrow sense, supervision connotes directing the activities of someone else. Effective supervision, however, needs to be more broadly defined to include concepts of access and collaboration between supervisor and supervisee. Productive relationships are developed through consistent application of the following procedures:

1. Regular and frequent information sharing between supervisor and supervisee through structured meetings, ready informal access, shared daily appointment calendars, mutual advice seeking, and so forth.
2. Clearly stated expectations, often committed to writing, that are revised and updated as job conditions change.
3. Delegation of as much responsibility as possible, consistent with job speci-

fications and agency objectives, including management tasks that were formerly done by administrators and can be accomplished as effectively by competent support personnel.

4. Authority commensurate with assigned responsibilities and appropriately formalized through statements in policy manuals, memos, and announcements in staff meetings.

5. Consistent reinforcement through formal procedures, such as pay raises, and informal methods, such as expressions of appreciation, acknowledgments in staff meetings, and verbal recognition of skills and contributions of individual support personnel.

Job satisfaction should be facilitated through consistent application of the above procedures. The relationship between job satisfaction and productivity is well documented. In an informative study of the job satisfaction of secretaries, Gordon, Miller, and Mindell (1976) found a surprisingly high degree of satisfaction in their sample of more than 1,200 secretaries. Approximately 91 percent of the sample reported having a "pleasant" or "very pleasant" relationship with their superior, and most indicated a high degree of satisfaction with their work. In analyzing their data the authors concluded that sources of satisfaction fell under three main headings: power, diversity, and supervision. Power as a source of satisfaction derived from the fact that many secretaries occupy pivotal positions in their organizations and have access to significant amounts of important information. Their key role in management grapevines and information-processing activities, with the resultant implied influence, related significantly to satisfaction. The diversity of the secretaries' responsibilities was also identified as a key source of satisfaction. Included were diverse work tasks as well as frequent opportunity for social and business contacts with a variety of people. The third source of satisfaction, secretarial supervision, focused less on formal direction and more on the secretaries' access to and involvement with their immediate supervisors. Interestingly enough, a primary conclusion was that the physical visiblity of the supervisor during a portion of the day was an important correlate of reported job satisfaction. Verbal access was also significant, including frequent opportunity for brief, informal discussion in which the secretary's advice was sought and planning was mutually carried out.

Although Gordon, Miller, and Mindell's study focused on secretaries, implications for other support staff in university and college counseling centers seem obvious.

Intern Staff

In chapter 17 of this handbook McCabe discusses the internship as a central component in the training role of the counseling center. This section will briefly discuss the intern as a human services provider.

Interns are neither professionals or paraprofessionals, and although the traineeship aspect of their role is generally emphasized, they are in fact an essential element in the staffing patterns of many larger counseling centers. The Counseling Center at the University of Utah is probably a representative example: during the winter quarter of 1977, interns comprised approximately 25 percent of the counseling staff and were working with 28 percent of the counseling clientele.

As is evident from McCabe's chapter, there are numerous references in the professional literature investigating the training aspect of the internship. Hardly any references at all, however, analyze the intern as a service provider.

Counseling centers associated with institutions that support one or more graduate-level academic programs in the helping professions more typically employ interns. Although part-time internships filled by local students undoubtedly remain the norm, an increasing number of centers are now offering year-long full-time internships that are nationally advertised. Among other activities, the recently organized Association of Psychology Internship Centers helps to coordinate and facilitate the filling of such internships.[1]

Counseling psychology students, generally in their third or fourth year of graduate study, often fill such positions, although candidates from other related disciplines are sometimes available and interested. Clinical psychology, social work, and psychiatry residency programs also represent potential sources of intern-level staff members. Potential benefits from developing such multidisciplinary relationships include: (1) the stimulation generated from bringing two or more related, but academically distinct, specialty areas at both professional and training levels; and (2) the development of training relationships with several academic departments and a related increase in the visibility and viability of the counseling center in the academic community.

The range of tasks performed by interns is as broad as that of professional personnel. In some instances, in fact, interns may end up being the major service providers in program areas in which full-time staff have little time, interest, or prior experience. Given this type of potential involvement, selection and training issues become crucial.

Competitive selection procedures are more congruent with the service goals of most centers than is simply taking whoever is referred by an academic department. A desirable arrangement is one in which the professional staff involved in an agency's training programs make annual selection decisions from a pool of applicants. Recommendations of practicum supervisors, work samples of various kinds, and personal interviews (with local applicants) are important in making such decisions. Full-time nationally advertised internships usually generate large numbers of applicants, and, hopefully, the same will be true in selecting interns from local academic departments. Joint appointments of counseling center professional staff with academic departments obviously facilitate both selection and training procedures.

McCabe's chapter details training and supervision issues. Suffice it to say that given the key role interns play as service providers in many agencies, adequate supervision is a tremendously important issue. Traditionally, supervision has emphasized regular one-to-one contacts between supervisee and supervisor. In addition, regularly scheduled, small consultation groups for staff working in various program areas are desirable. Examples include staff consulting groups that focus on outreach and consulting services, career development programs, group counseling, longer-term therapy, structured developmental workshops, and marriage and family counseling. A final important component in a comprehensive staff development program is regular in-service meetings that jointly involve intern and professional staff members. Such meetings serve to reinforce the interns' developing sense of professional identity and to facilitate integration into the agency's professional staff.

Note

1. c/o Dr. Sidney A. Orgel, State University of New York, Syracuse, New York 13210.

References

Allen, E. E. 1974. Paraprofessionals in a large-scale university program. *The Personnel and Guidance Journal* 53: 276–80.

Brown, W. F. 1965. Student-to-student counseling for academic adjustment. *The Personnel and Guidance Journal* 43: 811–17.

Carkhuff, R. R. 1969. *Helping and human relations.* Vols. 1 and 2. New York: Holt, Rinehart and Winston.

Carkhuff, R. R., and Truax, C. B. 1965. Lay mental health counseling: the effects of lay group counseling. *Journal of Counseling Psychology* 12: 426–31.

Crane, J.; Anderson, W.; and Kirchner, K. 1975. Counseling center directors' attitudes toward paraprofessionals. *Journal of College Student Personnel* 16: 119–22.

Dana, R. H.; Heynen, F.; and Burdette, R. 1974. Crisis intervention by peers. *Journal of College Student Personnel* 15: 58–61.

Delworth, U. 1974. Paraprofessionals as guerillas: recommendations for system change. *The Personnel and Guidance Journal* 53: 335–38.

———. 1972. The student paraprofessional in the counseling center: a tentative model. Paper presented at the meeting of the Western Psychological Association, Portland, Ore.

Delworth, U.; Rudow, E. H.; and Taub, J. 1972. *Crisis center/hotline.* Springfield, Ill.: Charles C. Thomas.

Gartner, A. 1969. *Do paraprofessionals improve human services: a first critical appraisal of the data.* New York: New York University, New Careers Development Center.

Geer, C. 1971. The paraprofessional—a panacea or a problem? Unpublished manuscript, Colorado State University.

Gordon, J. E. 1965. Project CAUSE, the federal antipoverty program, and some implications for subprofessional training. *American Psychologist* 20: 334–43.

Gordon, W. I.; Miller, J. R.; and Mindell, M. G. 1976. Are secretaries satisfied with their work? *Secretary* 36: 6–8.

Gravitz, H. L., and Woods, E., Jr. 1976. Multiethnic approach to peer counseling. *Professional Psychology* 7: 229–35.

Hamburg, B., and Varenhorst, B. 1972. Peer counseling in the secondary schools: a community mental health project for youth. *American Journal of Orthopsychiatry* 42: 566–81.

Hauer, A. 1973. Adjunct counselors in college. *The Personnel and Guidance Journal* 52: 43–46.

Ivey, A. E. 1971. *Microcounseling: innovations in interviewing training*. Springfield, Ill.: Charles C. Thomas.

Kagan, N. 1972. *Influencing human interaction*. East Lansing, Mich.: Michigan State University, Colleges of Education and Human Medicine.

Kozoll, C. E. 1974. Secretarial training for bosses. *Secretary* 34: 10–12.

Nicoletti, J., and Flater-Benz, L. 1974. Volunteers in a community mental health agency. *The Personnel and Guidance Journal* 53: 281–84.

Pearl, A., and Riessman, F. 1965. *New careers for the poor*. New York: Free Press.

Steenland, R. 1973. Paraprofessionals in counseling centers. *The Personnel and Guidance Journal* 51: 417–18.

Weber, G., and Palmer, D. 1969. New careers: problems and pitfalls. *American Education* 4: 26–28.

Wolff, T. 1969. Undergraduates as campus mental health workers. *The Personnel and Guidance Journal* 48: 294–304.

9

ADMINISTRATIVE CONCERNS: THE ROLE OF THE DIRECTOR

B. Mark Schoenberg

MEMORIAL UNIVERSITY

It is curious that the position per se of director of the college or university counseling center has not been the subject of extensive investigation. A full review of the literature was made, but the results of the search were most disappointing. If anything, the position has received only superficial treatment; it has never received the critical analysis that it deserves. This suggests one of two possibilities: (1) the position has not been studied in any detail at all, or (2) the position does not lend itself to generic investigation. It is probably not true that the position has escaped the attention of investigators; but it is probably true that attempts to define the position in terms of how it is managed at a majority of institutions is virtually impossible. The role of the director does vary from institution to institution, and therefore the kinds of administrative concerns will vary as well. The institution defines the role in large measure, but the director and the professional staff of the center contribute heavily to the definition as well. So do the needs—stated and perceived—of the student body.

In the final analysis the most worthwhile statement that can be made is the following: the position varies from campus to campus, the director is a powerful force in defining the programs and activities (and thus the campus impact) of the center, and the director must come to a knowledgeable understanding of the inherent strengths and weaknesses of the position. For instance, any number of variables can help to define the role of the director; among these are the size of the institution, the skills and prestige that the director brings to the position, and the support engendered by the center from all levels of the academic community. It is obvious that administrative support is important; but without enthusiastic student involvement in center activities and programs, the backing of the administration is to no avail and, moreover, will probably not continue for any length of time. The reverse position is equally obvious: that is, the ability to meet the needs of students depends on the quality of support that the administration is prepared to give. The director recognizes these realities as a kind of balancing act that must be continually performed—one aspect cannot be sacrificed at the expense of the other. I suspect that Warnath (1972) was indicating his concern with part of this balancing act when he warned that failure to determine what college counselors do on campus and how they do it is the largest professional issue. Examining many of the realities of college counseling, his critique ended on a somber note: unless critical issues are resolved, it is entirely possible that the next generation of college students will not have professional counseling services available to them. His is an alarmist position to be sure, but his fears are certainly not without foundation.

Activities and programs of the center must be comprehensive in the sense that they encompass the largest number of student needs, concerns, and issues; but in order to offer the broadest range of programs and services, directors must negotiate an accommodation with the administration of the institution. It is regrettable, and constitutes cause for concern, that not all centers offer a broad range of services, but it is probably too easy to infer that this is always the result of a fiscally stingy administration. It is just as probable that the directors did not press firmly enough for an adequate budget or became committed to the development of one area of service delivery at the expense of another. Several centers have been forced to close, and others have been absorbed into existing campus agencies. Although a simplistic—and possibly an unfair—reaction, questions must be raised as to what the directors were doing while these centers were being closed or absorbed. It occurs to me that if their directors had been promoting the centers to the degree that service organizations inevitably require, such outrageous end results would have never prevailed.

There is little doubt that the director of the college or university counseling center has one of the more ambiguous positions on campus, and a large measure of responsibility for this must be borne by the administration itself; it has never faced up responsibly to the placement of the center within the administrative structure. As Clark observes, "Where authority is broadly and ambiguously diffused, the proper channels may play a relatively small role compared to the informal exchange, the informal agreement, and the informal veto" (1962, p. 184). By way of explanation, directors frequently report to the vice-president of student affairs or to the dean of that department, if the vice-presidential title is not given. Other counseling center directors report to the chairperson of the Department of Psychology or even Educational Psychology (although, fortunately, this does not happen too frequently anymore). On other campuses it appears that directors are responsible to the dean of education. Clearly, having directors report to any of these officials is stretching the basic organizational premise of relationship, and the result is that directors are compelled to spend an enormous amount of time building the informal exchanges that ensure the authority of their position and their center—time that could be more productively utilized elsewhere.

In actual fact, of course, the director of the counseling center should report to the president of the institution. There are compelling reasons to justify this line of command, one of the more significant being the consideration of prestige. At this point in time, when the line of command is fuzzy as well as illogically placed, there is a problem in conceptualizing the position of director without considering the prestige of the individual holding the post. It is clear that the kind of leadership the director gives to the position frequently defines the parameters of counseling center impact. Indeed, it is not unlikely that centers have foundered because of weak or inept leadership provided by the director. The reverse situation should also command our attention: centers flourish when guided by directors who are able to provide dynamic leadership to the professional staff at the same time that they hold a position of respect on campus. Also, it would be a mistake to minimize the importance of the on-campus authority of the individual to whom directors report; for if directors lack prestige and if the individual to whom they report has no clout, their centers will encounter unavoidable problems in every area from budgeting to service delivery. As Preston pointed out, in chapter 5, reporting to the chief executive officer of the institution confers a certain amount of prestige.

Quite clearly, the issues of prestige for directors is not resolved completely by having them report to the president. Directors of centers must have the professional credentials as well as the knowledgeability and sensitivity that enable them to guide as well as to lead; but the direct-line relationship would most assuredly give added impact to this (prestige) consideration. This reasoning may not fully satisfy those who contend that there must be more logic in deciding the question of line and staff relationships, but I believe the argument is as valid as any other rationale currently in use to support the existing chain of command. Koontz and O'Donnell argue that "without definite lines of authority, the way is prepared for politics, intrigue, frustration, buck passing, lack of coordination, duplication of effort, vagueness of policy, uncertainty in decision making, and other evidences of organizational inefficiency" (1955, p. 277). The directors of counseling centers are regularly confronted with one—possibly all—of these difficulties. A direct link with the president's office would not solve all problems, but decisions affecting the center could most probably be made with greater ease. Such a direct link to the president's office would also ameliorate other contentious issues, most notably the absolute security of records and case reports. However, these and other advantages that might accrue are incidental to the reduction in the ambiguity of the position.

Not entirely unrelated to the issue of the authority to whom the director reports is the so-called legitimacy issue. This question of legitimacy is a very sensitive issue, one that we have not met with directness. The issue complicates all facets of the work of the center, contributes to the ambiguity of the position of the director as well as to the positions of the professional staff, and occasionally aggravates professional relations between members of the center and other members of the academic community. Stated very simply, the counseling center is not an easy fit within the college or university. The department is not an academic one in the same sense that other departments are considered academic: the teaching function is an obvious component of the counseling relationship, albeit a most subtle one. The center is not (nor should it be) a part of the administrative umbrella of the institution: surely the most effective way to destroy a center is to burden it with administrative responsibility. Moreover, regardless of the investment in psychotherapeutic procedures, the center is not perceived as a healing facility as is the campus medical health office, and most directors work diligently to avoid the design of the medical model for their centers. Finally, the counseling center is rarely in the forefront of departments investing in either pure or applied research.

Taken together, these facts define the counseling center as a facility like none other on campus. The unfortunate result too often is that this fact is recognized neither by faculty nor by administration, the net effect being that the solutions imposed are nothing more than trying to fit a round peg in a square hole. Surely the center cannot be expected to function autonomously or to earn campus-wide prestige if it is assigned a position as yet another vague department in the student affairs spectrum (along with financial aid and the housing office). I do not mean to suggest that the present system of having the director report to someone other than the president is unworkable: it is not, and if this individual is knowledgeable as well as sympathetic to counseling, the symbiotic relationship can be most satisfactory. However, this kind of arrangement does beg the issue of the counseling center being a singularly unique department requiring a distinctly different modus operandi.

A kind of lay mythology has grown up around the operation of the counseling center on the college or university campus, and it seems to me that educating the academic community out of this "mythicism" must be one of the director's primary concerns. Although our academic and administrative peers are neither inherently biased nor ill-informed, misunderstandings of what a center is and what it should be can create problems. For example, the placement of testing services within the activities of the counseling center rarely provokes any kind of discussion, because testing is generally acknowledged to be a function of counseling. However, beyond this one area there exists no such agreement. Detractors of the academic support programs pose arguments ranging from the perspective that students do not need these programs (if they do, they do not belong in college in the first place!) to the contention that if they are offered on campus at all they need be taught under the auspices of the English department! And so on. As a matter of cold hard fact, each and every program offered by the comprehensive counseling center can be criticized on the grounds that the program should not be offered on campus in the first instance and that, if it is, it should be offered by one of the academic departments.

Even worse, the term *counseling* itself is widely misunderstood. It would be interesting to conduct a poll of the academic community to determine how many of our colleagues would accept the word as a synonym (sometimes) for psychotherapy. According to Patterson, "Counseling (or psychotherapy) is a relationship, involving verbal interaction, between a professionally trained person and an individual or group of individuals voluntarily seeking help with a problem which is psychological in nature, for the purpose of effecting a change in the individuals seeking help" (1967, p. 82). Schofield (1964) terms psychotherapy as a conversation with therapeutic intent. Thus, it is clear to counseling practitioners that psychotherapy is an important facet of their very broad practice, but I suspect that people in general connect the term *psychotherapy* with psychiatrists. Inasmuch as counseling is concerned, too frequently it is considered a situation in which someone tells others what courses should be taken in order to qualify or what they should do with their lives. And so it goes: group programs are routinely assailed for any number of reasons; psychotherapy belongs in the physician-psychiatrist's office; biofeedback is in danger of capture by the johnny-come-lately medical associations; and even relaxation and desensitization procedures are the subject of discussion vis-à-vis their proper placement in the counseling center.

Therefore, it becomes clear that among the many administrative concerns faced by the director of the center, one of the most pressing is ongoing education of the entire academic community to the broad scope of services offered by the comprehensive counseling center. The aura of mystique enveloping the center must be removed, a task best done by the director and the professional staff through community education—some might call it public relations. The professional staff can take responsible roles in this educational mission, but the director must provide the leadership. The process is perhaps a bit less difficult on the small campus than it is on the large, and the means will undoubtedly vary from institution to institution. But the question of legitimacy of the center is a recurring issue—one that the director would be well advised to confront openly.

In times of institutional fiscal health the legitimacy of the center is not a very pressing concern. The issue can arise when the director seeks academic rank for the professional staff: for some unfathomable reason a relatively large number of colleges and universities resist awarding rank to counselors. But this is obviously an important issue for members of the professional staff of the center, so the director must press forward regardless of the invalid reasons mustered against awarding rank. The same situation can arise with respect to tenure or to granting of sabbatical leave. Every time a staff member of the center is accorded treatment unlike any other member of the faculty, the director must be prepared to engage the issue to a satisfactory conclusion. Wheelis may be correct when he observes that "institutional absolutes and the coercive power systems that protect them have never provided real security'' (1968, p. 36). Subjective feelings they may be, but on the college and university level it is generally acknowledged that rank, tenure, sabbaticals, and the like are privileges as well as rights of the academic community. Pretensions that counselors should not have these rights are foolish as well as dangerous. Yet it is precisely on these occasions when the director feels compelled to push for equal status with the rest of the academic community that the issue of legitimacy can be raised by administration and faculty.

Then, should the institution enter into a period of severe financial stress, the question is no longer one of rights and privileges, but becomes for the center a deadly serious one of survival. In the flurry of activity accompanying an announcement that the institution must find ways to economize come proposals ranging from cutting back on the services of the center to doing away with it entirely! This process has been repeated with an almost monotonous regularity at campuses across North America. Even having to undergo the deliberative process is ludicrous, for no institution interested in the welfare of its student body can afford to overlook their psychological interests. Yet when faced with possible threat to their own positions, some members of administration and faculty cast about, looking for a scapegoat. The center will have many supporters; and if the director and the professional staff have done a good job with the education of the academic community to the services and activities of the center, the threat should not prove to be a serious one. Still, it is helpful to realize that the rationales generally employed to support curtailment or abandonment of counseling services fall into two broad categories: (1) the lack of academic tradition, as embodied in the argument that the center does not have a primary investment in either teaching or research, and (2) the misrepresentation that other departments and services on campus can take responsibility for center programs, services, and activities. The important consideration here is that if directors have a keen awareness of the climate that might cause the issue to arise, they will be in a better position to mount a countercampaign.

It is not unlikely that the accountability issue has surfaced as a result of a genuine interest on the part of some administrators (and, indeed, some counseling center directors) to defuse certain of the criticisms regularly directed at the centers. Data on the number of clients seen are perceived by the administrative mentality as an indication of the impact the center is making on the campus. A large number of clients means that the center is really involved, while the implication is that a small number indicates that the center is not doing its job. The evidence is irrefutable to the bureaucratic mind, for who can argue with statistics? Guilford notes that ''some psychologists facetiously refer to the acceptance of some tests as a matter of faith validity'' (1954, p. 400). In considering the data collected to support the accountability thesis, I think we might do well to resurrect Guilford's term to describe any superficial appearance of validity resulting from accountability studies. The data might look good, but they probably mean nothing: if they pander to an administrative penchant for records keeping, perhaps it is worthwhile keeping them. There is little doubt that the total number of clients seen by most centers is impressive, but obviously numbers alone cannot reliably reflect the true investment. Cox states that "the crux of the accountability craze is the assumption that the physics concept of convertibility and conservation can be applied to education" (1977, p. 763). It is clear that the most important point for directors to remember is that this entire game of accountability is being played according to someone else's rules and regulations and that the data that are yielded are notoriously unreliable. If administration insists we play the game, then by all means let us play it. But let us not commit our time and energy beyond an absolute minimum, all the while maintaining the posture that the entire procedure is ridiculous as well as counterproductive from the perspective of wasted time, effort, and energy.

The administrative concerns considered up to this point have all been external, the kinds of pressure arising outside of the center. But there are the internal pressures to contend with as well, and, generally speaking, these kinds of pressures are tedious, time-consuming, and generally unnecessary. That this is true does not make them disappear or even make them easier to resolve.

The internal pressures on the director fall generally into three categories: (1) the programs and activities of the center, (2) the recruitment and maintenance of a highly professional staff, and (3) the budget priorities. These categories are not mutually exclusive: in fact, they are so entwined that it is difficult to recognize when one is moving from one to the other.

In large measure the programs and activities of the comprehensive counseling center are the result of ensuring that additional funds are available; that is, the budget must be adequate to support the proposed spending. But once the budget is assured, it becomes a matter of recruiting staff members who will be able to implement the programs. As an example, the center cannot offer training in biofeedback unless an individual with training and experience is available, nor can it proceed with the program unless sufficient funds are set aside to ensure the hiring of this individual plus the purchasing of suitable hardware and software. Thus it is clear that the director must press the administration of the institution for the required funding. Preparing the budget and having to defend it constitute an annual ritual that demands a tremendous amount of the director's time and energy.

The director bears the ultimate responsibility for the organization and integration of the programs, services, and activities of the center. Most centers are built on a broad base discriminated more or less equally into (1) vocation and career planning programs, (2) psycholinguistics and academic support areas, and (3) individual and group counseling. Special circumstances might dictate a tilt to one particular area, but on balance it is wise to keep the emphasis more or less even. I believe most directors would support the thesis that the broader the range of services, the less likelihood there will be for sustained criticism of center offerings. Relevance is also an argument for a broad range of services. Warnath

(1972) postulates that various categories of the counseling center's potential clientele are rejecting its traditional services. If this condition does exist to any degree, I would strongly suspect that the cause could be attributed to a narrow range of programs and services. Supported only by my personal observation (which I fully admit might be completely subjective), I sensed a tendency several years ago for strong investment by many centers in group (sensitivity or encounter) programs at the expense of personal counseling. It also seemed to me that much attention was being given to minorities on campus (for example, hard drug users) at the expense of other students. Nearly every campus in North America has witnessed a minority's "taking over" the student center at the expense of the majority (who no longer feel as if they want to participate at the expense of their own values). It seems to me that the same situation might befall the counseling center: a majority of students might perceive programs and services as catering to a minority. Regardless of the director's own area of interest, he or she remains the guarantor that the center's program is sufficiently diverse.

The professional staff that meets the needs of the clients of the center have been assembled by the director (in most instances) and thus reflect to a large extent not only the priorities of the center as perceived by the director, but also to manifest personality characteristics considered to be important. As suggested by a previous study (Schoenberg, 1971), counseling center directors believe that the ability to relate warmly to clients is the most important task of the counselor. Thus it follows that the professional staff will have been selected in large measure as a result of the preconceived notions (of the director, primarily) of desirable personality characteristics.

The subject of professional staff members is being treated elsewhere in the book, but I did want to make the point that the director has a responsibility to judge whether or not a prospective staff member has the ability to relate warmly not only to clients, but also to the existing staff. It is stating the obvious to say that the professional staff must be able to work together as an efficient team, but unfortunately situations do arise in which people simply cannot get on well with one another. A layperson might be surprised to learn that individuals who are trained in behavioristic areas have difficulty in their own interpersonal relations, and in a way it is somewhat surprising. However, tensions do come about from time to time, and it is the director's responsibility to see that the situation does not get out of hand. Usually the frictions are of the same variety that afflict any group of people who work together, which means that there is no set way to undertake the resolution of any given conflict. For the most part these tensions will work themselves out given time and goodwill, but directors should not hesitate to get involved if in their judgment the conflict is detrimental to the work of the center.

My experience suggests that the single largest area for potential conflict within a center is the divisioning off of professional staff members (as well as clients) into the academic/educational, vocational/careers information, and clinical areas.

I suspect that most directors have established such a breakdown of work load as well as responsibility for the professional staff. On the plus side, the organization of the center becomes much more manageable through the use of these arbitrary areas, which in fact do a creditable job of describing what goes on between the counselor-psychologist and the client. In short, the divisions do make sense, and the system can work very smoothly. However, problems can and do arise *if* the divisions are perceived by the professional staff members as definitions of their value within the center. The careers information specialist is as important to the center as is the clinician, and the work of the individual who specializes in the general area of teaching learning skills is of no less value than the person who runs groups. In short, all the programs, activities, and services of the center are of equal value. A director who encourages clinical prima donnas is courting disaster.

In chapter 15, Cochran makes the point that some psychologists have a tendency to believe that "depth" is the sole measure of the value of professional interaction with a client. This myth of psychological ascendancy has its beginnings in the course work provided for doctoral students in psychology, and the result is that very few students complete their final degree plans having any sophistication whatever in career planning or academic advisement. Preparing doctoral degree candidates to undertake the teaching of study skills courses has received an equal degree of selective inattention from those people responsible for establishing course work or training for the Ph.D. or the Ed.D., although it is probably safe to say that generally the Ed.D. programs are the more well-rounded. Given this reality, it is more the pity that Ed.D. programs receive a great amount of condescension from those who are involved in the structuring of course work for the Ph.D. programs. The stigmatization, begun in the graduate schools, of the Ed.D. counseling psychologist or Ph.D. educational psychologist as a quasi-psychologist is effectively promoted by state and provincial licensing boards and is demonstrated by the difficulty experienced by an educational or counseling psychologist who seeks state or provincial certification. Thus, it is no surprise, first, that students opt for the traditional Ph.D. (for who wants to work for a doctoral degree in psychology and subsequently find that the "professional club" is closed to them?) and, second, that there is a shortage of well-trained doctoral-level people to be plugged into vocational, academic, and career guidance programs. Given these "traditions" of perceived importance within the profession, it is not too surprising that subgrouping on the lines of clinicians versus the rest of the professional staff sometimes becomes an issue in the efficient and harmonious operation of the center. The issue spills over into the subject of the master's-level psychologist as well, and it would be an understatement to observe that the whole business can get extremely sticky.

It is difficult to understand why certain areas of psychology are so enamored with the medical model, but it is clear that the rationale infering that "depth means involvement" is an inevitable result of the attachment. Psychology's infatuation with internships (even the name is the same) is relatively harmless: if people want to play doctor, why not? Nevertheless, one must recognize that the clinical route is but one of several paths a psychologist can travel and that each specialization has equal significance in the total picture. A good beginning toward resolution of the issue would be to dismantle the state and provincial licensing boards that the professional organizations have been instrumental in creating. Failing this, the state and provincial boards must develop the machinery whereby psychologists of the several specializations can be licensed (without obstacles) in the particular area of their specialization. It is not likely that this latter course of action is the answer, because too many people have too great a vested interest in the maintenance of the status quo. No one would dispute that the public has a right to be protected, but the question that should be addressed to the American and Canadian psychological associations and to the state and provincial licensing boards that these organizations have created is, obviously, protected from whom? I am sorely afraid that the clinicians have found a lucrative Holy Grail and that divisiveness within the profession is of no concern to them as long as they hold the winning cards.

Perhaps I am being overly pessimistic, but having the machinery for certification and licensing so completely in the hands of the academic and clinical psychologists does not suggest an early end to the harassment of the counseling or educational psychologist. The blind allegiance to the psychiatric and medical models will not disappear simply because the existing reality dictates that it should. Perhaps a relatively new discipline like psychology needs the legitimacy provided by the identification with an older discipline like medicine. Yet the issue remains the same regardless of the cause, and the fact is that divisions and tensions do arise as a direct result of the bias against counseling and educational psychologists. It seems to me, therefore, that directors of counseling centers are required to be involved in this issue on two separate counts: first, they must be very alert to the potential damage that can be caused to their own centers as a result of subgrouping by specialization. Obviously, the way to guard against such a situation developing is to make certain that all specializations have equal input into policy. Second, they must be prepared to use their considerable prestige in effecting change in the professional organizations and in the state and provincial licensing and certification boards.

The regular office routine of the center will be administratively managed by the director's administrative assistant, an individual who must be carefully chosen not only for management skills, but also for an ability to get on well with the professional staff. This position does not carry the same amount of weight as the director's position, yet it can embody a tremendous amount of perceived—as well as real—authority. Thus, if the administrative assistant is unable to maintain good rapport with the professional staff, the position quickly becomes unmanageable—and the director will have to move hurriedly to straighten things out. Those affairs of the center which cannot be labeled routine will more than likely be resolved through consensus at staff business meetings. Such meetings should be chaired by the assistant director, with contentious issues being negotiated by the chair. The director will then be expected to announce policy decisions that stem from the consensus. Obviously, if agreement cannot be reached, it is the director's responsibility to affirm policy.

The maintenance of a harmonious working relationship among all members of the center's staff is another prime responsibility of the director. The administrative assistant is responsible for the output of the secretarial and clerical staff—but this reality in no way absolves the director of the responsibility for ensuring that the relationship between the clerical and professional staff is agreeable. Because the professional staff have been recruited to work in differing areas and because they have differing academic and work experience, occasionally their interests will be at variance. In other words, it can be anticipated that the professional staff working in group development will have differing perspectives from those involved in career planning and vocational guidance. There will be other conflicts in interest as well. As previously noted, the director must organize, integrate, and coordinate the working patterns of all staff members. People will be working independently while sharing the same physical facility. It is not impossible to bring together a number of people—regardless how many—into a smooth functioning unit: the overwhelming number of centers evidently accomplish this task with great success. Still, professional jealousies can arise when there is suspicion that center funds are not being used equally in the several program and service areas. Indeed, an uneven approach on any level is likely to cause a degree of friction, and certainly one of the most fractious is unequal disbursement of travel funds.

Yet none of these problems will arise if the director pursues a course that gives no reason to suspect partiality or bias in any internal matter. One of the most efficient ways to ensure this equality of treatment is the scheduling of staff business meetings at regular intervals, for it is from these meetings that the director receives feedback. An alternative to regularly scheduled business meetings is to establish a system whereby any member of the staff can request the administrative assistant to call a meeting any time that one seems appropriate. This latter approach does away with the tedium of regularly scheduled meetings in which a kind of make-work is the order of the day, but at the same time it guarantees that legitimate concerns can be brought to an open forum. Meetings in which case reports are given are quite a different matter and should be scheduled at regular intervals. In effect, they serve two broad purposes: (1) they promote discussion between professional psychologists who may have broadly varying backgrounds, and (2) they ensure that no one member of the center becomes so involved in his or her work that the larger issue of breadth of center service delivery is overlooked.

Since every member of the center's staff contributes to the image of the center that is held by all other members of the academic community, a disservice is done to the center when any staff member fails to conduct himself or herself accordingly. For example, the warmth and sincere friendliness that the secretarial and clerical staff projects to clients coming into the center are of critical import; but should this friendliness move onto a level more suggestive of a coffee klatsch than of an informal atmosphere, it is obvious that the emphasis is wrong. The image of professionalism is all-important, and this same barometer can be applied to the impact that the professional staff members have upon clients and the academic community at large. For this reason, I think, professional staff members who project an image identified with an "extreme" are failing in their responsibility to promote the center positively. It seems more likely that when counselors have a problem of identification with the center, the problem rests more with the counselors than with the center.

Warnath (1972) would probably draw the exact opposite conclusion. He seems to be saying that as increasing numbers of students reject the goals and standards of the middle class, there would be a turning away from the kind of helpful insights a middle-class counselor might be expected to provide. The same could certainly be said of hard drug users on campus. Additionally, Warnath takes note of the ethnic minority groups who complain that the "typical middle class counselor does not have the background or style to do more than assist [them] with factual information" (p. 233). He further observes that "one or two counselors may have contact with these groups, but their relations are generally due to the counselors' unique personal characteristics or life styles rather than their formal status within the counseling center" (p. 233). Thus he seems to be arguing in favor of counselor identification with an extreme, perhaps assuming the "background and style" in order to achieve rapport or playing the role of a rejectionist in order to be on common ground with those who appear to be rejecting. This reasoning would be consistent with the belief that the only physician who can effectively treat a pregnant woman is a pregnant obstetrician! It would seem to make more sense to approach the personality characteristics of counselors from the opposite direction, that is, an honest attempt to be the kind of professionals they were trained to be. The example of the student center that ceased being used by the majority of students once it had been taken over by a minority tends to support the thesis that the counseling center must provide a service for all students—with no tilt in any direction. It is clear that no one is in a better position to ensure equanimity than the director.

This chapter has only begun to touch on the subject of administrative concerns of the college and university counseling director. The position does not lend itself to either job description or even generalization from one campus to another. Although the institution defines the position, it seems that the director is also responsible in large measure for the definition. More important, the director is ultimately responsible for the health and well-being of the center; professional as well as administrative knowledgeability are the significant dimensions. Thus, it would seem in sum that the director's prime administrative concern is advancing the welfare of the center and that this is done best by an ongoing educational process directed at all levels of the academic community. The director of a center has no true guideline to follow because every campus presents a completely different set of given circumstances.

There is no doubt whatsoever that the question of legitimacy of the center demands more attention than it has received in the past, because the only reasonable way to bury the issue is to confront it squarely: wishing it away will not get the job done. Related arguments—that the centers are losing clients because of a loss of relevance or credibility with minority groups and/or that center services, programs, and activities can be absorbed into other campus organizations and departments—need to be countered equally forcefully. Toffler (1970) refers to the "Super Simplifier" and describes this individual as one who "invests every idea he comes across with universal relevance." It seems to me that trends are always starting, but it is also clear that trends are always fading out as well. To assume that the wave of the future can be charted because of one or two absorptions or several closures indicates little more than insensitivity and perhaps ignorance on the part of the institution's administration. A less acceptable, but equally possible, conclusion might be that those directors were not doing the job they should have been doing.

References

Clark. B. R. 1962. *Educating the expert society*. San Francisco: Chandler Publishing Company.

Cox, C. B. 1977. Responsibility, culpability, and the cult of accountability in education. *Phi Delta Kappa* 58: 761–66.

Guilford, J. P. 1954. *Psychometric methods*. New York: McGraw-Hill.

Koontz, H., and O'Donnell, C. 1955. *Principles of management*. New York: McGraw-Hill.

Patterson, C. H. 1967. The selection of counselors. In J. M. Whiteley, ed., *Research in counseling*. Columbus, Ohio: Charles E. Merrill.

Schoenberg, B. M. 1971. Personal characteristics of the successful counselor. *Canadian Counsellor* 5: 251–56.

Schofield, W. 1964. *Psychotherapy: the purchase of friendship*. Englewood Cliffs, N.J.: Prentice-Hall.

Toffler, A. 1970. *Future shock*. New York: Random House.

Warnath, C. F. 1972. College counseling: between the rock and the hard place. *The Personnel and Guidance Journal* 51: 229–35.

Wheelis, A. 1966. The quest for identity. In B. Rosenberg, ed., *Analyses of contemporary society*. New York: Thomas Y. Crowell Company.

PART III Formal and Informal Programs

10

THE ROLE OF INDIVIDUAL COUNSELING IN THE COUNSELING PROGRAM

John E. Hechlik and Robert D. King

WAYNE STATE UNIVERSITY

Individuals have historically been the primary subject of attention in the development of college and university counseling centers. This focus is consistent with counseling origins, which have roots in American government's traditional philosophic concern for the well-being of the individual. Scientific psychology has added its emphasis on the study of the individual as the basis for generalization about mankind. Applications of psychology to foster the well-being of people, whether by such diverse practitioners as Freud or Parsons, have grown from a focus on the individual as the basic subject for treatment. Higher education instituted counseling as a resource for individual students to complement their experience in an academic program that typically makes little other accommodation to individual differences.

However, Wrenn reflects a current trend in counseling when he states, "Although I have been a lifelong advocate of one-to-one counseling as the core of the counseling effort, I am convinced by now that we in counseling can no longer afford this luxury. Nor am I so convinced as I once was that we should go this route even if we could" (1973, p. 260).

Recent Influences on Counseling

In the past thirty years a number of developments within society, psychology, and education have led to the current questioning of the role of individual counseling in colleges and universities.

Growing student population showed greatly increased diversity of cultural background. Disparity between the needs of students and the ability of the traditional educational structure to provide for these needs resulted. Although counseling was expected to bridge the disparities between individuals and institutions, cultural traditions of many new students did not mesh with the verbal and intraceptive demands traditional to counseling. Nontraditional counseling resources developed rapidly to accommodate these new populations.

Social work and social psychology both recognized peer group influence upon individuals' attitudes and behavior and, conversely, the individual group member's potential to effect attitude and behavior change in the group. As the principle of utilizing the special empathy and understandings possible from subgroup identification developed, people with intimate knowledge of special problem areas—such as juvenile delinquency, draft resistance, and drug abuse—were recruited as personal helpers. In the college setting professional counseling personnel trained students and paraprofessionals with subgroup identity to add depth and sophistication to their helping orientations. These efforts added new dimensions to counseling.

Developments in learning theory also stimulated new ways of helping students. Behavioral techniques contributed step-by-step approaches directed toward clearly specified behavioral change. From specific, but common, problems came programs for general usage. These techniques were also utilized in individual counseling to work toward behavior change desired by the individual client. From a developmental perspective, behavior change has been viewed not as an isolated phenomenon, but as an element frequently crucial to personal development on a broader scale. Counselors have gained a new tool for assisting clients, and students have a new resource to supplement the counseling interview.

New developments in educational technology resulted in audiovisual devices and computer systems that program, interrelate, and present information previously conveyed less efficiently by counselors in the interview. Interactive computer programs, for instance, have related a great deal of research data to the characteristics of the individual person. These devices have made accessible to the total student population more information than individual counseling could give them.

Developments in administrative science demanded a clearer explication of the counseling mission, goals, objectives, techniques, and outcomes. As counseling began to articulate its discipline, new responses to student needs occurred, often not dependent upon individual counseling. Further, as government applied administrative science to the funding of higher education, it began to question the value of higher education relative to other social institutions and programs. Tighter scrutiny was given to the ways in which colleges and universities spend available moneys. Along with other departments and programs, counseling had to compete for its share of the budget. The value of counseling was no longer assumed; it needed to be demonstrated in relation to cost-effectiveness. Individual counseling in particular needed clearer justification at this point.

New Counseling Programs

As a result of these recent developments, counseling centers have developed a variety of new service modes. They serve many of the same purposes as did traditional individual counseling.

Group counseling practice has developed from group psychotherapy experience, from the social-psychological discovery of the effectiveness of groups in problem-solving situations, and from recognition of the personal value that group interaction has for many individuals. Counseling groups are typically problem-centered, growth-centered, or therapy-centered.

Workshops and seminars are more task-oriented, highly structured, leader-directed, and shorter in duration. Leader input, largely of a cognitive or didactic character, is directed toward helping group members understand something of a fairly specific nature.

Peer counseling, in the broadest sense, has probably existed since the invention of language. Research indicates that young people still tend to turn to friends first when they need help. In developing peer counseling programs, counseling centers utilize this informal assistance network, which reaches large numbers of students, and try to improve the quality of assistance by providing students with training in the use of empathy, problem-solving models, crisis intervention techniques, and human relations skills. Other nonprofessional persons are trained to operate within a more formal structure as paraprofessionals.

Programmed psychological education covers a wide range of topics such as values clarification, human relations, achievement motivation, decision making, problem solving, and goal setting. Within this category also fall interactive computer programs such as the Education and Career Exploration System (ECES), the System of Interactive Guidance and Information (SIGI), and the Computerized Vocational Information System (CVIS), all based on career education and decision-making models.

Individual Counseling and the New Programs

When contrasted with traditional individual counseling, new programs in college and university counseling centers show many advantages. They have been devised in response to the changes just described, they frequently operate at the developmental or preventive level, they can be organized to provide assistance in many areas of concern common to students, they can accommodate large numbers of students, and they can function at a relatively low cost per student.

The newer programs are generally limited, however, as a result of being structured to deal with a particular class of problem or population. To participate effectively in any such program, students must find the program area to be relevant to their own particular needs, be able to deal with those needs from a perspective that tends to isolate them from other experience, and be able to function effectively within the program's format.

Many students fall through the cracks of the structures upon which these programs are based. They frequently want help with aspects of their experience that are relatively unique within the student population. Their concerns are often so intertwined with other aspects of their life or self that a more holistic approach is necessary. Their own special characteristics often stop them from participating effectively in a program designed for a certain kind of person. Thus, although individual counseling makes its own unique demands on clients, for many students it represents a highly personal and flexible situation allowing them to deal effectively with highly personal and complex needs and problems. It may be the only means for some students.

While it is obviously good for counseling centers to reach more students through new programs, it is doubtful that higher education has reached a point of view that can rationalize the elimination of individual counseling. Individualized help is presently touted in tutoring programs, work-study assignments, financial aid packaging, and honors programs. At the same time, counseling centers are moving in the direction of the traditional teaching structure, which provides lectures, discussion groups, and laboratories as the nearly exclusive vehicle for learning.

Adaptation of Individual Counseling to Present Conditions

While it is useful to compare traditional individual counseling *versus* newer methods of counseling help, we must consciously avoid the implicit assumption that the two are mutually exclusive and that in these cost-conscious days we can only choose between them. To relinquish an established mode of service is to risk a shortsighted decision. Creative thinking has been startlingly productive in the general counseling discipline. Creative modifications *within* individual counseling are indeed scarce.

CHANGING THE CONTEXT FOR INDIVIDUAL COUNSELING

Can traditional individual counseling be modified to maximize its advantages and minimize its disadvantages? Any constructive thought must not compare it to other counseling programs, but must view individual counseling *within the whole context of counseling services*. It can best be seen as one of several options useful for students.

Since individual counseling is the most expensive form of counseling, a wide range of alternative programs are necessary. Each alternative complements and strengthens the others. Innovative programs from the 1974–1975 counseling centers Data Bank (1975) demonstrate this varied and complementary system:

Life-span planning for mature women and men
Death and dying
Test anxiety reduction
Communication skills
Life-planning workshops
Beating the system
Job-hunting strategies for survival after college
Biofeedback training
Paraprofessional programming
Weight control and body image groups
Race relations program
Assertiveness training
Self-management workshops
Career information programs
Comprehensive behavior therapy programs for essential hypertension
Computerized vocational interest inventories
Personal communications labs
Desensitization of the fear of public speaking
Relaxation therapy
Male-female communication groups
Psychobehavioral approach to weight reduction
Marital enrichment groups
Rape crisis clinics
Separation crisis programs
Sexual dysfunction counseling
Career development micro-labs
Listening skills training

If such programs are selected and developed on the basis of an honest and direct assessment of institutional needs, they can help many students who otherwise would need individual counseling time.

Supported by such alternate sources, individual counseling can be restricted to those students who must have it because of its personalized nature. Some requests for individual counseling are made because students are unaware of other resources equally or more appropriate for their counseling goals. Even students with a strong personal preference for individual counseling may not actually require it. They can be referred gently to alternative programs and counseled individually later if specific need develops. Inevitably, some students need individual help either because alternate programs have failed them or because such programs are manifestly inappropriate for them. In any case, new counseling center budgets require new screening approaches to select appropriate counseling options for students.

CHANGING THE STRUCTURE OF INDIVIDUAL COUNSELING

In the individual counseling situation several things can be done to maximize productive use of counseling time. It would be ideal to use individual counseling as an open-ended relationship with maximum freedom for the client, but most colleges and universities can no longer afford this, if indeed they ever could. Counselors need to structure the relationship in order to provide necessary limits and to facilitate movement and direction of the counseling process. Since discrepancy between client and counselor expectations is characteristic of many unsuccessful counseling experiences, these expectations need to be clarified initially with the client. In the initial interview the counselor can do these things:

1. Establish goals and evaluate feasibility (these may be modified as counseling progresses);
2. Clarify the duration of the relationship so that clients can mobilize their energies to work within these limits and pace their movement to maintain necessary personal controls;
3. Establish a contract about missed appointments, since individual counselor time is so expensive;
4. Clarify expectation that alternate counseling programs will be utilized when appropriate, even while individual counseling is proceeding;
5. Discuss "homework" assignments that may be anticipated as an adjunct to individual counseling;
6. Schedule periodic evaluation of counseling progress, to be made by client and counselor together. While evaluation of goals and progress will probably be tentative at many times, the regular evaluation of the counseling process supports both client and counselor and encourages progress.

Use and Development of Counselor Resources

Innovative use of counselor staff resources can contribute to better individual counseling. The important variables are counselor competencies, personality, and theoretical orientations. Although past research provides no systematic basis for matching counselor to client, a professional intake worker, sensitive to counselor staff characteristics, can make referrals of better quality than those which result from procedures based on administrative expediency.

Following referral is the theoretical orientation that the counselor decides will be most effective. Again, it is difficult to predetermine that one approach in the counselor's repertoire will be better than another. This must be left to the counselor's judgment as the relationship unfolds. However, if the counselor has only one orientation from which to interact with the client, the opportunity for adapting treatment to the client is limited.

Many theoretical orientations have special relevance to individual clients and special meaning to counselors. Personal counseling or psychotherapy offers psychoanalytic, Adlerian, client-centered, rational-emotive, behavior therapy, Gestalt, reality therapy, experiential, transactional analysis, encounter eclectic, and other orientations. According to Patterson (1966), five major groups emerge: psychoanalytic, existential, rational, perceptual-phenomenological, and learning theory. Theories of occupational choice and vocational development that provide background for counseling include not only trait-and-factor theory, but also need-drive and psychoanalytic theories and those formulated by Roe, Hoppock, Ginzberg, Holland, Tiedeman, and Super.

Although it is unrealistic to expect counselors to develop competence in more than a few of these approaches, it is reasonable to expect them to have an overview of most so that they can find orientations consistent with their personal style. They owe the client the flexibility that a variety of possible approaches supplies to the counseling relationship. Similarly, it is reasonable to expect a counseling center consciously to attempt to provide a staff representing a wide range of approaches.

While theoretical orientation provides a general set from which the counselors can respond to clients' unique behavior during counseling, there are many relatively direct techniques that counselors can introduce to facilitate client progress. Drawn from a variety of philosophical and theoretical frameworks, they are generally compatible with most theoretical orientations.

1. Problem-solving training helps the client learn how to break down confusing situations into manageable steps so that she can take into account as much data as possible relevant to herself, her situation, and the external environment.
2. Decision-making training helps the client develop effective decision-making strategies, such as clarifying the decision situation, considering possible alternatives, searching for information about possible outcomes of alternatives, and evaluating information in the light of personal values.
3. Autobiography can be used as a loosely structured creative writing experience through which client and counselor derive a greater understanding of the client and the effects of his life experiences.
4. Modeling provides direct experience of a live, simulated, or symbolic presentation of behaviors that the client can use in adapting his own behavior to similar situations.
5. Audiotherapy utilizes preprogrammed audio tapes and records to provide

the client with didactic framework for understanding mental health concepts, stimulus material for projection and identification of attitudes and feelings, and the modeling of behavior.

6. Logging involves the client's writing down her experiences and her responses to them to help in the process of self-discovery.

7. Achievement motivation training uses the personal characteristics, action strategies, and goal-setting techniques of high achievers as models to help the client learn to do things better, faster, more energetically, and more effectively.

8. Behavior contracting involves an agreement between client and counselor regarding specific client goals, the specific behavioral steps leading to the goal, the positive reinforcements involved, and the monitoring of the behaviors.

9. Mental imagery is a technique in which the client learns to establish cognitive, emotional, and behavioral associations that allow better adaptation to previously threatening situations.

10. Role playing is a form of dramatization in which the client acts out a role other than that which he perceives to be directly his own in order to explore a variety of live situations.

11. Relaxation training is a method of anxiety reduction that can be taught to the client either directly by the counselor or through use of tape-recorded instructions.

Special Administrative Considerations

Individual counseling, integrated with other services discussed here, involves development of many alternate counseling programs, selective referral *for* individual counseling, selective referral *to* individual counselors, establishment of structure within the counseling situation for greater efficiency, and provision of greater flexibility of orientation and counseling technique. Four administrative necessities emerge.

An intake procedure is essential to guide students toward appropriate counseling resources. This would require referral of students to counseling programs other than individual counseling when such alternatives appear relevant. It should be designed to help students clarify their understanding of individual counseling and to make possible referral to the most appropriate individual counselor.

Differentiated staffing of the counseling center is needed. Administrators, professional staff counselors, counselor trainees and graduate assistants, paraprofessionals, and peer counselors should play specialized roles appropriate to their level of training, expertise, and experience. Ideally, no staff members should work at a level below that appropriate to their qualifications and remuneration.

Staff development must be vigorously pursued in order to expand the possible orientations and competencies of individual counselors. Continual communication is also necessary in order to maintain awareness of the whole counseling program so that all staff can coordinate their own roles with those of other persons in the total center program.

A team concept must be considered in staff recruitment and staff development. Once the center's program dimensions are described and agreed upon, current staff strength can be evaluated. Recruitment of new staff members can be based upon their potential for providing orientations and approaches that the center wants to include.

Conclusion

Colleges and universities welcomed individual counseling at one point in their institutional development. Since then, society, technology, and education have changed dramatically. Counseling has, at the same time, added new approaches, techniques, and delivery systems to reach increasingly diverse target populations. The interaction of most new counseling programs with these new targets is positive.

Individual counseling continues to make a unique contribution to student development. However, if it is to survive as a counseling service, counselors and administrators must give creative thought to adapting it to counseling's new dynamic context.

References

Arbuckle, D. S. 1975. *Counseling and psychotherapy: an existential-humanistic view*. 3d ed. Boston: Allyn & Bacon.

Association of University and College Counseling Directors. 1967–1976. *Annual data bank*, ed. Thomas M. Magoon. College Park: University of Maryland.

Bordin, E. S. 1955. *Psychological counseling*. New York: Appleton-Century-Crofts.

Corsini, R. 1973. *Current psychotherapies*. Itasca, Ill.: F. E. Peacock.

Gallagher, P. J., and Demos, G. D. 1970. *The counseling center in higher education*. Springfield, Ill.: Charles C. Thomas.

Lewis, E. C. 1970. *The psychology of counseling*. New York: Holt, Rinehart and Winston.

Magoon, T. M. 1975. *1974–1975 counseling center data bank*. College Park, Md.: University of Maryland Counseling Center, Item 41.

Patterson, C. H. 1966. *Theories of counseling and psychotherapy*. New York: Harper & Row.

Peters, H. J., and Hansen, J. C. 1966. *Vocational guidance and career development: selected readings*. New York: Macmillan.

Robinson, F. P. 1950. *Principles and procedures in student counseling*. New York: Harper & Bros.

Shertzer, B., and Stone, S. C. 1971. *Fundamentals of guidance*. 2d ed. Boston: Houghton Mifflin.

Siegel, M. 1968. *Function, practice and technique: the counseling of college students*. New York: Free Press.

Stefflre, B., ed. 1965. *Theories of counseling*. New York: McGraw-Hill.

Toffler, A. 1975. *The eco-spasm report*. New York: Bantam Books.

———. 1970. *Future shock*. New York: Random House.

Walz, G. R.; Miller, J. V.; and Mintz, R. 1972. *Information analysis and targeted communications program for improving and expanding the amount of occupational exploration and career planning*. Final Report, project no. 1–0615 A, grant no. OEG-0-71-3581, U.S. Department HEW, O.E.

Warnath, C. F., ed., and Associates. 1973. *New directions for college counselors: a handbook for redesigning professional roles*. San Francisco: Jossey-Bass.

Wrenn, C. G. 1973. *The world of the contemporary counselor*. Boston: Houghton Mifflin.

Zaccaria, J. S. 1970. *Theories of occupational choice and vocational development*. Boston: Houghton Mifflin.

11

METHODOLOGIES OF STRESS-STRAIN MANAGEMENT

Charles R. Brasfield

SIMON FRASER UNIVERSITY

Definitions and Scope of This Chapter

Stress and strain are physical engineering concepts that have been increasingly applied to human functioning over the past several decades. When most people speak of being under stress, they mean that they feel pressured, put upon, frustrated, angry, subjected to many or conflicting demands, or a variety of other more or less idiosyncratically defined emotions. The engineers, more specifically, define stress as the amount of load placed upon the object or structure by the external environment; what happens to the structure when it is placed under stress is then defined as strain. Similarly, Harold Wolff (1953, p. 315) has described stress as "the interaction between organism and external environment, and strain is the alteration or deformation that then ensues." This general conceptual scheme of stress as environmental demand and strain as the resultant alteration or adaptation can be applied to machines, organizations, and, for the purposes of this chapter, people.

Given such a broad definition, a chapter on stress-strain management could conceivably deal with such diverse topics as physiology, nutrition, work, climatology, and so on. Most of these topics will be excluded here. This chapter will be restricted to discussion of methods of stress-strain management that might reasonably be applied to clients presenting themselves to a university or college counseling center. Specifically excluded will be methodologies involving gross physical alteration of the client (such as changes in diet and exercise regimens) or physiologically invasive procedures (such as surgery or medication). Certainly diet, exercise, medication, and remedial surgery are invaluable methods of stress-strain management, but they usually require collaboration with experts in fields rarely included in the university counseling center staff.

The stress-strain management methodologies that remain for discussion are primarily psychological in nature and may well be more easily and widely applicable than those excluded from discussion. That stress-strain management methodologies of whatever sort need to be more widely applied is very clear. Alvin Toffler, in *Future Shock* (1970), has written very persuasively of the stresses we face now and can expect to face in the future, while Hans Selye has already noted, "An ever increasing proportion of the human population dies from the so-called wear-and-tear diseases, or degenerative diseases, which are primarily due to stress" (1956, p. 275). Clearly, it is important, and perhaps imperative, for us to attend to stress and/or strain as a significant factor in the lives of our clients, our colleagues, and ourselves.

Development of Awareness of Stress-Strain

Perhaps the first step in dealing with stress or strain is to notice it; it is rarely possible for individuals to deliberately change something of which they are unaware. Yet all environments are stressful to some extent; and, after a time, we come to accept a certain, usual level of stress and strain as normal, and we no longer notice it. Indeed, there is an optimal level of stress that is necessary for the degree of arousal (strain) needed to perform any particular task to the best of our ability. It is quite possible, however, for the stress to gradually increase beyond the optimum without its being noticed. Then others may notice that we have become "normally" irritable, nervous, tired, or distracted. Some clients may have a vague feeling of being under stress without being able to specify at all what it is in their physical or social environment to which they are responding.

ENVIRONMENTAL STRESS MONITORING

As a first step in a stress-strain management program, it is often useful to have the client construct and keep a diary of all environmental events occuring over a period of a week or more. Holmes and Rahe (1967) have developed a "Social Readjustment Rating Scale" that is a landmark pioneering measure of the impact of a variety of life-change events. Their scale, however, is retrospective over the previous twelve months and includes many events (for example, marriage) that occur with a relatively low frequency for most clients. For most clients, what is needed is an index of stressful events that occur with relatively high frequencies. From a one-week sample of all events occuring to a client, it is often possible to pick out obvious stressors for further monitoring. For instance, one client's diary might include three nights of less than normal sleep, two parties, one argument with a boyfriend, one examination, submission of one essay just before a deadline, and one traffic ticket. Each of these events would then bear further monitoring and the frequency of their occurence could serve as a baseline for comparison with subsequent weeks.

STRAIN MONITORING

Because many clients are relatively unaware of the stressors in their lives, it is often important to teach them to monitor their *responses* to stressors in addition to, or instead of, monitoring stress events. A client might, for instance, be instructed to keep a tally of each time he felt tense, excited, frightened, angry, frustrated, cold, joyful, or tired each day. Each of these responses represents an adaptation to some environmental demand and is, thus, a strain response. The frequency of strain responses over a period of time could then be utilized as a baseline against which to compare with other periods of time.

In many cases it is useful to instruct the client to note not only frequency, but also intensity, of strain responses. Three instances of minor irritation with a salesclerk may be of considerably less import than a violent argument with a roommate. Utilizing both frequency and intensity of strain responses allows derivation of a simple numerical index of overall strain for any given period of time.

For some clients, only one or a very few strain responses may be of particular importance. For clients with tension headaches, for example, only the frequency and intensity of the headache activity may need to be monitored to gain an index of general levels of strain.

COMBINED STRESS-STRAIN MONITORING

Monitoring a variety of strain responses and noting for each response the concomitant environmental event provides an index of both the stress level of the client's environment and the degree of strain with which the client responds to stress events. In initial phases of stress-strain management this procedure is often important in order to determine what intervention strategy is likely to be most useful to the client.

Once the client (and counselor) has some idea of the amount of stress to which he is subject and the degree of strain with which he responds, two important concepts begin to emerge. These are the concepts of individual differences and response stereotype. For a variety of reasons (past experience, expectations, and so forth), different people respond to different events as stressors. Similarly, each individual tends to develop a particular response pattern to a variety of different stressors. A client with a history of academic failure, for example, may find herself responding with anxiety to a description of the grading system for a course in which she is enrolled, while her academically successful classmate may respond to the same event with only mild interest.

The principle of autonomic response stereotypy was clearly demonstrated some years ago (Lacey & Lacey, 1958), and more recent research (Sternbach, 1966) indicates that the principle applies most particularly to people with psychosomatic disorders, many of which are stress-related.

Behaviorally, one client may typically respond with anxiety to a variety of stressor events to which another client may usually respond with anger. In both cases, the responses may be similarly inappropriate, but the stress-strain management strategies the two clients might find useful would probably be quite different.

Environmental Stress Management

Because stress is defined as the demands of the environment upon the individual, environmental management or manipulation might be considered the only real method of stress management. Other management strategies might better be considered as strain management methods. Within the general area of environmental management, there are two basic strategies: stimulus control and arrangement of response consequences.

STIMULUS CONTROL

This concept refers to the idea that each individual responds to particular sets of stimuli with strain responses and that the frequency of the responses can be changed by simply changing the frequency of the associated stimuli. Which stimuli or events are to be controlled is determined through careful monitoring of stress events. There are some pitfalls to be avoided in the use of this technique, but it can be very useful. For example, if the client feels anxious to an extreme degree when involved in a typical university registration process, it is usually possible for him to avoid that whole stimulus complex either by registering early or late (and perhaps paying a nominal extra fee). In this manner, he has controlled to some extent the environmental demands (or stimuli) placed upon him.

Similarly, if a client finds unstructured social situations aversive, she can usually arrange her social life so that she is involved only in structured social activity through clubs and other organizations.

Both of these examples refer to behavioral stimulus control: this is a very useful strategy, but it can be inappropriately extended to the detriment of the client. People who are afraid of large, open spaces can avoid such stimuli to the extent that they are eventually confined to a single small room, for example. To avoid such pitfalls, it is quite possible to build perceptual controls of stimulus situations into the management program. A client can be taught to scan a stimulus array with the purpose of identifying and focusing upon the positive and nonstressful elements to the relative exclusion of the more stressful elements. This strategy does not, of course, change the actual environment, but it does change the client's perception of the environment and thus the environmental impact. This particular technique will be considered further under the section dealing with strain management.

ARRANGEMENT OF RESPONSE CONSEQUENCES

This idea refers to the fact that we all live in a continuing, more or less linear sequence and that it is possible to modify the sequence to some extent by prearrangement. Since all people have both aversive and rewarding events occurring during most days, it is often possible to help the client arrange for the aversive or stressful events that result in strain to be followed by relaxing events allowing for recovery from the strain response. For instance, completion of a final examination might serve as the signal to go home and have a relaxing, warm bath before beginning preparation for the next examination. In this instance, the strain response required by the examination has a *prearranged consequence* of relaxation.

Similarly, inevitable aversive events can also be prearranged as consequences to reduce strain. If a client finds, while preparing a difficult paper, that he is beginning to imagine receiving a failing grade and becomes anxious, that event of imagination can serve as the cue to take a short break and clean up his room, wash dishes, or complete some other minor aversive task. Thus the aversive, but inevitable, event serves as a distraction from another aversive event that produces more strain.

When one utilizes this approach, it is relatively important to ensure that rewarding events are prearranged to occur following a response the client *wishes* to make (even though it may be a strain) and that aversive events are prearranged to occur following a response the client *does not wish* to make. It is also important, in prearrangement of aversive response consequences, to make sure that the amount of strain entailed by the response consequence is less than the amount of strain entailed by the response itself.

Strain Management

As stress or environmental management is aimed at manipulation or control of the demands placed upon the individual by the environment, so strain management is aimed at managing the responses of the individual to his or her environment. However, just as environmental management does not totally eliminate stress, so strain management does not totally eliminate strain. It is a matter of response management, rather than response elimination.

It is useful to discuss strain in terms of the definition quoted at the first of this chapter—the "alteration or deformation" that ensues following interaction with the environment. Since the environment does not cease and at no point does the individual cease interacting with it, there is always some degree of alteration occurring. So what we are really discussing when we discuss strain is the degree or level of alteration occuring and whether or not it is appropriate to the environmental situation obtaining at that moment.

Obviously, a highly demanding environment would normally entail a high degree of alteration or strain to be utilized in coping with the environment. Once the environmental demand (or stress) has been dealt with or removed, the high degree of alteration (or strain) should return to something approximating normal. However, as noted earlier, under some environmental situations people may become "normally" nervous, irritable, or distracted just as if they were continually responding to a high stress situation. Malmo (1975) has suggested that when individuals are exposed to extremely demanding life situations over a prolonged period of time, their neurophysiological set-point (rather akin to a thermostat) "sticks" at a higher than normal level such that these individuals react to ordinary life situations as if they were emergencies. In such a situation, no matter how well the actual environment is managed, the individuals still respond with undue strain; clearly what is needed is some form of strain management.

Perhaps because acquisition of higher education is, in itself, a relatively demanding task and also usually occurs at a time when the individual is engaged in equally demanding developmental tasks such as establishing personal identity, independence, and intimacy, many students (and not a few faculty) show signs of undue strain. For those who present themselves as clients to a university or college counseling center, there are a variety of methodologies that can assist them in managing their levels of strain.

DIRECT STRATEGIES

As mentioned earlier, a necessary first step is to teach clients self-monitoring techniques that allow them to become aware of the amount and degree of stress and strain to which they are subject. Having done this, and perhaps having also rearranged their environment so that it presents the least possible stress, clients may still find that they are reacting with undue strain. At this point they may wish to apply one or more direct methods of strain reduction, such as progressive relaxation, meditation, or a particular form of biofeedback.

Relaxation Strategies

There are many relaxation methodologies in use today, but perhaps the best known is that described by Edmund Jacobson (1938). This approach teaches the individual to recognize and reduce residual muscle tensions that may be present even when lying or sitting in what is apparently a very relaxed position. Prescribed relaxation exercises progress from one relatively small muscle group to another until the individual has learned to relax the whole body deeply. This detailed and progressive approach to relaxation is somewhat similar to a less well known, but perhaps more extended, method of relaxation and strain reduction called autogenic training (Schultz & Luthe, 1959). Developed in Europe, this methodology involves frequent, short periods of detailed attention to particular body sensations while repeating subvocally a standard series of phrases intended to focus attention upon the body sensation involved. Like progressive relaxation, autogenic training progresses step by step until the client has developed the skill of becoming deeply relaxed at will.

There exist many other specific relaxation methodologies, and both of the methods described above have been modified by a variety of therapists and researchers. However, most of the relaxation methodologies have in common a relaxed posture, a specific set of relaxation instructions, and frequent practice of the technique. These same characteristics are also generally found in descriptions of meditative methodologies, which can also be utilized as a strategy for strain management or reduction.

Meditative Strategies

Probably some sort of meditative strategy, prescribed for a variety of purposes, can be traced throughout recorded history. In North America, at least since the 1960s, several meditative strategies associated with yoga, Zen Buddhism, and a number of other religious or semireligious movements have been known and practiced. Here I will discuss only the passive strategies of meditation, although there are others that make use of ritual activity.

Perhaps the best known of the passive meditative strategies is transcendental meditation, as introduced to the Western world by Maharishi Mahesh Yogi (1963). The technique of transcendental meditation (or TM) is relatively simple, involving silent repetition of a single sound (or mantra), over and over again, while sitting in a comfortable position and remaining passively inattentive to any distracting thoughts. Herbert Benson, one of the better known researchers of meditative techniques, has suggested that the particular sound used is less important than had been earlier thought and that the four basic elements of meditation are (1) a quiet environment, (2) an object to dwell upon, (3) a passive attitude, and (4) a comfortable position (1975, pp. 110–11). When an individual carries out such a meditative exercise for a period of twenty minutes or so, a variety of physiologic changes occur, which appear to be associated with a particularly restful state that Benson has termed "the relaxation response." He suggests that regular induction of this response can reduce physiologic strain and reduce the incidence of stress-related disorders. Benson notes that similar physiologic changes have been found associated with other passive meditative strategies, and it is likely that most or all passive meditative techniques can be utilized to reduce undue strain.

Biofeedback

In the last few years, *biofeedback* has become an overused word, a circumstance that has all too often led to this whole area of research and clinical application being dismissed as a fad. The word actually refers to a technique, often utilizing sophisticated electronics, of delivering to individuals accurate information about their ongoing biological functioning. The basic idea is as simple (or complicated) as using a mirror to shave or to comb one's hair. The idea that one can influence one's own physiology voluntarily, once given accurate feedback about it, is often presented as a novel innovation of biofeedback, but we have already been discussing voluntary influences of physiology in the sections on relaxation and meditative strategies.

Although biofeedback can be applied in a number of areas, only the application to strain management will be discussed here. Biofeedback becomes particularly important when we recall Malmo's set-point hypothesis and the idea that one can become "normally" strained without being aware of it. We might also recall the idea of autonomic response stereotypy and note that an individual might well have a particular pattern of strain responses to stressors. Putting these two ideas together, it then becomes possible for individuals to react with a particular pattern of physiologic strain to a variety of ordinary life events as though they were responding to emergency situations and yet to remain unaware that they are exhibiting undue strain. However, the strain responses are physiological alterations and, as such, can be measured with appropriate instrumentation.

The appropriate instrumentation, in many cases, is the same instrumentation that might be utilized in biofeedback training. This might include such instruments as an electromyograph (EMG), a skin temperature monitor, a monitor of the electrical conductance or resistance of the skin, a blood pressure monitor, an electroencephalograph (EEG), or a cardiotachometer, which gives a moment-to-moment measure of pulse rate. Such instruments can be applied diagnostically to determine the level of strain to which clients are subject and the body systems that are affected, even though the clients cannot specify either the level of strain or the body system with which they are responding.

In such a situation, showing clients the ongoing measurement of their own physiology would constitute biofeedback. When clients had been instructed to alter some monitored physiological parameter and actually were attempting to do so, the procedure could then be considered biofeedback training.

Once the strain responses are being monitored and clients are attempting to modify them to more appropriate levels, they might choose to employ one of the relaxation or meditative strategies already discussed or one of several others yet to be discussed, or they might develop their own strategies, which could be more effective for them and their particular response pattern. The great advantage of biofeedback is that clients can immediately *know* whether or not, and to what extent, the strain management strategies they are using are effective for them.

Clearly, biofeedback is an area of great promise. Barbara Brown (1974) has speculated on how it might be utilized now and in the future, and a great deal of research in the area is continuing (see Miller et al., 1974). But there remains much more to be done. The procedure seems to offer invaluable assistance in the area of strain management; however, it does require of the counselor or therapist a relatively high level of knowledge about motivation and learning theory, electronics, and physiology and anatomy, as well as good clinical skills.

INDIRECT STRATEGIES

While the direct strain management strategies are aimed at teaching clients methods of altering the inappropriate strain responses per se, indirect strategies are generally aimed at helping clients develop other responses that avoid or substitute for the undesired strain responses. Perhaps the oldest of these strategies is well known to every athlete and all actors: it is rehearsal.

Behavior Rehearsal

Many stress situations are those which call for individuals to *do* something actively to reduce the stress or resolve the situation. If individuals are skilled at performing the requisite behaviors, they are more likely to carry them out with a minimum of undue effort and a maximum effect on the situation. Once the required behaviors are known, the skill in performing the behaviors may be acquired through practice or rehearsal. For instance, if a student is required to give a class presentation, she may know exactly how she would *like* to sound, stand, gesture, or demonstrate. Yet if the presentation itself is the first time she has performed that particular set of behaviors, her performance is not likely to be especially successful. If, however, the actual presentation is the tenth performance of those behaviors, her chances of success are much higher.

Most people are aware that actors rehearse and athletes practice to ensure behavioral skill, but it may not be immediately apparent that the skill is increased in order to be applied effectively to high-stress situations and that the same techniques can be applied to their own behavioral skill in performing in high-stress situations.

There are, of course, some limitations to even the most elaborate dress rehearsal. Primarily, the target audience is not present and is not reacting to the performed behaviors; similarly, the performer is not reacting to the audience. A job applicant may be very skilled in performing the required interview behaviors he has rehearsed, yet quite inept in his response to an unexpected, and unprepared for, question. The smooth performance of his interview can, in this situation, quickly become highly strained. Such situations call for a different sort of strategy.

Cognitive Strategies

Even prior to behavior rehearsal, of course, it is necessary to think of the behaviors to be performed and to decide how they should fit together to make up the total performance. This sort of thinking ahead is a cognitive strategy, which might be termed performance planning.

Cognitive rehearsal need not, of course, be limited to thinking of specific behaviors to be performed at some time in the future. In many cases cognitive

strategies will also include thoughts, feelings, images, contingency plans, attention strategies, and the like. Thoresen and Mahoney (1974) have commented
extensively on the influence of thoughts and images upon human behavior.
Similarly, Meichenbaum and Cameron (1974) have discussed in some detail the
impact of what people say to themselves about what they are doing, the situation
in which they find themselves, and so forth.

In terms of strain management, cognitive strategies can be conceptualized as
being of utility before an expected stress, during the stress situation, and after the
removal of the stressor. Prior to the stress situation, a client can be instructed to
visualize mentally his behavior in some detail. He might also be instructed to
develop alternate performance plans for any of several possible changes in the
expected development of events. For instance, a client who will be entering a
public-speaking situation might mentally rehearse his speech and also decide in
advance how he will answer several probable questions. Further, the same client
might be instructed to scan his audience during the speech and to focus most of
his attention upon those members of the audience who appear to be interested. If
he finds himself becoming anxious during the speech, the client might also
follow the instruction to say to himself subvocally, "Relax, you're doing fine."
Finally, the client can be instructed to focus most of his attention after the speech
is delivered, upon the fact of completion rather than any inadequacies in his
delivery.

There are a variety of other cognitive strategies, not discussed here, that can be
easily applied to stress situations with the assistance of a skilled and innovative
counselor. The reader can probably quickly think of several additional cognitive
strategies that might apply to the public speaking example presented above.

New Skill Acquisitions

Sometimes clients must answer "I don't know" to the question "What would
you do if. . .?" This is a relatively clear indication that they need to acquire some
new skills. New skill acquisition can also serve the purpose of strain management.

It is probably clear that any of the stress-strain methodologies discussed so far
can be acquired as new skills. It may also be clear that there are a variety of other
skills, such as assertiveness training (see Smith, 1975), that can also be acquired
and applied to stress-strain management. Despite the current popularity of self-
help books and cassette tapes, the element usually common to acquisition of new
skills is instruction or coaching by someone who is expert in the area. This is the
element, of course, that maintains the existence of all professional (as opposed to
totally academic) training programs.

More specifically, a client might be coached by a counselor in relaxation
strategies and, quite separately, might take a course in public speaking as well.
The relaxation strategy combined with the new skill is much more likely to allow
the client to perform effectively than either strategy alone.

In most cities, courses are available in a variety of skill areas that may be useful to clients. The topics may vary from exercise management to dancing, public speaking to composing a resumé. Many such courses may not be of any particular value to a highly strained client in and of themselves, but combined with other stress-strain management programs, they can be invaluable.

Cautions and Other Comments

Clearly, all of the methodologies discussed in this chapter can be *taught* in a group setting. The advantages of such a program are obvious, but it should be remembered that the methodologies can be *applied* only individually. Each methodology is easily explained and discussed; equally easily, each methodology can be misapplied to the detriment of the client.

Self-monitoring, for example, can become so detailed that the client literally has time for nothing else. Similarly, stimulus control can be extended to such an extent that the client avoids almost all ordinary situations because they might be uncomfortable. In prearranging response consequences, it is very easy for a client to prearrange himself either into complete indolence with rewarding consequences or into a panic state with aversive consequences. Inappropriate application of relaxation or meditative strategies could either use up undue amounts of time or interfere with the degree of arousal necessary for optimal performance, while there is some suggestive evidence (Fowler, Budzynski & VanderBergh, 1976) that misapplication of biofeedback techniques could result in potentiation and possible toxicity of drugs that the client may also be utilizing. Too much behavioral rehearsal can also interfere with optimal performance, leaving the client feeling bored with the actual performance. Cognitive strategies can also be misapplied; a client can think of so many possible performance demands that he ends up imagining, and reacting to, all sorts of fantasized catastrophies. Or a client may focus her attention so inappropriately in an actual performance that she misses cues indicating a necessary change in her behavior, as in a public lecture that bores all but one member of the audience. Finally, acquisition of new skills can delay forever the doing of anything the client needs to do, but wishes to avoid.

The point of all these caveats is that even in group programs of stress-strain management each client must have *readily* available individual consultation with a counselor both competent in application of stress-strain management methodologies and aware of ways in which the same strategies might be misapplied.

MONITORING AND EXPERT CHECK-UP

Both because of the potential for misapplication of stress-strain management methodologies and because of the set-point hypothesis (suggesting that strain can become excessive without the individual being aware of it), it is strongly recommended that every client be encouraged to monitor closely occasional samples of behavior and experience. As discussed earlier in this chapter, such monitoring need not be continuous or even frequent so long as it provides clients with an index of how they have been functioning lately. If ex-clients find that their lives have changed in an undesirable way, they can then return to the counselor for what might be termed an expert check-up.

The concept of individual differences might also be remembered. Some clients will consistently misapply whatever management strategies they might be taught, while others will rarely or never do so. Many clients will find a more or less unique combination of management strategies useful to them. For all these reasons, skilled individual coaching must be very accessible for all clients utilizing stress-strain management methodologies.

FROM REMEDIATION TO PREVENTION

The procedure of using self-monitoring as a cue for remediation may be recognized as the strategy of prearranging response consequences. The utilization of a presumably remedial procedure (self-monitoring) in the absence of a known requirement for remediation may, further, suggest that all of the methodologies discussed here can be utilized preventively as well as for remediation of excessive stress or strain. This is indeed the case. Once clients have been taught and coached in the appropriate application of stress-strain management methodologies, it is quite conceivable that they may utilize exactly the same methodologies for prevention of excessive stress-strain. Other preventive programs are discussed later in this book.

Throughout the chapter it has been assumed that the stress and strain to be managed are undue stress and strain, but *undue* has not been defined. Determination of what is or is not an appropriate response involves a variety of areas other than stress-strain management, and it is mentioned here only as an index of one of many ways in which a number of topics relevant to stress-strain management have been omitted or oversimplified. Similarly, much interesting and relevant research has not been directly cited. The reader who is interested in pursuing a topic in detail is given only a starting point in the references that are cited.

Clearly, management of stress and strain will become a matter of increasing importance as society becomes more complex, and this chapter is intended only as an overview of some possible management methodologies; definitive treatment of the topic must be sought elsewhere. As universities and colleges become ever more involved with and influential in society, however, it seems fitting that they provide to society some means of handling the stress that is endemic. Accomplishing this task, in other than an academic manner, requires skilled counselors in a counseling center that is an integral part of the campus environment.

References

Benson, H. 1975. *The relaxation response*. New York: William Morrow.
Brown, B. 1974. *New mind, new body: biofeedback: new directions for the mind*. New York: Harper & Row.

Fowler, J. E.; Budzynski, T.; and VanderBergh, R. L. 1976. Effects of an EMG biofeed-back relaxation program on the control of diabetes: a case study. *Biofeedback and Self-Regulation* 1: 105–12.

Holmes, T. H., and Rahe, R. H. 1967. The social readjustment rating scale. *Journal of Psychosomatic Research* 11: 213–18.

Jacobson, E. 1938. *Progressive relaxation.* Chicago: University of Chicago Press.

Lacey, J. I., and Lacey, B. C. 1958. Verification and extension of the principle of autonomic response stereotype. *American Journal of Psychology* 71: 50–73.

Mahesh Yogi, Maharishi. 1963. *The science of being and art of living.* London: George Allen & Unwin.

Malmo, R. B. 1975. *On emotions, needs and our archaic brain.* New York: Holt, Rinehart and Winston.

Meichenbaum, D., and Cameron, R. 1974. The clinical potential of modifying what clients say to themselves. In M. J. Mahoney and C. E. Thoresen, eds., *Self-control: power to the person.* Monterey, Calif.: Brooks/Cole.

Miller, N. E., et al., eds. 1974. *Biofeedback and self control: 1973.* Chicago: Aldine.

Schultz, J. H., and Luthe, W. 1959. *Autogenic training: a psychophysiologic approach in psychotherapy.* New York: Grune and Stratton.

Selye, H. 1956. *The stress of life.* New York: McGraw-Hill.

Smith, M. S. 1975. *When I say no, I feel guilty.* New York: Dial Press.

Sternbach, R. A. 1966. *Principles of psychophysiology: an introductory text and readings.* New York: Academic Press.

Thoresen, C. E., and Mahoney, M. J. 1974. *Behavioral self-control.* New York: Holt, Rinehart and Winston.

Toffler, A. 1970. *Future shock.* New York: Random House.

Wolff, H. G. 1953. Life stress and bodily disease. In A. Weider, ed., *Contributions toward medical psychology,* vol. 1. New York: Ronald Press.

12

THE GROUP PROCESS

R. D. Archibald

OHIO STATE UNIVERSITY

Group programs have been common to counseling centers for a number of years. For a variety of professional and institutional reasons, group approaches to counseling have seemed attractive and economical. The relative emphasis placed on group or individual counseling on college campuses has generated considerable controversy in the past. That controversy has for the most part been resolved, as reasonable balances have been struck.

A larger issue, however, faces counseling today; the question of the role of counselors as primarily psychotherapists or as community mental health workers and consultants continues to draw differences of opinion from inside and outside the profession. Whether counselors are essentially healers or teachers and facilitators represents for many an open dilemma. Not only is a counselor's day-to-day work determined by his/her fundamental notion of him/herself as a professional, but students' perceptions of themselves are affected directly by their experiences with counselors. Regardless of the counseling approach used, whether individual counseling, group counseling, outreach, or workshops, the "world view" of the professional is communicated and pervades the situation. The underlying motives, or the basic rationale, for group programs obviously affect what will be communicated to students. Whether implicit or explicit, our attitudes do not remain hidden. As pointed out by Haley (1963), we cannot not communicate.

Since we are considering counseling on college and university campuses, several of the notions about group process expressed here are based on the assumption that students are in the institution to pursue an education and that services provided for students should support their overall learning objectives and be consistent with the mission of the institution. Services should be practical and useful for the students.

Most students need practical and somewhat temporary assistance as they struggle to learn more about themselves as learners, as people, as adults, and as contributors in life. Some require more extensive help. There are practical and impractical approaches to working with students, and there are times when a counselor may rush to assist a student with his/her woes, even though the frustration and stress may be important to the student's eventual self-understanding. There is a fine line between assisting in the struggles of the maturation process and rushing to heal the troubled person. It is in making fundamental decisions about group programs and in learning as much as we can about what is required that we must pay attention to what is known about the development of persons through the college years. Understanding such information and applying the knowledge directly in programming can help us work more carefully with the students at levels that will make sense to them.

Literature regarding the group process is extensive and has been part of most training programs and professional conferences in recent years. Rather than rehash the processes that generally occur in the many possible group programs used in counseling centers, the following discussion will focus primarily on what seems necessary in planning group programs from the point of view of the student consumers. Since important developmental phases and stages seem to be coincident with the college experience, the underlying experiences of students in our groups can contribute significantly to the changing concept of themselves or, on the other hand, can add to the confusion that many experience in college.

According to Perry (1970), there are different factors enhancing the learning environment at the different developmental stages in which we find students. To expect that a young, relatively immature student would be able to take advantage of the same learning environment found to be enriching by the more intellectually and emotionally mature student would be denying the existing evidence. It makes sense, therefore, that clear and studied reasons underlie our group programs in order to complement the developmental processes of our various students. Although extensive background in group process may be held by counseling professionals, if the students' ability to think about themselves and others at the levels required by the group situation has not been developed adequately, obvious discrepancies will result. An example may clarify this point. A few years ago a new professional, being fresh out of training and having had considerable experience with T-groups and encounter groups, was eager to develop group programs on a college campus. At that time few groups had been offered at the school, but the counselor was certain the response would be "overwhelming." The response was good (not overwhelming), and the groups began. Students of various ages and backgrounds were intentionally admitted, to ensure a good heterogeneous mix. Never before had undergraduates been included in such groups by the counselor, but his general enthusiasm helped him. He assumed that what had occurred in prior groups of graduate students would easily translate. The groups were designed with a low degree of structure, a high degree of ambiguity, and the full intent that learning would take place mostly through concentration on the here-and-now.

At times the group participants wanted to discuss their own social relationship problems. They were reminded that the emphasis was on the group and not on outside relationships. Several participants asked what they should be learning and how. They were told that the learning would evolve and that each person would discover unique things about him/herself and others through concentrating on the process within the group and on their own feelings. They asked what relationship this experience had to their frustrations, depression, or problems in school. They were informed that they needed to concentrate more on the here-and-now. Some students did not return after one, two, or three sessions. It was assumed that they did not really want to learn.

The counselors later recalled the long hours of frustration experienced by both themselves and the clients in the groups. At the time, it seemed incongruous that such a valuable learning and teaching technique as the T-group/encounter group/ Gestalt group format was achieving such mediocre results. In retrospect, the occurrences in those groups are not surprising. The setting was created with low structure and considerable ambiguity for everyone involved. From a developmental perspective, Perry (1970) would claim that younger students may not be prepared to cope with such a setting. They would be expected to require a much more concrete approach, a much more highly structured environment, and a clear notion of expected outcomes. In addition, subsequent research by Bedner and Lawlis (1971), DeJulio, Bentley, and Cockayne (1977), and Bedner, Weet, Evensen, Lanier, and Melnick (1974) points to the importance of structure as a variable in group performance.

The recent work on structure in groups seems to confirm what developmental theorists have been saying for a number of years. Developmentally, according to Perry (1970), Heath (1964), Erikson (1968), and others, people at certain stages or levels have not yet learned to think abstractly, especially about their own relationship to knowledge and events. They require a certain amount of initial structure in order to proceed in the learning environment. More careful consideration of intellectual and emotional development during the college years seems to shed light on what ought to be considered when planning group programs. If the structure is missing, the students' resulting insecurity may immobilize them or cause them to take flight.

Some theorists, such as Erikson (1968) and Chickering (1969), have studied the developmental tasks or functions of persons through certain periods of life. Others, such as Perry (1970) and Harvey, Hunt, and Schroeder (1961), have considered the stages through which persons develop in the way they handle learning and their own identity development. After studying college students over a number of years, Perry developed a scheme of development that is worth considering. Intellectual and ethical development were related to a set of stages occurring in sequence, with each stage representing a qualitatively different process or set of assumptions by individuals for both experiencing and dealing with knowledge, values, and their sense of themselves as persons. At different developmental stages people "experience" knowledge and perceive events, situations, themselves, and others differently. Depending on the developmental stage, they process their own world of events on a continuum defined at one end as absolute, right or wrong, concrete, and basically simplistic and at the other end as being pluralistic, complex, multidimensional, and changing.

Perry identified the way in which students at various stages processed knowledge. Knowledge was defined as it was perceived by the different students. That is, the person's assessment of his or her perceptual world was directly related to that person's developmental stage. Nine stages make up Perry's scheme, but they can be viewed as constituting three dominant phases. Dualism represents the first dominant phase. The dualistic learner "assumes" (perceives) information to be classified as either right or wrong. Uncertainty in any final form represents to the dualistic person a fundamental "error" in the system. Perceptually, an authority (teacher, professional, leader, and so on) qualifies information excessively, leaves interpretation open to question, or is abstract, is not to be trusted. That authority, in the student's perception of things, is either holding out some information to "spring on an examination" or has not prepared sufficiently. For such students, learning is a matter of finding the right answers and avoiding the wrong. The cognitive structure appears to be set and to need externally structured support. From early stages to later stages of dualism the student grows to accept more and more legitimacy in the fact of uncertainty, but has difficulty coping with the multiplicity of situations. Dualism comprises Perry's first, second, and third stages of development. The period represents a movement toward "modifying dualism," in light of the person's new experiences in the learning environment.

Stages four, five, and six represent the phase of "realizing relativism." Through this period the person's cognitive constructions of an absolute right or wrong world are displaced. The person begins to perceive uncertainty not only as pervasive, but also as more legitimate. Perceptually, however, knowledge and values seem to remain in an unordered state of mixed diversity. There is a move toward ordering the diversity, as knowledge, events, and thoughts begin to fit in some relativistic framework and to be seen in personal terms. A sense of one's place in a world of knowledge and values begins to unfold.

In the phase of relativism the student moves toward a sense of identity and begins to develop perceptual relationships between him/herself and the surrounding world. The person experiences the "creation" of him/herself as a person through numerous decisions, experiences, comparisons, commitments, and consequences.

In the Perry scheme, stages seven, eight, and nine are experienced more affectively. A constantly developing and changing identity through "evolving commitments" is discovered. Personal commitments are made based on one's perceptions of related events and factors. Ambiguity and diversity are not only accepted as legitimate, but seen as an integral part of life. This appears to be the phase that represents a level of cognitive complexity from which the person is able to risk openly accepting uncertainty, ambiguity, new commitments, and change, in order to seek renewal in life. From this latter position, when undertaking new events, uncovering knowledge, gaining new experience, or coping with stress, transitory periods of dualism, multiplicity, and early relativism are experienced. However, the phases are processed more readily. True to the scheme itself, development is not a discrete, singular set of events, but a way of describing a person's construction of his/her world conceptually, as learning to learn and cope with new knowledge and new events unfolds through the life span. It is Perry's contention that the developmental process is likely to unfold for the first time in a person's life during the college experience.

If the Perry scheme is taken seriously and applied to the counseling center setting and to the use of group programs, the work of Bedner, Melnick, and Kaul (1974) and others regarding the variables in group success is seen in a different light. No longer just interesting research findings—but, perhaps, representative of certain cognitive "tolerances" of students—the factors that predict success in groups become an important consideration. If students are developing through various stages of dualism, and unstructured or minimally structured group experience may be perceived as disorganization, a series of unrelated events, or the result of some error in the system or on the part of the counselor. The set of behaviors often referred to as "introspection" may be developmentally beyond the conceptual level of the dualistic learner. Such experiences as one would find in an encounter group or a Gestalt group, for example, may demand cognitive translations that are not yet developed. Along with the variables considered by Bedner et al. (1974) in their work on group structure, developmental readiness appears to represent an important overlay consideration.

In a 1977 study, Lamb found significant relationships between stages of cognitive complexity and levels of group structure in test anxiety management groups. When high-structure situations were presented, students demonstrating both higher and lower levels of cognitive complexity were shown to learn quickly, report less anxiety, and perform well on tasks that were previously anxiety producing. In the low-structure situations, those students able to think more abstractly improved significantly, while the students showing lower levels of cognitive complexity were less able to learn and adapt to the situation. High structure for students at more advanced stages of cognitive development was not aversive. Time has also been shown to be an important consideration in the process. Higher levels of structure seem important in the early stages of groups and in groups designed for short duration. Along several dimensions, low-structure groups that last over a longer period of time seem to eventually achieve similar levels of trust, cohesion, and risk taking. Time as a variable may indicate the ability of young learners to adjust to a specific low-structure situation. Time, however, is a luxury not available on most campuses.

Planning group programs in counseling centers may be seen as analogous to adapting classroom instruction to match the learner's developmental status as suggested by Hunt (1972). In such program development it is important to create learning environments that stimulate a readiness to learn and a resulting movement by the student toward more relativistic conceptualization. Since many of the values implicit in counseling programs (such as autonomy, introspection, independence, and interdependence) demand varying levels of abstraction and relativistic thinking, establishment of learning and therapeutic environments that complement development at various stages seems essential. Heath (1964), Sanford (1962), and others have emphasized the importance of fostering cognitive complexity among college students. Faced with diversity and pluralistic notions, students can take action that will help them develop cognitively. For dualistic thinkers, however, it appears to be important that materials and learning situations be selected and structured so as to guide them through the complex processes at first. As the students experience the guided sequences, they can then undertake more abstract comparisons themselves.

Although dissonance appears to be an important learning stimulus factor, excessive dissonance may be overwhelming and bring about retreat. The possibility of students being overwhelmed exists in counseling and classroom settings alike. The student develops by being confronted with pluralistic points of view. However, according to Heath (1964), the form taken by the confrontations is critical. Confrontations with new situations may bring about a sense of "overload" resulting in emotional retreat. Subsequent approaches by that person to similar learning environments become less likely. When the group or class is presented with reasonable degrees of structure, the student appears able to accept the learning environment and to develop the needed processes to stretch his/her perceptual world.

Sprinthall (1973) reported that students at concrete levels of thinking learned most completely when they were experientially involved in role taking as an addition to the subject matter structure. Although Sprinthall's work focused on the classroom, much of his work is directly analogous to group programs. The essential message is that when planning group programs, we must (1) determine the probable developmental level of the students; (2) structure the group format so as to guide students through that which is compatible with their current and developing levels; (3) involve students in role taking until they are able to translate the learning directly to themselves; (4) provide a series of encounters with diversity in a way that creates enough, but not excessive, dissonance; (5) constantly be aware of the developmental processes through which students are progressing in order to help them forge ahead to higher levels of abstraction, thought, and identity.

To be professionally sound, group programs in counseling centers require more than interest on the part of professionals. Not only must we take responsibility for developing clear objectives of intended outcomes, but the participants, our consumers, must be understood as thoroughly as possible. It seems not only desirable, but necessary to establish theoretical basis from our offerings and to test the theories underlying the programs in light of our experiences with each unique population and situation.

References

Bedner, R. L., and Lawlis, G. F. 1971. Empirical research in group psychotherapy. In A. E. Beign and S. L. Garfield, eds., *Handbook of psychotherapy and behavior change*. New York: John Wiley.

Bedner, R. L.; Melnick, J.; and Kaul, T. 1974. Risk, responsibility and structure: a conceptual network for initiating group counseling and psychotherapy. *Journal of Counseling Psychology* 21: 31–37.

Bedner, R. L.; Weet, C.; Evensen, P.; Lanier, D.; and Melnick, J. 1974. Empirical guidelines for group therapy: pretraining, cohesion and modeling. *Journal of Applied Behavioral Science* 10, no. 2: 149–65.

Chickering, A. W. 1969. *Education and identity*. San Francisco: Jossey-Bass.

DeJulio, S.; Bentley, J.; and Cockayne, T. 1977. The effects of pre-group norm setting in encounter groups. *Small Group Behavior*, in press.

Erikson, E. H. 1968. *Identity: youth and crisis*. New York: W. W. Norton.

Haley, J. 1963. *Strategies of psychotherapy*. New York: Grune and Stratton.

Harvey, O. J.; Hunt, D. E.; and Schroeder, H. M. 1961. *Conceptual systems and personality organization*. New York: John Wiley.

Heath, R. 1964. *The reasonable adventurer*. Pittsburgh: University of Pittsburgh Press.

Hunt, D. E. 1972. Matching models for teacher training. In B. Joyce and M. Weil, eds., *Perspectives for reform in teacher education*. Englewood Cliffs, N.J.: Prentice-Hall.

Keniston, K. 1971. *Youth and dissent*. New York: Harcourt, Brace Jovanovich.

Lamb, K. 1977. Matching Persons and Counseling Environments to Foster Self-control of Test Anxiety. Unpublished doctoral dissertation, Ohio State University, Department of Psychology.

Loevinger, J., and Wessel, R. 1970. *Measuring ego development:* Vols. 1 and 2. San Francisco: Jossey-Bass.

Perry, W. G., Jr. 1970. *Forms of intellectual and ethical development in the college years*. New York: Holt, Rinehart and Winston.

Sanford, N. 1967. *Where colleges fail*. San Francisco: Jossey-Bass.

———, ed. 1962. *The American college*. New York: John Wiley.

Sprinthall, N. 1973. A curriculum for schools: counselors as teachers for psychological growth. *School Counselor* 20 (May 1973): 361–69.

13

GROUP COUNSELING PROGRAMS

Robert I. Hudson

UNIVERSITY OF MANITOBA

My experience has been as a counseling center administrator in an agency that makes considerable use of the group approach to student counseling. Whereas I do not regard groups (or any other counseling modality) as a panacea and am aware of the potential abuses of such an approach, I do maintain a positive bias toward the inclusion of group activities in an agency's program of services. Rather than viewing this chapter as the assessment of one who is heavily immersed in the group movement, the reader is invited to examine group programs from a somewhat more objective posture, thus defining such programs as an integral part of a total service delivery system.

Definitions

Counseling has been defined in various ways. English and English refer to it as a "relationship in which one person endeavors to help another to understand and to solve his adjustment problems" (1958, p. 127). It is distinguished from psychotherapy in that the latter usually deals with a degree of mental disturbance or personality change (Tyler, 1969), while counseling is seen as having more of a developmental emphasis. However, most definitions of either process refer to a one-to-one relationship. More recently, references to group counseling have appeared. Glanz has defined it as "the establishment of a group of persons for the purpose of individual growth and development in the area of personal and emotional problem solving...normally employed with non-neurotic and non-psychotic persons within a developmental or growth climate" (1962, pp. 273–74). Like individual counseling, it is distinguished from group psychotherapy on the basis of the adjustment level of the participants and the goals of the process.

Programs using a group approach can generally be divided into two categories: (1) process-centered groups (group counseling, encounter or sensitivity groups,

T-groups, and the like), which focus on interpersonal communications and relationships; and (2) content-centered groups, which focus on the development of specific skills or the resolution of specific behavior problems. The latter will be covered extensively in subsequent chapters. However, it should be noted that the term *group* normally connotes a degree of interaction among members. Thus, a number of people engaged in similar activities in a given space, with or without leadership, but without interaction, does not constitute a group. Many skill development programs can be thus described. Such people are more properly termed as *aggregation*. We may then say that every group begins as an aggregation and becomes a group through interaction.

Goals and Expectations in Process-Centered Groups

Virtually all counseling processes are intended to assist clients to gain insight into their behavior. According to Corsini (1970), groups are aimed at any one or a combination of three gains: (1) intellectual, such as greater understanding of ourselves; (2) emotional, such as better feelings about ourselves; and (3) behavioral, such as better and more competent behavior. The group situation offers the type of acceptance that is essential to all counseling relationships, but multiplies it. The group also marshals the support of peers and provides a unique setting for the development of sensitivity to the attitudes and feelings of others. In this close group of people who share common concerns, one can learn to read the feedback and to obtain immediate clarification and correction of misunderstandings. The group also provides an arena for observing models of behavior, as portrayed by the leader or by other members, that may prove to be more satisfying alternatives for the learner. In attempting to emulate the behavior of these models, a member uses the group as a laboratory and can benefit from the immediate feedback mentioned above. In this accepting setting, patterns of behavior can be nurtured and developed to the point at which they can be effectively generalized to less accepting settings.

Rationale for Choosing the Group Approach

There are a number of other reasons for the selection of a group approach, rather than the one-to-one modality, as a means of resolving problems or developing personal competencies. First, to the extent that the counselor may be viewed as a paid listener, the client will feel that the group situation is less artificial than an individual interview. Second, if there is a tendency for the client to develop any type of dependency relationship, it will be diffused among the group members rather than being focused on a single person. Third, feedback from peers in a group can be expected on the basis of a mutuality of experiences and concerns, where feedback from a counselor is more likely to be accepted largely on the basis of the client's perception of the counselor as a superior observer and a knowledgeable authority. And finally, to the extent that such events occur, the group member is learning in an experiential mode; hence, the group becomes a microcosm of real life experience.

One possible limitation grows out of the counselor's role in a group as a facilitator, rather than a major participant. Since more verbal interaction is likely to take place between group members than between the counselor and any single group member, there is likely to be less emphasis on the development of verbalized insight into the causes of behavior and a correspondingly greater emphasis on the development of new and more satisfactory behavior patterns.

Group counseling is rarely, if ever, seen as a substitute for individual counseling. On the other hand, it may be regarded as a valuable supplement to a one-to-one relationship for many clients. New behavior patterns, tested in a peer group emphasizing sensitivity and behavioral development, require a transition to a broader range of contacts. The extrapolation should, in most cases, be more effective than the movement from an individual relationship emphasizing insight. Also, it would appear that the multiple insights available in a group setting allow for negative, as well as positive, feedback. A counselor might often avoid or delay the former. But in some cases the shock effect of such feedback is required to convince a person of the necessity for making substantial changes in interpersonal behavior patterns. At the same time it is delivered in an environment of basic concern, which can be expressed by others in the group.

Basis for Initiating Groups

The decision as to whether a counseling agency should initiate any type of group program may be influenced by several factors: evident needs of the client population, as estimated by counselors and/or indicated by direct requests from within the population; the desire to place more emphasis on preventive and developmental activities; or the skills and interests of counselors presently on staff. While the last observation may appear cynical, most counselors are not employed solely or even primarily to present group programs. In a period in which staff growth is minimal, progress in the development of group programs may well be limited by this factor.

One reason for the development of group approaches—often raised outside a counseling agency—is more efficient use of professional time. It is assumed that by establishing group programs an agency can serve a larger number of students at a lower cost per student. Although this may appear to be true on a superficial analysis of contact hours, one should bear in mind that the most effective functioning of many group programs requires the presence of two facilitators. Unless one of these is a paraprofessional, cost savings may be exaggerated. More properly, one should regard group programs as offering a qualitatively different experience that is justifiable on its own merits. The group experience presents different interpersonal vectors and thus implies the possibility of quite different effects from those usually expected from a one-to-one encounter.

Basis for Participation in Groups

The decision to participate in a group experience is a very important one and should be based upon a thorough understanding of the goals and purposes of a particular group and an awareness of the procedures, demands, and commitments implicit in group membership. The Guidelines for Group Facilitators in Higher Education prepared by the American College Personnel Association (1976) include the need for adequate screening procedures, confidentiality, and voluntary participation. Screening usually involves an interview with a group facilitator and may include a review of previous counseling contacts when this seems appropriate. Crucial factors in the screening process, which were well expressed in the Guidelines, include:

1. Applicants for group experience with particular physical health or mental health problems should not be included if there is a likelihood that they may be subjected to unnecessary risk or that because of their particular personal needs they may divert the group from its primary purposes.
2. Applicants receiving help from another professional person should be considered for group membership only after consultation between the group facilitator and the other professional person to consider the appropriateness of the experience for the applicant and the potential impact of the applicant upon the group.
3. Applicants selected for group participation after due consideration of [1] and [2] above will be of special concern to the group facilitator in order to protect the welfare of both the individual and the group (1976, p. 166).

In all counseling procedures confidentiality is a cardinal requirement. The development of mutual confidence, which is essential to the effectiveness of every group, must be based upon full acceptance by all participants of the principle that activities and expressions in the group must not be shared with persons outside the group. This requisite could, for example, present problems for a married person whose spouse does not belong to the group. Attention must be given to the resolution of such problems when they arise.

Required participation is an issue of particular importance because of the growing trend toward inclusion of group participation among the requirements for completion of preprofessional and in-service training programs. Involuntary participation, whether openly specified or more subtly required through the promotion of peer pressures, would seem to be in direct conflict with the emphasis on openness and humanism that is basic to most process-centered groups. The potential for compulsory participants to benefit from or add to the group process is questionable. Where group facilitators suspect the presence of such coercion or recognize its inevitability in some professional training programs, extra attention must be given to the protection of individual rights—a responsibility resting with the professional facilitator to a greater degree than with other group members. Since such situations may reveal themselves only in the early stages of group formation, facilitator vigilance becomes a specific ethical mandate.

Staff Roles and Requirements

Issues related to leadership have caused more controversy than any other aspect of the group movement. There seems to be a tendency toward an amoeba-like growth cycle in which some individuals who have participated in one or more group experiences consider themselves competent to become facilitators and feel compelled to "spread the word" by establishing groups whenever and wherever they find it possible to do so. Frequently failing to extend their newly developed sensitivity to a recognition of their own limitations, such individuals are often unable to recognize or to provide for the needs of those for whom the initial group experience has primarily negative effects. As a result of such developments, responsible group leaders have supported the establishment of standards or guidelines for the preparation of professional group leaders. Those prepared by the ACPA, previously cited, are representative of developments in this area. No educational institution should embark upon group programs without careful attention to these standards. Training focusing primarily upon individual counseling skills, whatever its level and quality, is *not* sufficient. However, supervised group experience is essential.

Apart from the issue of qualified leaders, the matter of paraprofessional leadership is often raised. One purpose of such staffing may be to reduce salary costs. In other situations, where homogeneous groups representing unique cultural backgrounds are involved, the assumption is made that a leader who shares that particular background will be more readily accepted in the role of facilitator. In the absence of fully qualified professional leaders having such identification, paraprofessionals are often selected. While few would deny the advantages of visible shared identity with a particular cultural group, that in itself is not a sufficient qualification. Although paraprofessionals may not have the same depth of education or background in the behavioral sciences, they should receive specific training in group procedures accompanied by supervised experience in group leadership. It seems reasonable to assume that such paraprofessionals, having gained reasonable experience in group processes, may also be able to play a unique reciprocal role in the training of professionals, since they will be able to point out the subtleties of language, nonverbal communications, and general attitudes that must be understood for effective work with specific groups.

All leaders, whether professional or paraprofessional, must recognize that their role in process-centered groups is quite different from that usually associated with more structured situations. To emphasize this difference, the term *leader* has been replaced with the term *facilitator*, emphasizing the primary goal of promoting communication and interaction between group members rather than between members and the leader. This difference in the attitude and behavior of leaders creates a mild source of role confusion for some group members; leaders must remain cognizant of the subtle, but pervasive, influence that they retain in the perceptions of many group members. The impact of their modeling behavior makes their ethical and philosophical awareness a matter of unquestionable concern.

Time Scheduling

In educational settings in which group members are available on campus on a daily basis, the most common arrangement is weekly meetings. The usual duration is between two and two-and-a-half hours, although the nature of the group process is such that rigid termination times are avoided. One of the first decisions each group should make involves the degree of rigidity or flexibility that members wish to maintain. Regardless of the decision made, facilitators should plan their own time in such a way as to be available either for extension of group meetings or for individual contacts that may be necessary after the end of a group meeting. In an institutional setting facilitators should, if at all possible, make themselves available for appointments with group members who are experiencing difficulty in entering into the full group experience. Such interviews, whether initiated by the group member or by a discerning facilitator, may make the difference between full participation and "going through the motions" or even withdrawal from the group.

It has been my experience that participation in daytime groups is difficult for some students because of heavy academic schedules. Consequently, group meetings tend to be scheduled during late afternoon and evening hours. It is also apparent that group facilitators, like individual counselors, require a certain amount of time for "homework" (reflection, record keeping, phone calls, and planning) in addition to their contact hours. This should be borne in mind when considering staff loads, working hours, and the like.

Some group programs, particularly those which are not directed to a previously identified population or utilize nonresident leaders, are based primarily on a series of sessions within a short period of time, often a weekend. These marathons, as they are aptly termed, usually involve not only more frequent sessions, but also much longer sessions than those described above. Since both duration and frequency of sessions are increased, the intensity of the experience has a significant impact on participants. Group facilitators often note both positive and negative effects of such intense experiences. In my organization the basic mode is that of weekly sessions. If a group at some point in its experience decides that more frequent or more extended sessions would be valuable, they plan them. However, none of our groups operate solely on the marathon format. It would appear that our approach has tended to enhance the prospects for positive outcomes and to reduce the risks of negative effects growing out of what may be an overly intensive experience for some participants.

Physical Settings

The effect of physical settings in facilitating or hampering group formation and development should not be minimized. In my agency, two rooms have been used for group meetings. One contains approximately 340 square feet and has lounge-type furniture. The other has only 240 square feet and no furniture. It is popularly known as the "pillow room" because of the large number of oversize pillows (at least two feet square) that it contains. Students sit on the carpeted floor and variously lie on, lean against, or hug the pillows as the mood suits them. They appear to find this highly relaxing. Somewhat lower-than-average lighting intensity (a floor lamp rather than overhead fluorescents) also tends to support the atmosphere of relaxation and informality.

Constraints and Precautions

With the relatively rapid growth of the human potential movement and other activities that stress affective behavior, there is need for an objective look at any possible negative effects of participation in group programs. Reference has been made earlier to the importance of informed voluntary participation and adequate preparation of facilitators. In addition to these basic requirements, the style of the facilitator and its effect upon group behavior must be considered. Some facilitators sincerely believe that the most important test of effective group progress and growth is the rate at which group members are able to develop complete openness with each other, to "let it all hang out." This would seem to resemble the concept of ventilation or catharsis that is frequently mentioned in more traditional therapeutic procedures. However, there is possible danger in the speed with which it is accomplished and the degree to which group pressures, spontaneous or facilitator-inspired, may lead to an openness that for some individuals is premature and frightening. The "Oh my God, what did I say?" reaction that hits some individuals after their first encounter, or more likely after their first marathon, may have severely negative effects. The highly desirable, long-range goal of increased openness may thus be defeated by pressure for too early and too extensive disclosure. Comfortable openness that can be generalized to other settings usually arrives well after individuals develop a feeling of warmth and belonging in the group. It should be noted in passing that some counselors will use tactics in a group setting to stimulate the activity of participants that they would quickly classify as overly directive in an individual interview. One wonders whether the issue in either case involves questions of ethics or of subtlety.

If openness is a primary goal, as most process-centered groups would suggest, we must then ask what the net effect of this emphasis will be on the behavior patterns manifested when individuals leave the group. Will their newly acquired and highly valued attitude of openness be accepted and reciprocated, or will they be highly vulnerable to both the verbal and nonverbal behavior of some less enlightened associates? Those groups which place considerable emphasis upon body contact may lead their graduates to send messages that are read by others in an entirely different context than that which was intended. The consequences need not be spelled out. It is essential that group members be able to accept their new attitudes and relationships in a realistic manner, recognizing that their approach to others must often move at a slower pace than that to which they have become accustomed in the group.

For many individuals a process-centered group meets needs for acceptance that have been long felt and rarely satisfied. In some cases this can lead to a dependency upon the group that, although diffused among a number of individuals, is very strong. Unless this can be carefully handled, such individuals may emerge from a group experience still unable to establish meaningful relationships with others in a less structured situation. They may be inclined to make adverse comparisons between their warm, close relationships within the group and those relationships developed outside it. As a result, they fail to pursue the latter to the point at which equally satisfying relationships may be established. For some the experience of a mixed-sex group may enable them to develop a degree of sensitivity and a number of approach styles leading to meaningful heterosexual relationships. For others, the group may be a refuge within which both the challenges and the rewards of a male-female dyad may be avoided. Group members should be encouraged to prepare themselves for the demands of normal living, including the development of one-to-one interdependent relationships.

Follow-Up

A number of the situations described above reveal the need for the establishment of adequate follow-up procedures for all group programs. As indicated in the ACPA position paper (1976), "the facilitator's responsibility for the group members does not automatically end with termination of the group experiences." In a number of cases individuals may need further assistance, either group or individual, in resolving their problems and further developing desired behavior repertoires. It should be the responsibility of the facilitator, either personally or indirectly through appropriate referral resources, to provide an opportunity for such further assistance as may be necessary. This obviously raises many ethical questions about transient marathon leaders who "drop in" to a community for a weekend and then disappear.

Community Acceptance

Leaders of group programs that stress the development of sensitivity in interpersonal relationships should themselves possess sufficient sensitivity to recognize the prevailing mores of various communities. Educational institutions are always under a substantial degree of public scrutiny. It would seem to be a self-defeating exercise to attempt to present, under the cloak of academic freedom, programs that run contrary to generally accepted local standards. For this reason, in employing group specialists some years ago, I felt constrained to mention, albeit unnecessarily, that I did not feel my institution and the community in which it was located were ready for nude encounter groups. Furthermore, I doubted whether they would ever be ready.

At the risk of raising the hackles of some very liberated group facilitators, I would venture the opinion that such encounters may well focus attention upon a very narrow band of interpersonal relationships, perhaps to the detriment of group members who must spend the major portion of their lives in a much broader range of activities. The proponents of such specialized encounters will probably be quick to suggest that their only purpose is to overcome antiquated taboos. If, in doing so, they tend to produce a degree of desensitization to certain types of visual stimuli, they may be creating more problems than they are resolving.

Conclusion

The introduction of group counseling programs into the repertoire of university and college counseling centers has added a new dimension to their ability to meet the needs of students. If properly staffed and ethically operated, these programs can expand our range of services. The relative proportion of staff resources that should be allocated to individual and group counseling facilities must be carefully considered in each setting. It should be remembered that group programs involve an initiating stance whereas individual counseling tends to be largely responsive. Both modes or operation have valuable contributions to make and neither should be ignored.

In addition to the items mentioned in the references, readers should direct their attention to the following:

The Clearinghouse for Structured Group Programs
Douglas M. Dahar, Coordinator
Counseling Center
University of Rhode Island
Kingston, R.I.
(Lists and occasional publications)

References

American College Personnel Association. 1976. The use of group procedures in higher education: a position statement. *Journal of College Student Personnel* 17: 161–68.
Corsini, R. J. 1970. Issues in encounter groups—comments on Coulson's article. *The Counseling Psychologist* 2: 28–30.

English, H. B., and English, A. C. 1958. *A comprehensive dictionary of psychological and psychiatric terms*. New York: David McKay.

Glanz, E. C. 1962. *Groups in guidance*. Boston: Allyn & Bacon. 1962.

Muro, J. J., and Freeman, S. L., eds. 1968. *Readings in group counseling*. Scranton, Penn.: International Textbook Co.

Solomon, L. N., and Berzon, B., eds. 1972. *New perspectives on encounter groups*. San Francisco: Jossey-Bass.

Tyler, L. E. 1969. *The work of the counselor*. 3d ed. New York: Appleton-Century-Crofts.

14

CAREER PLANNING PROGRAMS

John H. Russel

MEMORIAL UNIVERSITY

During the last two decades, colleges and universities across Canada and the United States have come to recognize the value and importance of assisting students in their career growth and development. Several authors (Sanford, 1966; Freedman, 1967; Perry, 1970; Chickering, 1969) have analyzed and reported various developmental activities experienced by the university-age student. Other authors (Stern, 1970; Pace, 1969; Astin, 1968; Holland, 1973; Clark & Trow, 1960; Newcomb et al., 1967) have contributed a great deal of valuable data on the relationship of the university environment to the student. In response to the growing quantity of data and to student and community requests, vocational psychologists and career counselors are being called upon to play a bigger part in career developmental programming for students at the college and university level throughout Canada and the United States.

The involvement by the career planning specialist has taken many directions. For example, the specialist may perform a unique consultative role with classroom teachers to assist them in ways of integrating the world of work into their specific subject. Tennyson et al. (1965) and Ashcraft (1966) suggest that a distinctive contribution teachers can make to the vocational development of students is to relate their particular subjects to the life environment of the present and future. Or the career planning specialist may assist faculty members improve and sharpen their advising skills. Several authors (Hale, 1974; Ross, 1975; Kirts & Fisher, 1973; Gelnick, 1974; Morehead & Johnson, 1964; Hardee, 1970; Tamminen et al., 1976; Russel, Sullivan, & Hadsall, 1976) have been involved in the development of teacher/advisor programs in which communication and interpersonal skills, group techniques, problem-solving skills, decision-making skills, and career development theory and information are emphasized.

Another direction that career planning specialists have taken in the performance of a consultative teaching function is the establishment of paraprofessional programs, whereby students are provided training to assist other students with career-related problems.

And finally, a major direction being pursued by career planning specialists is the development, refinement, and implementation of systematic career planning programs in which students either enroll for credit, receive some form of certificate or recognition, or simply participate on a volunteer basis. Many of these programs can form the content basis of a curriculum unit and can be used either in a group or on a one-to-one basis.

For the purpose of clarification and definition, in this chapter career planning programs are construed as counseling and instructional units couched in various theoretical approaches to vocational psychology and include goals with corresponding methods/techniques to help students achieve these goals.

General Considerations for Career Planning Program Implementation

In response to questions of accountability and justification for career planning program development and implementation, several issues need attention. This section will present data relevant to students' needs in the area of career development and will address some theoretical and philosophical considerations in career planning.

THE NEED FOR CAREER PLANNING PROGRAMS

Across Canada and the United States, students are indicating a need for career planning programs that will enable them to establish a direction in life and to acquire specific job-related and job-finding skills. Hitchcock (1973) observed that while the students of the 1960s were interested in examining values, the students of today are more concerned about establishing themselves vocationally.

Prediger, Roth, and Noeth (1973), in a survey of eighth- and eleventh-grade children in the United States, found that 78 percent indicated a need for career planning services. Furthermore, they found student-expressed need for help with career planning in sharp contrast to the amount of help students felt they had received. In conclusion, the authors suggested that if they had been speaking of physical development rather than career development, youth in the United States would be described as hungry, undernourished, and physically retarded.

Carney and Barak (1976), in a survey of Ohio State University seniors, found that 67.7 percent of the students were concerned with the choice of a major or a career. Specifically, 37.3 percent had experienced concern with such a choice, while 30.4 percent were somewhat concerned.

A survey of student characteristics and needs at the Memorial University of Newfoundland (Hedegard & Kirby, 1974) noted that 83 percent of the students listed choosing a major or a career as a priority. A high percentage of incoming students anticipated problems with a relationship between course work and career plans. In fact, "a large proportion of first year students are seriously bothered by the problems of deciding on a career, and seeing the connection between academic studies and future careers" (pp. 6, 37, 38).

THEORETICAL AND PHILOSOPHICAL CONSIDERATIONS IN CAREER PLANNING

The integration of career development programs on campuses—whether through the faculty/classroom teacher/advisor, through the trained peer, or directly through the career specialist—can be in part attributed to the recognition of their need by administrators, teachers, alumni, and community. Increasingly, the university years are viewed as providing a sound general and liberating education in which the living/learning environment encourages self-exploration, growth, and development.

Along with the transmission of knowledge, the basic intent of any university ought to be the development of the student's capability to solve problems and make decisions independent from others. And because problems and decisions are often laden with personal and social dimensions, the development of social and personal, as well as intellectual, capabilities is essential. Tripp (1972) proposes that counseling exchange the remedial model for a proactive model, and others suggest that programming be developmental rather than crisis-oriented. Such a philosophical outlook demands that planning go beyond the academic classroom setting through the implementation of developmental programming in all segments of the college and university environment.

From a theoretical viewpoint on sound systematic career planning, it is important to accept two premises: first, people are unique beings with different beliefs, values, wants, abilities, and interests; and, second, career development is a lifelong process. Through a process of self-exploration that includes an analysis of individual needs, interests, values, and abilities, students come to know and realize their inherent potential. In this light, then, the choosing of a career has become an extension and implementation of the self-concept (Super, 1957). Students search for various career alternatives that will allow them an opportunity to operationalize maximally their values, abilities, and interests. In order to facilitate this process, the Memorial University of Newfoundland Career Planning Team has developed a "Career Decision Making Guide" to pictorially assist students with relating personally relevant values, abilities, and interests to careers.

Certainly, it is difficult to regard the process of career choosing solely as an extension and implementation of self, for many personally uncontrollable factors can impinge upon this decision. Osipow (1973) suggests that the sociological approach to the consideration of career choosing and vocational behavior centers on the notion that elements beyond the individual's control exert a major influence on the person. To the sociologist, chance or "being in the right place at the right time" plays a major role in occupational decisions. To the psychologist, on the other hand, the chance factors represent an irritant that hopefully can be minimized so that nonchance factors can be brought under control by the individual.

From a sociological point of view, for example, Blau and Duncan (1967) suggest two extra individual variables that may affect vocational development. The first discussed is the relationship of father to son. The father passes along approximately two-fifths of his occupational advantage. In other words, if fathers are at 84 percentile in the occupational structure, their sons will almost all end up above 50 percentile. And at the other end of the continuum, sons inherit two-fifths of their father's disadvantage. The other variable concerns the effect of family structure on the individual's occupational aspirations and achievements. Additionally, Lipsett (1962) noted that social class membership, home, school, community, pressure groups, and role perception (that is, the degree to which self-perception is in accord with others' perceptions) have inhibitory effects on the individual's freedom to choose a career. Hart, Rayner, and Christensen (1971) have suggested that what appears to regulate career entry, especially at the lower levels of occupations, is unplanned. In their study, they noted a clear relationship between occupational level and career planning. And Osipow (1969) reported that a principle of "least resistance" in career development operates.

In addition to the myriad of social-environmental forces impacting on the individual, there are also psychological forces that hinder the student in the process of freely planning and choosing a career.

Lipsett (1962) touches upon a central concern when role perception is discussed. Individuals perceive and react to their surrounding environmental forces. Because in many instances individuals are discouraged from deviating from the norm of societal expectations, they are trapped in a collage of commonness. Dreyfus (1972) claims it is difficult to be authentic under such strong societal pressure and argues for a pluralistic society in which individuals do have the option to plan and to develop as unique persons. Walz (1976) labels as "personal empowerment" that behavior whereby individuals do attempt to assert control over those parts of the environment that can be controlled.

Because of the irrational beliefs they adopt, such as the overwhelming need to be loved and approved, individuals may not assert themselves for fear of rejection and the assumed proof of worthlessness (Ellis, 1972). Or a person may be inert because of a fear of failure (Beery, 1975). Powell (1969) suggests that what prevents individuals from asserting themselves is the thought that if they disclose themselves, they may not be liked, and that is all they have.

Korman (1966) noted that in comparison with low self-esteem individuals, high self-esteem individuals more likely implemented their self-concept through a career choice. Korman (1967) also found that a person's self-esteem is related to the perceived degree of difficulty of an occupation. In other words, a person with high self-esteem seeks high-ability and demanding situations.

In summary, the manner in which individuals perceive themselves as they react to and translate the various environmental stimuli is an important factor in the career choosing process. Low self-esteem and confidence can limit career options needlessly. However, through systematic career programming an individual can become more aware of both psychological and sociological forces and can plan for the future. Furthermore, Tiedeman and O'Hara (1963) and Miller and Tiedeman (1972) have suggested that though career development is affected by the external environment, it can largely be controlled by internal personal initiative.

Considerations in Developing Career Planning Programs

In this section several considerations in the systematic developing of career planning programs will be presented and discussed. The systems approach is not new to program development. Hare (1967) defined it as the selection of elements, relationships, and procedures to achieve a specific purpose, while Hosford and Ryan (1970) suggested that it is an approach directed toward attaining specific predetermined goals. And Russel, Shaltry, and Meredith (1974) reported that through the utilization of a systems method high schools can more effectively and efficiently deliver career development services. The primary advantage of using a systems approach is an increase in the probability that a given goal will be achieved (Campbell et al., 1971).

Applying systems methodology to the development of career planning programs involves seven phases: (1) conducting a needs assessment; (2) writing program goals; (3) preparing behavioral objectives; (4) identifying and analyzing career development methods and techniques; (5) implementing and evaluating program; (6) recycling decisions and program modifications; and (7) eventually conducting another needs assessment.

NEEDS ASSESSMENT

Along with a myriad of crucial developmental needs experienced by the university-age student, students themselves are indicating a strong need for the establishment of career direction, as evidenced by the data reported earlier in this chapter.

An initial step is to specifically identify what is meant by career planning. Does career planning cover all components from exploring oneself to exploring career alternatives, to making a tentative career decision, to learning how to write resumés, to interviewing for jobs, to preparing a job search strategy and outlining a job campaign? If career planning does include all of these aspects, then should all students, regardless of year level, be involved? Or should only first-year students or students experiencing a need for self and career exploration receive the program? And should the older students receive the more specific career preparation activities, namely, strategies of resumé writing, job interviewing, and preparing job search strategies?

From a theoretical and developmental point of view one might assume that first-year students need more help with the self and career exploration process and third-, fourth-, and fifth-year students with resumé writing, job interviewing, and developing a personalized job search strategy. In any event, it is important to determine the context in which your students function and the needs that may be particular to age levels or minority groups. With contextual evaluative data on which to base a career program it is possible to know if the students' needs are being ameliorated and if your intervention strategy is effective.

PROGRAM GOALS

Program goals, generally written in broad and comprehensive terms, are directional and terminal in nature. Ryan (1969) defines goals as "a collection of words or symbols describing general direction." Goals need to be written in such a fashion that all people concerned know what is expected and from whom. Directional goals should have the student as an actor and describe a concomitant behavior specifying what the student will know, understand, or do.

Suzuki (1974) defined the difference between product goal and process goal. A product goal definitely indicates what the student will learn, whereas a process goal describes what will be done by an individual or institution to enable a student to learn. Take, for example, the difference between two goals: "The student will understand herself" and "The counseling center will establish programs enabling the student to understand herself." The first goal specifically indicates the student as actor and describes what it is hoped the actor will accomplish. It is purposeful, directional, and terminal. Philosophically, it suggests that the student is important and needs self-understanding. In order to accomplish the terminal goal, necessary resources may need to be allocated or prerequisite activities such as in-service training or testing may need to be conducted.

The second goal is not nearly as clear, concise, or terminal. And, broken down, it consists of two goals, the first being an administrative concern of establishing programs and the second being a student-oriented concern for self-understanding. Having two goals in one statement makes it difficult to measure. Furthermore, the student does not seem to be the central concern, and the statement does not clearly indicate what the student will learn. For a career planning program for students to have direction, goals need to be stated forcefully, clearly, and concisely; thus, students, administrators, faculty, and counseling center colleagues are cognizant of its expectations.

BEHAVIORAL OBJECTIVES

Behavioral objectives specifying behavior, cognition, or affect more than adequately serve to respond to questions of accountability or to break down broad directional goals so that they are more specific, meaningful, and directional. Campbell et al. (1971) suggest that some of the major advantages of behavioral objectives are improving program efficiency, clarifying communication, facilitating specification of career guidance methods, assessing student performance and monitoring programs.

Behavioral objectives can have as many as four parts: an actor, a behavior, a condition, and a degree of success. For the purposes of organizing career planning program development, it is helpful to break behavioral objectives into two kinds, criterion behavioral objective and enabling behavioral objective. A criterion behavioral objective is directly related to the goal and is terminal insofar as its completion indicates completion of one aspect of the goal. Very much like the goal, a criterion behavioral objective needs to be clear and concise and has only the student as an actor. Bloom (1965) and Krathwohl, Bloom, and Nasia (1964) identify various kinds and levels of behavioral objectives. A criterion behavioral objective also specifies exactly what is expected of the student, indicates the degree of success necessary in order to have accomplished the objective, and identifies conditions necessary to facilitate accomplishment of the objective.

An enabling behavioral objective, on the other hand, indicates those prerequisite activities needed so that the student's achievement of the criterion objective will be accomplished. An enabling objective contains the same four parts and is directly related to the criterion objective. It also needs to be stated clearly and concisely, but does not need to limit the actor to just the student. It may be that for the student to accomplish a certain criterion objective, faculty members will need some in-service training. In this case faculty/teacher would become the actor in the enabling objective.

Depending upon the breadth and comprehensiveness of a goal statement, there may be several criterion behavioral objectives and, if necessary, corresponding enabling objectives. Where criterion objectives are necessary to the implementation of a goal, an enabling objective is not necessary to the implementation of a criterion objective. Or, if a program goal statement happens to be particularly narrow, then there may be only one criterion objective.

Let us assume that one of your program goal statements is "The student will acquire an understanding of himself." Depending upon your point of view, the self may be a combination of several components, such as interests, values, and abilities. If you are writing a criterion behavioral objective for career interests, then, it might be as follows: "Given the results of two career interest inventories, the student will list a minimum of five different careers that he would like to explore." In this criterion behavioral objective, "the student" is the actor, "list" is the behavior, "given the results of two career interest inventories" is the condition, and "a minimum of five different careers" is the degree of success. At least two enabling objectives are necessary in relation to the condition. One enabling objective would handle the administration of the interest inventories, while the second handles the interpretation of the results. If you are consulting with faculty who are administering an interest inventory in the process of advising students, then another enabling objective attending to in-service training of faculty advisors would be needed.

Another criterion behavioral objective might emphasize a guided fantasy to capture some interests of which the student was not aware, or it might be having speakers come to discuss unusual careers or life-styles.

In any event, the writing of behavioral objectives can enable one to improve program efficiency, clarify communication, and assess student performance.

METHOD IDENTIFICATION AND ANALYSIS

Method identification and analysis involves the searching and evaluating of career guidance methods currently available through publishers, colleagues, or journals. Career planning program development has experienced tremendous growth in the past several years. In fact, there are so many different exemplary methods in use and on shelves collecting dust throughout Canada and the United States that many individuals are completely unaware of them. Or if aware, they do not know how to evaluate their applicability. Trying to keep up with new developments would require constant vigilance and become a paramount task. Campbell et al. (1973) responded to this need through the development of *Career Guidance: A Handbook of Methods,* a compendium of over two thousand career guidance methods.

In attempting to evaluate the applicability of methods for use in a particular situation, one must ask five essential questions: 1) Has the method been evaluated by students, faculty, and administrators? 2) Is this method, which may have been applicable in another setting, applicable in yours? 3) How feasible is the method in terms of external assistance needed to implement it, availability of the method, and changes you might have to make to fit it to your needs? 4) Are there adequate resources (people, space, equipment, and materials), or would they have to be allocated? 5) Will your students, faculty, and administrators accept the method?

In addition to various texts on vocational psychology (Crites, 1969; Holland, 1973; Osipow, 1973; Zytowski, 1968; Super, 1957), the career planning team of the Memorial University Counseling Center has drawn upon several other useful documents. Recently annotated for inclusion in *A Guide to Self Improvement,* a booklet prepared by the Memorial University Counseling Center, these documents are presented here as possible methods, or learning activities, to assist in program development endeavors. For purposes of brevity, the documents are listed without the annotation.

General Guides in Career Planning

Birk, J. and Tanney, M. F. 1972. Career exploration for high school women: a model. Paper presented at the NEA Conference.

Bolles, R. N. 1975. *Quick job hunting map.* Berkeley: Ten Speed Press.

———. 1972. *What color is your parachute? A practical manual for job-hunters and career changers.* Berkeley: Ten Speed Press.

Campbell, D. P. 1974. *If you don't know where you are going, you'll probably end up somewhere else.* Niles, Ill.: Argus Communications.

Campbell, R.; Kriger, S.; Miller, J.; and Walz, G. 1973. *Career guidance: a handbook of methods*. Columbus, Ohio: Charles E. Merrill.

Chapman, E. 1976. *Career search: a personal pursuit*. Toronto: Science Research Associates.

Cosgrave, G. 1973. *Career planning: search for a future*. Toronto: University of Toronto, Toronto Guidance Centre.

————. *Career workbook* [a workbook supplement to *Career planning*]. 1973. Toronto: University of Toronto, Toronto Guidance Centre.

Crystal, J., and Bolles, R. 1974. *Where do I go from here with my life?* New York: Seabury Press.

Dickhut, H. W., and Davis, M. J. 1975. *Professional resume/job search guide*. Chicago: Management Counselors.

Djeddah, E. 1971. *Moving up: how to get high salaried jobs*. Berkeley: Ten Speed Press.

Ferguson, J. 1974. *The career guidance class*. Camarillo, Calif.: Walter T. Metcalf and Associates.

Figler, H. 1975. *Path: a career workbook for liberal arts students*. Cranston, R. I.: Carroll Press.

Ford, G. A., and Lippitt, G. 1972. *Planning your future*. La Jolla, Calif.: University Associates.

Gaymer, R. 1973. *Career planning and job hunting: a resource book for students*. Toronto: McLean-Hunter.

Gelatt, H.; Varenhorst, B.; and Carey, R. 1972. *Deciding*. New York: College Entrance Examination Board.

Gelatt, H. B., et al. 1973. *Decisions and outcomes*. New York: College Entrance Examination Board.

Irish, R. K. 1973. *Go hire yourself an employer*. Garden City, N.Y.: Doubleday & Co.

Kirn, A. G. 1974. *Life work planning* [includes student manual and instructor's manual]. Hartford: Arthur Kirn and Associates.

Malnig, L., and Marrow, S. 1975. *What can I major in?* Jersey City, N.J.: St. Peter's College Press.

Marshall, A. 1964. *How to get a better job*. New York: Hawthorn Books.

Mitchell, J. S. 1976. *I can be anything*. Princeton: College Entrance Examination Board.

Mullen, V. W. 1973. *Readings in life skills*. Saskatoon: Modern Press.

Nutter, C. F. 1970. *The resume workbook: a personal file for job applications*. Cranston, R.I.: Carroll Press.

O'Dell, F.; Abbey, R.; Chermonte, J.; and Demark, P. 1974. Values, decisions, careers: a group guidance program for girls. Paper presented at APGA.

Pietrofesa, J., and Splete, H. 1975. *Career development: theory and research*. New York: Grune and Stratton.

Prentice, B. 1971. *The back-to-work handbook for housewives.* New York: Collier Books.

Reardon, R. C., and Burck, H. D. 1975. *Facilitating career development: strategies for counselors.* Springfield, Ill.: Charles C. Thomas.

Scholz, N. T.; Prince, J. S.; and Miller, G. 1976. *How to decide.* Princeton: College Entrance Examination Board.

Simon, S. 1975. *Meeting yourself halfway.* Niles, Ill.: Argus Communications.

Stebbins, L.; Ames, N.; and Rhodes, I. 1975. *Sex fairness in career guidance.* Cambridge: ABT Publications.

Tippett, G.; Williams, J.; and Waite, N. 1974. *Creating a career* [includes student manual and instructor's manual]. Saskatoon: Modern Press.

Walz, G. and Benjamin, L. 1974. *Life career development system.* Human Development Services, Inc.; P. O. Box 1403, Ann Arbor, MI 48106.

Specific University-Age Related Career Planning Programs

Alberti, J. 1976. The business preparation program. *Blackburn College Bulletin* 4 (April 1976).

Barkhaus, R., and Bolyard, C. 1976. I'll buy that! A shopper's guide to career planning. Fort Wayne: Career Planning and Placement Center, Indiana-Purdue Universities; paper presented at APGA.

Bradbury, J. T.; Coinfeld, J.; Wertheimer, L.; and Harrison, K. Career planning and decision making: a developmental approach. College Park: University of Maryland Counseling Center; paper presented at APGA.

Brooks, G. 1974. Careers and life planning—a credit course. *Canadian Guidance and Counselling Association Newsletter,* 6: 4–5.

Carney, C.; Winer, J.; and Metts, M. 1975. Variations on a career planning theme. Ohio State University; paper presented at ACPA.

Hadsall, M.; Sullivan, T.; and Russel, J. 1976. Job search program. St. John's: Memorial University of Newfoundland.

Hazel, E. 1976. Group counseling for occupational choice. *Personnel and Guidance Journal* 55: 437–38.

Russel, J. H.; Sullivan, T.; and Hadsall, M. 1976. Planning your career. St. John's: Memorial University of Newfoundland.

PROGRAM IMPLEMENTATION AND EVALUATION

Upon the completion of identifying and analyzing methods appropriate to the setting, the next step in the systems approach is to implement the program goals. Based upon resource constraints, student needs, philosophical considerations, and types of evaluation strategies planned, the career planning program will be undertaken. If it is the first time in attempting the development of a career planning program, it may be advantageous to limit enrollment through the implementation of a pilot program; thus, if major revisions are required, large numbers of students will not suffer. Through the creative application of the methods, behavioral objectives will be attempted by the students, working either collectively or individually.

If it is necessary to know the effect of the particular program being implemented, then the collection of evaluative data is important. According to Guba and Stufflebeam (1968), process evaluation in the trial stages gives feedback, answering such questions as "Should new procedures be instituted?" or "Are there problems with time, budget, or design?" Upon completion of a career planning program, a product evaluation (Guba & Stufflebeam, 1968) is completed. During the product evaluation, individual attainment is compared with the predetermined goals and objectives set after the needs assessment.

PROGRAM MODIFICATION/RECYCLING

Based upon the process and product evaluation, decisions and changes are made concerning the program that was implemented. The heart of a systems approach is change. Planned change is based upon a deliberate and collaborative process involving change agents and those being changed (Fleming, 1966). Decisions might be made to continue the program exactly as it is, install a new method, rewrite a behavioral objective, or terminate the program completely.

Assume that a career program has been conducted with only 10 percent of the students achieving the behavioral objectives and, therefore, the goals. The reasons for failure may be numerous. For example, the students may find the method inappropriate or boring; the behavioral objective may not have been clearly and concisely stated; the degree of success may have been too stringent for the level of student involved; or, possibly, the goal was implemented out of sequence and the student did not have the prerequisite knowledge. Depending upon what the problem might be, the program developer recycles to the problem area, makes proper modifications, and offers the program again to other students. As modifications are made and resources become available, additional goals are implemented so that eventually all of the career planning goals and corresponding behavioral objectives will be implemented.

In summary, the use of a systems approach in the development of a career planning program can be an extremely effective tool enabling one to attain selected predetermined goals. After conducting a needs assessment, goals and behavioral objectives are written. Career guidance methods and techniques are identified to facilitate students' achievement of the behavioral objectives and goals. Next, the specific evaluation strategies are determined and the program is implemented; and, last, decisions are made concerning the program, and the program developer/ evaluator recycles to those areas needing change.

Conclusion

This chapter has dealt with some considerations involved in the implementation and development of career planning programs in Canada and the United

States. It is intended to serve as a guide and resource in programming endeavors. Two basic implementation considerations in career planning programs were mentioned and discussed: first, why career planning is important, and, second, theoretical and philosophical bases in career planning. The central emphasis to the section on program development considerations was a description of the use of systems methodology. The application of the systems approach to career planning program development assists in providing sequential and logical steps, facilitates student's attainment of goals, allows for program monitoring, and, generally, helps bring organization to nonexistent or disordered programs.

References

Ashcraft, K. B., ed. 1966. *Implementing career development theory and research through the curriculum.* Washington, D.C.: Report of Conference sponsored by the National Vocational Guidance Association, August 1966.

Astin, A. W. 1968. *The college environment.* Washington, D.C.: American Council on Education.

Beery, R. 1975. Fear of failure in the student experience. *The Personnel and Guidance Journal* 54: 190–203.

Blau, P. M., and Duncan, D. D. 1967. *The American occupational structure.* New York: John Wiley.

Bloom, B. S. 1965. *Taxonomy of educational objectives: the classification of educational goals. Handbook I: cognitive domain.* New York: David McKay.

Campbell, R. et al. 1973. *Career guidance: a handbook of methods.* Columbus, Ohio: Charles E. Merrill.

Campbell, R. E. et al. 1971. *The systems approach: an emerging behavioral model for vocational guidance.* Columbus, Ohio: Ohio State University.

Carney, C., and Barak, A. 1976. A survey of student needs and student personnel services. *Journal of College Student Personnel* 17: 280–84.

Chickering, A. W. 1969. *Education and identity.* San Francisco: Jossey-Bass.

Clark, B. R., and Trow, M. 1960. Determinants of college student subcultures. Mimeographed. Berkeley, Calif.: Center for the Study of Higher Education.

Crites, J. 1969. *Vocational psychology.* New York and Toronto: McGraw-Hill.

Dreyfus, E. A. 1972. *Youth search for meaning.* Columbus, Ohio: Charles E. Merrill.

Ellis, A., and Harper, R. A. 1972. *A guide to rational living.* Hollywood: Wilshire Book Co.

Fleming, W. G. 1966. Rational strategies for educational change. In *Emerging strategies and structures for educational change.* Toronto: Ontario Institute for Studies in Education.

Freedman, M. 1967. *The college experience.* San Francisco: Jossey-Bass.

Gelnick, B. 1974. Training faculty to do career advising. *The Personnel and Guidance Journal* 53: 214–17.

Guba, E., and Stufflebeam, D. 1968. Evaluation: the process of stimulating, aiding and abetting insightful action. Presentation at Phi Delta Kappa Symposium, Boulder, Colo.

Hale, L. 1974. A bold, new blueprint for career planning and placement. *Journal of College Placement* 34 nos. 2: 34–40; no. 3: 68–72.

Hardee, M. 1970. *Faculty advising in colleges and universities.* Student Personnel Series, no. 9. Washington, D.C.: American Personnel and Guidance Association.

Hare, V. C. 1967. *Systems analysis: a diagnostic approach.* New York: Harcourt, Brace and World.

Hart, D. H.; Rayner, K.; and Christensen, E. R. 1971. Planning, preparation and chance, in occupational entry. *Journal of Vocational Behavior* 1: 279–85.

Hedegard, J. M., and Kirby, D. M. 1974. *Report of the committee on junior studies.* St. John's: Memorial University of Newfoundland.

Hitchcock, J. 1973. The new vocationalism. *Change* 5: 46–50.

Holland, J. 1973. *Making vocational choices.* Englewood Cliffs, N.J.: Prentice-Hall.

Hosford, R. E., and Ryan, T. A. 1970. Systems design in the development of counseling and guidance programs. *The Personnel and Guidance Journal* 49: 221–30.

Kirts, D., and Fisher, R. 1973. Tripod: a systems approach to career planning. *Journal of College Placement* 33: 42–49.

Korman, A. K. 1967. Self-esteem as a moderator of the relationships between self perceived abilities and vocational choice. *Journal of Applied Psychology* 51: 65–67.

———. 1966. Self-esteem variable in vocational choice. *Journal of Applied Psychology* 50: 479–86.

Krathwohl, D. R.; Bloom, B. S.; and Nasia, B. B. 1964. *Taxonomy of educational objectives: the classification of educational goals. Handbook II: affective domain.* New York: David McKay.

Lipsett, L. 1962. Social factors in vocational development. *The Personnel and Guidance Journal* 40: 432–37.

Miller, A. L., and Tiedeman, D. V. 1972. Decision making for the 70's: the cubing of the Tiedeman paradigm and its application in career education. *Focus on Guidance* 5: 1–15.

Morehead, C. Q., and Johnson, J. C. 1964. Some effects of a faculty advising program. *The Personnel and Guidance Journal* 43: 139–40.

Newcomb, T. M. et al. 1967. *Persistence and change: Bennington College and its students after twenty-five years.* New York: John Wiley.

Osipow, S. H. 1973. *Theories of career development.* Englewood Cliffs: N.J.: Prentice-Hall.

———. 1969. What do we really know about career development? In N. Gysbers and D. Pritchard, eds., *Proceedings of the national conference on guidance, counseling, and placement in career development and education-occupational decision making.* Columbia, Mo.: University of Missouri.

Pace, C. R. 1969. *College and university environment scales (CUES)* [technical manual]. 2d ed. Princeton: Educational Testing Service.

Perry, W. G., Jr. 1970. *Forms of intellectual and ethical development in the college years.* New York: Holt, Rinehart and Winston.

Powell, J. 1969. *Why am I afraid to tell you who I am?* Niles, Ill., and Toronto: Argus Communications.

Prediger, D. J.,; Roth, J. D.; and Noeth, R. S. 1973. *Nationwide study of student career development: summary of results.* Iowa City: American College Testing Program.

Ross, M. 1975. College orientation: a three way street. *Journal of College Student Personnel* 16: 468–70.

Russel, J. H.; Shaltry, P.; and Meredith, C. 1974. Operation guidances: a career development innovation for high schools. Presentation at APGA, New Orleans, La.

Russel, J. H.; Sullivan, T. S.; and Hadsall, M. 1976. Faculty advising project. St. John's: Memorial University of Newfoundland.

Ryan, T. A. 1969. Defining behavioral objectives. Paper prepared for AERA, presession, Los Angeles, Calif.

Sanford, N. 1966. *Self and society*. Chicago: Atherton Press.

Stern, G. G. 1970. *People in context*. New York: John Wiley.

Super, D. 1957. *The psychology of careers*. New York: Harper & Row.

Suzuki, W. 1974. Program goals: a working paper. Paper presented to Career Planning Support System Staff, Center for Vocational Education, Ohio State University, Columbus, Ohio.

Tamminen, A. et al., 1976. Teacher advisors: where there's a skill there's a way. *Personnel and Guidance Journal* 55: 39–42.

Tiedeman, D. V., and O'Hara, R. P. 1963. *Career development: choice and adjustment*. New York: College Entrance Examination Board.

Tennyson, W. W., et al. 1965. *The teacher's role in career development*. Washington, D.C.: National Vocational Guidance Association.

Tripp, P. 1972. We can't go home again. *Journal of College Student Personnel* 13:

Walsh, W. B. 1973. *Theories of person environment interaction: implications for the college student*. Iowa City, American College Testing Program.

Walz, G. 1976. *Life-career development system*. Presentation at LCDS workshop, Chicago, Ill., April 1976.

Zytowski, D. 1968. *Vocational behavior: readings in theory and research*. New York and Toronto: Holt, Rinehart and Winston.

15

ISSUES IN THE DEVELOPMENT OF ACADEMIC SUPPORT SERVICES

Larry R. Cochran
MEMORIAL UNIVERSITY

Unquestionably, academic support services are of more potential value to a student population than any other program in a counseling center. The university is fundamentally oriented toward education, and the primary source of stress for students is apt to be connected with academic performance. Not only careers, but self-esteem and numerous other facets of personal experience can and often do rise and fall with the quality of academic endeavors.

Ideally, these services are concerned with academic excellence, with the information-processing plans, strategies, practices, attitudes, and the like that facilitate academic competence. They are concerned with learning to learn and learning to appreciate. More concretely, they are concerned with managing huge amounts of information for different purposes. Since students are apt to forget much of the content offered in their courses while retaining the capabilities refined in learning that content, services directed toward the enhancement of capability would or should be essential not only for university performance, but also in preparation for careers. Maintaining complex schedules or plans of action and managing huge, diverse amounts of information are indeed the burdens of the educated person.

Yet academic support services vary enormously in quality, with many, if not most, failing to fulfill the promise implicit in such services. They might be alienated from the mainstream of university activity, tucked away in some small room near the outskirts of campus where nothing much is thought to happen. They might be stigmatizing to students who qualify for service by their probability of failure. In this case, simply overcoming the stigma of participation is a consuming task for student and psychologist alike. And academic support services as well as the psychologists who run them sometimes enjoy the least status within counseling centers. Part of this lowly regard might be attributed to our unfortunate inheritance of the word *deep* from analytic psychiatry. Whatever you do, it should be deep. And particularly, when you are not achieving positive results, it must be deep. Regardless, however, of this perhaps dubious possibility, the lack of open admiration from colleagues might be richly deserved. Those programs which restrict themselves to offering simplistic and occasionally erroneous advice (for example, study in a quiet place) and to directing students to prepackaged programs are scarcely heady enough to compel the envy of colleagues.

But, of course, academic support programs need not be this way. There is no inherent reason why they should be alienated from university activities, stigmatizing to students, or undervalued by colleagues. Rather, they can be *made* this way. One way to view the manner in which academic support services are made is through the choice points that determine their development. As universities and colleges vary considerably in requirements for service, there is not apt to be a set of choices relevant to all settings. However, there are several broad issues that seem pertinent.

Remediation versus Enhancement

Should academic support services focus upon ameliorating weaknesses in learning capability or upon stimulating strengths? This issue is primarily one of appeal. Should services appeal only to those students who are failing, or should they appeal to everyone on campus? In relatively open universities at which entrance requirements are low, it is essential to offer remedial services, since they are important to a greater proportion of students. But directing services exclusively toward the failing student is likely to produce deleterious consequences.

If services are aimed predominantly at potential flunk-outs, university administrators and faculty may well treat academic support programs as humanitarian gestures (dispensable ones, at that) to the less fortunate and the less intelligent. They may be sanctioned, but with little expectation of success. (And what would success constitute, in most cases, but a failing student perhaps scraping by to graduation with a C-minus average?) This is not the type of student upon which an institution would ordinarily like to be judged. Prestige is won at least partially by the quality of graduates, by brilliant students learning brilliantly and demonstrating this background in future endeavors. But the C-minus student who scrapes by to graduation is a different kind of credit, one that is not of central importance to a university. Indeed, in some cases, it could be discrediting rather than crediting. After all, if students cannot make it in college, perhaps they should not be in college. It would be a travesty of the humanitarian impulse and a betrayal of public trust to grant degrees from an academic institution to students who demonstrate little academic competence. In directing academic support services only to failing students, professionals then can alienate themselves and their efforts from the mainstream of institutional activity and purpose, receiving benign neglect as a reward for service.

Also, when services appeal only to failing students, programs can all too easily become stigmatized settings in which vacuous advice is given. Participating in such a program becomes a matter of whether or not one *needs* it. And to admit that one needs it carries with the admission added difficulties of defining oneself as incapable, different from other students, or just plain dumb. Perhaps even more devastating is the practice of requiring students who fall below certain testing criteria to take study skills courses. Attempting to remove the stigma of such an assignment can require a major effort before the development of capability can take place. It is difficult to strive to make oneself into a competent student when fending off the definition of a dunce who perhaps does not belong in a university in the first place. In this situation, it is personally desirable to avoid having to define oneself as someone who needs academic support services, and it becomes unnecessarily difficult for a student to take advantage of those services.

Raising failing students to the average is emphatically not more important than raising average students to the excellent. Because failing students are often dismaying to themselves and to faculty members, it is all too easy to slide into or be pressured into providing service exclusively to them. The imminence of flunking out does not make their case more urgent than others; it merely makes the consequence more visibly immediate. Wasted capability at any level of competence is saddening. Certainly it is every bit as pathetic to witness a bright student assume the trappings of mediocrity as it is to observe an adequate student embrace the stigma of failure.

With the pressure of insufficient professional time and administrative demands for what they think they want, the temptation exists to design services for only a fraction of the student population. But this is a decision that should be resisted, for the consequences might involve even less institutional support, leading to even less personnel and time for a program spiraling into obscurity, irrelevance, and stigma.

Optimally, anyone within the university could benefit from academic support services. In better programs, it is not uncommon to help lawyers pass the bar examination, physicians prepare for a specialty examination, graduate students write a thesis or dissertation, and, indeed, professors process vast amounts of information more effectively. The impact of this message—that services are available not just for certain students, but could be available and beneficial for everyone—is difficult to underestimate in effecting constructive university relations and in establishing a program in which failing students can participate without handicap.

Correction versus Prevention

Should academic support services be primarily a reactive agency, providing services for those who have fallen on evil days? Or should they also be preventive, attempting to dissolve or resolve problems before they begin? Often problems that would be relatively easy to prevent are extremely difficult to resolve, particularly since academic problems are not isolated domains. They can have pervasive implications for oneself and one's career. A poor or puzzling grade can lead to self-doubt, which leads to worries, which hinder a person's ability to concentrate, leading to even poorer and more puzzling grades. Or it can lead to career indecision, strained family relations, and problematic peer relations, to name but a few consequences. It is worth reviewing these obvious points simply to stress that problems become embedded within the person's understanding of himself and relation to the world around him. And the sheer pervasiveness with which many difficulties are embedded makes them intractable to change.

The more preventive services a program can initiate, the better. One service concerns early provision of training. For example, on some campuses short courses in strategies of learning are designed to be delivered in freshman classes (for example, English classes are usually required of all students). This allows students not only to begin developing their capabilities further, but also to become more directly oriented to the notion that capabilities can be developed further.

A second area of service concerns the correction of mistaken ideas. Frequently among students as well as professors, intelligence is conceived unidimensionally as something of which each person has a fixed quantity. Good grades are due to intelligence, while poor grades are due to its lack, or so this idea is asserted in its simplest form. The dreadful consequence is that if this notion is accepted, there is often little that can be done about academic performance.

A third area of service concerns the sheer provision of information. Knowing that most of what one has learned (say, in studying a chapter for the first time) will be lost within a week's time can provide a powerful incentive both to review and consequently to give review a much larger role within one's plan of study. Or we might consider limited information processing capacity (for example, Miller, 1956). People are limited in the number of separate ideas they can manage simultaneously; and when the limit is exceeded, they feel overloaded. Information processing becomes increasingly fragmented, and performance deteriorates. In reading a new chapter, students (as well as anyone else) often reach a point of overload. Unfortunately, the overload feeling is subject to more than one personal interpretation. It should simply signal that it is time to organize and familiarize oneself with background material before adding new material so that the new ideas can be processed in a more orderly and more implicative fashion. However, what it often seems to mean to students is that the material is too difficult, that perhaps it is too boring ("I always learn things I'm interested in"), or that it provides evidence for one's own stupidity. As evidence of stupidity, for instance, overload can produce worries or distracting thoughts that further reduce one's capacity to process information. Reading can become a self-reinforcing feedback loop in which feelings, while reading, produce personal and distracting implications about oneself. Thus, the misinterpretation of the overload signal does not lead to an appropriate strategy for overcoming the difficulty and is apt instead to deteriorate performance further. It is understandable why some students dread studying.

A fourth area of service concerns influencing the university setting. As minor examples, some universities close buildings or lock classrooms at night, leaving students with few places to study on campus. Study facilities in the library are often inadequate, while some residence halls lack sufficient discipline to maintain an adequate climate for study. The emergence of community psychology and environmental psychology (Mehabrian, 1976, for example) may highlight a number of more subtle changes in university settings that might facilitate learning. In short, academic support services can also constitute something of an in-house lobby for desirable change, raising issues and influencing policy decisions.

Study Skills versus Cognitive Processing

Academic support services have developed primarily through reliance upon a body of evidence typically referred to as study skills literature. Over the decade since Neisser's publication of *Cognitive Psychology* (1967), there has been a spectacular development within the speciality of cognitive information processing. Yet even now, if a book on study skills and one on cognitive psychology are read side by side, one can look in vain for concepts that are held in common. Study skills material remains an extraordinarily isolated body of literature that has not changed to any significant extent for some years. Imagery in learning, hierarchical structuring, chunking, schema development and use, rehearsal, levels of information processing, processing limits, short-term and long-term memory, to name only a few—all are concepts and areas of investigation that appear to be virtually foreign to study skills literature.

Consider one example. Study skills books almost unanimously subscribe to the SQ3R method of study: survey, question, read, recite, and review. But it is one thing to know that you should do this and quite another to know how or to what end they should be done. For instance, what would a successful survey do? In study skills books, there are vague references to noting important points and following the author's outline. But how do you tell an important point from an unimportant one? What does an efficient organization or outline look like? To these questions, which are scarcely considered in most study skills texts, cognitive psychology can provide definite, although necessarily tentative, answers. Briefly, you scan to develop a schema, a hierarchical structure that will order or pattern the information in a chapter. You scan to develop what Ausubel (1968) has termed an "advance anchor" capable of subsuming and hence patterning information hierarchically from top to bottom. The purpose of ordering is to form expectations that will guide attention efficiently. As Neisser has noted in another context, "What is seen depends on how the observer allocates his attention; i.e., on the anticipations he develops and the perceptual explorations he carries out" (1976, p. 39). The importance of ideas depends upon their place within the hierarchical organization. The more subsumptive or the higher the placement of an idea within the hierarchy, the more important it is, since it provides not only a cue that makes the subsumed information accessible (for example, Meyer & McConkie, 1973), but also a basis for ordering that information. One can also scan to determine what strategies of processing are apt to be more effective. For example, a history chapter filled with concrete details would probably be more easily learned by constructing imagined sequences analogous to the flow of a movie, whereas a biology chapter on animal classification might require a purely conceptual hierarchy.

To take one more instance, the second phase of activity involves questioning. Yet the growing literature on the use of questions to control reading indicates that questions can both hinder and facilitate learning (for example, Frase, 1972). A question can direct attention inappropriately or focus on relatively unimportant details. To avoid belaboring the point, it might simply be observed that questions do affect learning, but that there is nothing simple about the generation of questions that will facilitate learning. Following the structural model, questions based upon more superordinate ideas would be expected to work well, but the form of the question requires considerable spelling out.

To sum up these illustrations, the traditional reliance upon study skills material is, I believe, inadvisable. Study skills books are not necessarily bad, although some are astonishingly vacuous. Rather, they are extremely incomplete in comparison with the richness of strategy and concept developed within cognitive psychology, which itself is incomplete. There is no definitive source to consult at all, so, at least for some time to come, reliance should be broad (covering a variety of areas inside and outside psychology), selective, and tentative.

Prepackaged versus Individually Developed Programs

Some academic support programs tend to rely almost exclusively upon prepackaged study skills programs to do the job of enhancing academic performance. Yet even for the best of these programs, one may have many reservations. Often they do not reflect contemporary knowledge on the subject; that is, they are subject to the same limitations as study skills materials in general. Diagnostic tests are not diagnostic enough, tending to direct one to areas such as grammar, spelling, vocabulary, and the like. They seldom consider ordering strategies, cognitive styles, and sheer conceptualization of what it is to learn. For instance, reading comprehension, writing coherence, and problem solving depend fundamentally upon cognitive representation. I am not aware of any prepackaged program that even begins to elaborate forms of representation and ways in which they might be developed.

Prepackaged programs can also decrease student motivation by concentrating on texts that are irrelevant to the student's course work. For example, it would seem obvious that showing a student how a chapter in one of her texts is structured would be more motivating than seeing how a carefully selected passage on an irrelevant topic is organized. Also, there is the question of professional motivation. The potential for laxness in leaving the program up to someone or something else can not be taken lightly.

In the end, academic support services cannot be left to a prepackaged program. Knowledge is accumulating at much too fast a rate for that. What can and is more frequently being done is building limited and highly selective portions of prepackaged programs into a more comprehensive service. At least, this places the burden of responsibility where it should be, upon the professionals who conduct the service.

Skill Development versus Personal Change

In the continual reference to academic support programs as study skills, there is a tendency to construe services in a truncated fashion. Skill development is certainly involved, but increased skill or know-how without personal change is like dancing without enthusiasm: although the techniques might be allright, the spirit is not simply lacking, but incongruous.

Fransella (1972) has convincingly demonstrated that therapeutic transformations (from stutterer to fluent speaker, from obese person to trim person, and so on) are not as likely to occur or to be maintained unless the person has endowed meaning upon the transformed position, that is, until the implications of the position have been drawn out and experientially consolidated. Now the transformation from poor student to good student, from underachiever to overachiever is certainly no less difficult and no less complicated. Orienting oneself to the world through the stance of an excellent student is quite different from maintaining the stance of a poor student. More might be expected of you. Increased future possibilities might be frightening and confusing; and reactions from friends can as often be threatening as supportive. A different orientation must underlie any drastic change in academic capability if it is to be maintained.

In many cases, a different orientation is required before any change in capability is likely to occur. For example, a student, who had been reared since childhood with the notion that he was quite intelligent, formed the belief that since he was intelligent, everything should come easily for him. If things were not learned quickly and easily, it would indicate that he was not intelligent. Since intelligence had become pervasively embedded in his personal orientation, feedback contradicting his assumed intelligence could scarcely be tolerated. He began to study even less, since he could always point to any grade and claim, "Look what I did when I just glanced at the book." The belief that intelligence exempts one from hard work could certainly be changed, but not without a considerable amount of personal change.

Another student entered psychological services to become more disciplined. Her poor academic performance could be attributed to laxness, and surely a better academic performance would stem from more discipline. However, upon exploration of her "implicit personality theory," it became apparent that to her a lax person was easygoing, friendly, joyful, liked, and happy, among other things, while a disciplined person was more like a dried-up prune with all the life squeezed out of her. In this context, laxness and poor grades became but an unfortunate consequence of living a fuller life. Particularly in view of her previous failures to maintain discipline (indeed, who would want to be drained of life?), it seems at least plausible that an alternative orientation might be necessary before skill development would be very successful. Certainly, some rather simplistic notions of scheduling fail to recognize that it is not so much study time that is being scheduled as a rather demanding life that is being managed.

In an unfortunately neglected series of studies, Arnold (1962) developed a motivational index for judging TAT protocols. This index, which classifies the import of story sequences, was developed empirically, but resulted in a scoring of motivational convictions bearing strong resemblances to the Puritan ethic. While this moralistic tenor has been the subject of some quite undeserved criticisms, it has also been validated by some of the most powerful correlational studies that have ever been published. Arnold reported two studies by Garvin that correlated the motivational index with grade point average for 50 male and 50 female college students. For the males, the correlation was .850. For females, the correlation was .832. Having demonstrated such an astonishing high correlation, he proceeded to test seventh-grade children. For a sample of 52 children, the correlation was .720. Respectively, the relationship of intelligence (ACE) to the motivational index was only .582, .470, and .468. Clearly, these results could not be attributed to overlap with intelligence. Perhaps in all of the psychological literature, there is no more striking demonstration of the importance of the personal orientations that underlie academic achievement.

If the objective of academic support services is construed along the dimension of skilled/unskilled, there is perhaps a tendency to neglect the person changing in favor of skills developing. Such a neglect can only be severely limiting of the service provided.

Required versus Elective Services

As a criterion for program evaluation, university administrators often and unfortunately use the head count. The more students who are provided with services, the better the program is thought to be. Coupled with this administrative demand is the professional difficulty of serving enough clients to avoid a budget cut. With programs that appeal primarily to failing students, the resulting stigma can virtually assure a low number of people who voluntarily request services. Professionally, the question then becomes, How can we reach the students who truly need these services? Administratively, the more desperate question becomes, How can we run enough students through the program to avoid the axe? Both questions have an immediate answer. Since the services are assumed to be beneficial, it is justified to require certain students to enroll. This policy must, I believe, be resisted. As argued previously, the stigmatizing imposition of services upon students can generate more problems than it can resolve. Also, the onus of responsibility has been shifted from the student to the professional. Required courses deprive students of the personal decision and commitment to take advantage of academic support services.

However, once involved in dwindling clientele and in administrative pressure, there still remain numerous alternatives to required attendance. For example, healthy faculty relations generate plentiful referrals. Faculty workshops on strategies of learning can do much to stimulate a working relationship between faculty members and academic support personnel. Also, added inducements can be built into formal course requirements. In lieu of doing a book report, term paper, or whatever, students can participate in learning programs. That is, participation can become an option in many courses, for which students will receive credit as well as institutional sanction. Or as another alternative, students can vote to have a designated number of classes devoted to learning to learn. In this case, academic support personnel can provide miniworkshops during regular class sessions. As yet another alternative, residence halls as well as fraternities and sororities can be offered the option of having learning workshops performed for their memberships. In short, alternatives to required attendance are limited only by imagination.

Comprehensive versus Specialized Services

The previous issue is partially self-generated, for if program appeal had been appropriate to begin with, there would most probably not be a lack of clientele. Indeed, with broad appeal and a quality program, there is more likely to be a problem of overload. With the perennial difficulty of small staffs and a wide variety of possible services, the question of what to offer is a pressing issue. It is pressing not only because administrators and students tend to expect a broad program, but also because the professionals involved desire it.

The scope of an academic support program depends upon practical procedures for conserving staff time and, in particular, for allowing more staff time for personalized assistance. (The necessity for personalizing services seems so obvious that it has not been made an issue in this chapter.) For example, some aspects of the program can be automated, freeing staff time for personalized instruction and counseling. Priorities can be established to encourage one type of clientele rather than another or to emphasize one type of service rather than another. Or the program can be constructed in modules. For example, academic support programs have frequently been divided into more or less separate domains such as reading, writing, vocabulary development, and the like. Such division is terribly redundant, for these activities have much in common. Each depends fundamentally upon forms of representation or patterns of organization; each depends upon strategies of use, ways to put patterns of organization into operation for purposes such as problem solving, writing, and comprehending. In short, one might stress the program's common core that leads into various refinements of purpose. But in the end, conservation measures may not be enough. With any reasonable demand for service, professionals will be faced with doing a few things well or doing many things inadequately.

It might seem that the ethical thing to do is to provide the best service possible for everyone, rather than turning some people away. But it is not particularly ethical, either, to knowingly stretch service capabilities so thin that the quality of the service as a whole suffers. An uneasy decision might have to be made.

The consequences of doing many things inadequately are well known. The reputation of the program can suffer, leading to diminishing respect from students and faculty members alike. Staff morale can suffer from the stress of doing too many things at once and from the frustration of never refining a particular service to the level of excellence. Lack of time increases the impersonality of the service, decreasing the involvement of all concerned. What began as perhaps a valiant effort to meet all needs can become a university expectation, locking the center into inescapable mediocrity. Taking a comprehensive service for granted can also deprive the center of one of its most potent bargaining points—the need to expand services. In these and many other ways, taking on more responsibilities than the center personnel are prepared to manage can lead to a general deterioration. For these reasons, if a decision must be made, it should be made for quality rather than quantity.

Means versus Ends

Should an academic support program be oriented solely toward increasing capabilities, toward the development of means? I think not. Certainly, enhancement of capability is the central concern of a program, but it is not the only concern. Capability is one thing; how it is put to use is quite another. Atomic power is one thing; how it is put to use is quite another, as we are all painfully aware.

Capability for what? Politically, the democratic ideal is to increase capability for becoming a better citizen, since democratic institutions rest presumably upon informed participation. Responsible participation is certainly a desirable ideal, particularly since it is or can be so at odds with practice. Some politicians are frequently successful in appealing to the selfish and the ignorant. And at least some political futures appear to be dependent upon irresponsible, uninformed, and self-interested participation. While there are apt to be a few politicians who would welcome an electorate made up of college professors, there are likely many who would welcome a more sophisticated public.

Personally, for a majority of students, the end is obvious. Capabilities should be enhanced to get good grades, to provide a basis for a successful career, or just to graduate. That is, the typical reasoning for enhancing capabilities is to get ahead in some fashion. While there is nothing particularly unworthy about getting ahead in some fashion, it is severely limited because it is extrinsic. Educational capability is enhanced for a noneducational end.

A university is not a trade school "writ large." Education is not simply a means for a good job. Fundamentally, education is concerned with the enrichment of life, the enhancement of one's capability to participate in life more fully, to become more involved in the world, and to experience in more variety and depth. Education is concerned with the elaboration of meaning. Clearly, this is an entirely different type of getting ahead.

A lay person looks at the face of a cliff, and he sees the face of a cliff, a mere bauble to capture his attention for a moment. A geologist looks at the face of a cliff and sees perhaps eons of time stretched out beautifully before her. A lay person looks at an ancient artifact, and there it ends. An archeologist looks at an ancient artifact and constructs an entire economy, technology, and perhaps spirit of living. A lay person observes a chess game and sees a move. A master might see a novel strategy fraught with trembling possibilities. The significance of living depends upon the significance that we are capable of endowing upon our actions and experiences.

To paraphrase Hanson (1969), to see what wise persons see, we must know what they know. Knowledge enriches experience and action. Being concerned with the communication of knowledge, education involves the enrichment of experience and action. Being concerned with the enhancement of a person's capability for a personal education, academic support programs facilitate or attempt to facilitate a person's enrichment of experience and action.

That academic support programs should be oriented toward styles of living might come as something of a surprise, but is no less accurate for that. From a getting ahead perspective, a particular course might represent simply another nonsensical hoop to jump through. From an enrichment perspective, the same course might be an invitation to adventure. There is no objective reality to a course as a hoop or an invitation but what construing makes it so.

It is not a center's business to impose ends upon students, but it is most certainly a center's business to introduce students to a range of purposes or to assist them in the exploration of purposes. That an end might be obvious to the majority of students makes consideration of unquestioned assumptions even more necessary. If academic support services are directed toward styles of living, there is also created a professional responsibility to go beyond the platitudes of educational goals toward a thorough consideration of styles of living and to incorporate those alternatives within professional efforts to enhance student capability.

Many more issues could have been considered within this chapter. But these issues and other ones can be reasonably subsumed by a concern for enlarged perspective and responsibility. There is, I believe, a great danger in construing academic support services too narrowly. It is undoubtedly prestigious to be narrow, to be specialized, to be an expert on some small aspect of human endeavor—and the smaller the better. But it is also isolating. Means are separated from ends; abstract skills are separated from persons; mechanics are separated from attitudes. The student can become an object to be worked on, a problem to be solved, rather than a person to be worked with. You take this part, and others take other parts, and somehow it is supposed to add up. I do not believe it does. Fragmentation in delivery and responsibility too often leads to a fragmented result. In this context, the role of academic support services should be integrative, to assist in bringing the separated strands of educational experience together in some common purpose and to offer a service that is comprehensive in spirit, if not in technical exhaustiveness.

References

Arnold, M. 1962. *Story sequence analysis*. New York: Columbia University Press.

Ausubel, D. 1968. *Educational psychology: a cognitive view*. New York: Holt, Rinehart and Winston.

Fransella, F. 1972. *Personal change and reconstruction*. New York: Academic Press.

Frase, L. 1972. Maintenance and control in the acquisition of knowledge. In J. Carroll and R. Freedle, eds., *Language comprehension and the acquisition of knowledge*. Washington, D.C.: V. H. Winston.

Hanson, N. 1969. *Perception and discovery*, San Francisco: Freeman, Cooper & Company.

Mehabrian, A. 1976. *Public places and private spaces*. New York: Basic Books.

Meyer, B., and McConkie, G. 1973. What is recalled after hearing a passage? *Journal of Educational Psychology* 65: 109–17.

Miller, G. 1956. The magical number seven, plus or minus two: some limits on our capacity for processing information. *Psychological Review* 63: 81–97.

Neisser, U. 1976. *Cognition and reality*, San Francisco: W. H. Freeman.

———. 1967. *Cognitive psychology*, New York: Appleton-Century-Crofts.

16

TESTING PROGRAMS

John T. Deines
TEXAS WOMAN'S UNIVERSITY

Counseling centers on many university campuses were given their start by the Veterans Administration's program after World War II and the Korean War (Kirk, 1966). Testing was the backbone of many of the programs, designed to assist the returning veterans to find the right niche in the postwar world. In this sense it can be said that testing was the parent of campus counseling centers. Given that premise, it has become a mature, sedate grandparent. Testing seems to be a permanent, though small fixture in most counseling center operations in the late 1970s.

Discussions of the subject of testing in counseling centers in the published, readily available literature is virtually nonexistent. A few references, cited later in this section, are the only recent, noteworthy exceptions.

In an attempt to assess the status of testing programs, a survey was mailed to 195 counseling center directors in the United States and Canada. The names were taken from the list of counseling centers represented at the Twenty-Fourth Annual Conference of University and College Counseling Center Directors (1975) at Kennebunkport, Maine, or the Twenty-Fifth Annual Conference (1976) at Snowbird, Utah. One hundred and forty-seven questionnaires (75 percent) were returned. Of the 147 returns, 16 were from directors at small institutions (full-time enrollment under 3,000), 96 from directors at medium-sized institutions (full-time enrollment between 3,000 and 18,000), and 35 from directors at large institutions (full-time enrollment over 18,000).

Rationale

Goldman (1972) likened the relationship between counseling and testing to a marriage that is in trouble. He attributes the failure to a basic misunderstanding of the needs of selectors versus those of counselors. Tests can meet more fully the needs of selectors, because they can be designed to predict success in specific situations—a particular employment or a specific school. Counselors, on the other hand, are concerned with prediction of success in much more generalized situations—a range not only of employment situations or careers, but also of educational institutions. This is asking too much of tests. He also laments that the behavior of some counselors indicates that they do not realize testing's limitations.

However, both Goldman and his adversary, Layton (1972), mention that tests can legitimately be used in counseling as means of providing clients with a tool for greater self-awareness.

To determine what rationale is given for use of tests in counseling centers, the directors were asked, "What do you feel is the principle rationale for using psychological tests in serving the needs of a college student population?"

The directors mention most frequently the same counseling use of tests as Goldman and Layton. Testing contributes to the self-understanding and assessment for the client, with the emphasis on the client's need for self-exploration as opposed to the counselor's need for assessment. The directors see a value in testing for the objectivity it provides through normative information. Next, testing is seen as a valuable starting point in the counseling and therapeutic process, because it frequently uncovers areas unknown to clients or provides clarification or additional information to areas already known. Information obtained from tests provides the meat of the therapeutic process itself in addition to a starting point. They are valuable tools for students to use in both personal and vocational decision making.

However, diagnosis and assessment of personality functioning are frequently mentioned as a rationale for using tests. The directors feel that the counselor needs tests for the assessment of emotional disorder and for planning treatment or making referrals. Some directors emphasize that tests are quick, efficient, and inexpensive means of aiding the counseling process in an era of cutbacks and tight budgets.

Less frequently mentioned are such things as using tests to assess values, to attract students to the counseling center, or to match client with therapist. Also infrequently mentioned is the use of tests for carrying out research or for providing information about students in academic difficulty.

A few directors cite rationales for *not* using tests. They note that tests have limited value in the area of student development; that tests are, more often than not, inhibitive of the counseling process; that clinical evaluations turn the student off; or that the student's own report—"verbal projectives"—is more valuable in eliciting data.

Testing Programs

The directors' descriptions of testing programs in their counseling centers are as varied as the rationales they present for using tests. The testing that is done generally falls into two categories—academically oriented, that is, assessment of intellectual functioning, study skills, or habits; and personality-oriented, that is, assessment of personal traits.

ACADEMICALLY ORIENTED TESTING

Academically oriented testing programs involve serving as the agency on campus for administering tests developed for nationwide assessment and for administering and interpreting other standardized or locally developed measures of academic ability or achievement. Some centers also provide machine-scoring services to academic departments (Oetting, Ivey, & Weigel, 1970).

Examples of tests developed for nationwide assessment are the American College Test, the Scholastic Aptitude Test, the Graduate Record Examination, the Miller Analogies Test, the Law School Admission Test, and the College Level Examination Program. (Canadian directors report that there are no Canadian national tests, but that their institutions do administer the tests originating in the United States.) Examples of standardized ability or achievement tests are the individual and group intelligence tests (for example, the Wechsler Adult Intelligence Scale or the Otis Self-Administering Tests of Mental Ability), reading tests (such as Nelson-Denny Reading Tests), or locally developed tests used for screening in specific courses.

Counseling centers frequently have been charged with supervision of at least some of the tests administered nationally. For the most part, this function has little relevance to the counseling process, as the test results are seldom the subject of counseling interviews. To find out the extent of counseling center involvement in administering national tests, the directors were asked if their centers have this responsibility. Fifty-four percent of the centers at large universities, 60 percent of the centers at the medium-sized colleges and universities, and 50 percent of the centers at small colleges and universities have this responsibility. Many of these centers administer only some of the tests, with other agencies or academic departments on campus assuming responsibility for the others.

In those centers where national testing programs are not administered (42 percent of those responding to the survey), the directors were asked, "What philosophy or events have kept national testing programs out of the counseling center?" Half of these directors respond to the question by saying that another agency or academic department has the responsibility for the programs. About one-third report that agencies or departments that predate the establishment of the counseling center retain the responsibility. Thirteen percent say that another institution in the area administers the tests.

Over a fifth of the directors at these institutions leave the impression that they view administration of national testing programs as an albatross around their necks. Among the comments they make are the following: the work carries responsibility with no reward; it is not relevant to the counseling process and should be used for research purposes only; testing is unpopular with students; the counseling center staff is too small to administer the programs; and the expense involved in their administration is too great.

The expense of administering the programs has become a concern of more and more directors. At the Twenty-Third Annual Conference of University and College Counseling Center Directors (1974) in Houston, Texas, there were extensive talks between directors and personnel sent to the conference by Educational Testing Service. The discussions centered on adequate reimbursement for administering the College Level Examination Program.

My conclusion is that assigning the administration of national testing programs is as much a function of chance or unknown events as it is a philosophy or rationale for where the testing programs belong.

The other phase of academically oriented testing is the testing of the university's own students, either on an individual basis or in groups (a rare occurrence) with standardized or locally developed tests. To discover the intent and scope of programs in this area of testing, the directors were asked to name the two tests most frequently used "to measure academic potential or achievement, excluding the nationally administered tests."

Forty-four percent of the directors who list tests mention the Wechsler Adult Intelligence Scale, by far the most frequently named test. The School and College Ability Tests is named by 28 percent of the directors, and approximately 15 percent name either the Otis Self-Administering Tests of Mental Ability or the College Qualification Test. Twenty-seven other tests are mentioned at least once. It is also notable that only three-fourths of the directors list any academically oriented tests at all. This, plus the comments of some directors, is an indication that overall these tests are seldom used in counseling students.

PERSONALITY-ORIENTED TESTING

The second major category of testing programs involves testing oriented to personality assessment. That 90 percent of the directors listed personality tests (as opposed to 75 percent listing academic tests) is evidence that these tests and the programs associated with them are used more frequently.

Most testing is done in conjunction with individual counseling, but occasionally counselors develop programs around a test and present the results in groups—sometimes using the psychomat format. Conversely, sometimes a segment of the university will conduct a mass testing program requiring all students in a school or department to take a personality test. Counseling center staff will then offer to interpret the tests on an individual basis or in groups for the students.

Directors were asked to "name the four tests most frequently used other than those used to measure academic potential or achievement." Every director who responded mentions using the Strong-Campbell Interest Inventory (SCII) or its earlier form, the Strong Vocational Interest Blank (SVIB). Forty-six percent of the directors mention using one of the Kuder tests, most of them mentioning the Kuder Occupational Interest Survey, Form DD. Next are the Edwards Personal Preference Schedule and the Minnesota Multiphasic Personality Inventory, which are mentioned by 43 percent and 41 percent of the directors, respectively. The 16PF is mentioned by 21 percent of the directors, the California Psychological Inventory by 12 percent and the Self-Directed Search by 10 percent. Thirty other tests are listed by the directors at least once.

The overwhelming use of the SCII and the Kuder DD, plus the comments of the directors, indicates that most nonacademically oriented testing concentrates on supporting the vocational counseling functions.

No other study eliciting the same information for counseling centers has been found by my efforts. However, for purposes of comparison, a similar study by Sundberg (1961) can be cited. He surveyed 185 psychological services, of which 23 were counseling centers. Of the latter, one-third were in colleges and universities. The three top ranking tests were the Kuder Preference Record, the Strong Vocational Interest Blank (Men), and the Otis Self-Administering Tests of Mental Ability. All other tests were either academically oriented tests, performance tests, or projective tests, none of which are mentioned in the present study, except the Minnesota Multiphasic Personality Inventory, which ranks tenth out of 32 tests.

Sundberg compared his findings with the findings of two previous studies. Although the two previous studies were not conducted in counseling centers, he noted that use of intelligence tests had declined significantly over a twenty-five year period.

Extent of Usage

A similar trend in counseling centers shows up between Sundberg's study and the present study, that is, a shift in emphasis from academically oriented testing to personality-oriented testing. An overall decline in the use of any tests in counseling has been noted by Layton (1972) and has been alluded to in the comments of the directors. To further clarify the issue, the directors were asked, "In what percent of students who are served by your center is testing a part of the counseling process?"

Ninety-three percent of the directors responded to the item. The median percentage of students for whom testing is part of the counseling process is 30, while the semi-interquartile range is 14; therefore, the middle 50 percent of the directors report that testing is involved in the counseling of between 16 percent and 44 percent of their clientele. However, the number of those who indicate less than 10 percent, is disproportionately high (19 percent), and only one director marked 95 percent. Thus, there is an abnormally great percentage of centers in which the use of testing seems deemphasized.

This deemphasis seems especially true in centers in smaller colleges and universities, nearly one-third of which marked that testing is a part of the counseling process for 5 percent or less of their clients. This phenomenon may be a function of the small sample size in this category; more likely, the recent training of these directors, most of whom are young, deemphasized testing.

Financial Expenditure

An attempt was made to determine the cost of materials and supplies used for testing by asking the directors two questions: "What percent of your non-personnel budget is allotted for testing materials, supplies, etc.?" and "What is the dollar figure?" If we judge from the lower number of respondents (60 percent from large centers, 79 percent from medium-sized centers, and 86 percent from small centers) and from comments made by a few directors, obtaining these figures presented some difficulty. For example, the definition of nonpersonnel budgets differs from center to center, and in some centers testing materials are not a separate budget item, or expenditures for them vary greatly from year to year. Some centers include expenditures for scoring as well as materials, and other centers charge students for this scoring and do not include it as a budget item.

Table 1*

PERCENTAGE OF NONPERSONNEL BUDGET OF COUNSELING CENTERS SPENT ON TESTING

	Large Universities	Medium-Sized Universities	Small Colleges
Highest	100	100	80
3rd quartile	25	30	20
Median	12	12	15
1st quartile	6.5	7.5	7.5
Lowest	.05	.01	1

DOLLARS SPENT ON TESTING BY COUNSELING CENTERS

Highest	5,500	13,000	4,000
3rd quartile	3,000	2,000	1,250
Median	2,000	1,000	605
1st quartile	876	350	400
Lowest	250	50	120

*Highest, Lowest, Q_1, Median, and Q_3 responses are in answer to the questions, "What percent of your non-personnel budget is allotted for testing materials, supplies, etc.?" and "What is the dollar figure?"

The summarized data, presented in table 1, are fairly uniform despite these discrepancies. The percentages are strikingly similar, and the dollar amounts are consistent with the sizes of the universities. The median percentage is 12 percent for large and medium-sized universities and 15 percent for small colleges. The median dollar amounts are $2,000 for large universities, $1,000 for medium-sized universities, and $605 for small colleges.

It should also be noted that the distribution for expenditures is positively skewed. The same positive skew was noted in the data for percentage of students in which testing is a part of the counseling process. It follows that centers that report serving a small segment of their student population spend less money for testing. Thirty-three percent of directors reporting from large institutions spend less than $1,000, while 29 percent of directors at medium-sized institutions report spending less than $500.

Bearing the expense of scoring tests has been alluded to previously. Since the Strong vocational tests (SVIB and SCII) and the Kuder Occupational Interest Survey have a separate scoring for each occupation or college major, computer scoring is the only feasible method. The directors were asked who bears the cost of scoring the test, the university or the student. Of the directors at large universities (91 percent responding), 75 percent report that the university bears the expense, while 19 percent say it is the responsibility of the student, and 6 percent claim that both bear the expense. In medium-sized universities (98 percent reporting), the distribution of responses is the university, 76 percent; the student, 22 percent; and both, 2 percent. In small colleges and universities (81 percent reporting), the distribution of responses is the university, 69 percent; the student, 23 percent; and both, 8 percent. Overall, the university bears the expense at three-fourths of the reporting institutions.

The Future

The final question the directors were asked was, "Is testing (excluding ACT, GRE, etc.) as an adjunct to the counseling process on the increase? remaining the same? on the decrease?" The responses from the directors at the medium-sized institutions and those of the directors as a whole are the same. Sixty percent marked "remaining the same," while 20 percent marked "on the increase" and 20 percent marked "on the decrease." An even greater percentage (71 percent) of directors at large institutions marked "remaining the same," while less than half (46 percent) of the directors at small institutions indicated that they see no change. For all practical purposes, the directors at large and small institutions were also balanced on the issue of increasing or decreasing use of tests.

It seems, therefore, that in college and university counseling centers testing programs will remain the same. Local needs or an innovative director or staff could create the conditions for change. The positive skew noted above for the distributions of percentage of clients served and for dollar expenditure indicate that in many institutions testing will be a small part of the overall counseling program. This relatively steady state of programs in counseling centers seems to parallel the leveling off in development of new tests noted by Kirk (1966).

Summary and Conclusion

A survey was conducted among directors of counseling centers in the United States and Canada to determine the status of testing programs in their institutions. It was found that in the area of academically oriented testing just over half of the centers have responsibility for national testing programs. When directors were asked to indicate which tests were in greatest use, every director mentioned the Strong-Campbell Interest Inventory or its predecessors, and just less than half mentioned the Kuder Occupational Interest Survey. This extensive usage of vocational tests suggests that testing to help students make career decisions is the backbone of counseling center operations.

Other tests frequently used are the Weschler Adult Intelligence Scale, the Edwards Personal Preference Schedule, and the Minnesota Multiphasic Personality Inventory. The directors said that testing is a part of the counseling process for one-third of their clientele. Overall, directors spend about 15 percent of their nonpersonnel budget on testing materials.

Most directors see test usage in counseling remaining the same, and the number who see testing on either the increase or the decrease balance each other. In the future testing is expected to be an important, though relatively small, part of counseling center operations.

References

Goldman, L. 1972. Tests and counseling: the marriage that failed. *Measurement and Evaluation in Guidance* 4: 213-20.

Kirk, B. A. 1966. The challenges ahead in counseling and testing. In G. J. Klopf, ed., *College student personnel work in the years ahead*. Student Personnel Series, no. 7. Washington, D.C.: American College Personnel Association.

Layton, W. L. 1972. Symposium: tests and counseling. II. A basis for a lasting relationship between tests and counseling. *Measurement and Evaluation in Guidance* 5: 403-07.

Oetting, E. R.; Ivey, A. E.; and Weigel, R. G. 1970. *The college and university counseling center*. Student Personnel Series, no. 11. Washington, D.C.: American College Personnel Association.

Sundberg, N. D. 1961. The practice of psychological testing in clinical services in the United States. *American Psychologist* 16: 79-83.

PART IV Other Activities

17

EDUCATION AND TRAINING ROLE OF THE CENTER

Sheridan P. Mc Cabe

UNIVERSITY OF NOTRE DAME

Earlier chapters have documented the diversity that exists among counseling centers. However, the basic common denominator shared by all is existence in an institution of higher learning. The basic purpose of the college or university is the education of the students enrolled there, and all agencies of the institution must relate more or less directly to this purpose. At the present time, institutions of higher education typically have been caught in a financial squeeze of escalating inflation, decreasing enrollments, and increased competition for research and endowment dollars. Fiscally motivated retrenchments are the order of the day, and frills are being searched out and eliminated by administrations. Drum and Figler describe this situation:

Schools and colleges are beginning to feel the effects of restricted funds. This has led to an examination of existing programs, and counseling services cannot demonstrate that they are helping a significant portion of the student body, despite the fact that they have waiting lists. The passive-reactive, prescriptive model is too limited and archaic. Even when the demand for services far outstrips a counseling service's ability to deliver, educational administrators are unimpressed because counselors still are talking about a small fraction of the student body.... A growing number of educational administrators are requiring counseling services to demonstrate that they are relevant to the larger portion of the student body and that they operate in the mainstream of the educational institution (1973, p. 74).

Unless the counseling center operates and is perceived as contributing to the main purpose of the institution, it will risk becoming an endangered species.

The point of view to be presented in this chapter is that this state of affairs is not an entirely unmixed evil. By increasing its commitment to its education and training role, the counseling center can become a more vital unit, improve the quality and quantity of the services it offers, and assume a more central position among the agencies of the college or university. The compatibility of educational and therapeutic goals will be considered, and several modalities of specific educational and training activities will be treated.

Over the past decade or so there has been a definite trend among counseling centers to move away from a clinical model, which concerns itself with clients who seek out help, to a more proactive model featuring efforts at prevention and developmental counseling: "most counselors do not occupy a vital role in their educational communities because they provide extensive service to only a small number of troubled students and superficial service to a number of others trying to make educational and occupational decisions" (Drum & Figler, 1973, p. 29). The clinical model provided excellent service to a relatively few in great need, but only by neglecting a great many more students whose need, although individually less, was collectively much greater.

At the same time, there has been a growing awareness of the importance of developmental theories in educational programming. The work of Erikson (1968), Chickering (1969), and Perry (1970), among others, is increasingly cited in the literature of higher education. Miller and Prince (1976) emphasize the central importance of the awareness of the developmental tasks faced by college students in designing their educational experience. The goals of education involve the development of the whole person and his/her total functioning and are not limited to theoretical knowledge and cognitive functioning.

Thus motivated by institutional pressures and equipped with relevant theoretical models, counseling centers are increasingly oriented toward serving the entire campus community and aligning themselves more closely with the educational mission of the institution. The educational role of the counseling center is not a new one by any means. On campuses that have graduate programs in clinical or counseling psychology, the counseling center is frequently involved in providing a supervised practicum experience. The viewpoint that I would like to share in this chapter has been shaped by ten years of experience in directing a center with a primary function as a practicum training agency. The primacy of this role led to a conscious effort on our part to develop an interpersonal climate and way of interacting that would facilitate development and skill acquisition by the graduate students. These efforts led to the enhancement of many of our service programs in observable ways.

An effort was made to create a climate of openness and freedom among the staff, faculty and graduate students alike. The emphasis is on growth and development, rather than on evaluation and performance criteria. Graduate students are expected to use well the skills that they already have, rather than to pretend to have skills they have not yet acquired. They are encouraged to develop new skills and are supported in the process. This open atmosphere tends to form the staff into a cohesive group, and the spirit is readily evident to those who visit the center. It is our impression that this makes the entry by a prospective client more comfortable and the initial participation in developmental groups more enthusiastic.

Supervision, which is the keystone of our training effort, is not so much a critique of the student's performance as it is a mutual exploration of the issues and dynamics of the case or project in discussion. Efforts are made to integrate this exploration with what has been acquired in the classroom and what can be found in the professional and research literature. Alternative ways of conceptualizing the issues are pursued and translated in possible strategies or action plans. Both the supervisor and the student are expected to stimulate and challenge each other and to contribute according to their respective knowledge and experience.

Thus the students' experiences in the counseling center are a direct extension and augmentation of what they learn in the courses and seminars of their degree program. One useful conceptualization of what we are trying to accomplish is provided by Argyris and Schon (1974), who discuss the theoretical framework for increasing professional effectiveness. They distinguish between "basic theory" as taught in the classroom and "theory in practice," an effective application of basic theory in a practical professional situation. Their book explores in detail the steps necessary in building an effective theory in practice. A careful probing of the inconsistencies and discontinuities between espoused theories and theories in use is necessary, a process that can best occur in a practicum situation under a set of optimum conditions that they refer to as Model II.

The goal of our practicum training program includes an effort to assist students to acquire proficiency in particular counseling techniques and professional procedures, but goes well beyond it to include an orientation to all phases of a counseling agency. Students are considered as members of the staff and are expected to participate as responsible staff members. They are listened to, and their viewpoints are valued. The expectation is that they will identify themselves with the center and be committed to its mission and goals. In this way they grow in confidence and skill appropriate to their level. Participating in the articulation of the goals, values, standards, and norms of the center, they become more aware of themselves as professionals and have a clearer perception of their ideals and limitations.

Students are incorporated into the center in this way, but are assigned tasks and responsibilities proportionate to their capabilities. First-year graduate students who have had only introductory course work as a background generally participate as observers in the programs and services of the center. As they become oriented and acquainted with the procedures, they serve as helpers, especially in the structured group programs. Toward the end of their first year, they act as cocounselors and as coleaders of groups.

Second-year students are given progressive responsibility for individual counseling cases, and they assume more direct responsibility for leading structured groups. In this regard, they participate in the planning of new programs. Particular emphasis is placed on including in every new project a well-developed evaluation component designed to assess its effectiveness. In addition to program assessment, second-year students are more involved in testing and clinical assessment.

Third-year students continue their involvement in one-to-one counseling with cases involving more than routine complexity. In addition, they are given administrative experience in the form of coordinating a developmental or preventive project. Through this experience they have the opportunity to participate in the supervision of first-year students and, of course, are supervised themselves in this task. It is our belief that a learner's learning is enhanced when he/she assumes responsibility for the learning of others.

In general, the practicum students participate on a basis of ten to twenty hours per week, concurrently with their academic course work. We have the advantage of a particularly close relationship with the program faculty. The sequence of academic courses pursued by the students is designed to prepare the students in a timely way for this progressive participation in the center, and the experiences in the center prepare the student for more advanced courses. This situation optimizes the process of students' developing effective theories of practice. When students complete the third year, they should have acquired a reasonably well developed repertoire of techniques and skills, an appropriately critical attitude toward their effectiveness, a measure of aplomb and self-confidence, and a theory of practice suitable for their level.

At this point, students undertake an internship. We expect that this will be a full-time experience in which interns function with the full range of duties that would characterize a regular staff member. The major difference is that interns will be afforded a rich experience both in the diversity of their work and in the supervision and other opportunities for continued development that will be provided to them.

Many of the specifics of this sequence will, of course, not be practical for other centers. However, some general principles can be identified that could be applied in most centers, even those not directly involved with the training of graduate students. Many centers have paraprofessional programs. A number, too, are involved in in-service training programs for staff or contribute to the orientation, training, or development programs for other staffs, such as those of residence halls. But all counseling centers have in one way or another to identify themselves with the central mission of the campus—education.

Probably the basic ingredient in attaining effectiveness as an agency with a significant role in education and training is that the facilitation of learning is a priority goal of the center. Education and training must be valued activities and not be relegated to a subordinate rank in terms of the other activities of the center. Often this is made difficult by the pressing demands on staff time in the form of long waiting lists of individuals needing counseling services. In addition, it is important that this role of the center be a shared enterprise among the staff, pervading all functions of the center and not being assigned to a subunit. This activity entails a point of view that will be open to and encourage innovation. The staff will be stimulated to keep up with the current literature and to keep abreast of new developments and practices in the field. The impetus will be present to reflect on one's own activities and their effectiveness and to engage in systematic efforts to evaluate the results and outcomes of the services offered. Finally, as a shared enterprise, the education and training role will facilitate the exploration of the relationship between theory and practice. In order to communicate effectively what we are about, it is necessary to arrive at conceptualizations that can be articulated.

The second essential factor in implementing this role is the establishment of a climate for effective supervision. This is equally the case for the supervision of staff members, graduate students, or paraprofessionals. Such a climate is characterized by trust and openness, and it encourages personal and professional development. It is in this kind of a climate that supervisors and supervisees can articulate long- and short-range goals for development. One of the main functions of supervision is providing and receiving feedback on performance in a way that fosters goal attainment. It is essential that the goals and procedures of the agency are very clear and that the way in which these relate to overall institutional goals and values is articulated. Otherwise anxieties and frustration will ensue, impeding both effectiveness and development of the person. An effective climate is one in which the participants appropriately are engaged with one another and in which collaboration, rather than competition, is the norm of interaction.

A program of staff development is an important basis of the education and training role. When the center holds the education and training of others as a major priority and expects its staff members to share a commitment to this, it needs to show a high level of concern for the continued education and development of its own staff. Provision will be made for staff members to participate in conferences and workshops enabling them to enhance their skills or to develop new ones. Opportunities will be developed within the center for ongoing seminars and training sessions in which the staff can help each other by exchanging insights or viewpoints. Often this is done by regular case conferences or discussions of current journals. Inviting outside presenters to speak to the staff or to lead workshops for them is especially effective in bringing a fresh perspective to the staff.

Research is an activity that is generally highly esteemed in counseling centers, due in part to the training of many staff members as psychologists and to the overall commitment of the college or university to research as a basic academic pursuit. However, research is the one activity that is the most likely to fall by the wayside under the pressure of service demands. In my opinion, research as a function flows directly from the individual counseling service. In the process of rendering service, counselors come into direct and immediate contact with evidence of system dysfunction on the campus. Students who seek counseling help are often experiencing personal confusion or unusual academic pressure in their efforts to pursue their education. Others are in crisis stemming from their social life or living situation. In working with these students in need, the counselor frequently gleans very unique insights into the inadequacies and sources of stress inherent in their experiences on the campus at large. Because of the unsystematic character of this information—obtained mainly from those not coping well with the system and bounded by the confidentiality within which counseling takes place—the counselor is often at a disadvantage to provide other components of the campus with the necessary information to improve their functioning.

However, by systematically gathering data by well-designed studies to verify the hypotheses derived in the counseling process, the counseling center can serve a most effective function in sharing this information to upgrade the quality of the overall educational program of the campus, both in the classroom and in the residence halls. Research on student characteristics or on the impact of various programs and situations on effective student development and documentation of the results of new approaches or programs can form the foundation for the very important function of consultation.

Like research, consultation has been considered an important function in many centers over the years. All too often, however, this has been concerned largely with mental health consultation. Center staff would consult with faculty or residence hall staff on understanding and responding to students who manifested indications of emotional or adjustment problems. It would seem much more meaningful to broaden the scope of this consultative function to pertain more to the issues that touch the lives of all students and not merely those in distress. The foundation of this consultative function should be not only the staff member's expertise in the behavioral sciences, but also actual data assembled in the ordinary scope of the counseling center's activities. It should be data both based on and relevant to the concerns and activity of the consultee. In this way, the counseling center can become an effective change agent on the campus, not so much to enlist other components of the campus in the mission of the center—the improvement of mental health on the campus—but to assist the various units of the institution to be more effective in their pursuit of the goals and objectives of the institution as a whole.

As an illustration of how this activity can function, I will describe a program operating in the counseling center on my campus. We offer a program to residence hall staffs centering on the environment of the hall. Our campus is a largely residential one, and the goals and values of the institution feature not only academic excellence, but also formation of the whole person of the student and development of interpersonal skills and consciousness of personal and social values. The residence hall staff is entrusted with the responsibility of creating and managing an environment that will foster student development along these lines. At the invitation of the hall staff, we will meet with them to share our perspective based on our experience and our knowledge of the research and theoretical literature on the impact of living environments on the development of the student. We then gather data from the hall residents using objective instruments such as the University Residence Environment Scale (Moos & Gerst, 1972) or other environmental assessment techniques. The results of the survey are then shared and discussed with the staff of the hall. Ways in which the hall environment might be changed to facilitate student development are explored in terms of changes in hall management or programs. Any modifications that are made are followed and evaluated. Changes in hall environments can be documented and assessed. Similar programs could be instituted in almost all aspects of the campus including academic programs, student services, and the endeavors of student government.

The most recent addition to the pattern of services in the typical counseling center are outreach programs. When these are developmental in purpose, as more and more of them are, they serve to augment the education and training role of the center. They are designed to assist larger numbers of students than can be reached by traditional counseling programs and have as their purpose enhancing the overall participation of the students in their pursuit of an education. In some places, these take the form of courses for academic credit. This trend in counseling centers documents the movement toward increasing centrality of the educational and training role in its overall mission.

In this chapter an attempt was made to examine the education and training role of the counseling center as it has developed out of the traditional services of individual counseling, training of graduate students, and research and consultative activities. The movement has been one of natural development, but one that has been fostered by changing patterns in higher education and evolving needs and expectations of the center by the campus at large. The emphasis has been on serving larger numbers of students, establishing a relevance to the central mission of the campus, and not restricting the services to a small minority of the student body. The experience and reputation of counseling centers as contributing to the formation of future counselors by training practicum students and interns can be extended to contributing to the development of human effectiveness of students at large.

These concepts are not particularly new. The Proceedings of the Twenty-Fifth Annual Conference of University and College Counseling Center Directors included as an appendix a summary of the presentations and discussions of the first conference held in 1950. It is interesting to note the principal themes: (1) the role of the counseling center in training counselors-in-training, (2) the need for research and consultation, and especially, (3) the importance of relating the objectives of counseling to the objectives of the institution in which the counseling is done. At the present time these developmental trends are converging, and the education and training role can emerge to rank with the individual counseling function as a major aspect of the counseling center.

References

Argyris, C., and Schon, D. A. 1974. *Theory in practice: increasing professional effectiveness.* San Francisco: Jossey-Bass.

Chickering, A. W. 1969. *Education and identity.* San Francisco: Jossey-Bass.

Drum, D. J., and Figler, H. E. 1973. *Outreach in counseling.* New York: Intext Educational Publishers.

Erikson, E. H. 1968. *Identity: youth and crisis.* New York: W. W. Norton.

Miller, T. K., and Prince, J. S. 1976. *The future of student affairs.* San Francisco: Jossey-Bass.

Moos, R., and Gerst, M. 1972. *University residence environmental scale manual.* Palo Alto, Calif.: Consulting Psychologists Press.

Perry, W. G., Jr. 1970. *Forms of intellectual and ethical development in the college years: a scheme.* New York: Holt, Rinehart and Winston.

18

REFERRAL AND CASE MANAGEMENT CONSULTATION

David H. Mills
UNIVERSITY OF MARYLAND

The counseling center articulates with many other campus (and off-campus) agencies concerning administrative, fiscal, educational, and personnel issues. However, in the area of client referral and case management, the center and its personnel move into critical interactions with other agencies and individuals regarding making the best possible service available to particular clients. Terminology in this domain is somewhat confusing; the following definitions are offered in an attempt, at least for the purpose of this chapter, to clarify and to make this discussion internally consistent.

Referral refers to the process whereby individuals (clients or patients) who have had contact with the counseling center are directed for assistance to another agency or professional (usually outside of the counseling center); the persons being referred set up a relationship directly with the agency/individual to whom they are referred without the information involved in that contact having to be sent to or interpreted to the individual by the counseling center. In other words, clients set up a new helping relationship with someone outside the center and, for the purposes being referred, deal directly with the non-counseling-center person to whom they have been referred. They become, therefore, that person's client or patient.

Case management consultation refers to the situation in which the counseling center maintains its relationship with the client but asks for advice, special procedures, or confirmation of existing plans from a third party (the consultant). The consultant may function with direct contact with the client (as in a medication review) or without such contact (as in a typical case conference). In distinction to the referral, in which the primary relationship with the client shifts from the center to the person or agency receiving the referral, the primary relationship with the client during case management consultation remains with the counseling center. The term *consultation*, especially since the advent of the community consultation movement, organizational development, "eco-mapping", and the like, is used with more frequency than precision. For this paper, I am reserving it for third-party assistance in the management of a particular case.

Referral

A client is referred from the center when the presenting problem is not one that is appropriate for the center to manage. This includes a number of reasons and types of situations.

First, and probably most critical, is the client who appears to need, or who probably will need, psychiatric hospitalization. This is not to say that many counseling center personnel do not have skills and training in handling difficult cases (for example, borderline or ambulatory schizophrenics) and treating such cases very successfully on an outpatient basis. However, there are cases that probably need (or will shortly need) some kind of inpatient care (or protection), and since few counseling center personnel have admission and hospital privileges, it is important for the client's protection to refer such clients quickly to someone who does. Such referrals should, first, be made quickly and, if possible, before treatment has started in the counseling center and, second, be made with a formal written referral (even if such is written subsequent to a telephone referral). These referrals, if made on campus, typically are to a health or mental health facility such as a student health center or infirmary. If such is not available on campus, community resources must be used, for example, a local hospital or physician (preferably a psychiatrist).

Early referrals are critical in order not to give the client a feeling of being shuttled around or of being abandoned, in order to get definitive treatment for the client as soon as possible, and, last, in order to avoid having to refer in the midst of a crisis. Too often, relations between counseling centers and their medical referral agencies (even under the best of conditions) are strained. This can occur on occasion because of a feeling from our medical colleagues that center personnel "get in over their heads" (sometimes true) or that we "dump" our failures on them. On the other hand, counseling center personnel sometimes do not use their physician referral sources adequately because of a feeling that it is a sign of ineptness to "ask for help" (which is not true) or because of a fear that the medical agency will "steal the client" (which does happen, but rarely). Good relations between counseling and medical agencies on any campus are of critical importance, and this issue of referral (both ways) is often difficult unless addressed in an ongoing and collegial manner.

A second kind of medical (usually psychiatric) referral may be made when prospective clients are under intercurrent medical treatment for a psychological problem, for example, taking lithium salts or some other medication. It seems more parsimonious to have one person handling the monitoring of the medication and the counseling/therapy. Such a referral seems most appropriate when such clients initially present themselves to the center. If clients have medication prescribed for them in the midst of counseling, it seems unnecessary to refer at that point, provided that the medication is being appropriately (and medically) monitored on a consultative basis.

A second area of referral relates in part to some college students' belief that the counseling center will perform the same functions as their high school counselor. Accordingly, these clients present concerns over grades, course enrollment, or departmental rules, concerns that would better be answered by their academic advisor or department. Good liaison between the counseling center and the academic structure of the college or university, as well as a well-trained and knowledgeable receptionist, will facilitate such referrals (which rarely need to be formalized in writing). The sophistication of the receptionist will also help in identifying those clients who in a circuitous manner are asking for educational-vocational assistance even though they sound initially as though they need to be referred to an academic office. Parenthetically—and obviously—the counseling center receptionist needs as much skill and training in the university structure and functions as she or he needs in human relations. The receptionist is one of the most critical persons within any counseling center!

Somewhat similiar are the persons who are asking for assistance in non-counseling-related matters such as financial aid, housing, or job placement. However, it is important to differentiate this group of persons into two subsets, one who does not know where to go and simply needs that information and the other, more critical, group who have been shuffled from office to office and who in desperation turn to the counseling center. This latter group needs more assistance, often an attempt at intercession by a member of the professional staff. The center and its image suffers if it is seen as "just another office that doesn't really care about students." A little patience and a small amount of time can be very helpful to this nonclient. Good relationships with and knowledgeability of the other student affairs offices (again, by both professional and receptionist staffs) are necessary to facilitate these referrals. Too often, unfortunately, there is an implicit pecking order in student affairs that translates into counseling center personnel's dealing with their student affairs colleaues in a cavalier or condescending manner ("remember, we often have Ph.D.'s and they usually have bachelor's or master's"); to do so, however, can undermine easy referrals and communication with these agencies.

There is also an intra-agency referral, from one staff member to another, which is too often overlooked. This type of referral is critical when the counseling center is a training agency with short-tenured practicum students or interns who see clients (under supervision) for training purposes. The duration of counseling often extends beyond that of the trainee, and unless dealt with early and directly by the trainee and the supervisor (who does have the professional responsibility for the counseling of the trainee), there may be a last-minute attempt to find a new counselor or the counseling may be prematurely terminated with less than satisfactory results. Another kind of intra-agency referral, which will not be dealt with here, is the transfer of a client from one professional staff member to another often "because I can't work with that kind of client." Such referrals are too often a result of bad case assignment or of the narcissism of the counselor. Most counseling center professionals would like to deal primarily with "YAVIS" clients (Young, Attractive, Verbal, Intelligent, Sensitive), but unfortunately all of our clientele do not fit into this category. Some clients, for example, are boring, some not psychologically minded, and some not very bright. These characteristics (which may be a substantial part of the presenting problem) are not adequate reasons for referral. These clients are as needy and as eligible for service as their more attractive peers.

A potentially difficult referral situation occurs when prospective clients request (or demand) to be seen by a member of their own race or ethnic background. There is, unfortunately, no general agreement within the helping professions as to the efficacy of such pairings, for example, black with black, Chicano with Chicano. Therefore, in the absence of guidelines, intake personnel must exercise their best professional judgment in case disposition—some members of minority groups work very well with nonminority professionals, and some do not. If the prospective client comes from a particularly rigid or isolated subculture (and is generally still adhering to its rules), it would seem typically appropriate for that person to see a professional with similar antecedents (to borrow a phrase from cultural anthropology, someone who is a member of the "third culture," the culture that bridges the other two). On the other hand, if the client's background seems not qualitatively disparate from that of the "majority" culture, then the client may be able to work with a wider variety of professionals. The referral decision usually does (and should) rest with the staff persons who have the initial contact with the client. If they are not members of a minority group, however, it is often valuable for them to consult with a colleague who is. There may also be reality factors at play that will help in the decision making; for example, the Chicano counselor may have a longer backlog of prospective clients than the agency in general, a fact that may alter the preferences of the new client. Of course, the minority professional staff needs to be highly involved in the parameters of case assignment so as to get the mix of clientele best suited to their needs and training.

Another set of clients present problems for which the treatment is within the capacity of the individual staff member, but outside the treatment guidelines of the counseling center. This situation most typically occurs in an agency that delivers only short-term treatment,—no more than, six or twelve or twenty sessions, for example—when a client presents difficulties that can only be resolved in longer-term treatment. An early referral of such cases is extremely important. If referral seems unlikely, then a very explicit contract for a maximum number of sessions needs to be entered into with the client. However, clients can so easily enter into our own rescue fantasies and (mistakenly) give us the feeling that "you are the only person who can help me" that we, too, often buy into demands that conflict with agency policy. Few agency rules should be inviolate. However, in this type of case the best way of deciding whether we are in truth acting in the best interests of the client or satisfying our own needs (by abridging policy) is to have such cases accepted only after substantial peer review of the case. Lacking that, the client should be routinely referred.

Case Management Consultation

Despite the ongoing nature of a particular case, there are a number of reasons to ask for consultation for assistance in case management.

The first of these is a need for assistance in an area outside of the treating counselor's area of expertise. One of the most common situations occurs when the counselor feels a particular client might benefit from medication (for anxiety, depression, and so on). If such is the case, a formal, written medical consult is usually made, outlining the client's symptomatology, any recent changes in status, the nature of the counseling, and the reason for the request for review. It would be, of course, as inappropriate for the counselor to tell the physician what to prescribe (or if to prescribe) as it would be for the physician gratuitously to tell the counselor how to treat the client. While physician's styles differ, it is not appropriate to expect them either to prescribe anything without physically seeing the client or not to plan to see the client under medication for review. However, some ongoing interaction between the counseling center staff member and the medical person doing the prescribing is dictated if the client is continuing on medication.

A second area is that of consultation with regard to client dynamics and/or treatment strategies, a typical case conference situation. A formal protocol should be written when a case is being presented to one's colleagues and/or an outside consultant. Occasionally, audio or video recording of case sessions with the client will augment the case protocol. Typical questions revolve around diagnosis, the way in which to break an impasse in treatment, difficulties with termination, future directions for counseling, and so forth. Parenthetically, it should be noted that the organizing of case material (and one's own thoughts) and the review of the course of counseling prior to writing it up can be one of the most (if not the most) valuable parts of the case conference for the presenter. Informal case conferences, without written material, can be valuable, but are most helpful in conjunction with the more formal ones. In the absence of case conferences, a staff member may, as in the request for a medication review, ask an outside professional (for example, a psychologist or psychiatrist) for assistance in answering similar questions. Such consults have to be written (though typically not in as detailed a manner as the formal case conference protocol) and an appointment set up for the client with the consultant. It must be reemphasized that the staff member making the referral must receive the consultant's report and then interpret that report to the client. Basically, this kind of consultation is to help counseling center professionals do their job with clients.

There is another domain that really fits between the areas of consultation and referral. Occasionally, there will emerge during counseling an issue that is important enough to address but falls outside the counselor's realm. The client needs to be referred for assistance with that circumscribed area while the counseling continues as before. Examples of such concerns—which are important but may not be central to the counseling—might be requests for educational-vocational counseling, specific questions about the job market or resumé writing, which should be handled by the placement or career development center; difficulties in writing, studying, or reading skills that could be referred to an academic skills laboratory; valid concerns over religious issues, which an appropriate member of the clergy could handle (and which counselors too often ignore, downgrade, or interpret). It is, obviously, not ethical to deal with issues or concerns outside one's area of training or competence. However, it is important when such issues appear not to ignore them, but to seek assistance for the client in dealing with them.

General Issues Concerning Referral and Consultation

Open lines of communication need to be maintained and constantly monitored between agencies that interact continually on a referral or consultative basis, probably the most critical dyad being the counseling center and the campus health/mental health agencies. If there is antipathy or mutual distrust, not only is the referral/consultation function made more difficult (or, at worst, impossible), but ultimately, and more importantly, the client suffers. Among others, three potential sources of difficulty between counseling and medical agencies are common.

First, inadequate collateral information is sent to the medical agency by counseling center staff. Unfortunately, all too often the counseling center staff members are not trained or knowledgeable in appropriate referral/consultation procedures. Hence, it can appear that center personnel are demanding certain consultative activities,—for example, prescribing medication—when they should be, or actually are, asking for the medical professional's opinion as to whether such medication is necessary. We need to be scrupulous in making sure that the agency we are referring to or asking for consultation (1) knows what it is that we are asking for; (2) is told why we are asking for it; and (3) receives enough information about the case to facilitate the referral/consultation.

When dealing with a medical agency especially, this information should be in writing (even if there has been prior telephone contact). The earlier telephone information may have not been given to the appropriate professional at the other end, it may have been too terse, or it may have been forgotten. All of this can lead to a feeling among our medical colleagues that we are "not professional" or are "dumping" clients on them. One way of dealing with these potential difficulties is to have, once or twice yearly, joint staff meetings to talk frankly of these issues and to set up procedures to obviate them. These joint staff meetings should then be followed by more regularly scheduled meetings (weekly or biweekly) between representatives of each agency to deal with specific difficult issues as they arrive. Unfortunately, there is a long history of mistrust, if not antagonism, between the counseling/psychology and psychiatry professions so that this continued contact is necessary to keep things running as smoothly as possible. It is of vital importance in these meetings that the participants be open, frank, and able to admit mistakes when they occur. To try to cover up such mistakes, rather than to learn from them, will serve only to increase the distance between the counseling center and other agencies.

A second potential source of difficulty is, paradoxically, believing too often that what clients report is always literally true. Clients being referred (or being consulted about) are often frightened, anxious, or angry. Because of these feelings they may distort or misrepresent one agency or professional to the other. Certainly, professionals and agencies do err, do handle things badly or cavalierly, and these situations should be rectified; however, it is of critical importance both to check client reports carefully to determine their accuracy and to give feedback to the agency involved. The weekly or biweekly meeting between agencies is a good vehicle for such interaction.

Third, agencies have experienced difficulty in "informal" referral, that is, when persons are told (typically by the counseling center receptionist) that they probably should go to another agency rather than the center because of the kind of request they are making (for example, "I need to get some tranquilizers"). These individuals then arrive at the second agency (in this example, the health center), saying they have been referred to it by the counseling center; the health center (or any other similar agency) then feels aggrieved because the counseling center is "referring" people to them and not informing them of the referral or the reason thereof. This kind of ambiguity can never be completely taken care of, but alerting the receptionists (and the professional staff) to this potential source of difficulty and brainstorming ways around it for a particular campus can be very useful. In addition, the feedback loop from the other agency (including the two receptionists' knowing each other and feeling comfortable in communicating directly) can help.

Another general consideration regarding referrals to other mental health professionals relates to the manner in which the referral is presented to the client. Effective referral consists as much as possible of making the person being referred a part of the process. It is a temptation for some counseling center personnel to try to "pull their punches" and to soften the referral so as to make the client feel more comfortable. This can be done to the point of making the referral reasons too bland and too imprecise for the client to sense the reason behind (and the importance of) the process. If it is important to refer a client, that importance has to be presented directly to the client (obviously continuing to be sensitive to cues that might panic the client or give her a feeling that "she's too sick to treat"). Difficult referrals may well take some time and perseverance, well beyond a single session. They can include a great amount of encouragement and active assistance on the counseling center professional's part in order to be successful. It is important not to capitulate at the first indication of negative or ambivalent feelings on the client's part. Instead, one must attempt to work directly with those feelings so that the referral is completed and, further, the client arrives at the new treatment setting ready, as much as possible, to begin work.

Ethics

Of critical importance in the area of consultation and referral are the ethical standards in counseling and in psychology intended to safeguard the client's welfare. These ethical standards are published by the American Psychological Association (1963, amended in 1965 & 1970) and by the American Personnel and Guidance Association (1974). The areas of "professional competence," "confidentiality," "client welfare," and "interprofessional relations" are particularly important to the counseling center professional who is making a referral or asking for consultation. All counseling center personnel subscribe to these standards (and adherence is one of the requirements of the International Association of Counseling Centers, the counseling center accrediting organization). However, the specifics of the standards may not be immediately available and easily remembered.

Using the APA ethical standards as a guide, the following areas seem germane to this discussion:

1. The professional must recognize the areas of his/her competence and is required to refer problems outside his/her area of expertise or to consult when necessary (principle 2c).

2. The professional must safeguard information obtained in his/her counseling practice. Information received in confidence should be revealed only if there is "clear and imminent danger to an individual or society" (principle 6a), but then only to appropriate professionals or agencies. Such information may be shared with other professionals (orally or in writing) only if such persons are "concerned with the case" (principles 6a & 6b). In some states (for example, Maryland) a psychologist has "privileged communication" with his/her clients, so the confidentiality has both ethical and legal support. Prior to releasing information about a client, a written release from the client must be obtained.

3. The counselor should terminate a relationship nonbeneficial to the client (principle 7c), and a referral may be appropriate. If a client is referred, the referring person maintains responsibility for the case until the referral is

effected or until the counselor/client relationship is mutually terminated (principle 7e).

4. If a person being referred is continuing to receive psychological services from another person, additional psychological service should not be rendered unless the other professional agrees or terminates his/her relationship with the client (principle 11b).

This section is in no way intended to be definitive with regard to professional ethics in consultation or referral. Instead, the attempt is more to alert readers that the ethical issues in referrals or in consultation are extremely important and to refer them to the basic documents published by the American Psychological Association and the American Personnel and Guidance Association.

Examples

A. CASE MANAGEMENT CONSULTATION
   To: Mental Health Unit
   From: David Mills, Ph.D., Counseling Center

   1. Identifying Information (Please note that this person has an appointment at 2 p.m., Wednesday, July 13, with Dr. Smith.)
   Mary J. is a 21 year old, single female who is a senior in Elementary Education; she is the oldest of three sibs in a Maryland suburban family (father is a pharmacist and mother teaches junior high school). Family relationships seem solid, and there is no family history of significant psychological or psychiatric difficulties. Client is scheduled for graduation this June.

   2. Course of Treatment
   The client has been seen weekly since September 1976 for a total of 15 sessions. Her initial concerns related to a public-speaking phobia, which responded extremely well to systematic desensitization. Her concerns have subsequently shifted to her making plans for postgraduation. She feels that she must stay in this geographic area (where her family and friends are), get a job, and begin paying off school loans. She is dating and is quite emotionally involved with a young man who has one year remaining in his master's program in business—this is a major part of the impetus to stay and seems to be a serious relationship, one which provides her with a marked amount of emotional support. However, the job market for elementary teachers in this area is extremely tight, and she is starting to experience great concern over getting a teaching position.

   3. Current Status
   Over the past approximately 6 weeks this articulate, bright young woman has become increasingly anxious and depressed; she cries easily, has marked difficulty sleeping, and reports that she has lost approximately fifteen

pounds. Her problem centers very specifically over her feeling that she will not be able to get a teaching job for next year ("I just know that this time next year, I am going to be the best educated cocktail waitress in College Park"). While we are working on these professional concerns in conjunction with the University Placement Office, I am concerned about the difficulty in sleeping and the weight loss. She reports feeling (and looks) very run-down and is starting to do poorly in class, she says, because of this (up to this semester she has maintained a B+ cumulative average). There is no suicidal ideation.

4. Reason for Consult
I have two reasons for this consultation. The first relates to the possibility of her getting some medication in order to help her sleep. Secondly, because of the marked recent weight loss, I would appreciate your advice regarding her physical condition (it has been ten months since she had a full physical, the results of which were negative).

B. CASE REFERRAL
To: Dr. P. S. Wasserman
From: David Mills, Ph.D., Counseling Center

This is a formal referral for Robert——— about whom we spoke on 3/17/77 and whom you are scheduled to see next Thursday.

The client is a new freshman at the university who came in through our intake process last Wednesday asking for long-term therapy (which had been suggested to him by his last therapist, Dr. ———, whom he had been seeing weekly since beginning high school). That therapy was terminated because of Bob's leaving home to attend the university. We explained that we have a 12 session limit on personal counseling or therapy here at the Counseling Center and offered him that option as well as referring him off-campus to someone who could see him privately for a longer period of time. Bob selected the latter option, hence the current referral.

Because we did not pick the client up for treatment, the material that we have is somewhat sketchy. Bob is an 18 year-old, unmarried male, the only child in what he describes as a very wealthy family. He was referred to therapy by his headmaster four years ago because "I didn't have any friends and spent all of my time by myself." He has become very dependent upon his earlier psychologist and is very fearful of being here at the university, away from home, and "on my own." The prior therapeutic relationship, he says, has given him some insights into the distance that he feels from his father and stepmother (his mother died when Bob was three years old) but, even in the way he describes this "insight," one senses that there is still much strain in these relationships. He still feels lonely much of the time, though it is difficult to separate out the problems typical to entry to the university from the preexisting character structure.

He is "treatment-wise" and uses a lot of psychological jargon in describing himself and other persons. However, these psychological "insights" seem somewhat brittle and not well integrated. Clinically, he appears to be bright, verbal, and somewhat awkward in manner. His range of affect seems somewhat limited (though not blunted) and there were no indications of a significant thinking or mood disorder. He appears to be highly motivated for and experienced in treatment.

C. CASE CONFERENCE PROTOCOL

Client: Betsy, 28 year-old married woman, currently separated from her husband, a local businessman; a junior in Spanish, working part-time in a local bookstore.

Intake notes from 9 months ago: "Betsy is in a great deal of pain. She gives the appearance of a rather well-composed 'lady' sitting on a volcano and talks nonstop, apparently as a way of communicating her pain before falling apart. For the past two months her husband has vacillated almost daily with regard to leaving her. She says that she doesn't feel strong enough to tell him to leave though feels that the marriage is a very bad one; they married because it 'was the most convenient thing to do.' She reports some thoughts of suicide though she is convincing when she says that she will not act on them. She appears strong on the surface, though her defenses are rather brittle. Her husband refuses to come in for counseling. She is given a priority appointment with Dr. ———."

Treatment: The client was picked up one week after the above intake and Betsy has been seen at the current time for 18 individual sessions.

Background: Betsy grew up in a small, rural community in the Middle West, the oldest of three children in a poor farming family "halfway between sharecroppers and landowners." The family, very religious and conservative, lived in a run-down house that her mother kept very badly and that did not have electricity until the client was in high school. She and her sisters worked the farm (as much as 18 hours a day), and she reports very few friends because "I was embarrassed to ask anyone home." Her happiest memories were of being by herself reading. Her mother is described as being rather borderline and continually accused the father of "running around," which Betsy says was absurd ("he didn't have time for anything but work"). Betsy describes herself as being very submissive. Nonetheless, she did go away from home after high school and worked her way through two years of a local state college. There she met her husband, and they married. Until her courtship she had not dated, even though she was voted the "prettiest girl" in her high school graduating class. She was overwhelmed by her husband's attentions, and they decided to get married because "it was too expensive to maintain two apartments." After the marriage she worked as a typist until he got his degree, and they moved here to a larger city, where he has become a manager of a local clothing store. In retrospect, she sees the marriage as "my ticket to get away from my family."

Marriage: Her husband is described as being a very controlling, compulsive, and protective person who, nonetheless, reinforced Betsy's feelings of low self-esteem, e.g., he told her that she was uninteresting socially and bought her an encyclopedia to enliven her social talk. He worked very long hours at the store and expected her to organize her life around them. Their sex life, which she reports had been very satisfying, deteriorated because of his lack of response. He began to have long, unexplained absences in the evening, which, from information that she got from a neighbor, she believes were due to his having an affair with one of the persons in his store. She began to unload her problems on this neighbor (a male), and the two of them began a sexual relationship of their own. At this time, she precipitated a separation from her husband (who doesn't know about her affair). Her neighbor's marriage itself is extremely bad, but he refuses to leave his wife because, he says, of feelings for his children. There is no doubt that he has been very supportive of Betsy in her transition from her own marriage, but she is currently very afraid of being "left alone."

Course of treatment: The above represents much of what we have dealt with in the treatment to date. I do not think that therapy has begun yet, but we are about to begin (I hope!). Most of our work has been in dealing with the real life demands of the marriage, the separation, the affair, and their effects on her life to include her schooling and job.

   She presents herself as a verbal, articulate, but not psychologically minded person. Her range of affect, while appropriate, is somewhat limited and heavy on the social/positive end—she is a denier, and while she talks of being depressed, she does not show it. There is in this woman an intense strength that she uses, but does not acknowledge. While she professes to feel quite inadequate and inept, her behavior and manner are not congruent with these feelings (which she acknowledges come in part from messages that she has gotten over the past four years from her husband). She is a physically attractive person, but there is a distance and a superficiality to her that attenuate her attractiveness; in many ways she reminds me of a grown-up sorority girl.

Questions:
1. Should I have moved in quicker to the business of therapy with this woman; and, if so, with the myriad intercurrent crises in her life, how? I am

wondering if part of the reason I did not was some feeling of voyeurism on my part (I don't sense this, but it may be there).

2. Having not done so, what is the best way to "shift gears" now?

3. Any assistance in handling the case from now on?

References

American Personnel and Guidance Association. 1971. Ethical standards. *The Personnel and Guidance Journal* 50: 327–30.

American Psychological Association. 1953. *Ethical standards of psychologists.* Washington, D.C.: American Psychological Association.

19

UNIVERSITY RELATIONS

David L. Jordan

BROCK UNIVERSITY

The survival and effectiveness of professional counselors in higher education increasingly will depend on the relationships that center directors and their staffs develop with other sectors of their institutions. The model centers, against which many centers compare their own functioning, emerged out of the battles that early directors fought for confidentiality and center autonomy (Oetting, Ivey, & Weigel, 1970). Relative isolation from the academic and administrative sectors has been a frequent accompaniment of the struggle for autonomy. Now, pressures from within the profession for greater impact and pressures from without for greater accountability mean that, more than ever, counseling centers need supporters among the faculty and administration of their institutions.

While few counselors in service settings would likely dispute this conclusion, the professional literature has not acknowledged it until recently. As Warnath points out, the counseling theory literature assumes that counselors in higher education "work in settings untroubled by human relationships and organizational pressures which affect other working people" (1971, p. 2).

In a more recent publication Warnath and others (Halleck, 1973; Stubbins, 1973; Warnath, 1973b) examine the social context in which counselors work. Their insights and conclusions are not always comforting, but they are internally consistent. Counselors are not autonomous agents in the service of their student clients. Rather, they are part of bureaucratic organizations, playing a role in these organizations and relating to other parts in an interdependent manner. The problems that some students bring to counseling arise, in part, from the environment in which both clients and counselors function. The type of help that counselors offer will be influenced by their views of that environment.

Acknowledgment of this interdependence suggests a more intentional approach to relationships with faculty and administrators. Making such a suggestion to counselors seems like recommending birth control to someone who feels that "sex is allright if it happens spontaneously, but I don't want anyone to think that I plan on it." However, the importance of being prepared cannot be overstated. Fortunately, planning the development of support need not jeopardize counselors' personal or professional integrity. Goals, such as humanizing decision-making processes, can keep the counselors' integrity intact. Planning points of entry should increase the counselors' effectiveness.

Counselors must develop relationships with other sectors of their institutions. Initially, these relationships will have to be informal, rather than formal or contractual. The faculty, administrators, trustees, and students who actively influence campus policy and functioning should become known to counselors and come to know counselors. The specific people (or positions) with whom counselors should increase contact will vary from campus to campus. Rather than enumerating potential targets, this chapter examines some difficulties that counselors may encounter in their pursuit of expanded influence. The opportunities that informal relationships offer for the development of effective services are considered as part of this examination.

In the past five to eight years, we have entered a period of economic constraint resulting in increased emphasis on accountability and on a sense of professional responsibility to recognize the limitations of traditional counseling models (Kopplin & Rice, 1975; Magoon, 1973). In response to these pressures, a number of counselors have argued for increased involvement with campus power structures. The goals of increased involvement include extending the reach of counselors (for example, Kopplin & Rice, 1975; Magoon, 1973; Oetting, Ivey, & Weigel, 1970), becoming agents of social change (Banks & Martens, 1973; Ivey & Leppaluoto, 1975; Schwerner, 1975; Warnath, 1971), and establishing a base of support (Kopplin & Rice, 1975; Warnath, 1971). The methods through which increased involvement is to be achieved range from psychoecological research, consultation, and outreach programming to social activism and Nader-style confrontation.

It is not within the scope of this chapter to review or evaluate the suggested methods. The authors cited earlier present excellent discussions of alternative approaches and models. A counselor's selection of particular methods will be a matter of personal choice and institution needs, rather than professional dictate. Whatever methods are selected, their success will depend not on acceptance by counselors, but on acceptance by faculty and administrators. Counselors cannot successfully consult, instruct, train, or present research to people who have not acknowledged a need for such services or a counselor's competence to offer them.

The immediate problem seems to be of the chicken-or-the-egg variety. Counselors need to adopt new methods in order to increase their impact and to build support, and they need support for these initiatives. The dilemma can be resolved through gradual entry (or reentry) into the institutional community. Herein lies the value of informal relationships, relationships in which counselors meet faculty and administrators over common interests, joint projects, shared responsibilities, or a glass of beer.

Once counselors decide to move out of the counseling cubicle, they will encounter a number of resistances; their own as well as others'. Involvement, according to Schwerner, "means getting one's hands dirty, taking risks, and sometimes losing" (1975, p. 121). More than a distaste for losing, counselors' fears regarding their academic and administrative colleagues' view of counselors may inhibit moves into the community. In this regard, Schwerner suggests that "some faculty often do not listen to counselors. . .and consider them irrelevant" (1975, p. 123); Warnath states that most faculty have little interest in a counselor's activities, while some view counseling as "little more than coddling and look on the center with contempt" (1971, p. 41); and Oetting, Ivey, and Weigel suggest that "stereotypes of counselors and their activities can create resistance [to consultation]" (1970, p. 35).

These feared perceptions do exist. They are both a hindrance to and a reason for increased involvement. Perhaps counselors need to counsel themselves to check their assumptions (projections), avoid stereotyping faculty and administration, and, if necessary, take small steps. Most counselors who have ventured out of their cubicles have found a few friends.

Moving out will also raise fears of becoming involved in "responsibilities which will interfere with counseling" (Oetting, Ivey & Weigel, 1970, pp. 43, 47). Added to this concern is the knowledge that increased visibility inevitably leads to increased referrals. Less time for counseling and more demand for it do not constitute a circumstance many counselors will want to encourage, since innovations such as paraprofessional programs—while valuable for other reasons—have not proved successful as responses to waiting lists.

Along with outreach, Warnath suggests that a "fundamental change in counselors' attitudes toward the focus of their services and toward their own capacities" is necessary before meaningful changes can occur in the services that are offered (1973a, p. 291). Part of this fundamental change involves dropping or significantly reducing the current priority given to individual counseling. Warnath's suggestion will be too extreme for many counselors. The gradual entry into the community encouraged in this chapter may delay a reassessment of the role of individual counseling, but it will not avoid it. It may permit the emergence of solutions that avoid radical surgery.

Additional inhibitions arise from the knowledge that interpersonal influence is normally a reciprocal process. If counselors increase contacts in order to influence other components of their institutions, they also risk being influenced by these components. Their marginal status on many campuses may make them seem more vulnerable. This is a switch for the counselor who is normally in control of the one-to-one counseling relationship with a student-client. However, the mutual influence process should not be viewed as entirely negative. Kopplin and Rice have noted that the "similarity of good teaching, good counseling, and good consulting [and I would add good administration] means mutual benefit for counselors and faculty [and administrators] of increased contact with communication" (1975, p. 372).

Involvement with administration has been questioned on the grounds that it seriously risks student trust (for example, Hanfmann, et al., 1963, p. 121). Those of us who have worked on small campuses are vividly aware of this risk. However, if we have become involved at all in outreach programs, we are also aware of the impossibility of avoiding multiple role involvements. Students who are seen in counseling on Monday show up as student representatives at a committee on Tuesday and for peer-helper training on Wednesday. While these arrangements involve some discomfort, role conflicts can be handled. In my own experience, open acknowledgment in a counseling session of these conflicts and discomforts often increases trust. Not infrequently, such acknowledgments served as a vehicle for productive work. The understanding between client and counselor can serve both parties in their committee and training roles.

Those who fear loss of student trust should also consider the image that is created by remaining isolated when issues of critical import to student development are involved. Individual client confidences must be maintained; but on issues that affect students generally, counselors have things to say that should be heard by faculty and administrators (Schwerner, 1975, p. 121; Magoon, 1973, p. 179).

With increasing involvement outside counseling offices the counselor risks getting caught in the middle of intramural fights between faculty and administrators (Russell, 1970, p. 233). Counselors have little direct power in these battles. Their "organizational fence sitting" makes them "marginal people in both power systems and unlikely to be a loyal team member in either" (Warnath, 1971, pp. 39, 43). While this fence sitting may be frustrating (some might say it causes pain in particular anatomical areas), it also gives counselors a unique opportunity to add a third voice—a voice that presumably can interpret students' needs (Russell, 1970, p. 244) or facilitate constructive decision making. If counselors have made some friends (that is, faculty and administrators who understand "where they're coming from"), their impact may be substantial.

Conflicts between students and administration (or faculty) may present some of the greatest challenges to the counselor. Here the inherent duality of their position (Halleck, 1973; Stubbins, 1973; Warnath, 1971, 1973b) becomes painfully clear. Counselors are, by training and inclination, providers of services to their clients—the students. However, counselors serve at the pleasure of the administration. So long as the counselor is committed to helping clients find their own resolutions through individual counseling, the duality of the counselor's role is easily ignored. The duality looms larger with moves out of counseling offices and into more public arenas. However, it has always been there, and the clearer view of it available from outside their offices should be sought by counselors.

In each of the circumstances of conflict between two or more sectors of the campus, counselors potentially have the advantage (and difficulties) of a third party. The counselors' dilemma seems analogous to that of the child therapist who adopts a family therapy model. Overidentification with any member of the family ties the therapist's hands, whereas adoption of a (family) systems focus allows the therapist to move freely toward correcting barriers to growth for all parties. Many of the authors previously cited suggest or imply an "institution as client" approach to increased involvement.

Most counselors lack direct training in consultation and organizational development. Unaware of bureaucratic functioning, most of them are ill equipped as politicians. Their recognition of these lacks will inhibit movement into the community, and their actual shortcomings could preclude success for those who do venture out.

But counselors do have skills and knowledge. Interpersonal skills, problem-solving skills, and observational skills are part of many counselors' repertoires. Knowledge of group processes, interpersonal dynamics, motivation, and learning are included in the training of professional counselors. For some counselors, only the application to institutional concerns is lacking. Warnath (1973a, p. 293) suggests that counselor training programs must be modified to include these applications. For counselors already on the job, he suggests workshops and short courses.

Informal relationships offer counselors opportunities for increased awareness of their campuses. Even more than short courses, such relationships seem a necessary first step to overcoming the deficiencies of earlier training. Among the friends whom counselors might seek are those colleagues whose backgrounds in social psychology, organizational psychology, and sociology might complement their skills and knowledge. Collaboration with related disciplines—later with more distant fields—offers contact without the overlay of superior-inferior that seems inherent in consultative or other helping relationships. The absence of a hierarchical component in the relationship may reduce many of the inhibitions for all parties.

The suggestion of collaboration may involve its own barrier to outreach. Counselors have typically tried to translate a private practice model to their counseling function on campus (Warnath, 1973b). The "independent practitioner" may be somewhat unskilled in seeking help from and in working together with other professionals. Again, counselors possess the basic skills. In-house planning of counseling programs provides some practice in collaboration, so translation to joint ventures with related professionals need not involve a major overhaul.

One further difficulty is suggested by Oetting, Ivey, and Weigel: counselors will encounter "individuals on campus who tend to be destructive influences on students" (1970, p. 35). Further, these individuals are often the "most resistant to change." Here, the intentional (or planned) approach to increased involvement is especially indicated. Counselors need to apply their own principles of intervention, specifically, intervene first in those areas in which the discrepancy between current functioning and desired functioning is smallest (Carkhuff, 1969, p. 50). In other words, maximize chances for success in early ventures out of the office.

This examination of inhibitions to increased involvement has suggested that tentative, exploratory ventures through informal relationships should provide a vehicle for effective outreach. Implicit in this suggestion is the assumption that counselors need to become involved first as participating members of a community. This type of involvement will have two effects. First, it will increase the counselors' awareness of the campus on which they work. Second, it will increase their credibility among faculty and administrators. Other members of educational communities may acknowledge counselors' expertise within the counseling office, and they may also assume that counselors have some valuable insights regarding student behavior. They will not assume, and most counselors have not demonstrated, that counselors are concerned about where the institution is going (Brayfield, 1972, p. 75; Schwerner, 1975, p. 123).

At the outset, a values dilemma—regarding the intention to make friends in the right places—was noted. In the discussion of difficulties, it was generally assumed that effectiveness and survival were complementary. While it is comforting to assume that doing a good job will guarantee survival, this is probably naive. When survival and effectiveness seem to conflict, effectiveness must be the criteria for guiding action. Becoming more involved will make some friends and some enemies. For long-term success, counselors' goals cannot be to make friends, but rather to become effective contributors to the development of their institutions. When they attempt this, they will bring needed skills and knowledge to the problems they encounter. This will not guarantee survival. But, counselors' current isolation from their colleagues provides no greater security, and the effectiveness of this approach is increasingly under attack from within and without.

In concluding, I must state that what I have set out is a result of my own reading of the current scene and a projection of where I hope to go—not a description of past success. I am keenly aware that in my own center we have no consistent program of consultation, only sporadic efforts; we have no routine training programs for faculty or administration, only occasional offerings when time permits; our committee participation and attendance at meetings is on the increase, but slowly. So, in sharing my experience, I share a conviction that we need to relate to the institutions we work in; I share a keen awareness of the difficulties in doing this; and I share considerable uncertainty regarding the outcome of following this course.

References

Banks, W. and Martens, K. 1973. Counseling: the reactionary profession. *The Personnel and Guidance Journal* 51: 457–62.

Brayfield, A. H. 1972. Counseling psychology and higher education. *The Counseling Psychologist* 3: 74–76.

Carkhuff, R. R. 1969. *Helping and human relations.* Vol. 2. New York: Holt, Rinehart and Winston.

Halleck, S. 1973. Counselor as double agent. In C. F. Warnath & Associates, *New directions for college counselors.* San Francisco: Jossey-Bass.

Hanfmann, E., et al. 1963. *Psychological counseling in a small college.* Cambridge: Schenkman.

Ivey, A. E., and Leppaluoto, J. R. 1975. Changes ahead! Implications of the Vail conference. *The Personnel and Guidance Journal* 53: 747–52.

Kopplin, D. A., and Rice, L. C. 1975. Consulting with faculty: necessary and possible. *The Personnel and Guidance Journal* 53: 367–72.

Magoon, T. 1973. Outlook in higher education: changing functions. *The Personnel and Guidance Journal* 52: 175–79.

Oetting, E. R.; Ivey, A. E.; and Weigel, R. G. 1970. *The college and university counseling center.* Student Personnel Series, no. 11. Washington, D.C.: American College Personnel Association.

Russell, N. M. 1970. Relationships of counseling center personnel to faculty, administrators and students. In P. J. Gallagher and G. D. Demos, eds., *The counseling center in higher education.* Springfield, Ill.: Charles C. Thomas.

Schwerner, S. A. 1975. The counseling service and academic politics: a case for delivery of services. *The Counseling Psychologist* 5: 121–24.

Stubbins, J. 1973. Social context of college counseling. In C. F. Warnath & Associates, *New directions for college counselors.* San Francisco: Jossey-Bass.

Warnath, C. F. 1973a. Can counselors make a difference? In C. F. Warnath & Associates, *New directions for college counselors.* San Francisco: Jossey-Bass.

———. 1971. *New myths and old realities: college counseling in transition.* San Francisco: Jossey-Bass.

———. 1973b. Whom does the college counselor serve? In C. F. Warnath & Associates, *New directions for college counselors.* San Francisco: Jossey-Bass.

Warnath, C. F., & Associates. 1973. *New directions for college counselors: a handbook for redesigning professional roles.* San Francisco: Jossey-Bass.

20

THE COUNSELING CENTER AS A HUMANIZING INFLUENCE

Donald A. Brown
UNIVERSITY OF MICHIGAN-DEARBORN

Roberta E. Brown
UNIVERSITY OF MICHIGAN-ANN ARBOR

This chapter is intended to suggest some of the concrete, ''nut and bolt'' activities that can be implemented by a counseling center staff to minimize the dehumanizing and bureaucratic impersonality of our educational institutions, thus assisting students in developing their human potential and realizing all that they can become. The activities suggested involve both the counseling center per se and other individuals and units of the institution that constitute the student's educational environment.

When the wide variety of services provided by counseling centers are studied, eight counseling center models can be identified (Oetting, Ivey, & Weigel, 1970). Though these models vary greatly, the recommendations in this chapter have applicability to all of them, as well as to the other units of the educational institution dealing with human services.

Modern Technology and Impersonalization

As our modern technological society has evolved, it has brought with it a crisis that requires new and creative approaches if humanity is to survive. Recognizing this crisis almost a half century ago, Charlie Chaplin depicted the dehumanizing effect of the factory production line on the individual worker in his motion picture *Modern Times*. Charlie, little more than a cog in the machinery, is finally engulfed by a huge machine. Unfortunately, no Charlie Chaplin has come along to alert us and to draw a comparison between the factory and many of our institutions of higher learning. The tens of thousands of people, huge physical plants, research facilities, budgets, accountability—the list is endless—all document the similarities. And when the football stadium is not in view, a casual glance at campus facilities emphasizes this likeness.

Negative effects of the factory production line on worker productivity and mental health have been well documented. The negative effects of the university production line on the learning and mental health of students have caused less concern. This paper will examine some of the more dehumanizing practices of the educational institution and will make some suggestions for their correction.

The impersonalization of our colleges and universities can be attested to by students seeking to find their way through the bureaucratic maze that often impedes their academic progress and peace of mind. Many professors and other staff members mean well in their attempts to facilitate student progress, but they frequently are as impotent as the students in accomplishing this goal.

One expression frequently made in jest among university employees is "This would be a great place to work if it weren't for the students." What these individuals are saying is that students are low on their list of priorities. Research, publications, graduate seminars, administrative tasks, and community service too often take priority over the needs and concerns of the young undergraduate. They forget that without the students there would be no institution.

In conversations with deans and vice presidents of student affairs from a number of private and state institutions, it becomes apparent that much of the energy of their staffs is dissipated, first, in conflict with the rest of the institution and, second, in what appears to be an almost adversary relationship with the students. Necessity may dictate that they expend their resources in these ways; however, it would appear that if they could redirect their energies into meeting the needs of students, their relationship both with the students and with other university units as well would improve. Oftentimes counseling and other student services fail to see the trap into which they have fallen. Perhaps the realities of the university's internal power struggle and of infighting are such that the individual units like counseling are forced to "play the game"; however, if the counseling center and the other student services are to exert a positive, humanizing influence, they must get their own house in order.

A variety of reasons have contributed to the adversary relationship that often exists between students and university employees—the campus militancy of the 1960s, the continuing hostility of a small percentage of students, and the general budget squeeze. Symptoms of this malady would be an excessive number of regulations and procedures, inflexibility, "passing the buck," and all of the other behaviors that show a general lack of caring and compassion for students.

The educational giants have not been totally oblivious to student concerns, having used a variety of approaches to minimize and compensate for their size and impersonality. The residence hall system with its relatively small units, the residential college contained within the parent institution, and the branch campus immediately come to mind as attempts to lessen the problems stemming from size. However, these efforts often affect only a small percentage of the student body.

Efforts to Humanize the Counseling Center

One institutional unit that can have a considerable influence on the university community, although generally perceived in a more limited role, is the university counseling center. Just as David slew Goliath, the counseling center—though only one small part of the university community—can ultimately have greater impact than its size would indicate. Before the counseling center can have this pervasive, positive effect, it must necessarily be humanistic in its own operation; therefore, it seems appropriate first to examine the functioning of the center per se and then to consider how to facilitate its influence throughout the university.

Directors of counseling (and this would apply to other administrators as well) have to recognize that a major part of their energy may have to be devoted to acting as a buffer between the uncaring, impersonal bureaucracy and their own unit. They must continually strive to prevent negative attitudes and practices from filtering down and affecting their staff. In areas of budget and certain personnel policies, they may be limited in the degree to which they can block and ameliorate; but if they approach their leadership role with this protective attitude, they can minimize the negative influence of the institution.

To continue with putting the internal affairs of the counseling center in order, it might be helpful to look at the unit from the students' perspective. It is not uncommon to see students enter an office, approach the reception desk, and find that they are ignored because the receptionist is busy talking on the phone or is engaged in some clerical activity. Obviously, students cannot help but feel demeaned and sense that their needs are not viewed as important by this representative of the university. Once identified, however, this situation can easily be remedied. All staff members, both professional and nonprofessional, must be cognizant that students are their most important business. When students enter the center, they must be immediately attended to or at least informed that they will receive attention as soon as the other business is completed.

Once students have stated their needs to discuss their problems with a counselor, they are often given appointments several days or even a week or two in the future. Obviously the institution does not regard students as very important if they are asked to wait an extended period of time before they can voice their concerns. If all students can be scheduled—but only after a specified amount of time—then it seems logical to assume that with stepped-up counselor activity and better planning they could be seen almost immediately. There may be exceptions, but the center that forces students to wait is contributing to the dehumanizing process.

This time consideration applies to more than just the initial interview: all problems should be handled as expeditiously as possible. Matters dependent upon logistical considerations, such as the mailing of tests to a scoring center, often slow the delivery of services. But again, the greater the delay in meeting student need, the more likely the significance of their request is deprecated.

In reviewing the procedures that can foster a humanizing influence, one recognizes that they are not unique or particularly creative, and for this reason they may be dismissed as unimportant. However, it might be valuable to review each of these suggestions, realizing, of course, that they must be adapted to the local situation.

STAFF MEETINGS

Staff meetings generally should be held on a weekly or biweekly basis. A block of time (generally an hour is adequate) should be available to avoid interruptions or feelings of being rushed. Although it may be threatening to the director or top administrator, the meeting should be run in a democratic, open climate. The inclusion of secretaries and other nonprofessionals will endorse the "team" concept. If the group becomes larger than fifteen or twenty persons, it may be necessary to restructure the organization. A rotating chairperson helps to encourage staff involvement. Some tentative agenda should be announced in advance, but other matters of business can be introduced without prior announcement.

These meetings might be perceived negatively by the staff; therefore, it is necessary to critique them continually and to make the changes necessary to ensure that everyone's needs are being met and that everyone is made to feel important. If this is accomplished, staff members hopefully will reflect this feeling of improved morale in their dealing with others in the university. The staff meeting also provides the setting for communication to occur, the time for values to be examined and priorities to be established. A few minutes can be set aside periodically to evaluate the extent to which goals are being met.

The staff meeting is not the panacea for all problems that confront the organization, but it can be a useful first step. As a management tool, it should be seriously considered.

IN-SERVICE TRAINING

In keeping with the attempt to humanize the center, in-service training for all staff is mandatory. By *all staff* we mean professionals, nonprofessionals, and everyone associated with the operation. Research has shown that in addition to achieving the learning objectives set forth, a general placebo or "Hawthorne effect" occurs. Realizing that the institution cares and is concerned usually improves staff performance. For example, if the need for telephone etiquette is apparent, in-service training could consist of a representative from the telephone company being invited to discuss appropriate telephone behavior. There is no more effective way to alienate someone than to mismanage their telephone inquiry.

To the extent that the budget allows, staff members should be encouraged to attend professional meetings and conferences and should be subsidized when possible. This would include nonprofessional personnel as well. When employees feel positive about themselves and their work, this attitude will be reflected in their contacts with the public.

ACCOUNTABILITY

Given the budget pinch and the increased competition for existing funds in recent years, there has been an effort to establish accountability, often as a protective measure to justify the continuation of an organization or one of its programs. Frequently, the result has been attempts to quantify a variety of organizational activities. To identify how funds are expended and to determine costs of various programs obviously make good fiscal sense; however, an overemphasis on accountability can have a stultifying effect on creative endeavors and can introduce paranoia. For example, when the number of clients seen becomes the criterion for measuring job performance, it is apparent that quantity, rather than quality, of treatment is given priority. Some cases will be shunted aside because they do not lend themselves to compiling an impressive statistical record. Obviously, some balance must be met between accountability and provision to staff members of the freedom to be creative. There must be developed criteria for evaluation that are not based entirely on quantitative results.

COMPENSATION

The lack of adequate compensation plays a major part in contributing to poor employee morale. When it is recognized that employees are receiving inadequate wages for their contribution, it is the supervisor's responsibility to attempt to remedy the situation. Due to a variety of reasons she frequently may be unable to do so. In that event, the employer might discuss the situation with the employee, explain her inability to increase the remuneration, and assure the employee that the inequity is not her fault and should not be taken personally. Often some compensatory measures can improve morale—allowing additional time off to attend professional meetings, encouraging publication, or suggesting a community service that might be financially rewarding. A compliment for a job well done as well as pleasant working conditions often will more than compensate for financial inequities.

COUNSELING CENTER DECOR

The importance of office decor cannot be minimized. The counseling center should not reflect the cold, austere, impersonal look that characterizes so many university offices. On the other hand, it need not look like a rock band's "pad" or a modernistic brothel. Facilities vary considerably, and budgetary considerations limit what may be done. In any event, the use of bright colors, inexpensive plants, and attractive posters can transform the most unappealing environment into one that is warm and inviting.

CONFIDENTIALITY

The importance of maintaining confidentiality probably need not be stated. However, it is not uncommon to find counseling offices that are insufficiently soundproofed. Clients who wish to discuss important concerns cannot help but feel uncomfortable and, as a result, become reluctant to express their feelings. Soundproofing can be expensive if architects, engineers, and building crews are involved. If a budget is inadequate to finance this procedure, then informal methods may be implemented. Draperies, inexpensive carpet padding on the walls, cork, egg cartons, and caulking compounds are all materials that can be installed by amateurs and yet be effective. A radio playing in the background often will serve to obscure conversations. The staff should assess their facilities and then take the appropriate actions.

CLOTHING AND ACCESSORIES

Many individuals, because of a belief in democracy and the equality of all individuals, look with disdain upon the use of clothing to achieve social status or the adaptation of their attire to help achieve some objective. However, the impact of one's appearance cannot be denied. A recent book, *Dress for Success* by John T. Molloy, explores in detail how clothing and one's appearance affect the way in which a person is perceived. In the space allotted here, it is impossible to discuss this topic in depth. Nevertheless, counselors should recognize that their clothing is important and affects in some degree how students and other members of the university community react to them. The middle-aged counselor who dresses like an eighteen-year-old may look ridiculous and may "turn off" many students. On the other hand, the counselor with the Wall Street image may produce a similar effect. The answer is very likely some sort of balance between the two extremes. Also, if the counseling center is heterogeneous in terms of age, sex, race, and life-style, then students should be able to find someone with whom they are comfortable.

The Counseling Center as a Humanizing Outreach Agent

It is difficult in every case to classify a given counseling center activity as being basically a task internal to the center or basically an "outreach" activity. Some of the following activities are ambiguous in terms of category, but have been listed here because they seem to have a definite outreach quality.

THE COUNSELING CENTER ADVISORY BOARD

One step the counseling center can take to publicize its activities and to spread its humanistic philosophy is to create an advisory board. The members of the board should represent every major unit of the institution. A typical representation would consist of members from each college, (for example, engineering, business administration, education, liberal arts), several students representing different interest groups, the psychiatric consultant, a representative from the student health service, and several individuals who have some particular area of competence or political clout. Some boards include an alumnus or a member of the community. In addition to the outreach benefits, the board can help develop policy and contribute their special expertise to the center's operation. On occasion, when the center is under bombardment from some specific group, the board can act as a buffer, moderating the intensity of any attack. Responsibility for action or lack of action cannot be attributed to the center's staff alone, but must be shared by the board. Obviously, the members of such an advisory board should be very carefully selected.

In addition to the advisory board members' representing the various units, they should have the personality traits and student orientation to constitute a positive, rather than a negative, force. The exception would occur when very non-student-oriented, unsympathetic individuals are purposely selected with the hope that pressure would cause them to become more aware of student needs. Adding such members to the committee could sabotage the entire effort. So the counseling center establishing its first advisory board should probably be conservative in its selection of members, limiting it to include only those who will be concerned and motivated and yet who will avoid making rash decisions or recommendations that could be damaging or destructive to the center. For example, from the staff standpoint, it would be ill advised to establish an advisory board that would recommend their dismissal or the transfer of the counseling center's functions to other units of the institution.

MEETINGS WITH UNIVERSITY OFFICIALS

The counseling center director and staff should meet periodically with university deans, departmental chairpersons, and others in the bureaucratic hierarchy. A rationale for the meeting might be "How can we improve our services to your unit?" or "How can we improve communication between university offices?" These meetings, in addition to fulfilling their own public relations function, can promote and contribute to the development of humanistic policies and procedures. To the deans or university officials whose days are generally concerned with budgetary and other administrative and housekeeping functions, this meeting, particularly if done over lunch or cocktails, can serve as a pause in which they can take time to set new priorities and develop new perspectives.

The problems of students that could lead to further controls and repressive measures can often be explained and remedied with a minimum of effort and fanfare.

MEANS OF KEEPING THE FACULTY INFORMED

A variety of methods should be used to keep the faculty informed of the services provided by the counseling center. This could include individual and group meetings as well as a letter sent at the beginning of each school year to the entire faculty to explain the services available. Included with the letter should be the center's brochure, listing its services and a detailed procedure for referring students to the center. Several widely publicized open houses should be held each year, and, once again, individual invitations should be sent to each faculty member. Requesting a few minutes to make a presentation at a departmental faculty meeting is another way to disseminate information. In addition to familiarizing the faculty with the center's services, such a talk can discuss the problems of students and promote humanistic solutions and procedures. Often, just making faculty members aware of existing services will cause them to seek assistance in dealing with student problems in a less arbitrary, more humane way.

THE "EXIT INTERVIEW"

One function the counseling center staff can effectively perform is the "exit interview." Having no vested interest—at least not to the extent of a faculty member or department head—the counselor can dispassionately explore with students their reasons for withdrawing. From the perspective of the students, the act often comes only after some personal problem, failure, or frustration of such magnitude that they are willing to pay the financial penalty and loss of time and credit. On occasion, the counselor can help resolve the particular problem and the student need not withdraw. In any event, the counselor can help them with their feelings and can encourage them to return when their problems are resolved. Often the counselor's handling of the exit interview determines the students' perception of their entire educational experience at the institution and plays a significant part in whether or not they ever return.

Records should be maintained regarding the reason for student withdrawals. This data can periodically be compiled into a report that is disseminated among the officers of the institution, department heads, and faculty. Hopefully, the report will lead to policies and practices that would reduce the need for students' leaving the institution.

THE COUNSELOR AS OMBUDSMAN

Too often students come to the counseling center as a last recourse after having experienced frustration elsewhere in the institution. Frequently bordering on tears, feeling angry and bitter, students seek a counselor in the role of ombudsman. With their knowledge of the institution and of the idiosyncracies of other university employees, and with the influence stemming from their position, counselors can sometimes ameliorate or circumvent the bureaucratic red tape and can counteract the insensitive treatment that students have experienced. Their ombudsman actions often play a major part in improvement of the students' attitude and even in the continuation of their education.

Many colleges or universities do not have adequate grievance or appeal procedures that students may use to resolve problems. If it does exist, such a procedure often is so complicated and takes so many months to process that it is practically worthless. Counselors should work for the development and adoption of a procedure that is simple in administration and rapid in the processing of the complaint.

OUTREACH ACTIVITIES IN THE RESIDENCE HALL

The residence hall program with small housing units has already been mentioned as an attempt to respond to the impersonalization associated with size. The success of such a program is limited because often only freshmen or, generally, no more than 15 to 30 percent of the student body live in the residence halls. In spite of this limitation, the dorm units can most effectively contribute to making students feel that they are more than a number, that they are actually personal and significant parts of the university.

An abundance of material has been written about the staffing and organization of residence halls. Obviously, the hall director and the various staff and student assistants should have the personality characteristics and work habits that will contribute to the humanizing objectives of the housing unit. The counseling center staff can contribute to the success of the residence hall program in a variety of ways. They can provide in-service training for the staff, serve as consultants in specific problem areas, or assist with programming within the housing complex. These services will be described in greater detail later in this chapter. The counseling center can assign counselors to residence halls on some regularly organized basis, such as one or two days or several evenings a week. After becoming known, the counselors can reach a variety of students who would not venture to some central counseling center.

PROGRAMMING AS AN OUTREACH ACTIVITY

The counseling center can provide a variety of outreach programs, which invariably cause students who otherwise would not do so to come to the center. The types of programs offered will necessarily reflect the interests and competencies of the staff, but can include a wide range of topics.

Vocational Information

Students generally need information about career opportunities and the world of work. Such information can be disseminated in a variety of ways. Working in conjunction with the career planning and placement office, the counseling center could, on a biweekly or monthly basis, publish a bulletin or newsletter that would provide such information.

A format can be developed around a weekly program concerning such general vocational areas as medical service, civil service, legal careers, accounting, insurance, law enforcement, counseling, teaching, conservation, and agriculture. It might be advantageous to organize other programs along more specialized lines, such as the health professions—medicine, nursing, pharmacy, and dentistry. Obviously, the number and organizational possibilities are endless. Students could be polled to determine their particular interests and the areas about which they are lacking specific information.

Sex Education

Our Judaic-Christian tradition, with its almost phobic attitude regarding anything sexual, has played a large part in keeping society ignorant in the area of human sexuality. Medical and nursing schools as well as other professional programs are only now beginning to provide their students with specific training in this area. There is still some feeling by both professionals and lay people that sex is "dirty" and is not a topic for "polite society." Consequently, students invariably need information, often to correct the misinformation they acquired from their peers.

Typical areas for programs would include contraception, physiology of sex, value clarification, homosexuality, and sexual dysfunction. Generally on a campus or within the community are resource persons who can contribute to the development of learning experiences. A number of good films are available. Because films vary considerably in their degree of explicitness, they should be previewed to ensure their suitability.

The Returning Woman Student

The returning woman student, in addition to having the needs of other students, often requires assistance in clarifying her roles as wife, mother, and student. She frequently does not fully understand her reason for wanting to continue her education. She may feel a lack of fulfillment or a need to grow and leave the family cocoon. Her children may no longer be in school or may be grown, so her maternal role is no longer as important. Her husband can be reaching the zenith of his career and may be demanding an attractive, exciting partner. Or the other extreme may prevail: he may have accepted the rut of mediocrity and be locked into a life syndrome consisting of beer, television, and an occasional night with the boys. The marriage may be deteriorating, and she is little more than a housekeeper; yet it is easier to continue than to face reality.

Often the housewife returning to school is exposed to new role models, both male and female. She may have her first contact with the liberated and sexually free female. She often meets professors and other males who see her as more than a *hausfrau,* are exciting intellectually, and have more interesting life-styles than her spouse. Her husband and children are often bewildered by her changing attitudes and values and her desire for changes in her marriage. Divorce is not infrequent.

During this metamorphosis she needs counseling to help her explore her options and the consequences of her actions. Counseling for the entire family may be necessary. Her age, vocational opportunities, financial situation, and family responsibilities must be carefully examined. The counselor can provide invaluable assistance during this period.

Study Skills and Reading Improvement

Most students could improve their general study habits as well as their reading and comprehension rate. In the event that the institution does not have a study skills center, the counseling staff can provide assistance in this area. Some students, unless their skills improve, will not survive the rigors of the academic program.

The counselor must keep in mind that academic problems are sometimes symptomatic of more deep-seated personal concerns; therefore, before plunging into some remedial program, one must carefully examine the student's situation.

Counseling Groups

There is a constant demand among students and staff members for group counseling experiences. Value clarification, group encounter, self-exploration, and other group experiences are possibilities that may be provided. These activities are often helpful in giving the isolated, lonely individual a sense of belonging and kinship. They lend themselves particularly well to residence hall programs.

The counseling staff that sit idly in their offices and complain for lack of clients could stimulate activity by becoming involved in these types of outreach programming.

Specialized Programs

The interests of students are almost infinite. Their interests can be polled or surveyed periodically, and, to the extent that resources allow, programs can be developed to meet their needs. The list of specialized programs is endless, examples of which are assertiveness training, anxiety reduction, and weight reduction. Often a student will receive psychological strokes, satisfaction, and sense of belonging and self-worth from these experiences.

PEER COUNSELORS

Peer counselors are becoming increasingly recognized as a useful component of the counseling team. Generally highly motivated, altruistically oriented, possessing excellent personal qualifications, and frequently working toward a professional career in some area of the helping professions, they bring an age perspective and a relevance that compliments the qualifications of the professional staff. Through their daily association with their student peers they can inform them of available counseling services and help to balance the impersonality and size of the institution.

Any center considering the use of peer counselors will find that a considerable literature exists regarding all phases of their selection and training. Also, some grant money has been available for the establishment of peer counseling programs.

COMMITTEE ASSIGNMENTS

Educational institutions generally have a number of standing committees that meet regularly. Typical committees would include space allocation, food service, budget, safety, employee selection, academic standards, and grievance. Counseling center staff members should make every effort to serve on these committees. Not only are they able to make favorable public relations contacts, but they also can add a humanistic dimension to committees that are often biased in terms of budgetary and other materialistic considerations.

USE OF THE MEDIA

The counseling center can reach the student body and the university community through the use of a variety of printed media. The university announcement and the student newspaper are useful publicity tools. An attractive, carefully designed brochure should list counseling center services, staffing, office hours, and other relevant information. It may be helpful to send one with a cover letter to each incoming freshman and transfer student as well as to faculty and staff. Inexpensive, colorful flyers featuring cartoon characters can be used economically to supplement more costly brochures. As opportunities present themselves, press or news releases can be given to the local newspapers or radio and television stations.

Conclusion

After reviewing the above recommendations, a small counseling center staff may wonder if they have sufficient resources to implement these ideas. Obviously, it will take time. However, even if conditions are such that the institution rejects all efforts by the staff, the counseling center, by maintaining its own humanizing attitude, can become a growing force in assisting the university community in becoming more student-oriented. Once students perceive the center in this way, they may regard the institution as having a heart.

References

Molloy, J. T. 1975. *Dress for Success*. New York: Peter H. Wyden.

Oetting, E. R.; Ivey, A. E.; and Weigel, R. G. 1970. *The college and university counseling center*. Student Personnel Series, no. 11. Washington, D.C.: American Personnel and Guidance Association.

Ohlsen, M. M. 1974. *Guidance services in the modern school*. New York: Harcourt Brace Jovanovich.

Reardon, R. C., and Burck, H. D. 1975. *Facilitating career development: strategies for counsellors*. Springfield, Ill.: Charles C. Thomas.

Sinick, D. 1970. *Occupational information and guidance*. Boston: Houghton Mifflin.

21

PREVENTIVE PSYCHOLOGY AND THE COUNSELING CENTER

Beatrice G. Lipinski

SIMON FRASER UNIVERSITY

The prevention of disorder and the enhancement of well-being are central to the development of community mental health (Caplan, 1964). The parallel development of preventive programs in the university and college community is essential if counseling centers are to contribute to the kind of environment that fosters positive mental health, an atmosphere of vitality, and keen interest in intellectual mastery on our campuses.

The principle of preventing dysfunctional anxiety, emotional turmoil, and excessive stress is both simple and extraordinarily complex. Many preventive programs, including public health measures such as vaccination and fluoridation, often collide with the value systems of North American culture, with its emphasis on individual freedom of choice and resistance to invasion of privacy. Ethical issues abound in this difficult area, particularly when social planning related to the prevention of emotional distress is proposed and/or instituted. Decisions are often made at political as well as professional and personal levels. A game of "Power, power, who's got the power?" sometimes ensues, consuming inordinate amounts of time and energy. The impetus to introduce preventive intervention programs on a campus occasionally encounters similar difficulties, perhaps reflective of resistance to ruffle a reasonably comfortable status quo. Very often, an ounce of prevention is worth a pound of politics.

Definitions in the preventive area are legion. In their excellent review of primary prevention, Kessler and Albee conclude that "practically every effort aimed at child rearing, increasing effective communication, building inner control and self-esteem, reducing stress and pollution, etc.—in short, everything aimed at improving the human condition, at making life more fulfilling and meaningful—may be considered to be part of primary prevention of mental or emotional disturbance'' (1975, p. 557). Describing the literature search of the area of prevention as something akin to exploration of the Okefenokee swamp, they comment, ''After this heady experience we still remain enchanted, although not overanxious to make the same trip again soon'' (p. 558). To guide the reader to some contributions in the field of preventive psychology, the following abbreviated list of references will prove useful: Bindman & Spiegel, 1969; Caplan, 1964; Caplan, 1970; Caplan and Killilea, 1976; Cook, 1970; Grunebaum, 1970; Zax and Specter, 1974.

Caplan's influential preventive psychiatry model has identified three major areas. Primary prevention is directed toward reducing the probability of social and emotional problems. The aims of secondary prevention include early identification and treatment of disorders in order to alleviate distress and hasten recovery of health, while tertiary prevention involves attempts to ameliorate and minimize long-term effects of social-emotional distress as well as to promote health in general. Many readers will recognize this tripartite approach as similar to public health paradigms of prevention, treatment, and rehabilitation. The interrelated areas of preventive intervention in community psychology, community and social psychiatry, and community mental health attempt to embrace all environmental forces that might affect most members of a community with a view to alleviating misery while at the same time promoting positive mental health (Jahoda, 1958).

Preventive intervention is defined by Wagenfeld (1972) as a body of knowledge directed toward affecting the balance of physical, social, cultural, and psychosocial forces that influence a society, as well as intervention in inevitable transitional stages of individual development and in inevitable life crises. Caplan and Grunebaum (1970) also discuss long-term and short-term factors that affect the adaptive energies of individuals and, cumulatively, of society. Long-term resources include optimal physical, psychosocial, and sociocultural factors. According to Caplan and Grunebaum, provision of these resources involves social and political planning to modify communities and societies in many ways in order to provide healthful ecology, positive family environments, and enriched sociocultural opportunities. Short-term resources include the capability to cope with, and to learn from, crisis situations. The techniques they have suggested to maximize preventive efforts include ''education of caregivers, mental health consultation, education of the public, crisis intervention, and anticipatory guidance'' (Cook, 1970, p. 65). Comparative analyses of approaches to general health care and of allocation of resources in Canada and the United States have been presented by Andreapoulos (1975). It is within the context of the development of national priorities in preventive care that model programs will flourish, especially on campuses.

Preventive Psychology on Campus

The notion of preventive mental health efforts on a campus is not new. Farnsworth (1962), writing within the context of campus psychiatry, viewed preventive intervention as having great potential for improving the quality of life and the environment of a campus, for encouraging the capacity of students to engage in academic and creative endeavors by increasing their sense of "affectance" (active mastery) and competence (see White, 1963), for identifying incipient problems, and for changing attitudes of the campus community toward emotional distress. The principles enunciated by Farnsworth have also been explicated by Falk (1971) and Warnath (1971), both of whom have stressed in vigorous terms the need for counseling centers to reach out into the campus community, to be actively involved as stress diagnosticians, to be visibly involved in the total life space of the campus, and to move with deliberate speed to emphasize preventive and developmental programs in addition to remedial efforts. Many counseling centers in North America have embarked on innovative, developmental programs that have preventive aspects. (Some of these programs will be mentioned later in the chapter.) Although most of these efforts have been directed toward the student population, the persuasiveness of general systems theory encourages the extension of preventive approaches to all interrelated constituencies on campus—students, faculty, and staff.

Students, as a group, are vulnerable to a great number of stresses. Entering postsecondary academic life is a significant transitional event with many attendant changes in life-style. The sheer number of life event changes predictably results in strains on adaptive energy through extended, excessive emotional arousal. Most students must work through identity crises (Erikson, 1959), intellectual grappling with new ideas, challenges to established values, questions about sexuality, separation from home, and performance anxiety in competition with a highly selected group of peers. During the academic years, the emergence into a delayed adulthood and the need to achieve a sense of active mastery in some field of work are other developmental tasks for the student. In a milieu of rapid change, many students will develop psychophysiological impairment, while others will grow and thrive.

The kinds of stresses that students must cope with—or defend against, in the psychodynamic sense—are not simply theoretical. Reid (1970) has presented statistics reflecting a higher incidence of emotional disorders among students than the general population. Farnsworth (1966) estimated that 1,650 of 10,000 students may require professional help for a variety of distressing circumstances, 20 may attempt suicide, while 25 may require hospitalization. An American College Health Association survey of mental health programs in 1973-1974 (1976) has reported a mean rate of 8 known suicides and 75 known suicide attempts per 100,000 students. Approximately 246 students per 100,000 left school in 1973-1974 for mental health reasons, as compared with 492 per 100,000 who left for "other medical reasons." These data reinforce the identification of the student population as a high-risk group that includes many thousands of persons experiencing considerable distress during their university and college careers. Admissions personnel might be well advised to say to incoming frosh, "I am not promising you a rose garden."

Although stress has been identified as necessary and even beneficial to the quality of life (Selye, 1974), excessive prolonged stress affects capacity to cope and adaptive energy is depleted over time, with structural changes constituting a possible outcome. A person's changes in life-style, whether negative or positive in affective tone, require expenditure of psychophysiological energy to restore a state of equilibrium. When life change events reach a critical level (Holmes & Rahe, 1967), the majority of people become susceptible to illness of various kinds. The social readjustment rating scale developed by Holmes and Rahe includes a variety of life event changes, providing a cumulative score that would identify many incoming students as particularly vulnerable to illness. The prevention and treatment of psychosomatic disorders and stress-related problems will become a challenging area for interdisciplinary collaboration (Groen, 1974).

In the application of community psychology principles, the campus may be viewed as a microcosm of the extended community, with the same potential for identifying and ameliorating dehumanizing and stressful factors. Because most campuses are staffed with care givers, such as counselors, physicians, chaplains, residence advisors, and so on, there is a reservoir of talented, interested professionals who are willing to embark on preventive ventures and to include indigenous members of the community in this effort. Although the service aspects of preventive intervention may not be universally welcomed, a campus provides an excellent training ground for students in preventive-community psychology, both on- and off-campus. Because of their intensive contacts with stress points on campus, counseling center staff can design realistic preventive programs that have both training and service functions.

Counselors may not be confirmed futurists in the mode of R. Buckminister Fuller or B. F. Skinner. But they can play a role by trying to influence the educational process to incorporate new ways of learning as described by Toffler (1970), through "alternatives" programs or some modifications of the free university. They can also encourage the development of a more personal, human educational environment in order to minimize rigid rules and regulations, an inordinate emphasis on competitive examinations and grading, and other stress factors that tend to overlook individual needs and circumstances. The cumulative effect is to involve counselors in an attempt to gain an intimate awareness of the campus community and to develop a rapport with it (Robertson, 1968). The desired result would be both to decrease stress vulnerability for students, faculty, and staff and to increase opportunities for self-determination and a keen sense of cognitive competence in an academic setting.

In seeking enhancement of quality of life on campus, counselors or community psychologists assume a number of possible roles, some of which may be uncomfortable: the advocate-professional, who is supplementary to the scientist-professional model (Simon, 1975); the "consultant" in the form of organization person, ombuds-service provider, or facilitator; the organizer of the oppressed; or the "visionary" (Pearl, 1974). In assuming these roles, members of the counseling center need to be prepared for resistance from other members of the campus community (Brigante, 1965).

Psychological Consultation and Crisis Intervention

Tasks confronting the mental health consultant seem formidable. Workable definitions of the disorders or problems that one hopes to prevent, the need to evaluate programs undertaken, and other practical issues influence the effectiveness of preventive intervention. "The mental health consultant is concerned with gaining entry into a client system, assessing what expertise is appropriate to the client system, being aware of the public visibility of the undertaking and realizing personal consequences of failure," reports Gump (1973, p. 133).

An excellent overview of psychological consultation to a university community through the auspices of a psychological services department has been presented by Waxer (1974; Waxer & White, 1973). This university, located in central Canada, had been designed to avoid some of the alienating features of large multiversities by building smaller college units. Epidemiological and social survey data suggested that the college goal of social affiliation was also associated with the level of student distress. The aim of the intervention program was to attempt to modify physical, social, and academic features of the colleges and to encourage social affiliation through a variety of outreach programs.

The particular model that was adopted involved "securing sanction to consult; developing entry points; eliciting problems; and developing solutions" (Waxer & White, 1973, p. 258). After initial contact with the administration of each college was made, the consultative program was advertised. Points of entry included a variety of contacts, such as conferences, conversations over coffee, overnight visits at a residence hall. The most effective entries appeared to depend on the rapport developed by the individual counselor-consultant with the unique characteristics of the particular college.

Consultative programs were developed for the approval of each college. One program served to increase the accessibility of the college to commuting students by helping with such practical problems as obtaining sleep-over accommodations. Another project involved the consultant in working with a financial aid committee to provide financial counseling along with aid. At a third college, the consultant worked with a group of students concerned about the goals and functions of the college. A videotape, which showed students expressing their ideas about the particular college and the entire university system, formed the basis for discussion during open meetings. A great deal of the discussion involved the issue of student-faculty relationships. These open meetings stimulated the formation of an ongoing leadership group to look at the goals and structure of the collège. Waxer and White were pleased with the evolution of this program since it involved indigenous leaders and members of the college community, another goal of preventive community psychology.

Although most of the programs appeared successful, a few did not jell. These less successful outcomes seemed to be related to lack of mutual trust with administrative personnel. Waxer and White emphasized the need to gain initial sanction to consult so that territorial and power questions are minimized or worked through. In most situations, they recommended rather formal contractual arrangements to reduce mutual frustrations and poorly defined roles of both the consultant and consultee in the development of programs of preventive intervention. Waxer (1974) has also discussed community psychology programs involving the psychologist-consultant as an integral member of the campus community. Drawing upon ecological principles from organizational psychology, Waxer has showed how identification with, and participation in, the campus community can be facilitated for all its members. Kysar (1966), Kalafat and Tyler (1973), and others have developed the community approach on campus, including programs such as telephone counseling services staffed by student volunteers. For a brief overview and conceptualization of the consultation approach, the reader is referred to Rhodes (1974), as well as Schroeder and Miller (1975). Levinson (1972) has also provided a critical review of the state of the art.

Crisis intervention and preventive strategies before crisis occurs are principles of preventive efforts that need to be developed in the same manner as community planning and mental health consultation on campus. Caplan (1964) has discussed the significance of life crises and of crisis events that have a sense of urgency and immediacy, such as marriage breakdown, suicide attempts, impulses to hostile acting out, and so on.

A number of preventive programs may be implemented by viewing crises in terms of developmental phases. Such programs might include counseling related to premarital relationships and marriage, family planning, parenting, sexuality and interpersonal relationships, and the meaning of aging, death, and dying. These developmental programs may be implemented on individual and/or group bases with the goal of encouraging a sense of competence, self-determination, and positive mental health (Kessler & Albee, 1975).

In crisis situations with more immediacy, such as withdrawal from school because of fear of failure, loss of an intimate relationship, death of a parent, or injury in an accident, principles of crisis intervention involve the need for immediate counseling, usually on an intensive basis for a relatively short period of time while the crisis is being resolved. Liaison with, or building of, support systems for the person in crisis is important (Caplan & Killilea, 1976). On many campuses, hot lines or crisis lines, often staffed by students with counseling or health service back-up, provide immediate access to responsive care givers. The theory and methodology of crisis intervention are more fully discussed by Aguilera, Messick and Farrell (1970).

Some Preventive Programs in Campus Communities

Zax and Specter (1974), in their chapter on prevention in the college community, have discussed in depth several preventive programs outlined below, citing both positive outcomes as well as drawbacks. For example, Webster and Harris (1958) instituted a program of professionally led, small group discussions for frosh with the goal of enhancing interpersonal relationships. They discovered that members of a control group sought psychiatric help more than students in the discussion groups or average frosh. Group discussions were viewed as one method for preventive intervention with a consequent possibility of lessening demand for individual counseling. Although the use of the group format has been encouraged by some as economical in saving time, energy, and funds, this is not necessarily the case. As Warnath (1971) has pointed out, a number of factors related to the total group process suggests that group approaches be instituted on a sound theoretical level rather than on the basis of questionable economics.

Wolff (1969) also worked with male frosh volunteers in discussion groups focused on interpersonal relations. The groups were led by students rather than professionals (a feature often given undue credibility). The group experience appeared to have favorable effects in term of the ways in which students were perceived by their peers. Another interesting finding was that group members made minimal use of the health service for individual counseling.

Spielberger and Weitz (1964) attempted to identify a high-risk group of incoming students whose responses to two anxiety scales of the MMPI suggested a high probability of academic difficulty or failure. Those vulnerable students who regularly attended group discussions performed better academically than controls, while "low attenders" did least well on their first-semester grades. This trend continued on follow-up in the second year. Participants commented on the supportive aspect of the program, showing that they were not unusual or unique in experiencing dysfunctional anxiety related to academic performance. As is often the case, the program did not reach the underachieving students with high anxiety who appeared to need help most. Psychodynamic questions of a clinical nature obviously come into play here.

A highly sophisticated effort to implement primary, secondary, and tertiary preventive efforts was conducted at the University of Florida by Barger and his colleagues (Barger, 1963; Barger, Larson & Hall, 1966). As in Waxer's work, research was conducted to identify environmental influences on students, including values and attitudes incongruent with the campus. Difficult courses and performance evaluation were identified as principle causes of stress and distress, while participation in recreational and athletic programs provided considerable relief and release. Research findings were communicated to administrators and faculty, resulting in some changes, including an enriched orientation program for frosh.

Secondary prevention efforts in the University of Florida program focused on early diagnosis and effective treatment of emotional disturbance as identified by MMPI profiles. Of the 10 percent of incoming students identified as significantly distressed, one-third accepted therapy. More effective was a program to involve the key people ("signal receivers") on campus who might recognize signs of distress and make appropriate referrals. At the tertiary prevention level, the program included customary counseling treatment modalities, including individual and group therapy, crisis intervention, and so on. Students were also seen on a walk-in basis, another important preventive principle.

A number of counseling services have either encouraged the formation of or provided training and/or back-up consultation to student-run crisis lines and drop-in centers. It is difficult to evaluate the impact of student-initiated preventive programs, which frequently experience discontinuity of function. These programs may grind to a halt, awaiting the arrival of a new group of highly motivated student volunteers. In general, there is evidence that a well-designed, student-run hot line or telephone counseling service can be effective, especially in serving lonely, alienated students who reach out to empathic listeners through the anonymity of the telephone call (Kalafat & Tyler, 1973).

Because a separate discussion on paraprofessionals in this chapter is sacrificed to other topics, the reader is referred to the literature on several aspects of their involvement in preventive programs. Mutuality of care giving through support systems and self-help programs is discussed by Caplan and Killilea (1976), while Kalafat and Tyler (1973) and Wasserman, McCarthy, and Ferree (1975) point out benefits derived by students through helping others. Benign skepticism and criticisms about the involvement of paraprofessionals are discussed by Steisel (1972). Peer self-help programs are described by Dumont (1976) and Hurvitz (1974), as well as by Glaser (1976) in relation to the women's movement.

Other Preventive Programs and Strategies

A multitude of preventive programs and strategies can be considered and implemented, depending on the most pressing needs of the campus and the resources available through the counseling service staff itself and in collaboration with other key persons and care givers on campus.

Preventive strategies may tie into national policy and programs such as "Operation Lifestyle," currently being implemented by the federal government in Canada (Lalonde, 1976). Alternatively, they may draw on the integrative work of such authors as McCamy and Presley (1975), who focus on body-mind unity in terms of four areas of prevention and enhancement of well-being: nutrition, ecology, exercise, and stress reduction through relaxation. Identifying cognitive competence as important to mental health, Kuriloff and Rindner (1975) have described four ways in which a sense of cognitive mastery may be acquired through psychological education curricula. The majority of preventive programs, because they are aimed at groups more than individuals, utilize a small group format, occasionally as a bulwark against alienation (Sager, 1968).

Although there are profound philosophical questions regarding behavior modification and behavioral therapy, the field is burgeoning and, combined with sensitivity and clinical competence, has a definite role to play in preventive programming. Poser (1970) has suggested that principles of learning be used in a variety of preventive psychological approaches. He has provided examples of prevention of addictive and obsessive behavior as well as exposure of high-risk people to learning experiences that will enable them to be more effective in facing crises, separation anxiety (as in impending marital breakdown), stage fright, and so on. Poser's ideas are similar to the concepts of anticipatory guidance and emotional inoculation proposed by Caplan (1964).

The model of a "human services community," as described by Bierman and Lumley (1973), may be implemented on a campus with modest expectations of providing a growth-enhancing, supportive setting as well as involving both professionals and paraprofessionals in service and training functions. Budman (1975) has developed "psychoeducational" groups directed toward preventive intervention. He has provided a cognitive and experiential modality for families and individuals in life crises, including veterans, hypertensives, and new parents. A sophisticated ecosystem model utilizing an ecological approach to foster positive features of campus environments has been developed by the Western Interstate Commission for Higher Education (WICHE) through its program, "Improving Mental Health Services on Western Campuses" (Aulepp & Delworth, 1976).

Employing a learning model, Gump (1973) has enlisted the aid of counseling service personnel to meet with large groups of parents of frosh. Their reactions to the transitional phase in family life as well as such crises as drug abuse and abortion were discussed, apparently with uneven results.

Although preventive activities are mainly directed to students on campus, there is considerable merit in establishing a closer liaison with secondary school personnel to help prepare students for entrance to a university or college (Medway, 1975). When students have arrived on campus, an alertness to those exhibiting special risk of failure or underachievement may prompt the development of enriched or individualized orientation sessions, special skills training, anxiety reduction programs, and so on, preferably in conjunction with others in the support system (interested faculty, chaplains, and residence coordinators, among others.)

Because the faculty-student relationship is a vital one in the experience of students, preventive measures including consultation about teaching and tutorial techniques, small group dynamics, and referral procedures are some measures that a counseling service can offer to faculty (Kennedy & Seidman, 1972). The administrative and support staff of a campus community are often overlooked in discussion of preventive programs. As with faculty, they influence the ethos of campus life and have a great deal of contact with students, often making the difference between a human or an impersonal climate for the student. In addition, administrators and other staff face life crises and have their own personal problems requiring access to a counseling service (Dauw, 1968; Spiro, Siassi, & Crocetti, 1975).

Because the current student population includes more older students and married students than in previous years, preventive measures are often made available in such modalities as marital enrichment groups (Sauber, 1974). Some students are single parents who might benefit from either a professionally led or a self-help group initiated through a counseling service (Weiss, 1976). A great many universities and colleges provide or support day care centers, some of which may evolve into "family life centers" integrated with counseling services and general health services (Sharfstein, 1974). Spoon and Southwick (1972) have described a program to strengthen healthy families through family life education. Some of these families may in turn become "trainer families" to help other families attain an improved family self-concept (Carnes & Laube, 1975).

Groups in cultural transition may find considerable help in coping with academic and personal demands through preventive programs for ethnic minorities (Cohen, 1972), women (Glaser, 1976), returning military personnel on campus (Borus, 1973), foreign students coping with culture shock (Weinberg, 1967), gay people (Caplan & Killilea, 1976), aging students (Braceland, 1972), and others. Although preventive programs directed toward self-defeating behavior—misuse of alcohol, tobacco, eating patterns, and so on—are available in most communities, a considerable number of counseling centers have excellent resources, especially in collaboration with campus colleagues, that can be made available to control or minimize such problems (Sorenson & Joffe, 1975; Whitehead, 1975).

A model with a great deal of potential for development of campus preventive programs is exemplified by a program developed at the University of Cincinnati (Weiss & Kapp, 1974), where collaborative efforts of an interdisciplinary team from counseling and health services provide short-term therapy, crisis intervention, and community outreach on a cooperative basis.

Problems in Preventive Intervention

Barriers to preventive measures on campus, as elsewhere, can be formidable (Broskowski & Baker, 1974). Lombardi (1974) has surveyed the resources assigned by 128 counseling centers to preventive and remedial activities. The centers indicated that, ideally, they would devote 34 percent of their resources to preventive activities, as compared with the reported 25 percent. Lombardi concluded that counseling centers are not disposed to altering their mission as they perceive it. Often, the problems are philosophical and practical. Many, perhaps most, counselors do not perceive themselves as change agents, ombuds-service providers, community psychologists, or advocate-professionals and are uncomfortable in the more assertive, reaching-out kind of activities often involved in preventive programs. Understandably, they prefer to do what they do best, which is individual and group counseling in the clinical mode. Because of potential friction within counseling centers, preventive activity and service delivery may need to be separated with a differential use of professionals (Perlmutter, 1974), a risky solution in terms of its possible effects on cohesiveness within the counseling service. Also, many counselors are aware of the dangers inherent in romanticizing their rescue fantasies in a complex network of campus community life (Hersch, 1972).

Although sound arguments have been put forward regarding the economic advantages of primary prevention (Harper & Balch, 1975), they are not accepted by many administrators and probably not by a majority of counselors who respond to individual distress rather than group intervention processes. In addition, many counselors recognize that the effectiveness of preventive programs depends on individual involvement and motivation to persist toward a goal of optimal health. Other problems involved in prevention are described by Denner (1974) and Henderson (1975). There does seem to be a sign of optimism in a survey of attitudes toward institutional goals of personnel in postsecondary institutions in Canada (Piccinin, 1976): academic development and intellectual orientation as well as individual personal development through academic life were perceived as primary goals by various sectors of campus communities.

One of the most serious impediments to the development of preventive programs—along with theoretical, territorial, financial, and other concerns—is the question of evaluative research in this complex field. Excellent resource books on evaluation are available (Suchman, 1967; Wiess, 1972), and a number of preventive programs already described have included evaluative research of outcomes. Schwartz (1969) has stressed the need to evaluate the effectiveness of preventive programs in terms of "health in general." Freeman and Sherwood (1965) have presented a model examining the impact of intervention programs as compared with the more traditional focus on the extent and quality of services, which has provided ballast for accountability over the years. Many counselors are not enamored of complex statistical analyses of program outcomes that divert valuable time from their service roles; and others are apprehensive about the evaluation of their work and the impact that any negative findings may have on their self-esteem (Page & Yates, 1974). Directors of counseling centers may feel that evaluation is frequently based on oversimplified principles with a potential negative effect on budgets. However, whatever the consequences, accountability has arrived.

Training in Preventive Psychology

Much of the emphasis on the development of perspectives in training originated with a report of the Boston conference on the education of community mental health psychologists, perceived as generalists (Bennett et al., 1966). Lesse (1971) has espoused the development of an interdisciplinary field that he has termed "psychosociology," and Asken (1975) would encourage the growth of medical psychology. A very interesting and promising training model has been described by Levine (1970): a "service commune" of senior staff, their families, and approximately twenty graduate students from different disciplines (including sculptors, novelists, architects) is established. The students are trained in prevention and amelioration of problems of living in the commune as well as in group dynamics and therapy. The entire group is involved in decision making and establishment of policy.

Some of the training programs associated with clinical study include George Peabody College, University of Rochester, City College of New York, Yale University, and the University of Colorado. Multidisciplinary training programs include Harvard School of Public Health, the University of Texas, Duke University, and Boston University. A new specialty area in health psychology will be offered in the fall of 1977 by the Graduate Group in Psychology, University of California, San Francisco.

Some Current Trends in Preventive Programs

The Data Bank for college and university counseling centers, coordinated by Thomas Magoon, University of Maryland, has included information regarding innovative, developmental programs implemented by various centers. In addition, a small number of counseling centers in Canada have indicated the kinds of programs they have mounted in terms of a format that is based on life skills, life themes, and life transition and was developed by Douglas Daher, University of Rhode Island, coordinator of a Clearinghouse for Structured Group Programs in North American Counseling Services. Although the range of programs reported is very broad in scope, some trends are discernible.

According to the Data Bank survey for 1975-1976, service trends have included increases in group work, crisis intervention, consultation efforts on campus, marriage counseling, use of cassette tape programs, and vocational/career guidance. These trends have obvious preventive implications.

Counseling centers in North America report an emphasis on programs related to career exploration, life planning, values clarification, improvement of study skills, and reduction of performance anxiety. Stress management through relaxation and increased mastery of problem situations, both academic and emotional, is offered. Personal growth groups, including self-assessment, assertiveness training, and "self-improvement," are provided by a considerable number of centers. Groups directed toward marital enrichment, parenting and sexuality, and communication skills tend to be very popular. Environmental assessment, consultation with various campus resources, and involvement in decision-making committees and campus governance also provide opportunities for counseling services to have an influence on the campus climate that is conducive to a positive way of life (Albee, 1976).

Examples of Preventive Programs

Many students experience uncertainty and confusion regarding their life goals. The following is a vignette of a career exploration group.

Life planning consisted of a series of six sessions for students who were feeling vocationally lost: "I don't know what to do with my life." Through a series of structured exercises suggested by the group leaders, students were given an opportunity to look at the past in a brief exploration of some of the experiences that had helped to form them; to look at the present ("Who am I now? What is important to me?"); and to look at the future ("What do my past and present tell me about my future?"). The group discussions did not focus on vocational decision making per se, but rather on gaining more personal awareness of values, dreams, hopes, and fears—and how these related to one's direction in life.

Follow-up interviews with the students who participated in the small group discussions revealed that most of them had very positive feelings about the experience, felt they know themselves better, and had more confidence in themselves and a better sense of how to clarify their own values and directions in life.

Another group program, involving guidance by a professional counselor and a support system of peers, involved single parents, who represent a growing number of students.

A single parent group was initiated by a client who, during individual counseling, frequently focused on issues of parenting and the role of a single parent. Sharing experiences, feelings, and problem resolution with the therapist—also a single parent—was valued by the client, who suggested a focused group for single parents on campus.

Group sessions, attended by about twelve students, staff, and faculty, were held once weekly. By consensus, the format was one of sharing of information and experiences on an informal basis along with programmed events, including a session with a lawyer who belonged to the Family Law Commission and a screening of the film *Separation and Divorce*. The group was a verbal one, and the assumed role of the group leader was that of participant-facilitator.

Initially, the group focused on practical issues, and, as trust developed, discussions shifted to child-rearing philosophies and practices. Then sessions became more personalized, with considerable attention focused on interpersonal attraction, rivalry, and self-doubts. This phase required a great deal of clinical acumen on the part of the leader in order to work through the sense of threat experienced by some group members. A group decision was made to return to more focused discussions related to practical issues, a choice that proved supportive to the group, most of whom have maintained contact with the counseling center for several years and have encouraged others to attend similar groups.

Another kind of preventive outreach program, responding to stated needs and involving interdisciplinary efforts, is exemplified by the women's safety program described below:

Because of concern expressed by female clients for their safety and concern in the community at large about an increase in violent crimes against women, a counseling center initiated a program on women's safety in collaboration with campus security, the women's caucus, the rape relief center, and representatives of local law enforcement agencies. The campus administration was sympathetic to the need for such programs, recognizing that a sense of threat can be individually and collectively unsettling, and arranged to provide time-off during regular working hours for staff to attend the program. Publicity for the program was also directed to the off-campus community.

Approximately 300 women and a few men (students, staff, and faculty) attended the program, which involved a film and a discussion by a panel composed of a policewoman, a representative of a national police force, and a member of the rape relief center. A lively question period followed, and many members of the audience lingered to continue discussion with panel members and, in some instances, to discuss career possibilities with the policewoman.

The program, with modifications, has been repeated on campus at the request of women in several departments and has been extended in a variety of ways to the larger community. Evaluation of such a preventive program is very difficult. It evoked a great deal of interest and awareness and informed a large number of women about precautionary measures they could take to reinforce their sense of physical safety and emotional security.

Many facets of prevention that can enter into the academic career of a student are traced in the following vignette.

Mark, a thirty-five-year-old married student with one child, entered university as a special entry mature student after having served in the armed forces for many years. Following his acceptance, Mark was also advised to attend a workshop for students reentering an academic setting. Through group discussions regarding what to expect at the university, Mark derived an increased self-confidence and a sense of community with the group leader and other mature students. He and several others formed a "mature student rap group" to provide information and support to others like themselves. This group was instrumental in encouraging other mature students to become involved in a longitudinal study, which indicated that mature students do well academically.

Because Mark had been away from a formal academic setting for many years, he enrolled in programs designed to improve reading, study, and writing skills. When he panicked during a difficult examination even though he knew the material well, Mark became involved in individual and group counseling aimed at controlling examination anxiety. Gradually, he developed a sense of competence in his academic work.

While Mark was engrossed in his science courses, his very capable wife, Marie, began to feel left out and to resent his obvious enjoyment of university life. Although she was a graduate nurse, she had never felt fulfilled in that role and now began to consider ways to further her education in another direction. After serious financial problems were resolved through campus and community resources, Marie also entered the university and placed their child in the exceptionally well run day care center. With a budding interest in special education aroused through a life planning group, Marie collaborated with day care staff, interested parents, and members of the campus community to establish an informal family life center with both cognitive and experiential features.

During their second year at the university, Mark and Marie found that, for a variety of reasons, they were having difficulty in respecting their rights to develop as individuals. Conflicts between them began to interfere with their generally superior academic performance. Marie perceived Mark's general attitudes as chauvinistic and joined a group discussing women's issues to gain some perspective on both her own situation and their future as a couple. In a complementary fashion, Mark found a group of men eager to discuss how the changing status of women affected them and how they could be assertive without being dominant. After several months, Mark and Marie entered a couples group, led by a professional counselor who focused on issues such as mutual caring, communication, sexuality, and decision making. They began to live and learn more effectively as a couple.

Conclusion

It is unfortunate that this chapter on prevention is being written during a time of financial constraint, when evolving programs are vulnerable to—and sometimes the victims of—budgetary restrictions or cuts. The promise and potential of prevention is vast, awaiting energetic and creative endeavors by campus counselors currently engaged in the field and those being trained in different ways in new programs. The need for individual service will continue, and the demand may continue to increase. In addition, there is an apocryphal tale, apparently based on some Parkinsonian law, that the more preventive programs and services are provided, the more the demand for service increases. The resources of counseling centers will be strained to the limit.

Although the efficacy of preventive programs may not be satisfactorily established at this time, new efforts in evaluative research will approach the problem in sophisticated ways by taking into account the multiple factors that go into making a program work. Occasional discouragement is inevitable, because preventive work is rarely glamorous. Many of us have wishful fantasies about magic cure and immediate benefits. But all of us hope that preventive efforts will enlarge possibilities for lives to be reasonably free of distress and filled with a zest for loving and working.

A great deal of this chapter has focused on preventive measures related to the personal growth of the student, my hope being that universities and colleges become community leaders in this area of prevention. Academic success may follow from preventive programs geared specifically to improve scholastic performance, but it is at least as reliant on a sense of personal competence and well-being. As Zax and Specter have expressed it: "The most significant challenge for workers in the college community will be the need to discover ways to make that setting a truly growth-enhancing environment which, in many respects, is altogether in keeping with the goals of the educational enterprise" (1974, p. 465). We are moving toward an ideal.

References

Aguilera, D. C.; Messick, J. M.; and Farrell, M. S. 1970. *Crisis intervention: theory and methodology*. St. Louis, Mo.: Mosby.

Albee, G. W. 1976. Innovative roles for psychologists. In P. J. Woods, ed., *Career opportunities for psychologists: expanding and emerging areas*. Washington, D.C.: American Psychological Association.

American College Health Association. 1976. Summary report: mental health annual program survey, 1973–74. Unpublished manuscript, Evanston, Ill.

Andreapoulos, S., ed. 1975. *National health insurance: can we learn from Canada?* New York: John Wiley.

Asken, M. J. 1975. Medical psychology: psychology's neglected child. *Professional Psychology* 6: 155–60.

Association of University and College Counseling Directors. 1967–1976. *Annual data bank,* ed. Thomas M. Magoon. College Park: University of Maryland.

Aulepp, L., and Delworth, U. 1976. *Training manual for an ecosystem model*. Boulder, Colo.: Western Interstate Commission for Higher Education.

Barger, B. 1963. The University of Florida Mental Health Program. In *Higher education and mental health*. Gainesville, Fla.: University of Florida.

Barger, B.; Larson, E. A.; and Hall, E. 1966. Preventive action in college mental health. *Journal of the American College Health Association*. 15: 80–93.

Bennett, C. C., et al., 1966. *Community psychology: a report of the Boston conference on the education of psychologists for community mental health*. Boston: Boston University Press.

Bierman, R., and Lumley, C. 1973. Toward the humanizing community. *Ontario Psychologist* 5: 10–19.

Bindman, A. J., and Spiegel, A. D. eds., 1969. *Perspectives in community mental health*. Chicago: Aldine.

Borus, J. F. 1973. Reentry: III. Facilitating healthy readjustment in Vietnam veterans. *Psychiatry* 36: 428–39.

Braceland, F. J. 1972. The mental hygiene of aging: present-day view. *Journal of the American Geriatrics Society* 20: 467–72.

Brigante, T. 1965. Opportunities for community mental health training within the residential college campus context. *Community Mental Health Journal* 1: 55–61.

Broskowski, A., and Baker, F. 1974. Professional, organizational and social barriers to primary prevention. *American Journal of Orthopsychiatry* 44: 707–19.

Budman, S. H. 1975. A strategy for preventive mental health intervention. *Professional Psychology* 6: 394–98.

Caplan, G. 1964. *Principles of preventive psychiatry*. New York: Basic Books.

————. 1970. *The theory and practice of mental health consultation*. New York: Basic Books.

Caplan, G., and Grunebaum, H. 1970. Perspectives on primary prevention: a review. In P. E. Cook, ed., *Community psychology and community mental health*. San Francisco: Holden-Day.

Caplan, G. and Killilea, M., eds. 1976. *Support systems and mutual help: multidisciplinary explorations*. New York: Grune and Stratton.

Carnes, J., and Laube, H. 1975. Becoming us: an experiment in family learning and teaching. *Small Group Behavior* 6: 106-20.

Cohen, R. 1972. Principles of preventive mental health programs for ethnic minority populations: the acculturation of Puerto Ricans to the United States. *American Journal of Psychiatry* 128: 1529-33.

Cook, P. E., ed. 1970. *Community psychology and community mental health*. San Francisco: Holden-Day.

Dauw, D. C. 1968. Mental health in managers: a corporate view. *Personnel Administration* 31: 42-46.

Denner, B. 1974. The insanity of community mental health: the myth of the machine. *International Journal of Mental Health* 3: 104-26.

Dumont, M. P. 1976. Self-help treatment programs. In G. Caplan and M. Killilea, eds., *Support systems and mutual help*. New York: Grune and Stratton.

Erikson, E. H. 1959. Identity and the life cycle. *Psychological Issues Monograph* Vol. 1, no. 1. New York: International Universities Press.

Falk, R. B. 1971. Innovations in college mental health. *Mental Hygiene* 55: 451-55.

Farnsworth, D. L. 1962. Concepts of educational psychiatry. *Journal of the American Medical Association* 181: 815-21.

————. 1966. *Psychiatry, education and the young adult*. Springfield, Ill.: Charles C. Thomas.

Freeman, H. E., and Sherwood, C. C. 1965. Research in large-scale intervention programs. *Journal of Social Issues* 21: 11-28.

Glaser, K. 1976. Women's self-help groups as an alternative to therapy. *Psychotherapy: Theory, Research and Practice* 13: 77-81.

Groen, J. J. 1974. The challenge of the future: the prevention of psychosomatic disorders. *Psychotherapy & Psychosomatics* 23: 283-303.

Grunebaum, H. 1970. *The practice of community mental health*. Boston: Little, Brown.

Gump, L. R. 1973. The application of primary preventive mental health principles to the college community. *Community Mental Health Journal* 9: 133-42.

Harper, R., and Balch, P. 1975. Some economic arguments in favor of primary prevention. *Professional Psychology* 6: 17-25.

Henderson, J. 1975. Object relations and a new social psychiatry: the illusion of primary prevention. *Bulletin of the Menninger Clinic* 39: 233-45.

Hersch, C. 1972. Social history, mental health, and community control. *American Psychologist* 27: 749-54.

Holmes, T. H., and Rahe, R. H. 1967. The social readjustment rating scale. *Journal of Psychosomatic Research* 11: 213-18.

Hurvitz, N. 1974. Peer self-help psychotherapy groups: psychotherapy without psychotherapists. In P. M. Rowan and H. M. Trice, eds., *The sociology of psychotherapy*. New York: Jason Aronson.

Jahoda, M. 1958. *Current concepts of positive mental health*. New York: Basic Books.

Kalafat, J., and Tyler, M. 1973. The community approach: programs and implications for campus mental health agency. *Professional Psychology* 4: 43–49.

Kennedy, D. A., and Seidman, S. B. 1972. Contingency management and human relations workshops: a school intervention program. *Journal of School Psychology* 10: 69–75.

Kessler, M., and Albee, G. W. 1975. Primary prevention. *Annual Review of Psychology* 26: 557–91.

Kuriloff, P., and Rindner, M. 1975. How psychological education can promote mental health with competence. *Counselor Education & Supervision* 14: 257–67.

Kysar, J. E. 1966. Preventive psychiatry on the college campus. *Community Mental Health Journal* 2: 27–34.

Lalonde, M. 1973. Beyond a new perspective. *APA Monitor* 4: 9–11.

Lesse, S. 1971. Prophylaxis and psychotherapy. *Canada's Mental Health* 19: 21–23.

Levine, M. 1970. Some postulates of practice in community psychology and their implications for training. In I. Iscoe and C. D. Spielberger, eds., *Community psychology: perspectives in training and research*. New York: Appleton-Century-Crofts.

Levinson, H. 1972. The clinical psychologist as organizational diagnostician. *Professional Psychology* 3: 34–40.

Lombardi, J. S. 1974. The college counseling center and preventive mental health activities. *Journal of College Student Personnel* 15: 435–38.

McCamy, J. C., and Presley, J. 1975. *Human life styling: keeping whole in the twentieth century*. New York: Harper & Row.

Medway, F. 1975. A social psychological approach to internally based change in the schools. *Journal of School Psychology* 13: 19–27.

Page, S., and Yates, E. 1974. Fear of evaluation and reluctance to participate in research. *Professional Psychology* 5: 400–8.

Pearl, A. 1974. The psychological consultant as change agent. *Professional Psychology* 5: 292–8.

Perlmutter, F. 1974. Prevention and treatment: a strategy for survival. *Community Mental Health Journal* 10: 276–81.

Piccinin, S. 1976. Results of student services goals inventory. Paper presented at the meeting of the Canadian Association of College and University Student Services, Brock University, Ontario, June 1976.

Poser, E. G. 1970. Toward a theory of "behavioral prophylaxis." *Journal of Behavioral Therapy & Experimental Psychiatry* 1: 39–43.

Reid, K. E. 1970. Community mental health on the college campus. *Hospital and Community Psychiatry* 21: 387–89.

Rhodes, W. C. 1974. Principles and practices of consultation. *Professional Psychology* 5: 287–92.

Robertson, B. 1968. Primary prevention: a pilot project. *Canada's Mental Health* 16: 20–22.

Sager, C. 1968. The group psychotherapist: bulwark against alienation. *International Journal of Group Psychotherapy* 18: 419–31.

Sauber, S. R. 1974. Primary prevention and the marital enrichment group. *Journal of Family Counseling* 2: 39–44.

Schroeder, C. S., and Miller, F. T. 1975. Early patterns and strategies in consultation. *Professional Psychology* 6: 182–86.

Schwartz, A. D. 1969. Evaluation of mental health: three suggested approaches. In A. J. Bindman and A. D. Spiegel, eds., *Perspectives in community mental health.* Chicago: Aldine.

Selye, H. 1974. *Stress without distress.* Philadelphia: J. B. Lippincott Company.

Sharfstein, S. 1974. Neighborhood psychiatry: new community approach. *Community Mental Health Journal* 10: 77–83.

Simon, G. C. 1975. Psychology and the "treatment rights movement." *Professional Psychology* 6: 243–51.

Sorensen, J. L., and Joffe, S. J. 1975. An outreach program in drug education: teaching a rationale approach to drug use. *Journal of Drug Education* 5: 87–96.

Spielberger, C., and Weitz, H. 1964. Improving the academic performance of anxious college freshmen: a group counseling approach to prevention of underachievement. *Psychological Bulletin Monographs,* vol. 78, no. 5.

Spiro, H. R.; Siassi, I.; and Crocetti, G. 1975. Cost-financed mental health facility: III. Economic issues and implications for future patterns of health care. *Journal of Nervous & Mental Disease* 160: 249–54.

Spoon, D., and Southwick, J. 1972. Promoting mental health through family life education. *Family Coordinator* 21: 279–86.

Steisel, I. M. 1972. Paraprofessionals—questions from a traditionalist. *Professional Psychology* 3: 331–34.

Suchman, E. A. 1967. *Evaluative research: principles and practice in public service and social action programs.* New York: Russell Sage Foundation.

Toffler, A. 1970. *Future shock.* New York: Random House.

Wagenfeld, M. O. 1972. The primary prevention of mental illness. *Journal of Health and Social Behavior* 13: 195–203.

Warnath, C. F. 1971. *New myths and old realities: college counseling in transition.* San Francisco: Jossey-Bass.

Wasserman, C. W.; McCarthy, B. W.; and Ferree, E. H. 1975. Student paraprofessionals as behavior change agents. *Professional Psychology* 6: 217–23.

Waxer, P. 1974. Community psychology in colleges: II. Psychologist as administrator. *Canadian Psychologist* 15: 251–57.

Waxer, P., and White, R. 1973. Introducing psychological consultation to a university community. *Canadian Psychologist* 14: 256–65.

Webster, T., and Harris, H. 1958. Modified group psychotherapy: an experiment in group psychodynamics for college freshmen. *Group Psychotherapy* 11: 283–98.

Weinberg, A. A. 1967. Mental ill-health, consequent to migration and loneliness, and its prevention. *Psychotherapy & Psychosomatics* 15: 69.

Weiss, R. S. 1976. The contributions of an organization of single parents to the well-being of its members. In G. Caplan and M. Killilea, eds., *Support systems and mutual help.* New York: Grune and Stratton.

Weiss, S. D., and Kapp, R. A. 1974. An interdisciplinary campus mental health program specializing in crisis-oriented services. *Professional Psychology* 5: 25–31.

White, R. 1963. Ego and reality in psychoanalytic theory. *Psychological Monograph* no. 11.

Whitehead, P. C. 1975. The prevention of alcoholism: divergences and convergences of two approaches. *Addictive Diseases: An International Journal* 1: 431–43.

Wiess, C. H. 1972. *Evaluation research: methods of assessing program effectiveness.* Engelwood Cliffs, N.J.: Prentice-Hall.

Wolff, T. 1969. Community mental health on campus: evaluating group discussions led by dormitory advisors and graduate students. Unpublished doctoral dissertation, University of Rochester.

Zax, M., and Specter, G. A. 1974. *An introduction to community psychology.* New York: John Wiley.

22
TRENDS AND DIRECTIONS

William A. Cass and
Janet C. Lindeman

WASHINGTON STATE UNIVERSITY

What is in store for university and college counseling centers five, ten, fifteen, twenty years from now? "The Shadow knows," to quote from a popular radio program of thirty-five years ago. Aside from a visit to your friendly, neighborhood psychic, partial answers to the question can be investigated from three relatively independent frames of reference:

1. The counseling process: What future trends may be anticipated within theoretical systems or schools of counseling and psychotherapy?
2. Counseling center programs: What kinds of services may be offered by the staffs of future student counseling centers?
3. Counseling center survival: Will university and college student counseling centers still be a viable entity five, ten, fifteen, or twenty years from now?

The Counseling Process

Is there a new Carl Rogers lurking somewhere over the horizon? Will counseling centers be turning their individual interview offices into sophisticated electronic control centers for biofeedback procedures? Will Freud come full circle and reemerge as a powerful therapeutic school under the title of "modern psychoanalysis?" Will centers install an in-house yoga expert?

To review the rich literature on the theoretical foundations of psychotherapy and counseling is far beyond the scope of this chapter, or even of this book. For example, some years back Harper (1959) wrote a delightful volume reviewing the various schools of psychoanalysis. Even after he had thus narrowed the field, he presented thirty-six systems. Corsini's recent publications (1973) is a good example of the many surveys available to the student of counseling theory. He invited authorities to write summary, in-depth chapters on twelve current theoretical systems. Each advocate implied that the school being represented was not only making a significant contribution to present counseling and psychotherapy practice, but would continue to do so in the future. One is forced to conclude that a prediction of the trends and directions in the counseling process would most likely be a reflection of personal bias. We choose not to follow that course.

Counseling Center Programs

Are the days of individual, one-to-one counseling numbered? Will college counseling centers forsake career counseling and, in effect, turn it over to college placement centers? Will the offices of future counseling centers merely serve as home bases for staffs of human development consultants, outreach programmers, and institutional environment modifiers? Will college health services assume responsibility for students' personal, social, emotional, and marital adjustment problems, leaving counseling center staffs to grapple with developmental problems and career decisions?

These are issues that have been, are currently being, and will continue to be hotly debated by counseling psychologists. Avis and Stewart, for example, plead for "a basic reconceptualization and restructuring of the college counselor's role so that their expertise would become available to the entire campus community" (1976, p. 77). Nejedlo et al. reported a change in name for their service from "Counseling Center" to "Counseling and Student Development Center"; this "signified a basic change in direction and philosophy from a traditional therapeutic model to a broader model that includes remedial services but emphasizes developmental and preventive counseling interventions" (1977, p. 257).

Again, space limitations preclude surveying the extensive literature exemplified by the two references above. We are electing, rather, to report on data from Lindeman's 1977 study and from item response comparisons of the annual Data Bank sponsored by the Association of University and College Counseling Center Directors (1967–1976). Further, we cannot overlook the opportunity to offer a few of our own crystal ball observations.

TRENDS AND DIRECTIONS

The 1970s have been marked by economic crises and increased unemployment. Students entering institutions of higher learning have become more concerned than in the past with preparing themselves for a competitive job market. College personnel claim, appropriately, that these same entering students are presenting lower academic achievement scores and more minimal reading and study skills than in the past. Such trends are not likely to show radical change within the next few years. How will all of this affect student counseling services?

Study Skills and Learning Resources

Lindeman (1977) surveyed 83 public, four-year colleges and universities and found that 81 percent of the institutions provided special study skills and learning resource facilities. Clearly, institutional personnel are concerned with the need for remedial services.

The 1969–1970 Data Bank (Association of University and College Counseling Directors, 1970) reported that about 44 percent of large, four-year universities and colleges had reading and study skill services that were apart from the counseling center. The Data Bank studies for the three years between 1973 and 1976 (1974, 1975, 1976) noted that on the average between 7 and 9 percent of professional counseling center staff time was devoted to providing these specialized services. Further, the 1975–1976 Data Bank (1976) indicated that most centers were "uninvolved" or only "slightly involved" in providing study skills or reading training. Although universities and colleges are making more of these types of services available, student counseling centers have tended not to pick up this load. We can make the easy prediction that such will be the case in future years, despite some expressed increasing interest in the developmental model.

Vocational and Career Counseling

On many a campus the old student placement center has changed its name to something like career services and placement office. Offering career counseling over the four years of college, such offices often sponsor, sometimes jointly with the counseling center, special career topic workshops and career development groups and classes.

Does this mean that vocational counseling, as a service provided by the counseling center, is diminishing? Apparently not. The 1975–1976 annual Data Bank (1976) indicated that less than 10 percent of counseling centers were "uninvolved" or only "slightly involved" in vocational and educational counseling. In Lindeman's survey (1977), 93 percent of the respondents listed "vocational/educational" counseling as one of the counseling center's services. On the other hand, 79 percent of the same respondents stated that student counseling center "counselors frequently help students simultaneously with both vocational/educational and emotional/social problems" (p. 56).

In some areas computerized career information systems are being experimentally used in high schools as well as in colleges and universities. The technology is already available for huge amounts of centralized information to be made instantaneously accessible to students all over the nation. However, computerized systems are very expensive, and ways of effectively integrating them with personal counseling have not been worked out.

What then do we see as the trends for vocational counseling services? Career counseling will continue to be given greater national attention. Placement services will widen their career concerns to all college years and not concentrate on just the senior and alumni groups. Placement staffs will continue to expand the career choice development model, either in cooperation or in competition with counseling services. Although college students are raising more and more questions about the career value of four years or more of higher education, such thoughts run afoul of parental and societal reactions. Thus, vocational counseling will move even further away from the old mechanistic (that is, trait-factor) model to a more complex counseling of a total individual with ambivalences, conflicts, and adjustment needs. And, because of ever present budget problems, most counseling centers will rely on the printed word, painfully collected at minimum cost for use in their vocational libraries, at least for the next several decades.

Emotional and Social Counseling

At the same time that students are becoming more concerned about practical, vocationally directed, higher education, they are also becoming more open to experimenting within personal relationships and are challenging their parent's sexual and social mores. The norm is now increasingly to include, rather than exclude, sex as part of normal dating behavior. Couples often live together and discover both their complementary and their uncomplementary relationship patterns prior to getting married. More older and married students are able to attend college with the broadening of GI bill and student loan programs. "Relationships" or "couple" counseling is available at student counseling centers for unmarried as well as married couples in increasing numbers. Sexual dysfunction counseling, patterned after the treatment programs of Masters and Johnson and of Helen Kaplan, is also becoming more prevalent and accepted by students. Gay liberation groups are becoming more vocal, and increasing numbers of students are experimenting with bisexuality or homosexuality as possible sexual identity choices. Students are increasingly seeing counseling centers as places to receive help with any of these concerns.

According to the 1975–1976 annual Data Bank (1976), most of the counseling center staffs from the larger universities and colleges were "highly involved" or "moderately involved" in the following:

Individual personal counseling/therapy	99%
Group therapy/counseling	84%
Counseling/therapy with students with normal personal-social problems	99%
Counseling/therapy with students with severe psychological problems	71%
Short-term counseling/therapy	100%

It seems evident that the vast majority of most counselors' time is being spent in individual and group counseling and psychotherapy. We predict, despite the pleas of Avis and Stewart (1976) and Nejedlo et al. (1977), that individual and group counseling over the total range of student concerns will continue to be the major activity of counseling centers in the years ahead. A proviso to this statement will be discussed later in this chapter.

Outreach

All the rapid academic and social changes have led many counseling center staffs to become increasingly interested in outreach. Common directives include "Get out where the action is"; "Solve the little problems before they become big problems"; "Work with those who work with students"; and "Make our expertise available to all." Increasing attention is being paid in the professional literature to training paraprofessionals and peer counselors to work with students. Generous amounts of program time in the Annual Conference of University and College Counseling Center Directors are devoted to outreach.

But it is possible to exaggerate these trends. In the Lindeman survey (1977) 81 percent of the respondents reported increased outreach services from 1971 to 1976. The average amount of time, however, the staff members spend in outreach work was reported to be only one to four hours per week. We anticipate that outreach activities will increase somewhat over the next five to ten years, but that individual and group counseling will remain the major responsibility of the staff.

STUDENT HEALTH SERVICE COOPERATION

Recent psychopharmacology discoveries have had a subtle impact on educational institutions and point up a pressing future need for greater working cooperation between student counseling and student health services. Students developing clinically defined schizophrenias, manic-depressive and depressive psychoses, and debilitating anxieties are often able, with the help of psychotropic medication and psychotherapy, to continue successfully their college and university educations.

The availability of these new medications and the growing governmental acceptance of the "community mental health center" model have served as stimuli to the development of services within student health centers that parallel those of student counseling centers (Glasscote & Fishman, 1973). Lindeman (1977) found that 66 percent of her respondents reported an increase in mental health services by student health centers, with 36 percent noting that extensive psychotherapy was offered by psychiatrists and/or psychologists employed by the health center.

Glasscote and Fishman (1973) indicated that the service overlap between the health and counseling centers can be seen as quite advantageous, since a wider range of students are being served. We would agree, provided there is solid working coordination between the two service centers. Unfortunately, Lindeman's survey (1977) found that coordination is usually limited to only occasional individual counselor-physician contacts regarding specific students. Only 15 percent of the respondents reported having weekly or monthly joint staff meetings. Of equal concern is that 42 percent of respondents reported that there was no psychiatric case supervision at the student counseling center. This was true despite the fact that 71 percent of the centers were reported as working with students with severe psychological problems. We can only hope, but not necessarily predict, that the future will find a better and closer cooperative working relationship. We fear that failure to do so on our part may well becloud the future of student counseling centers.

The overlap of student counseling and health center services has not yet created sufficient problems to have received much attention in the student services professional literature. Mental health, however, is currently covered by public health insurance in Canada (Lindeman & Cass, 1977) and is proposed for national insurance coverage in the United States. If national health insurance becomes a reality, the overlap of services between the two centers will raise many questions. Some of these will be dealt with below.

Counseling Center Survival

"Did you know that John Bagley's center was closed because of budget cutbacks?" "I hear that both the George Adams University and the University of Lincoln student counseling centers are required to charge students fees for counseling services." "Hey, what is going to happen to us when national health insurance is adopted?" The concerns evidenced by these questions and comments appeared not only on the formal programs, but also during the informal give-and-take in the dining halls, cocktail lounges, corridors, and guest rooms at recent Annual Conferences of University and College Counseling Center Directors. These are survival issues. The director or staff member of a college counseling center who does not feel anxiety pangs relative to the survival future of counseling centers and their staff is playing the old ostrich head-in-the-sand game.

We predict that a revolution in student services during the 1970s and 1980s will much more likely occur, at least in the United States, in the area of financial support systems than in the types of services rendered. Even in Canada, where public health insurance systems already exist, questions are being raised as to who should be paying for student counseling services and how (Lindeman & Cass, 1977).

REDUCED STATE AND PROVINCIAL FUNDING

The executive vice-president of a good-sized university has publicly and explicitly stated that he cannot understand why university students should receive free health and counseling services. After all, the student's nonstudent peer must seek such services from the community and for a definite fee. He does not respond to arguments that physical and mental health are closely related to academic attainment and that the university should assume the responsibility for assuring that students have optimal conditions for learning.

One need only read an occasional issue of the *Chronicle of Higher Education* to become aware that colleges and universities no longer enjoy the status and prestige that they had in the 1950s and early 1960s. Then, legislative bodies and private funding sources provided higher education with just about everything it could ask for. Now, legislative bodies in both Canada and the United States are casting a jaundiced eye at college and university budget requests. The legislators indicate that they are simply passing on a clear message coming from their constituents. Higher education is in for tough times on the budget front.

The expected responses from administrators and faculty are "We must tighten our belts"; "Students will have to pay for a larger percentage of their education through increased tuition and fees"; "First things first; we are here to teach"; "Auxiliary services must absorb a disproportionate share of budget reductions in order to preserve as much of academic department teaching programs as possible." The student counseling or student health center that does not feel a discriminatory budget crunch in the years ahead can consider itself extremely lucky—and probably living on borrowed time.

FEES FOR SERVICE

One of us served for over a year as the only nonphysician member of a university student health service task force studying student health service funding, budgets, salaries, and physical facilities. It is a rare student health center that does not receive a significant portion of its funding directly from student tuition and fees. Many of these centers provide "basic" health services financed largely by mandatory student fees, with further health services available to those who pay an additional voluntary fee or subscribe to special student health insurance. Still other health centers have initiated fee-for-service charges for services over and above the basic level. One gets the clear impression that student fees, student insurance, and fees for service are used in varying combinations as the major funding sources. Support from legislative bodies is strictly secondary, is decreasing, and is often limited to providing and maintaining physical facilities on the university campus. A number of health services are setting up plans to collect for student health care from the private health insurance policies of the students or their parents. The American College Health Association (U.S. Congress, House of Representatives, 1975) is making ongoing efforts to assure that student health centers will be able to receive national health insurance benefits, should they be implemented. Canadian student health centers currently receive reimbursements for student health care from provincial health insurance programs (Lindeman & Cass, 1977).

Hurst, Davidshofer, and Arp (1976) surveyed 225 institutions as to the current fee-charging practices and perceptions of college and university counseling centers. Approximately one-third of the institutions surveyed received financial support for counseling centers from student tuition and general fees. Only 4 percent of the institutions charged fees for specific counseling sessions, and only 3 percent had any part of their services covered by an insurance plan. Over half the directors surveyed had recently discussed the issue of whether or not to charge fees, but 81 percent stated a flat opposition to the practice.

In many ways we agree with the feelings expressed in the Hurst, Davidshofer, and Arp survey, and we undoubtedly answered it at the time in the majority direction. In view, however, of the financing problems within higher education, the trends evidenced within student health services, and the likely arrival of national health insurance, we can only anticipate that the question of fees for counseling services, testing services, and outreach consultation will face many a counseling center director in the coming years. It seems inconceivable that university administrators will overlook such nonlegislative funding sources for very long.

NATIONAL HEALTH INSURANCE

Public health insurance is a fact of life for Canadians, and national health insurance is a likely part of the future for the United States. It takes little perception to recognize the question that seems not to be *if* national health insurance will be enacted, but *when* and *how*. And again, the question is not *if* mental health coverage will be included, but *how much* and for *what types of professional services*.

Both the Republicans, through the Nixon/Ford Comprehensive Health Insurance Plan (U.S. Congress, House of Representatives, 1974) and the Democrats, by way of the Kennedy-Mills Health Security Act (U.S. Congress, 1975), have introduced major national health insurance plans. The 1976 Democratic platform and President Carter have pledged to introduce some form of national health insurance system during the current administration. The present economic slump and the determination of a fiscally sound delivery system seem to be delaying factors, but not permanently inhibiting ones.

Private insurance companies are increasingly including outpatient mental health services in their coverage. Medicare and Medicaid are already covering mental health services in approved community mental health centers, and both the Republican and the Democratic proposals included mental health coverage for outpatient services. The Health Security Act mentioned above proposed the creation of health maintenance organizations that would be local decision-making groups for all services covered by the insurance. Institutions and nonprofit organizations could apply to the Health Security Board for eligibility for coverage and, if approved by the area's mental maintenance organization, could receive payments for mental health and health services rendered. Universities and colleges would likely qualify. If a student counseling center were affiliated with a comprehensive mental health organization, which requires a total range of services including crisis intervention and hospitalization, its outpatient mental health services could be covered.

If this source of funding becomes available, it seems likely that university administrators will rush to drop health and mental health services from their already sagging budgets. But, how will the mental health services eligible for national health insurance coverage be defined vis-à-vis educational and vocational counseling services? What educational and vocational counseling services will universities be willing to continue to fund? And, what will a dual funding base do to the present integrated fashion in which educational, vocational, and personal counseling is delivered at most student counseling centers?

Lindeman (1977), asked student counseling center directors, student health center directors, and vice-presidents or deans of student affairs at 83 universities for their opinions on how national health insurance should cover student services, and how universities should respond to this coverage. The majority of the 167 respondents felt that national health insurance should cover counseling for individuals who have attempted suicide, are severely depressed, are sex offenders (against minors or nonconsenting adults), are drug and alcohol abusers, are psychotic, have marital and family difficulties, are recommended by the court, or have serious relationship problems. They felt national health insurance should *not* cover counseling for individuals who are in conflict about an important developmental task, have vocational direction questions, or are deciding on an academic major. Ninety percent of the respondents felt, however, that the university should *not* change its responsibility for offering emotional/social counseling and crisis intervention counseling as well as vocational/educational counseling for its students. Services in the first two categories were simply seen as eligible for national health insurance reimbursement at both the student counseling center and the student health center.

Seventy-four percent of the survey respondents indicated that the university should *not* respond to national health insurance by locating vocational/educational counseling in one place and emotional/social counseling in another. Evidently, the vast majority of student services personnel were satisfied with the integration of services and would like to continue it. They recommended a dual funding base for student counseling centers as a way of dealing with the advent of national health insurance, rather than a separation of types of counseling services.

As might be predicted, the counseling directors favored coverage of licensed psychologists without requiring medical referral and psychiatric consultation, while the health directors favored coverage with those limitations. The health directors seemed less strong in their attitude, however, than were the counseling directors.

There is considerable division between the professional groups as to who should and who should not be trusted to deliver insured mental health services. So far the national health insurance proposals have all based eligibility for mental health coverage on some sort of institutional or nonprofit organization affiliation, except for private psychiatrists. They have proposed to address quality control issues for all but private psychiatrists not through a system of professional licensure and supervision, but through a system of organizational licensure by the Department of Health, Education, and Welfare.

Canada already has public health insurance systems that are operated by each of the provincial governments (Lindeman & Cass, 1977). Under these mental health coverage systems, only private psychiatrists and provincially run hospitals and mental health clinics are eligible for provincial health insurance reimbursement. Therefore, Canadian university student counseling services depend on general university funding, and university student health services depend on provincial insurance reimbursements.

Lindeman and Cass (1977) surveyed 27 Canadian university counseling center directors. Almost all of them indicated offering services very similar to centers in the United States. Only 7 out of 27 universities reported having vocational/educational counseling services separate from emotional/social counseling services. All respondents noted that students tended to use university-based mental health services rather than off-campus services. Several respondents suggested that although students could use private psychiatrists or community mental health centers with 90 to 100 percent coverage under provincial insurance, they rarely used these services. This was due to long waiting lists and the frequent unavailability of long-term individual psychotherapy.

The Canadian directors were asked for general comments on the effect that public health insurance has had on student mental health services. Their comments underscored concerns already expressed in this chapter. University administrators have become more hesitant to finance university counseling services, because they feel they should collect 100 percent from provincial insurance for mental health services. They are actually able to collect only about 40 percent, since counselors and psychologists are not eligible for third-party payments under Canadian insurance acts. This has resulted, on at least one campus, in considering putting more counseling services under a new Family Medical Health Center umbrella that could collect more health insurance reimbursement. The model of offering psychological services closely integrated with educational and vocational services would be left behind in a quest for financial security. This approach would be clearly against the Lindeman (1977) survey recommendations that insurance and university funds be combined to support student counseling services, but only in such a way as to continue the integrated service system now existing on most campuses.

Summary and Conclusions

The 1970s and the 1980s will likely see more changes in the financial support of student counseling centers than in the types of counseling services. Already apparent are some innovative methods of delivering services such as peer counseling, thematic small groups, and study and reading skill clinics. These innovations seem small, however, in comparison to the likelihood of major financial changes.

University general funds are being stretched tighter and tighter, squeezing out more and more support services. Realistic questions of student counseling center survival are looming over the horizon. Student fees are going up in order to cover services that would otherwise be dropped. Debates rage over which services warrant inclusion in general student fees and which services are limited to only some students and therefore should require a specific admission or fee-for-service payment by the user. Canadian provincial health insurance covers psychiatric and government clinic services, but not student counseling services. National health insurance for the United States is increasingly imminent, but it is unclear how it will cover psychological services and how counseling centers will be involved.

Ideally, the following conditions can be anticipated: the 1970s will herald a time when all United States citizens will have access to the kind of comprehensive, quality services that so far have been available to most university and college students. These services will be more broadly defined than they have been in Canada so that university and other nonprofit organizations already offering such services will be able to benefit from the national health insurance funding system. Universities will continue to exercise responsibility for offering counseling services to students and will work closely with insurance offices to devise ways to provide educational, vocational, social, and emotional counseling in an integrated fashion. And an increasingly secure financial base for emotional/social counseling will allow universities to direct their own counseling dollars to improve educational/vocational counseling methods.

Potentially, however, other conditions could occur: changing state and federal funding systems could have divisive and deteriorating effects on student counseling centers. National health insurance could narrowly define its mental health coverage, and counseling psychologists could be excluded from eligibility for insurance payments. Universities could drastically reduce their counseling budgets, erroneously concluding that these services would be provided elsewhere. Educational/vocational counseling could be split off from emotional/social counseling services.

Much will depend on the ability of student services personnel in general and counseling center personnel in particular on each campus (1) to get together and determine what is in the students' overall best interests, (2) to rally student counseling, student health, and student administration professional groups behind such interests, and (3) to impact state, provincial, and federal legislation.

If vocational/educational counseling continues with university funding, it will have to be well integrated into the university's overall academic, residential, and placement services. Career and educational information will have to be easily accessible, accurate, and available to counseling psychologists, peer counselors, and faculty in classrooms, dorms, and counseling centers.

If emotional/social counseling is to continue for students in an integrated fashion with educational/vocational counseling, national health insurance and university administrators will have to work out dual funding systems that enhance, rather than divide, services. Professional groups will have to work out procedures for controlling the quality and costs of services. Of special importance is the development of uniform standards for certifying psychologists and of acceptable procedures for medical referral and psychiatric consultation. Doctoral clinical and counseling psychology training programs will have to address such issues as whether to require clinical diagnosis and somatic treatment methods courses in order to qualify graduates to work within a national health insurance system.

All of these changes will present a major challenge for the future. Will we be able to listen to each other, trust each other, and cooperate with each other? Will we avoid losing sight of the major goal of a student service system—that any student should be able to "cry for help" in any way, in any place on campus, and be personally guided to receive the most appropriate kind of help from the most appropriate person, without consideration of his or her financial status?

References

Association of University and College Counseling Directors. 1967–1976. *Annual data bank,* ed. Thomas M. Magoon. College Park: University of Maryland.

Avis, J. P., and Stewart, L. H. 1976. College counseling: intentions and change. *The Counseling Psychologist.* 6: 74–77.

Corsini, R. 1973. *Current psychotherapies.* Itasca, Ill.: F. E. Peacock.

Glasscote, R., and Fishman, M. 1973. *Mental health on the campus: a field study.* Washington, D.C.: Joint Information Services of the American Psychiatric Association and the National Association for Mental Health.

Harper, R. A. 1959. *Psychoanalysis and psychotherapy: 36 systems.* Englewood Cliffs, N.J.: Prentice-Hall.

Hurst, J. C.; Davidshofer, C. O.; and Arp, S. 1976. Current fees charging practices and perceptions in college and university counseling centers. Unpublished paper, Colorado State University.

Lindeman, J. C. 1977. Implications of national health insurance for university student counseling services. Unpublished doctoral dissertation, Washington State University. The author acknowledges the valuable assistance of LeRoy Olsen and James Shoemaker, Department of Education, Washington State University.

Lindeman, J. C., and Cass, W. A. 1977. A survey of mental health counseling services for Canadian university students. Unpublished paper, Washington State University.

Nejedlo, R. J., et al. 1977. A good trip: from counseling center to counseling and student development center. *Personnel and Guidance Journal* 55: 257–59.

U.S. Congress, House of Representatives. 1974. H.R.12684, *A Comprehensive Health Insurance Plan.* 93d Congress, 2nd Session, February 6, 1974.

———. 1975. Committee on Ways & Means, Subcommittee on Health. *Statement of the American College Health Association.* 94th Congress, 1st Session, December 3, 1975, pt. 3, pp. 1732–36.

U.S. Congress, Senate. 1975. S.3, *The Health Security Act of 1975.* 94th Congress, 1st Session, January 15, 1975.

APPENDIX

A List of Professional Organizations of Interest to Counselors

Academy of Certified Social Workers (ACSW)
Academy of Psychologists in Marital Counseling (APMC)
Adult Education Association (AEA)
American Academy of Psychotherapists (AAP)
American Association of Adlerian Psychologists (AAAP)
American Association for the Advancment of Science (AAAS)
American Association of Marriage and Family Counselors (AAMFC)
American Association on Mental Deficiency (AAMD)
American Association of Pastoral Counselors (AAPC)
American Association of Sex Educators, Counselors and Therapists (AASECT)
American Association of University Professors (AAUP)
American Board of Professional Psychology (ABPP)
American College Health Association (ACHA)
*American College Personnel Association (ACPA)
American Educational Research Association (AERA)
American Group Psychotherapy Association (AGPA)
American Institute of Group Counseling (AIGC)
American Orthopsychiatric Association (AOA)
American Psychological Association, Division 17 (APA)
*American Rehabilitation Counseling Association (ARCA)
*American School Counselor Association (ASCA)
American Society of Clinical Hypnosis (ASCH)
American Speech and Hearing Association (ASHA)
Association for the Advancement of Behavioral Therapies (AABT)
Association for Clinical Pastoral Education (ACPE)
*Association for Counselor Education and Supervision (ACES)
*Association for Humanistic Education and Development (AHEAD)

*A division of American Personnel and Guidance Association

*Association for Measurement and Evaluation in Guidance (AMEG)
*Association for Non-White Concerns in Personnel and Guidance (ANWC)
Association of Religion and Applied Behavioral Science (ARABS)
Association of Rehabilitation Centers (ARC)
*Association for Specialists in Group Work (ASGW)
Canadian Bureau for International Education (CBIE)
Canadian Guidance and Counselling Association (CGCA)
Canadian Psychological Association (CPA)
Canadian University and College Counselling Association (CUCCA)
Council for Exceptional Children (CEC)
International Association of Counseling Services (IACS)
International Association of Rehabilitation Facilities (IARF)
International Reading Association (IRA)
International Transactional Analysis Association (ITAA)
National Association of School Counselors (NASC)
National Association of Social Workers (NASW)
National Association of Student Personnel Administrators (NASPA)
National Association of Women Deans, Administrators and Counselors (NAWDAC)
National Career Information Center (NCIC)
*National Catholic Guidance Conference (NCGC)
National Conference on Social Welfare (NCSW)
National Council on Family Relations (NCFR)
National Council on Measurement in Education (NCME)
National Education Association (NEA)
*National Employment Counselors Association (NECA)
National Rehabilitation Association (NRA)
National Rehabilitation Counseling Association (NRCA)
*National Vocational Guidance Association (NVGA)
*Public Offender Counselor Association (POCA)
Society for Clinical and Experimental Hypnosis (SCEH)
Society for Clinical and Experimental Hypnosis (SCEH)
Society for Personality Assessment (SPA)
Student Aid Division (SAD)
Veterans Administration (VA)
Young Men's Christian Association (YMCA)
Young Women's Christian Association (YWCA)

NAME INDEX